THE POLITICS OF ENGLISH NATIONHOOD

The Politics of
English Nationhood

MICHAEL KENNY

OXFORD
UNIVERSITY PRESS

OXFORD
UNIVERSITY PRESS

Great Clarendon Street, Oxford, OX2 6DP,
United Kingdom

Oxford University Press is a department of the University of Oxford.
It furthers the University's objective of excellence in research, scholarship,
and education by publishing worldwide. Oxford is a registered trade mark of
Oxford University Press in the UK and in certain other countries

First Edition published in 2014

Impression: 1

Published in the United States of America by Oxford University Press
198 Madison Avenue, New York, NY 10016, United States of America

British Library Cataloguing in Publication Data

Data available

Library of Congress Control Number: 2014931674

ISBN 978-0-19-960861-4

As printed and bound by CPI Group (UK) Ltd, Croydon, CR0 4YY

For Euan, Orla, and Luke—members of the next English generation

Acknowledgements

The award of one of the Leverhulme Trust's Major Research Fellowships enabled me to complete much of the research and writing which this book has involved. This scheme affords the kind of opportunity to reflect, research, and write, while less encumbered by the proliferating demands of academic life, that is increasingly rare. Given the scale and scope of the topic addressed in this volume—which requires engagement with a range of distinct and sizeable literatures, and different kinds of source material—I am all the more appreciative of the Trust's generosity.

The book has its origins in research I began some years ago, initially in partnership with Richard English and Richard Hayton. We completed a small project examining how intellectuals and pundits were becoming increasingly animated by the re-emerging question of Englishness. This was an enormously collegial and stimulating collaboration, and represented the genesis of a number of trains of thought that I have subsequently pursued. I was then able to reflect further on the policy implications of the resurgence of English nationhood during the course of a visiting Senior Research Fellowship at the Institute for Public Policy Research. I learnt much from the talented and shrewd colleagues I encountered there, and am grateful to my collaborators Guy Lodge, Rick Muir, and Katie Schmuecker. The research we conducted was generously supported by the Joseph Rowntree Charitable Trust.

I began the research for this volume while I was teaching, first, at the University of Sheffield and, latterly, at Queen Mary, University of London. I am especially grateful to my new colleagues at QM for the interest they have shown in my work, and for the stimulating intellectual environment that is lodged within the School of Politics and International Relations at Mile End. George Currie proved assiduous, intelligent, and thoughtful in tracking down materials for me at a late stage in proceedings. I also had help with sources from John Curtice, Elizabeth Kenny, Andrew Mycock, and Andrew Pinnock.

I took the liberty of pestering a number of experts on various subjects covered by this book, asking for their comments on particular chapters when they were in draft form. Everyone I asked agreed to my request, and for that alone I am very grateful. Each then supplied me with thoughts and suggestions that have improved the quality of the manuscript quite considerably. Any errors that remain in the text are my fault, not theirs. Given that they all have innumerable demands upon their time, I want to underline how much I appreciate their collegiality and goodwill. They are: Arthur Aughey, Christopher Bryant,

John Denham, Patrick Diamond, Richard English, Jim Gallagher, Sunder Katwala, Guy Lodge, Andrew Mycock, Nick Pearce, Nick Stevenson, and Ben Wellings.

During the course of the various projects I have undertaken in relation to this topic, I have been involved in conducting interviews with a number of politicians, policy-makers, commentators, and opinion-formers, and have also had access to transcripts of interviews conducted by my collaborators. Quotations from these figure at various points in the text. All of these encounters provided a surfeit of stimulating and important reflections upon the issues covered in this volume. I would like to signal my gratitude to these interviewees—Arthur Aughey, Liam Byrne, David Cannadine, Kenneth Clarke, Jon Cruddas, Iain Dale, Philip Dodd, Frank Field, Simon Heffer, Chris Huhne, Tristram Hunt, Sunder Katwala, Krishan Kumar, Gordon Marsden, Andrew Marr, Sir Malcolm Rifkind, Roger Scruton, Michael Wills, and Gareth Young. In addition, I organized several workshops on identity-related issues with community stakeholders during 2008 and 2009, and had access to transcripts of several others conducted by colleagues at IPPR. These were held in Barking and Dagenham, Brighton, Central London, and Leicester. I would like to thank all of the participants in these events, which taught me much about the kinds of anxiety and hope which people often identify in expressions of English national identity. One particular collaborator and good friend deserves a special mention. Guy Lodge prompted me to write this book, and has been an astute sounding-board for the arguments contained within it. Dominic Byatt has been enormously supportive too, as well as patient. His professionalism, astute judgement, and sense of humour make him an ideal editor. I remain particularly grateful for the enthusiasm with which he responded to my initial proposal, and for the stream of good advice he has dispensed ever since. Thanks also to Sarah Parker and Lizzy Suffling at Oxford University Press.

Finally, I owe a debt to my family that is not easy to put into words. Euan, Orla, and Luke continue to show a healthy indifference to their dad's interest in politics, but are increasingly interested in what it means to be English. And Becky has provided a very rich bounty of love, support, and patience. They have all sustained me in different ways during the completion of this book, often without knowing it.

M.K.
Cambridge, July 2013

Contents

List of Tables   xi

Introduction: England as an Imagined Community—Myths,
Ideas, and Politics   1

1. Crisis over Nationhood: The 1990s Reconsidered   27

2. Interpreting Englishness: Views from Right, Left,
   and the British Centre   50

3. Englishness as a Mass Phenomenon: Evidence and
   Interpretation   78

4. The Cultural Politics of Englishness   131

5. Answering 'the English Question': Party Politics,
   Public Policy, and the Nationalist Fringe   171

6. Political Intimations of English Grievance: West Lothian
   and the Barnett Formula   205

Conclusions: Reconfiguring the Politics of English Nationhood   232

Notes   245

Index   289

List of Tables

3.1 Trends in 'forced choice' national identity, England 1992–2009   82

3.2 Trends in national identity, England 1997–2007   83

3.3 Trends in 'free choice' national identity, England 1996–2007   83

3.4 Constitutional preferences for England, 1999–2009. 'With all the changes going on in the way different parts of Great Britain are run, which of the following do you think would be best for England?'   85

3.5 Attitudes towards the 'West Lothian' question, 2000–2007: 'Scottish MPs should no longer be allowed to vote on English legislation'   86

3.6 Attitudes in England towards the financial relationship between England and Scotland, 2000–2009. 'Compared with other parts of the UK, Scotland's share of government spending is . . .'   86

3.7 Trends in 'forced choice' national identity, England 1992–2011   89

3.8 National identity: Moreno results by region of England, 2011   90

3.9 National and regional identity, Moreno results: England in comparative context   90

3.10 Attitudes in England towards how England should be governed, 2011   91

3.11 Attitudes towards the 'West Lothian' question, England 2000–2011 'Scottish MPs should not be allowed to vote on English matters'   92

3.12 Forced choice national identity by ethnic origin, England 1997–2007   101

3.13 National identity, Moreno results by ethnicity, England 2011   102

6.1 Index of identifiable spending per head, minus social protection, across the nations of the UK, 2003/04 to 2008/09   227

Introduction

England as an Imagined Community—Myths, Ideas, and Politics

INTRODUCTION

Whether the English have begun to develop a stronger sense of their own national identity, and what might be the wider political ramifications of such a trend, are questions that have been posed with ever greater frequency and urgency in recent years. Even within mainstream political debate, where national and constitutional questions are typically seen as secondary to economic and social issues, they have become more familiar and pressing. Yet, despite their increasingly ubiquitous character, and the volume of evidence and research which have been compiled about English nationhood, this remains a subject which is usually skirted rather than directly engaged, and is mainly confined to the margins of political analysis. There are still only a few academic books devoted to this question, and English national identity has been studied much less extensively than its Scottish and Welsh counterparts.[1]

There are several reasons for this reticence. It may in part be a reflection of the difficulty which liberal thinking and commentary has with English nationhood, a subject on which I reflect throughout this volume. For many commentators, Englishness is irretrievably tainted by its regressive, conservative, and ethnically charged character. The prospect of a significant shift in attitudes away from familiar forms of Britishness and towards an avowed sense of Englishness is not welcomed in some quarters. A further reason for the relative lack of academic engagement with this issue, among political scientists in particular, arises from an unease with issues and affiliations that are rooted in identity, rather than individual or collective interest. This is supplemented by a tendency to consider 'the English question' as a narrow matter of constitutional policy, rather than a theme that connects with broader shifts in the nature of collective identity and contemporary forms of belonging. It may also stem from some of the difficulties associated with the appraisal of trends that are still, as we shall see, significantly disputed. Developing a balanced and proportionate assessment of shifts in mass sentiments when it comes to nationhood is a difficult enterprise, and is made all the harder by the emergence of a number of competing, polemical interpretations of the nature and extent of Englishness. Put simply, these tend either to exaggerate the extent to which a sense of nationalism has spread among the English or radically understate the extent and character of recent shifts.

A related fault of these, and other familiar, judgements about Englishness is that they treat its political dimensions in a reductive and simplistic fashion. Many assume that an upsurge in Englishness reflects a rightward shift among the electorate. Other commentators, as we shall see, regard the most likely cause of the reassertion of English identity as the result of a backlash against the asymmetrical character of the model of devolution introduced by the first Blair government after 1997. Neither of these contentions is borne out by the available evidence, I will suggest. In their place, I explore a rather different interpretive conclusion—that the language and sentiments associated with resurgent ideas of Englishness have a more complex set of causes than devolution itself, and have afforded considerable opportunities for those seeking to promote a variety of political agendas and arguments. These include an emerging discourse of anti-system populism, as well as an embryonic attempt to recast England in a self-consciously multicultural vein.

These are not the only perspectives that appeals to English nationhood have bolstered. I draw attention as well to a new alignment between several long-established ideological traditions within British politics and the language associated with a self-consciously English lineage, and highlight the continuing impact of embedded forms of conservative and liberal thought. I also place emphasis on the need to disentangle some of the main interpretations of Englishness from the phenomena they seek to explain, suggesting that this kind of critical exercise is a precondition for establishing a more proportionate and balanced overview of national sentiment in this case. Overall, I give more weight to political considerations and traditions than do many other accounts of Englishness, the majority of which presume that it is essentially cultural, and not political, in character. But I also supplement the conventional manner in which the politics of Englishness has been explored by observing the various cultural arenas and sources from which a renaissance of English national sentiment has emerged.

The final chapters of the book turn to questions of policy, representation, and normative principle as I consider how the main political parties have, gradually and reluctantly, come to recognize that the consent of the English for the constitutional arrangements and forms of governance under which they live can no longer be taken for granted. And I explore the emergence of new kinds of democratic principle in British politics on the back of these shifts in national consciousness.

The abiding aims of this volume are twofold. First, I seek to reveal the limited and partisan manner in which the question of Englishness has been considered in academic terms and public discourse. And I set out, in contrast, to bring to bear insights and ideas generated by work that has emerged from various disciplinary backgrounds. While not all of these studies can be neatly or easily combined, I aim to offer a judgement about the political dimensions of Englishness which represents a synthetic overview of the various kinds of research which have been conducted into it. This is offered in counterpoint to the unduly narrow and partisan views that tend to dominate debates in this area. More generally, my reliance upon insights and ideas generated by sociologists and social psychologists, as well as political scientists and policy analysts, stems from a commitment to the idea that the multi-faceted dimensions of English national identity, and the different kinds of political effect they have had, cannot be captured by a single theory or discipline. Each of these fields of study has brought insight to different aspects of Englishness, and its relations with contemporary politics.[2]

My second, related ambition is to reach beyond the specialist communities of scholarship, campaigning, and punditry which have grown up around this issue, and highlight the various ways in which the English question, broadly conceived, illuminates aspects of British politics and government that have been overlooked or neglected. This approach generates a better appreciation of the gradual waning of some of the leading orthodoxies about British government, and the wider national forms of thinking in which they are encased. But it also suggests that some of the major traditions of thinking associated with modern British politics retain considerable power and resonance, and have been renewed, as much as challenged, by the revival of the English question. Engaging with this, and indeed other, national questions in the UK, is to appreciate a challenging instance of a broader phenomenon which the academic study of British politics has yet to grasp fully: the increasing importance of the dynamics of identity and culture as sources of political allegiance, sentiment, and thought, and the challenges these pose for a party system that still reflects the social structure and cultural assumptions that emerged out of the industrial revolution.

In this introductory chapter I review some of the well-worn caricatures with which Englishness is still encrusted. These reflect the continuing influence of some of the ideas about national character which historian Peter Mandler has identified as influential from the late eighteenth to the mid-twentieth centuries.[3] I then proceed to examine the widely held proposition that the prevalence of a familiar stock of national folk mythologies and nostalgic references in the

English cultural imagination reflects a form of nationality that is regressive and pre-modern in kind. I suggest, in contrast, that these be seen as important materials which have been appropriated in different ways by some of the main rival characterizations of the English nation. Towards the end of this chapter, I explore the rationale informing my own approach to the vexed issue of conceptual terminology.

In Chapter 1 I consider questions of chronology and causation. Specifically, I cast doubt upon the guiding assumption of political scientists and commentators that devolution has been the main source and cause of a revival of Englishness. Instead, I draw attention to a number of different developments and dynamics which coalesced during the 1990s, triggering a sustained bout of soul-searching in public life, sections of the academy, and the political world, about the future and viability of the UK. One of the main outcrops from this set of debates was a growing focus upon the merits and nature of Englishness, at both elite and popular levels.

I focus in Chapter 2 upon the three main broad perspectives that have come to dominate the field of interpretation in relation to English national identity. The leading expressions of these are set out and critically evaluated, and the limitations of their guiding assumptions stressed. I draw particular attention to their collective unwillingness to consider the different, competing ways in which Englishness is expressed in political terms. In Chapter 3, I turn to consider the mass of available evidence contained in many different polls and other recent qualitative studies which have shed light upon the development and character of this form of nationality. Sifting the many surveys that have been conducted on this issue, I highlight some important changes in the pattern of national identification of the English, as well as recent signs of constitutional disaffection. But I also draw upon qualitative studies that tend to confirm the proposition that a rising sense of national self-awareness has arisen from other social changes and trends, and is not primarily driven by constitutional issues. This chapter also considers whether there are abiding social and demographic characteristics attached to a growing identification with English identity.

In Chapter 4 I consider those somewhat overlooked arenas and sites where ideas about the English have been most fully explored and challenged. These are cultural in kind, and span the specialist worlds of artistic production and everyday life. I also draw attention to the various political narratives of Englishness that have developed during this period. And in Chapter 5 I proceed to consider the public policy dimensions of the English question. First, I recount the attempts of the main political parties to come to terms with the interlocking set of national questions that devolution has released into the political ether. I also consider the efforts of various organizations to mobilize a sense of English-focused grievance in recent years, pausing to explore why these endeavours have yielded so little reward. And then, in Chapter 6, I explore two increasingly symbolic issues—associated with the West Lothian problem and the Barnett formula—where there is growing evidence of English disaffection. In both cases I explore the nature of the difficulties which these embody, and the normative and political prospects for their resolution. In my Conclusion I seek to draw together some of the main strands of argument and consider how the English question is likely to unfold in political and normative terms, and I reflect, more generally, on some of the interpretative challenges associated with this subject.

HABITS OF UNDERSTANDING

It is widely recognized that national identities call upon, and promote, particular ideas about the national past. Yet it is rarer than is often supposed for any single version of the national story to achieve a position of unchallenged dominance. Invariably, different versions of the past are in competition with each other, and these narratives are usually harnessed to different ideas about the character of, and prospects for, the nation in the present. In the English case, this is an especially significant observation given the recurrent tendency to see Englishness as defined solely by the regressive and Arcadian images through which it is often evoked. Such a judgement makes the mistake of regarding the recurrent cultural form in which the national spirit is evoked as the sole determinant of the meanings generated by its evocation. In fact, historical ideas about the development and character of the English people have shaped different visions of the nature and prospects of English nationhood.

One of the principal arguments that I set out in this book is that this more salient sense of avowedly English nationhood has not resulted in a straightforward rejection of a sense of British affiliation or disconnection from the traditions at the heart of the British model of government. The growing Anglicization of English culture and politics for the most part represents a shifting emphasis within the combined and overlapping loyalties associated with England and Britain. In order to understand the new versions of Englishness that have become salient, and their continual reliance on established traditions of political thinking, it is imperative to stand apart from the numerous layers of prejudice and interpretation with which English nationhood has become encrusted. A familiar set of characterizations of the nature and temperament of the English have dominated discourse upon national identity, and have generally had the effect of narrowing, rather than opening up, this topic in terms

of critical understanding. In his major recent study Mandler has illustrated
how central ideas of the English personality were to elite political discourse
from the eighteenth century onwards.[4] And he observed the disappearance
of the terminology associated with 'character' in the last half-century, and its
replacement by the conceptual language associated with national identity. He
may well, however, have underestimated the continuing role that assumptions
about the English temperament, and its abiding cultural expressions, have
continued to play since the middle years of the twentieth century.

A host of clichés, caricatures, and canards are indissolubly attached to the
subject of Englishness, and a number of these have their roots in the earlier
period that Mandler excavates. Their combined effect has been to signal that
an interior core, made up of a bundle of unchanging inclinations and disposi-
tions, lies at the heart of this form of nationhood. In addition to the empirical
difficulties attendant upon such a conception, this manner of characterizing
Englishness is vulnerable to a normative challenge which this vernacular literature has tended to avoid: what about those who do not display these particular attributes? In what sense, and with what consequence, do they become
less English than their fellow citizens? *of it is ethnicity?*

In contrast to such essentialism, a more historically inclined approach sheds
light on the many different ways in which Englishness has been 'decontested'
in political and cultural terms.[5] This study takes this observation as its starting point, and treats Englishness as more akin to an 'empty signifier', which
has been painted in various cultural and political colours and corralled in the
service of a surprisingly wide range of arguments and ideas. The recurrent
appearance of a pretty standard set of national images, mythologies, and folk
references in English cultural life has also led many commentators to the erroneous conclusion that English nationhood can be characterized in simplistic,
reified terms. One of the secondary ambitions of this book, therefore, is to
illustrate how mistaken such an assumption is, and to prompt fresh thinking
about the different kinds of meaning and resonance achieved by assertions
and expressions of the English idea.

A more rounded and probing analysis of the provenance and purchase of
current ideas about the English is attainable if we desist from relying upon
stock characterizations of this people and identify more carefully those traditions of feeling and thought that have endowed these with plausibility, and
ensured their perpetuation. It is particularly important to appreciate that
such observations about the English character, or references to other common mythologies—about the iconic significance of the English countryside,
the provenance of the 'free-born Englishman', or the idea of the Norman yoke,
for instance—have a polysemic, rather than singular, character.[6] This means
that they have been recuperated by various different ideological perspectives,

rather than simply reinforcing an established view. I give emphasis at different points in this study, therefore, to the competitive appropriation of a common stock of mythological and folkloric elements. I part company too with those scholars and critics who see the ubiquity of ancient, mythical, and folkish themes in references to English culture as by-products of a national imagination that is inherently backward-looking and nostalgic in kind, and which remains fundamentally inadequate as the basis for a modern sense of nationhood. Some of the ideas which deploy these elements may well comply with such a characterization; but many do not. In contrast, I maintain that it is in part through the recuperation of these well-worn myths and vernacular ideas that rival versions of 'the nation' seek to establish authenticity and resonance. Mythological and folkloric elements are integral parts of the construction of different kinds of modern nationhood, and their persistence does not constitute a priori evidence that Englishness lacks the capacity to be conceived as an inclusive and democratic identity.

As well as stressing its essentially contested character, my assessment of current forms and expressions of Englishness adopts a broadly historical approach, even though my attention is largely upon the recent past. Taking the longer view enables an appreciation of the sources and patterns of current thinking, and offers a helpful vantage point from which to evaluate many of the polemical and partial interpretative responses that Englishness has elicited. It also provides a sense of perspective upon the different purposes served by such ideas, as well as throwing light on the enormous variety of different, and often conflicting, traits and attributes that have been projected onto the English as a people.

In the course of this analysis I highlight the recurrence of several particular mythologies. One is the often repeated assertion that this is a people who are congenitally unwilling, and perhaps unable, to define who they are in national terms. This, for instance, is the sentiment encapsulated by a character in Ronald Harwood's resonant recent play *An English Tragedy*: 'The English have never understood why anyone should be concerned with the mystery of identity. That's because they're so certain of their own. The notion of belonging is alien to them because they belong.'[7] Or, as literary critic David Gervais put it: 'Not only do the English resist articulating their "Englishness", they feel truer to themselves by *not* articulating it.'[8] This canard is an almost ubiquitous accompaniment to discussions of the collective identity and character of the English. Its familiarity should not, however, disguise its paradoxical quality, given that its many proponents are so easily able to identify this as a defining feature of the English. Equally, the empirical validity of such an assertion is not hard to call into question, given the great number of occasions on which attempts have been made to represent the quintessential qualities and character of the

English. Mandler, by contrast, has highlighted the 'periodic bouts of obsessive self-scrutiny' which the English have displayed since at least the middle of the eighteenth century.[9] Nevertheless, innumerable writers have reasserted that the latter are, by nature, disinclined to articulate their shared national identity in an ordered or explicit manner, and have accordingly been happy to accept the wilful muddling of British and English identities upon which the edifice of modern British nationhood has been built.

Such continually reiterated, commonsensical thinking has been buttressed, as Krishan Kumar has observed, by the trope which stipulates that nationalism happened to other people but never quite made it across the English Channel.[10] Such an assertion has provided a common point of reference in both elite and popular cultures over the last three hundred years, and continues to figure in discussions of English culture and identity. But the proposition that the English populace is temperamentally immune to the lures of nationalism is also open to challenge, in empirical and historical terms, and tells us more about the governing frameworks shaping ideas about the English than the sentiments of its people. Yet, exposing its falsity does not necessarily destroy the resonance of these characterizations. For nationally rooted mythologies of this sort gain meaning and traction only in part from their historical verifiability.[11] They perform important roles too as elements within a much broader web of national thought and sentiment.

The disavowal of nationalism and the insistence that Englishness consists of ingrained characteristics, not a reflective sense of shared identity, underpin the prevalence of many of the commonsensical observations which are so hard to prise apart from Englishness, and which render its analysis so difficult. Social psychologist Susan Condor has shown how this kind of mythology mediates the relationship between English people and their sense of identity. In several of her studies, English respondents who exhibited a broadly liberal set of values were typically reluctant to talk about, let alone define, themselves in national terms. They often condemned expressions of nationalistic pride, and were prone to deny that being English defined them in any important way.[12] And yet this reluctance is best explained, she has argued, by the fact that, for these respondents, overt expressions of nationalism are associated with forms of chauvinism that conflict with their own, preponderantly liberal, values. And, as sociologist Steve Garner has observed, there may be a further complicating factor at work here—the delicate entanglement of nationhood and class distinction in England which means that nationalist sentiments are identified as the natural expressions of the lower orders, representing an idiom that 'respectable' citizens are keen to disavow.[13] England, therefore, remains for many a place where 'hot nationalism' and its deplorable consequences have supposedly been avoided, and, as Condor concluded, this claim exerts a

significant influence upon perceptions of its national identity. Leading sociologist of nationalism Michael Billig has also observed how English people often
distance themselves from patriotism as a way of distinguishing themselves
from those who are seen as indulging in vulgar displays of national pride and
greatness.[14] Such representations have themselves become a factor influenc-
ing and inhibiting perceptions of the nature of the national identity that it is
deemed legitimate to hold in England.

THE ENGLISH AND THEIR LISTS

Several commentators have noted that attempts to capture the essence or spirit
of the English are often expressed in particular idiomatic forms. One especially
revealing mode of national reflection is the habit of listing those practices,
pastimes, and cultural features which are said to be unique to the English.[15]
This genre illustrates the highly particularistic and exceptionalist manner in
which English culture and nationhood is often conceived. It also suggests the
powerful connection that has been established between a specific set of objects
and practices and the values deemed to be integral to this particular nation.
Authors compiling such lists have often been content to reproduce items listed
by their forebears, as well as adding new ones to these, typically without comment or justification. This was most obviously true of Prime Minister John
Major, whose much derided foray onto this territory in a speech he made in
April 1993 ushered in a period when a growing number of political actors
and commentators were drawn towards the themes of nationhood and patriotism.[16] What Major termed the 'unamendable essentials' of English life had
all figured on the lists compiled by a previous Conservative Prime Minister
in the 1920s, Stanley Baldwin, and various other prominent national intellectuals throughout the twentieth century, including T. S. Eliot, George Orwell,
and John Betjeman. More recently, new lists have been offered by high-profile
commentators Peter Ackroyd, Christopher Hitchens, and Jeremy Paxman,
and the English habit of list-making has been satirized in Julian Barnes's novel
England, England.[17]

The recurrence of these lists, and many of their contents, is suggestive of a
sense of the *patria* that is acquired through experience of the habits, assumptions, and artefacts of a culture, rather than a nationalism that is actively
propagated, defined, and stipulated. It also expresses the proposition that this
cultural tradition is continuous in its evolution, and can be seen as akin to a
club with subtle and non-intrusive rules.[18] But this seemingly non-stipulative

form of association actually implies secure possession of a shared cultural hinterland, enabling appreciation of the iconic value of the references included on these lists. And this assumption is an increasingly contentious one in a context of growing cultural diversification and social division.

These lists arose from a rich seam of national self-understanding that has long found favour with intellectuals, politicians, and commentators in England. That produced by George Orwell remains the most widely cited, notably his 'solid breakfasts and gloomy Sundays, small towns and winding roads, green fields and red pillar boxes'.[19] Writing a decade earlier, the American-born, but impeccably Anglicized, Eliot defined culture itself through the particular forms he encountered in England, characterizing it as 'Derby Day, Henley Regatta, Cowes, the twelfth of August, a cup final, the dog races, the pin table, the dart board, Wensleydale cheese, boiled cabbage cut into sections, beetroot in vinegar, nineteenth-century Gothic churches and the music of Elgar'.[20] For Betjeman, broadcasting on the BBC during the Second World War, England conjured up:

> the Church of England, eccentric incumbents, oil-lit churches, Women's Institutes, modest village inns, arguments about cow parsley on the altar, the noise of mowing machines on Saturday afternoon, local newspapers, local auctions, the poetry of Tennyson, Crabbe, Hardy and Matthew Arnold.[21]

Each of these collections includes some of the iconic objects, practices, and artefacts that have, over time, become integral to leading forms of English national mythology. All make reference to the countryside, which has recurrently been invested with an enormous degree of symbolic significance as the crucible of the national spirit. The village, the country house, the thatched cottage, and the garden are itemized within numerous reflections on the character and culture of the English. And these highly familiar elements have once again become prominent in recent years. Yet, for all their ubiquitous, even hackneyed, character, they have been put to a multiplicity of uses in ideological and cultural terms.

These lists are also notable for what they do not include. There are few signs of Empire, the industrial revolution, high politics, or commercial activity within them, despite the undoubted impact of all of these episodes and dynamics upon England and its people's consciousness. Instead, since the early twentieth century, as historian Alison Light has demonstrated, English nationhood has been typically imagined through reference to objects that signify the commonplace, the domestic, and the particular, with dashes of nostalgia and pastoral fantasy added to the mix. The grandeur and expansiveness that were hallmarks of the Englishness that was projected during the era of Empire are implicitly identified, through their absence, with the separate history and institutions of the British state. As we shall see, features of this style of national reflection have re-emerged in the current period, as a swathe of nostalgic and elegiac appeals to a disappearing England have filtered into contemporary culture.

INTERPRETATIONS OF ENGLISHNESS

A reaction against the parochialism and Arcadianism associated with these and other related expressions of Englishness has animated an important counter-tradition of critical thinking. This reflects a deep scepticism about the viability of redeeming Englishness from the nostalgic and retrospective tones in which it is typically expressed. This mode of critical thinking has also been powerfully rejuvenated in the current period. It has been harnessed to great effect in the work of Tom Nairn, who has supplied a widely influential account of the pathologies of contemporary Englishness, and the stunting effects that the persistence of the British 'state-way' has had upon the English imagination.[22] His thinking is examined in detail in Chapter 2.

A separate, more nuanced, perspective upon English nationhood, which has been too readily overlooked in the increasingly polarized debates that this subject attracts, strikes a very different note altogether. This maintains that the qualities and attributes that are commonly identified with Englishness represent one side of a more varied national coinage. Its flip side consists of an unbroken affiliation with the institutions, rules, and purposes associated with Britain. Various commentators in these years observed the growing appeal of England as a meaningful and attractive point of identification, the source of a more intimate and rich sense of belonging. 'Britain', by contrast, came to carry a very different set of overtones—being more official and formal in character. But for the most part, these different forms of national identification were seen and experienced as inter-related, and sometimes synonymous, rather than as rivals to each other. On this view, the various strains of whimsy, sentiment, and nostalgia associated with Englishness form the inner elements of a layered sense of nationhood which also possessed an outer shell defined by the institutions and codes associated with Britain. What is often derided, notably by progressive critics, as an abiding sense of confusion about where Englishness ends and Britishness begins, is in fact a reflection of an enduring and hybridized form of national consciousness—what Anthony Barnett has termed 'the strange half diffusion of Englishness with Britishness and the many elisions to which this leads'.[23] This kind of understanding enabled Britain to be, often unthinkingly, imagined in English terms, and reinforced the notion of the national temperament as pragmatic, adaptive, and moderate. One of the major questions which the current focus upon Englishness raises, therefore, is whether this mode of understanding has now broken down at both elite and popular levels, or whether it is still intact, though with an altered balance between its internal elements.

These three broad perspectives upon English identity—comprising a highly particularistic form of everyday conservatism, a progressive scepticism towards its merits and implications, and a residual loyalty to an Anglo-British form of nationality—have become prominent in the context of a recent upsurge of interest in English identity. In addition to them, a more aggressive and populist national idiom has moved into the political mainstream, and a counter-opposed attempt to recast England as a multicultural nation has also become visible. Each of these perspectives builds upon older traditions of thought, and all call upon an overlapping set of national mythologies, while also putting these to different political uses. These include the age-old claims that: the spirit of England lies in the countryside, rather than the urban behemoths generated by the industrial revolution; Englishness tends towards quiescence and decay, until the moment when the nation is in danger; the English are an island race, dispositionally unable to join the alliances associated with other great powers; and this people developed a unique form of political liberty which was the product of gradual historical evolution, not major revolutionary rupture. Each of these axioms has been subjected to significant historical challenge, yet each continues to figure prominently within current ideas about, and expressions of, Englishness. One of the themes I stress in the concluding chapter of this book is that extant debates about Englishness underestimate the different uses served by the language, sense of cultural authenticity, and rhetorical opportunities afforded by appeals to the beleaguered, but resurgent, English nation.

In several of the chapters that follow, therefore, I highlight the continuing appeal of various iconic, mythical, and folkish references, and point to a renewal of interest in the lineage of English pastoralism in particular. These have been vital elements within a rich seedbed from which current ideas have been compiled. I give particular emphasis to the growing importance of references to place in general, and to localities and landscapes in particular, within the revival of the English imagination. The idealization of the national landscape, and the sense of belonging it has been said to embody, have afforded a symbolically rich and resonant language within which to express a sense of social alienation and political disenchantment, both of which have become powerful motifs in contemporary public discourse. Place, landscape, and cultural tradition have also been important points of reference for a renewed set of conservative and radical claims on behalf of the English nation which, we shall see, have become prominent within the political system in recent years. For the most part, the conclusions drawn from these currents of thought have proved difficult for the political parties to accept, though many of the themes and concerns associated with them—including references to the position of the countryside, the decline of traditional institutions, and the perils of over-centralized governance—have bubbled to the surface of political life in this period. But the main barrier to the growing influence of the voices of Tory and radical England has been the continuing presence of a lineage of constitutional orthodoxy, itself rooted in both liberal and conservative values, underpinning the doctrines of British parliamentary government.

Liberal constitutionalism has its roots in Whiggish ideas about the exceptional and exemplary character of the British constitution which date back to the nineteenth century.[24] This broad mode of thinking has tended to stress the 'civilizing', non-nationalistic qualities of the English people, as exhibited by their identification with values such as freedom and tolerance. England, on this view, was a cultural nation which divested its sovereignty to the institutions and forms of the British state.[25] There are good reasons to think, however, that this vein of sentiment began to fade, as a pessimistic view of Britain's place in the world and relative economic position gained ground from the 1950s onwards. Claims about the unique and exemplary features of the British state and the English people were increasingly lacking in appeal in a context where the UK was being outperformed by other states, in economic and geo-political terms. And yet, weakened as it may be, this Whiggish-liberal lineage continues to shape the thinking of political actors and public servants overseeing the British state, and still gives life to the idea that a British form of nationhood retains uniquely valuable qualities, not least its ability to obviate the kinds of nationalist sentiments that have proved so disruptive and challenging elsewhere.

PROGRESSIVE FEARS

This mode of thought has in recent decades shown increasingly obvious signs of decay. And, as the idea that an avowed sense of English nationhood is being renewed has become prevalent, commentary has increasingly revived a number of long-standing fears about some of the properties associated with Englishness, especially among liberals and leftists. In his 2006 novel *Kingdom Come*, for instance, J. G. Ballard evoked the concerns of those who have long seen the English psyche as suffused with irrationality, populism, and a latent violence.[26] The English have become a disparate collection of consumerist junkies, inhabiting a society where the lower orders are consumed by bursts of atavistic nationalism. The novel's hero Richard Pearson travels to a suburb close to the western edge of London's M25, and reflects on a ubiquitous new presence: '[e]verywhere St George's flags were flying, from suburban gardens and filling stations and branch post offices, as this nameless town celebrated its latest victory'.[27]

Many other writers and commentators have echoed and amplified these fears. Scottish author Andrew O'Hagan offered an even more hostile account of the state of English consciousness in a public lecture he delivered in 2009.[28] What counts as culture in England now, he argued, is the detritus left behind by the disappearance of the stolid independence and self-reliance of its working class. In its place has emerged a loud, rude, and self-interested individualism which occasionally erupts in the form of chauvinistic nationalism. For such critics, the once great nation that was England has lost its soul and sense of direction. Its people now exhibit a 'riot of individualism with no real sense of common purpose and no collective volition as a tribe'.[29] A good deal of commentary has concurred, though without adopting quite such condemnatory language. O'Hagan's critique painted English nationalism as the pathological consciousness of a declining and resentful working class. For others, too, it is axiomatic that a greater emphasis upon Englishness reflected the lowest aspects of the English temper. One recent academic study of its role in sport, for instance, cited the tendency to display the '*English* flag of St George rather than the *British* (Union) flag' as a self-evident cause of a rise in aggression among English supporters, without feeling the need to supply any evidence for such a contention.[30] And, according to one of the leading contemporary progressive thinkers, David Marquand, no one has advanced a positive case for Englishness 'based on a moral vision of what England and the English stand for', and this is because there is no meaningful 'English national myth'.[31] The abiding assumption that the pre-modern roots of the form of nationhood have inhibited its development as a species of modern nationalism is ubiquitous within many academic studies, political speeches, and comment pieces.

Yet, disagreement on this score has opened up in progressive circles as a small, but growing, band of writers, artists, and politicians has sought to revalue English nationhood and stress its positive potential and implications. This sensibility has been most extensively and creatively developed in various artistic and cultural quarters, as we shall see in Chapter 4. For instance, in Rachel Joyce's 2012 novel *The Unlikely Pilgrimage of Harold Fry*, we encounter a protagonist who undertakes a modern-day pilgrim's progress through contemporary England.[32] In the course of his journey to see an old friend, now dying in hospital, the novel's hero walks the length and breadth of England. In the process he reconnects with forgotten parts of himself and enlightens many of those he encounters. Joyce's treatment breathed new life into the well-worn trope of making sense of England and the English in relation to different places and landscapes, and illustrated that the quest for roots which this form of national reflection evokes can provide the basis for decidedly modern ideas about community and identity. Other commentators have concurred that an England shorn of Empire, and the baggage associated with the British past, may flourish anew, and more generous and culturally capacious ideas of the England nation might now be forthcoming.

These divergent lines of progressive thinking about Englishness—emphasizing cultural decline and mass pathology, on the one hand, and its recuperative potential, on the other—have become entrenched polar opposites in an emerging field of debate and contestation. Other commentators have insisted upon the multi-faceted manner and ambivalent fashion in which the English nation has been reimagined. This, for instance, was the position taken by John McLeod, in his introduction to a recent volume on English culture: as the social conditions of England have changed, he argued, so too has the content of its self-images evolved over time.[33] Such a characterization supplied an important counter-weight to the tendency in public discourse to narrow, rather than stimulate, the imagination when it comes to ideas about English identity. As McLeod maintained, England has been continually refashioned and reclaimed in imaginative terms. There is an abiding plurality to the range of cultural and political meanings that can be hung onto Englishness.

DIVERSITY AND THE ENGLISH

This is an important point to bear in mind when considering one of the touchstone themes at the heart of recent debates about Englishness. How much diversity can the English sense of nationhood bear? And how deep is the sense of cultural commonality that Englishness entails? A key, related question is whether this mode of nationality carries ethnically exclusive connotations. For many, this represents the most troubling and revealing aspect of the renewal of Englishness, which is sometimes framed as a retreat into the defensive laager of 'whiteness'. Rather strikingly, as we shall see, the rhetoric associated with multiculturalism has been hijacked and redeployed by populist tribunes for the downtrodden indigenous people, and the 'white working class' depicted as a seething mass of resentment lacking a voice within representative politics.

And yet, as we shall also find, a more optimistic reading has also become prevalent, insisting that the diversity of the inhabitants of England is gradually imprinting itself on the wider national culture.

This debate returns to an age-old set of arguments about the racial and cultural character of the English. The leading expressions of the English spirit that emanated from the influential Edwardian 'moment' identified by Kumar (which is discussed in detail in Chapter 2) have, for the most part, traded upon the fantasy of England as an ethnically pure, rural nation. And many contemporary analysts insist that little has changed on this score. Yet long-running counter-arguments have always contested this picture, maintaining that the English are a hybrid people, forged out of the patchwork of migratory movements onto the country's shores ever since the Norman conquest. One of the leading cultural authorities on English culture, Ackroyd, reflected that 'Englishness is the principle of diversity itself. In English literature, music and painting, heterogeneity becomes the form and type of art. This condition reflects a mixed language comprised of different races.'[34]

The tradition of thinking which Ackroyd invoked has also been prominent in the recent period. It has sometimes been signalled through reference to Daniel Defoe's iconic poem from 1701, *The True Born Englishman,* in which the illusions of nativism were heavily satirized and the emergence of an idea of nationhood founded upon a common life, spanning cultural and ethnic differences, was glimpsed:

> The Scot, Pict, Britain, Roman, Dane, submit,
> And with the English-Saxon all unite:
> And these the mixture have so close pursu'd,
> The very name and memory's subdu'd:
> No Roman now, no Britain does remain;
> Wales strove to separate, but strove in vain:
> The silent nations undistinguish'd fall,
> And Englishman's the common name for all.
> Fate jumbled them together, God knows how;
> What e'er they were they're true-born English now.
> The wonder which remains is at our pride,
> To value that which all wise men deride.
> For Englishmen to boast of generation,
> Cancels their knowledge, and lampoons the nation.
> A true-born Englishman's a contradiction,
> In speech an irony, in fact a fiction.
> A banter made to be a test of fools,

*Engtish identity based on a sense of history of
class struggle? (Peterloo, Tony-Pandy, 1974, 1984, 1386 ...)*
Introduction 17

(actually Wales) (England from
below.
Which those that use it justly ridicules. Another) -Thomas Paine
A metaphor invented to express list, -Shakespeare. -John
A man a-kin to all the universe.[35] -Ian Brown Lennon

This vision has been reanimated, as we shall see in Chapter 5, by various practical endeavours and projects that have set out to reimagine England in a cosmopolitan and multicultural vein.

PLACE, EMPIRE, AND RACE IN THE
ENGLISH IMAGINATION

A growing number of campaigners and advocates have stressed that the
English can only regain a sense of purpose and rootedness by rediscovering
the national past, and by reconnecting with the places and landscapes that
define the history and character of the country and its people. Most of the
debates about who the English people are, and what they have in common, are
typically conducted in a retrospective mode, and are littered with references
to iconic authors, figures, texts, and periods from the past. And while this is
fairly typical of modern forms of nationhood, in the English case the themes of
place and landscape have played a particularly important role in the retelling
of the national story. As Ackroyd put it, 'English writers and artists, English
composers and folk-singers, have been haunted by this sense of place in which
the echoic simplicities of past traditions sanctify a certain spot of ground.'[36]

Historical geographer Ian Baucom has set the recessive appearance of these
themes in a striking interpretative perspective, arguing that prior to the nineteenth century Englishness was mostly expressed in relation to locally rooted
mythologies, iconic places, and a romanticized sense of landscape.[37] This mode
of reflection was displaced, first, by the expansionary and outward-looking
thinking demanded by Empire, and, more recently, by a new sense of national
mythology which ascribed a fixed set of ethno-cultural characteristics to the
English. This approach, he argued, was disseminated following the rise of the
New Right in British politics, and put into circulation the fiction of England
as an ethnically and culturally homogeneous national community.[38] In this
view, the division in the English imagination occasioned by Empire has had
momentous consequences. It set in motion a recessive split between the kind
of national outlook which Kumar termed 'missionary nationalism'[39]—a uni-
versalizing idea of an England that will be discovered in overseas lands, just
as much as in England itself—and a more parochial and insular sense of

nationhood defined in relation to the unique properties of physical landscape and locality. This bifurcation, Baucom suggested, established a deeply rooted, enduring split within the English psyche, and still haunts debates about who the English are. Intellectuals and politicians remain fundamentally uncertain about whether a consciousness forged in the era of Empire is still secreted within the national psyche, and needs to be restrained by the civic culture and laws associated with Britain, or if English nationhood is rooted in the innumerable forms of particularity associated with its locales and places. If so, it might be reconstituted as an inclusive sense of identity founded upon these elements, rather than as a nationalistic ideology in which ethnicity is predominant.

The growing estrangement between these distinct forms of national thinking has given rise to open antagonism on only a few occasions, as, for the most part, these modes of reflection have developed on separate lines. One such moment occurred when figures from the 'little Englander' current of the early twentieth century offered a powerful critique of the emotional and cultural costs to the nation associated with the drive to imperial expansion.[40] Another was when Enoch Powell in the late 1960s redefined England as a country defined by a set of institutions and mores that were not amenable to the immigrant populations of the former colonies who were laying claim to a common British citizenship.[41] But, in the most recent period, a further point of overt disagreement has developed. This takes the form of an Anglo-British form of liberal internationalism—in which the UK remains a moral leader and civilizing influence in world affairs, on the one hand—and a desire to scale politics back from the state and to reconnect it with the communities and places that ground the conservative instincts of the English people, on the other.[42]

More generally, the burgeoning academic and public debate about the genesis and meaning of Englishness would benefit considerably from a more nuanced sense of the values that are promoted through reference to place, landscape, and heritage. A renewed interest in folk aesthetics, as we shall see in Chapter 4, has contributed to the revival of the English cultural imagination in recent years. Simply dismissing such elements as dewy-eyed expressions of a regressive national imagination tells us little about why they have once more gained appeal among a wider set of audiences. Kumar's historical account of the origins of modern Englishness offers some important pointers in this regard.[43] He identified the vitality of national sentiments associated with a wide-ranging body of writing, poetry, art, and rural preservationism which emerged in the Edwardian era and established the template for Englishness as a sensibility that was always on the verge of disappearing. But this extended 'moment' of national consciousness was, he suggested, predominantly cultural, and not political. In key respects it complemented, rather than

challenged, the parameters of a British-focused tradition of liberal constitutionalism. The nostalgic and pastoral themes that Kumar observed may not
have become central to party politics in the early twentieth century, but they
were nevertheless put to a wide range of rhetorical and political uses. As historian Julia Stapleton has shown, leading cultural figures, such as John Betjeman
and Arthur Bryant, began, during the inter-war period, to harness appeals to
the value of the English countryside to a conservative opposition to new forms
of urban planning and the pattern of ribbon development associated with suburban expansion.[44] These trends were deemed to be jeopardizing the forests,
villages, and landscapes that formed the crucible of Englishness. This seam
of thinking provided an important precursor for some of the most resonant
declarations of English grievance in the last few years.

The national consciousness that emerged from the Edwardian period
involved a subtle dialogue between the historical past and the present, with the
past often presented as the more authoritative interlocutor. This characteristic
has remained troubling for critics who discern at the heart of these sentiments
the consciousness of a people who dream only of living in an old country, and
are incapable of fostering the kind of inclusive modern nationality that would
enable them to deal with the realities of the present. This kind of criticism
(which is considered in greater depth in Chapter 2) insists that the democratic
aspirations of the English people have been stymied by their loyalty to the
institutions and codes of the British state, on the one hand, and the lures of
nostalgic Englishness on the other.

But an important counter-perspective has long insisted that England is an
age-old political and institutional entity, having developed a centralized state
form earlier than any of its European counterparts. The British state was grafted
onto the style of governance and network of institutions that had originally been
devised to rule England. Several leading historians maintain that as early as the
eleventh century an English nation-state, founded on a 'substantially uniform'
system of national government, was instrumental in defining and inculcating a
common Englishness.[45] A larger number have tended to argue that it was during the late medieval and early modern periods that the idea of England as a
nation developed.[46] But, over time, they suggested, the English hold upon this
system was gradually loosened, to the point where the benefits of union were
available only to elite groups that were increasingly wary of ideas of English
sovereignty, while being ever more disposed to ensure the quiescence of the
non-English territories through resource transfers and the granting of limited degrees of legislative autonomy. This perspective has become much more
prominent in recent years, as a growing band of campaigners, scholars, and
commentators have insisted that current signs of a rebirth of English nationhood signal a renewed appetite for an English political community.[47]

Proponents of this perspective are increasingly inclined to argue that the English are the last, unwilling subjects of a state that was forged around the imperatives associated with its external and internal empires. Historian and broadcaster David Starkey has consistently argued that what sets England apart from the other countries of the UK is not its cultural symbolism or romantic heritage but its political inheritance—the institutions which have been claimed as British, but are, in essence, English. The notions that the English are starting to wake up to the reality that they have, over time, lost their own national sovereignty, and are denied the opportunity to celebrate their own traditions, have been aired ever more loudly in recent years. In a situation where the rest of the UK enjoys varying forms of self-government, and the Westminster parliament is caught between its roles as a UK-wide body and legislature for England, such complaints have acquired a readily defined target. For many proponents of this view, it is only by granting the English an equivalent form of devolution that the kind of civic nationalism that has become established in Scotland and Wales might emerge.

This major intellectual divide between the vision of England as, on the one hand, a perpetually regressive form of imagined community, and, on the other, a once great political nation which might yet be regained, runs throughout public and scholarly debates on this issue. One of the main questions I consider throughout this book is whether either of these stances generates a sufficiently plausible and nuanced understanding of the political dimensions and ramifications of English identity. The starkness of the alternatives they represent has, I will argue, served to obscure the complex, shifting relations between the cultural and political imaginings of England. As Aleks Sierz has observed, 'Englishness or Britishness is a state of mind, an imaginary place, a fictional way of being, a set of stories we tell ourselves.'[48] It is my contention that some of the leading story-lines of the current period have come to carry an increasingly political charge.

Both of these views have become more prominent as a result of the dawning realization that some important changes have been happening to English sensibilities and perceptions in the recent period. Elsewhere in this volume I review the large body of data on these issues supplied by a considerable number of academic studies and numerous opinion surveys. And, while I caution against simplistic or unidimensional accounts of what are fluid and complex trends, I conclude that there is a considerable body of evidence to support the conclusion that an avowed sense of English national identity has become more salient and meaningful for many people, and that this has developed at a greater distance from an established sense of allegiance to Britain. This emerging pattern of national identity may well turn out to constitute one of the most important phases in the history of the national consciousness of the English since the eighteenth century. Its consequences are already starting to become apparent. Whereas, until recently, the question of where Englishness ended and Britishness began could be confidently dismissed as of little relevance, a pervasive interest in considering whether and how these categories might be delineated has become apparent. Such an impulse has led to frustration when interpreted as the retrieval of an unsullied Anglo tradition, potentially detachable from the many different influences that have shaped English culture. But it is more typically regarded in a less purist manner, signalling an intuitive interest in establishing roots for, and pre-existing points of connection with, contemporary national sensibilities. Such a perspective can bolster a gloom-laden declinism which stipulates that the best years of the nation's history are in the past. But it can also inform the claim that this is an old country now being discovered afresh, unburdened by the weight of the British past.

CONCEPTUAL TERMINOLOGY

It has long been suggested that the confusion associated with the interchangeable use of the terms English and British is a telling symptom of the absence of a clearly delineated and self-conscious sense of nationality, or indeed nationalism, among the English. The assumption on which this conventional wisdom rests—that a clear distinction between these terms is both meaningful and desirable—provides one illustration of the type of complexity associated with the selection of linguistic terms in relation to the issues under consideration here. The question of conceptual terminology has itself become a prominent part of scholarly debates over Englishness. In this section I set out the broad approach that I adopt in relation to it. Readers who are familiar with some of the well-worn debates about these questions will be aware that in some accounts the object of enquiry is taken to be 'English nationalism', yet in others it is the question of whether the English possess a 'national identity' that is central.

One other familiar term—'Englishness'—continues to be widely used. This undoubtedly needs to be employed with greater care than it generally receives. Its standard usage tends to convey a settled, interior core, which has often been imagined as a bundle of national characteristics and a related set of cultural proclivities. The essentialism which shadows the use of this term makes it irredeemably suspect in some critics' eyes. Yet it remains of value, I suggest, as a term referencing a field of contestation and debate, rather than a set of fixed qualities and character traits. I deploy it in the first of these fashions, and seek to separate the term from any one of the leading accounts and interpretations that have been imprinted upon it.

I rely too upon the terms nationhood and nationality which are broadly amenable to my emphasis upon the importance of long-standing traditions of national thought and pre-modern elements within these. And I reserve the epithet 'nationalism' for those occasions when particular sentiments and arguments have been aired in a manner that conforms to nationalist precepts about the cultural character and political rights of the nation.[49]

In order to ground my interpretation of the ways in which English nationhood has been imagined and contested in the recent period, I draw upon the insights of those theorists of nationalism who have stressed its imaginative properties and implications. Benedict Anderson's work, for instance, has highlighted the importance of the political and ideological resonances associated with patterns of national awareness, and provided a valuable framework for reflecting upon the archaic mythologies and historical references that crop up within modern national formations.[50] It is especially helpful in reminding us that there are always competing versions of the nation in play, each of which offers a distinct combination of social, geographical, and historical ideas and images and contributes to the shifting, contested, and layered sense of an 'imagined community'.

One further reason for my more circumscribed employment of the concept of 'nationalism' concerns the interpretative influence of the proposition that nationalism is primarily defined by its reaction against various external 'others'. Such an emphasis on the supposedly constitutive process associated with alterity has increasingly been presented as the central dynamic of English nationalism in the last few decades. Florence Reviron-Piégay speaks for many commentators when she argues that:

> Depending on the Other which it challenges, Englishness itself takes on different garbs. Its rivalry with the Continent has adopted many forms, aesthetic, intellectual ideological, religious and political: the Continent is the main entity against which Englishness developed and still does, with the European Union seen as a threat to its sovereignty.[51]

Yet, even if various kinds of otherness are discernible, the nature of the recoil that is assumed to have occurred, and the degree of repulsion to 'the other', is likely to have varied quite considerably over time, and to differ in character for different social groups and actors. Often invoked as a quasi-universal law, the role of otherness in establishing identity among nations has been successfully challenged in various historical studies. David Cannadine, for instance, has demonstrated that attraction, as well as repulsion, can inform the development of collective identity.[52] More generally, it is clear that those influences that leading forms of national identification are taken to be defined against vary in quality and meaning for different people and groups. The ways in which Englishness has been construed have at times shifted rapidly, without any major change in the character and identity of its 'others' being apparent.

Moreover, the focus upon the exterior dynamics of alterity has served to occlude the integral character of *internal* contrasts within the English imagination. Several significant, binary cultural oppositions have done as much to structure and shape the leading notions of English nationhood, as we shall see in Chapter 3. And, as with external kinds of 'othering', the relations between these opposites are not merely defined by antagonism and recoil. Rival forms of English identity, associated with entrenched differences rooted in class, region, ethnicity, and the urban/rural divide, have left a major imprint upon the imaginative dimensions of English nationhood. The a priori notion that Englishness invariably takes the form of an aggressive and exclusionary nationalism is inaccurate and misleading.

I do, however, point to the emerging influence of nationalist conceptions of England in this period, and chart their growing political resonance. This paradigm is closely, and somewhat misleadingly, associated with debates about the declining position and identity of the 'white working class'. Nationalist discourses have been important, I argue, in contributing to the rhetoric associated with a rising tide of populist sentiment in the last decade, much of which frames the English as a people who have lost control of their own country and are denied the right to celebrate their own culture. As a participant in a recent workshop on these issues put it: 'because we feel that our Englishness and our identity are being suppressed, we now feel the reason to celebrate it'.[53] But, for many others, claims made in relation to English nationhood signal a less defensive nationalism, and express a desire for a greater sense of cultural community that reaches across the lines of class and ethnicity. I characterize these kinds of sentiment as signs of a new, more expansive approach to the imagining of English nationhood. More generally, I place particular emphasis on the different, competing ways in which the English nation has been understood and represented in recent years.

NATIONHOOD AS IDENTITY

Much of my focus in this book is upon arguments about, and characterizations of, England as a community of imagined attachment. These ought not to be confused with empirical claims about the national identity of the English, which can only be gauged by an assessment of the various sedimented layers of feeling, culture, and thought from which such an identity is assembled.[54] Mandler has sounded a usefully cautionary note about the danger of confusing the increasingly intense focus upon questions of nationhood and identity among the political elite and broader trends in popular identification and sentiment. As he put it:

> A steady drumbeat of commentary from journalists and politicians has summoned historians to consider the alleged 'crisis' triggered by the 'break-up of Britain', mostly to show how and why 'Britishness' was so fragile and then either to refurbish it or to exhume versions of 'Englishness' from the past that might serve as substitutes. This agenda, implicit or explicit, has not been friendly to methodological refinement or definitional clarity (but neither has the reaction against it, which asserts that 'national identity', instead of being inevitable, is the great modern psychopathy).[55]

The obsession with national identity, he contended, needs to be dethroned from its elevated place within the modern political imagination and historical scholarship. His strictures offered an important caution against the assumption—which has undoubtedly crept into the academic literature devoted to national identity in the UK—that the nation has become more encompassing and important as a source of identity than the many other attachments and loyalties that citizens hold dear. Indeed, one question arising from Mandler's observations, which is raised in subsequent chapters, is whether the forms of English nationhood that have become prevalent are encompassing in character, or may, in fact, be worn more lightly than politically focused commentary has tended to allow.

Mandler's further contention—that national identity is declining in importance for many of the English—is less persuasive. There are different kinds of evidence to support the proposition that in England, as in many other parts of Europe, a sense of 'the national' has become a more central part of people's individual and collective identities. This trend should not be seen as antithetical to the proliferation of ties and identifications associated with cultural life, more generally, in this period. A growing emphasis on Englishness represents, for many, an additional element within a personal portfolio of identities, and it is only among a minority that a commitment to Englishness overrides other kinds of loyalty and attachment. The growing prominence of the nation in British social culture and public discourse is less a product of the fevered imagination of intellectuals and politicians, and more the result of a shift towards the themes of belonging, identity, and culture since the 1990s.[56] Ideas and invocations of English nationhood have served as vehicles for this broad trend, and have provided a rich vernacular and vivid set of cultural references for various kinds of political argument.

Instead of supposing that a renewed sense of Englishness is the catalyst for other attitudinal changes, therefore, we would do well to explore its importance in aiding the expression and negotiation of other socially rooted impulses, such as a heightened sense of anxiety of both cultural and economic kinds. The reconfiguration of English identity is a vital dimension of a much broader turn within the ethical and cultural imagination of British society. A national frame of reference offers an especially powerful heuristic since it is so securely embedded in the vernaculars and practices of daily life, whereas other familiar registers—associated with class or political allegiance—have waned in appeal during this period.[57] Ideas of 'the nation' invoke visionary elements, forms of consolation, and redemptive narratives that would once have been located within the ideologies and traditions of party politics.

UNDERSTANDING THE ENGLISH NATION

This study of some of the leading expressions of, and ideas about, the English nation, and of the copious evidence relating to its strength and salience at mass level, is not, therefore, informed by a strong allegiance to either of the two main camps of interpretation associated with the study of modern national-ism: the so-called modernist and primordialist approaches.[58] I tend to side with those historians who consider that nations arise from forces and cultures that are both 'ethnic' and 'civic' in kind, and believe that a focus upon con-tinuities in the history of national communities—in terms of common kin-ship, symbols, and rituals—should be combined with an appreciation of the invented character of national traditions.[59] I therefore take seriously the mod-ernist epistemological claim that the traditions which are said to lie at the core of Englishness are, in fact, deliberate acts of recreation and renewal, which need to be understood in relation to different kinds of political context and intention. But I also borrow the primordialist insight that, without an appre-ciation of the underlying traditions of belief that provide the resources and contexts available to individual authors and audiences, we cannot understand how national thinking and sentiments develop and gain their meaning.

Faced by the multitude of mythologies, Arcadian references, and folk narratives that recur in the contemporary English imagination, I propose an approach that takes a far less prescriptive stance towards them, and con-siders why and how it is that their appeal has been renewed. As theorist

Tim Edensor has argued, such 'cultic' elements, which have often been seen as antithetical to the construction of a modern sense of nationhood, have typically been integral to the development of distinct webs of national understanding.[60] He has also identified the appearance within nationalist thinking of appeals to 'an idealised folk culture' which is typically conceived as supplying a 'a sense of belonging, of knowing one's place in an organic world, a pre-urban *gemeinschaft* where one's identity was part of an ingrained and unquestioned way of being'.[61] Alternative understandings of the national lineage were often sustained, in his view, through the appropriation of these elements. National cultures are forged from a rich mixture of elements that traverse the increasingly irrelevant distinction between high and low cultures. But modern ideas of nationhood are constructed and reproduced through reference to different, competing accounts of the historical past, via practices and pastimes that offer individuals a multi-faceted national story. They typically rely on a distinctive set of mythologies, and invoke a multiplicity of symbolic images, rituals, sites, and artefacts. As various historians have demonstrated, nationhood often emerges from below, as well as being propounded and policed from above, in modern societies—and this insight is highly pertinent in the English case.[62] John Hutchinson, for instance, has cautioned against excessively state-focused and political accounts of the genesis of nationalist formations, pointing to the importance of culturally generated ideas that propose the moral regeneration of the nation against, or outside, the parameters of the state. In these cases, it is typically historians and artists, rather than politicians and legislators, who play the role of national intellectuals and moral innovators, recycling stock images of the national tradition in response to emerging dilemmas.[63]

Such observations are highly suggestive for an appreciation of recent developments in English national consciousness. A renewal of interest in the national past, ranging from the debates sparked by professional historians to the revival of folk aesthetics in artistic circles, has been of considerable importance in supplying an anchorage for a contemporary sense of national awareness. More generally, I will suggest that the nature and implications of this transformation have been most fully and creatively explored within the realms of culture, the arts, and the creative industries, rather than the arenas of politics, policy-making, and political thought.

•Yeah, but where does "Graham" get his culture and art from?
• Middle class nationalists?

Also Englishness didn't go away?
– Author thinks English identity is resurging, I think people who identify as English instead of British

1

Crisis over Nationhood

The 1990s Reconsidered

INTRODUCTION

Much of the commentary devoted to English national identity in the recent period takes the introduction of devolution as both a chronological and causal point of origin. The reforms that Labour introduced were widely viewed as a watershed, seen by many as unwittingly instigating a reactive and resentful sense of English nationalism. This chapter considers the years prior to the late 1990s, and points towards a very different chronology and pattern of causation in relation to the renewed focus upon English nationhood. It does so by exploring the implications and impact of a developing set of debates about the prospects and future of the UK—both as a viable state and as an encompassing form of nationality—which broke out during the early and middle years of that decade.

These rather angst-ridden reflections can be seen, I suggest, as a local instance of a much broader return across Europe to forms of belonging associated with historic forms of national and regional identity. They emerged also in the context of the growing sense of turbulence and uncertainty associated with changes in the global economy and geo-politics of that period. The British-focused debates I evaluate reflected and accentuated a deepening crisis of confidence within elite circles as politicians and policy-makers saw themselves increasingly caught between a constitutional paradigm that was palpably weakening and the reassertion of older forms of nationhood in different parts of the UK. The introduction of devolution was itself a response to this growing sense of strain. In explaining the emergence of this major moment of national uncertainty and the early signs of a growth of English self-awareness, I point to a number of important exogenous factors. These include the appearance of

European integration as an issue of intense political concern, which has been pinpointed by Ben Wellings as the major cause of the renewal of Englishness.[1] I supplement his analysis with a consideration of several other important factors, and highlight a gathering sense of intellectual scepticism about established, exceptionalist ways of thinking about the British state, and a deepening loss of confidence in the UK. Several other recent accounts of this period argue that a declining sense of certainty among the political elite about the rationale for, and connections between, public institutions and constitutional structures in Britain created openings for nationalist currents outside England.[2] I add to these observations the argument that this process also had significant, though less immediately apparent, reverberations for the self-understandings of the English.

There was nothing inevitable or predetermined about the regeneration of a more avowedly English sense of identity and culture at this point in time. It was, I suggest, the contingent interaction between the waning of established ideas about Britain and the emergence of new pressures and uncertainties generated by changes in the international economy, and the dislocation associated with Britain's rapid transformation to a post-industrial economy during the 1980s, that created the opening for this significant shift in national gestalt.

The first signs that those understandings of constitution and nation which had been at the heart of the British political tradition were beginning to falter can be detected as early as the 1970s when figures on both right and left attacked the exceptionalist thinking that had underpinned ideas about the purpose and nature of the British polity.[3] But, in the run-up to the millennium, a more pervasively sceptical mood became palpable in a number of intellectual communities, and triggered a wider debate about the prospects for Britain, given its tradition-bound nature and weakened economic position. These themes were debated with increasing intensity against the backdrop of various exogenous pressures, including a new phase of economic globalization which brought in its wake an argument for the UK to align with a drive towards greater integration within the European Union. This was also a period in which questions of belonging and nationhood were becoming increasingly salient, and when a focus upon the merits of, and threats to, national cultures were also prominent as new waves of inward migration concentrated minds upon the challenges associated with cultural and religious diversity. In response to these pressures, a rather whimsical recourse to the romantic, imagined community of 'England' became palpable, presaging the more emphatic trends of the subsequent decade.

In particular, a current of scholarly opinion began to question the value and viability of the Whiggish narrative of British political development, which infused elite thinking about the state and constitution. Various commentators cast the historical development and territorial settlement associated with the British state in a radically new light in these years, and some questioned the plausibility of the continuation of a sense of British nationhood.[4] These shifts in mood were increasingly percolating into public discourse, and chimed with a more generalized sense of cultural insecurity and anxiety in these years.

This multi-causal account of the factors that created the conditions for the re-emergence of a discernibly English sense of nationality challenges the conventional assumption that, aside from developments in its peripheral territories, Britain remained cut off from the nationalist wave that swept across large parts of Europe in these years. In England, just as elsewhere, there emerged a growing desire to reconnect with forms of belonging and identity that appeared to offer answers to the pressing questions being posed by changes rooted deeply in both economy and society in this period.

AGAINST THE EUROPEAN UNION: THE REBIRTH OF ENGLISH NATIONALISM?

In his recent book-length study, and various associated essays, Wellings has also contested the presumption that devolution prompted the current renewal of Englishness.[5] Instead, he has suggested that the recoil against the drive for greater European integration in the early 1990s provided the seedbed for a new nationalist orientation among sections of the English public. In his account, the unwillingness of the Conservative party under the leadership to John Major to set itself against the demand for European integration was a major catalyst for a shift in national awareness among the English. This was increasingly expressed in populist and nationalistic tones as Euroscepticism gathered momentum.

This emerging nationalist mood was, somewhat paradoxically, animated by loyalty to the core principle of the sovereignty of the Crown-in-Parliament, the axiom which had been central to the British tradition of government. But, as Eurosceptics came to regard none of the major political parties as trustworthy guardians of the British parliamentary tradition, a new populist imperative to preserve the national interest against the pro-European sentiments of politicians gained ground.[6] This side of the Eurosceptic outlook was increasingly expressed through the emphatic demand that the people of Britain should be granted a referendum on whether the UK should remain in Europe. This demand had come to symbolize the populist conviction that the 'general will' of the people needed to be reasserted against the machinations of political and corporate elites. The project of European integration thus came to crystallize a powerful set of reactive fears about the apparent inexorability of Britain's decline, a sentiment that had been only temporarily abated by the patriotic rhetoric of the Conservative governments in the 1980s. Increasingly, the blame for Britain's fall was laid upon the faint-hearted response of the political elite and its apparent lack of conviction that the country could prosper outside the confines of a federal Europe.[7] National redemption was conflated, in Eurosceptic discourse, with the triumph of the popular will associated with the granting of a referendum.

Wellings has provided an illuminating and fertile analysis of the linkages that were forged in parts of the popular mind between an Anglicized sense of nationhood and growing scepticism about European integration in these years. Whether the sentiments that he identified were unique to the English within the UK is, however, a debatable point.[8] He contended too that the Tory party leadership's decision to accept the devolution settlement introduced by the Labour government after 1999 was fateful, as it locked a growing and increasingly resonant body of national sentiment outside the political mainstream. A sense of Englishness was increasingly central to the generalized hostility that arose in the shires and semi-rural towns of England to the Labour government's handling of such issues as fox-hunting and the countryside more generally, as well as Europe. Some of the same activists moved from campaigning against Europe to involvement in the Countryside Alliance.[9] Out of these various developments, Wellings suggested, a more nationalist consciousness began to gel, and was increasingly expressed as a need to provide cultural protection for groups feeling threatened and marginalized by a liberal, metropolitan elite which promoted its anti-English values through the codes and conventions associated with 'political correctness'.[10]

Wellings's contention that important shifts in national consciousness began to take place prior to devolution is a persuasive one, even if the extent and nature of the English nationalism he detected may have been overstated. While Europe was undoubtedly a divisive issue within Conservative politics in these years, Euroscepticsm did not at this point generate a major challenge to the political system. The strands of sentiment which, he argued, grew out of the European issue had only minor political effects in these years, including the founding of the short-lived Referendum party in 1995 and the United Kingdom Independence Party (UKIP) in 1993, both of which were initially small parties of protest focusing upon this particular issue. Other organizations committed to developing a political case for English recognition have, as we shall see in Chapter 5, remained small and disparate, and the various campaigns that Wellings identified as the crucible for English nationalism waned more than they waxed during the 1990s and 2000s.

TOWARDS A MULTI-CAUSAL ACCOUNT OF
ENGLISHNESS

Europe was undoubtedly an important arena within which a new national sensibility was beginning to stir in these years. But other dynamics and pressures also played a key role in creating the conditions in which a renewed sense of Englishness could flourish. Some of these related to the continuing impact of major changes in the structure of the UK economy and the opportunities afforded by its labour markets in the wake of the rapid decline of parts of the manufacturing base during the 1980s, and the growing focus upon service-based production.[11] The movement of key sectors within the UK economy towards a model based upon a combination of low wages and skills, notably in such sectors as retail, leisure, and catering, had major consequences for many people's experience of employment and patterns of family life. More generally, Thatcherism had bequeathed a polarized economic geography within England, with many zones where affluence, spending, and employment opportunities were concentrated, and areas where deindustrialization had entrenched high rates of unemployment and lower levels of educational attainment. An expanding retail sector was organized around a number of supermarket giants and a steady transformation of the look and feel of the high streets of many towns and cities was under way.[12]

As the recession of the early 1990s gave way to an extended period of growth, many people's lifestyles and personal expectations were significantly altered by the opportunities associated with expanding consumer markets and new leisure choices. But for those working in the lower echelons of this economy, work was longer and less well remunerated in relative terms. For many on lower incomes, a self-perpetuating cycle of low skills, low wages, and shrinking opportunities for social mobility was increasingly hard to escape.

In this socially polarized context, the notion that the traditions and institutions that were most readily associated with Britain represented an impediment to the achievement of the good life gained a foothold among the wealthier echelons of society, especially the professional classes. This emerging perspective, which regarded globalization as signalling positive opportunities—in both cultural and economic terms—chipped away at the notion that Britain's future lay in the institutional structures and established traditions of its past. And this shifting perception helped engender a climate that was more culturally cosmopolitan and pro-European in its orientation.[13] Michael Ignatieff captured this emerging mind-set:

> Out of de-colonization, immigration and genteel economic decline there emerged a new style of national identification which enjoyed and celebrated Britain

precisely because it was essentially post-nationalistic, because the demands it
placed upon individuals were mild and thin enough to enable each to be as British
as he pleased.[14]

The growing inclination among liberal thinkers and progressive commentators to champion the merits of post-national and cosmopolitan thinking
resulted in a tendency to regard 'the national' as the locus of the kinds of
sentiments and values that progressive politics needed to transcend.[15] The
very idea of the nation as a viable and desirable ethical and political community came under increasing intellectual pressure in these years.[16] This
stance was translated in political terms, in an era of considerable excitement
about the possibilities and challenges associated with globalization, into the
dictum that Britain's future lay in opening itself up to the tides of economic
change, and jettisoning those facets of its identity rooted in tradition and
nostalgia.[17]

On the political left, Britishness was imagined in these years in the light of
this shifting intellectual mood. It was increasingly celebrated as the underpinning of a civic and legal nation that had defied the limitations associated with
nationalist forms of identity, and was unusually amenable to ethno-cultural
diversity. In his influential study of Britishness, Paul Ward provided a historical grounding for this perspective, arguing that this had been a highly adaptive
and impressionable identity that had fluctuated in its connotations as different social groups made claims upon it.[18] Critical of those historians who had
overstated the decline of familiar forms of British identity, he suggested that a
more flexible and plural version of it had, over time, replaced the traditional
forms that had prevailed in the first half of the twentieth century. He argued
too that new arrivals to the UK were increasingly inclined to identify with
Britishness, a trend that has resulted in its increasingly resonant 'civic' associations. This vision of British nationhood became more prevalent in progressive
circles during the 1990s. For adherents of this perspective, the advocacy of
Englishness appeared almost antediluvian, a retreat to the pre-industrial fantasies peddled by proponents of 'Little England' at a time when interdependency
and cosmopolitanism were the favoured motifs of progressives. Such a stance
was encapsulated by the casual confidence underlying playwright David Hare's
observation in 1999 that: '[m]ost of us look with longing to the republican
countries across the Channel...We associate "Englishness" with everything
that is most backward in this country.'[19]

This abiding intellectual duality—in which Britishness assumed the mantle
of a progressive, or even post-national form of nationhood, and Englishness
was deemed to be its insular, irredeemable opposite—supplied an influential,
organizing framework for a good deal of liberal thinking about questions of

territory and nationhood from the 1980s onwards.[20] These positions were also shaped by the fundamental divisions affecting British society in this period, as values such as mobility, openness, and tolerance chimed with the experiences of the more affluent. But for those in insecure forms of employment or living on low incomes, these norms could feel alien and out of reach, bound up as they were with perspectives that appeared to celebrate the conditions in which insecurity and inequality were thriving.

Labour's identification with the two major exogenous forces of this era—the global economy and Europeanization—placed it on the post-national side of an emerging set of debates about the prospects of the nation-state in general, and Britain in particular. Across Europe a myriad of older historic forms of identification, associated with locality, region, and nation, were being reconstituted and retrieved in these years, as citizens sought the bearings and sense of security provided by the imagined communities they heralded.[21] In their reflections on the British Social Attitudes survey conducted in 1995, Lizanne Dowds and Ken Young pinpointed those factors which had ensured that 'The 1990s could be said to be a decade characterised by a search for a more elemental sense of identity than the years immediately preceding it; moreover an identity made special by ties of "blood and belonging".'[22] They emphasized the growing salience of national forms of identification across the UK, and pointed to a heightened competition between different understandings of the nation in these years. Specifically, they distinguished between a small group of 'supra-nationalists' who were wary of the symbols and values of the nation, and three other larger groups of patriots. These included: well-educated and broadly libertarian citizens who identified with their locality and were located in the centre-ground of politics; more assertive and conservatively minded patriots, who were typically more working-class in origin (labelled 'belligerents'); and a small number of 'John Bulls', who were more socially authoritarian and nationalistic in temper.[23] These authors saw no clear consensus in public opinion about whether Britain remained a meaningful or viable nation, and concluded that the sense of mental and emotional separation between state and nation which many commentators applauded among the Scots and Welsh, was becoming apparent too among many of the English.

Increasingly, long-held orthodoxies about the merits of the British model of governance, and assumptions about its legitimacy, were now being called into question. And these doubts were increasingly reflected across public debate and cultural discourse, just as they were also ignited, as Wellings suggested, by lightning-rod issues such as Europeanization, as well as growing anxieties about rising levels of inward migration. Throughout the 1990s, there was a palpable drift towards those ideas and forms of nationhood that appeared to offer a more resonant and rooted sense of belonging and security.[24]

SCEPTICISM RISING

One source of this uncertainty related to the declining deference elicited by some of the core institutions associated with the British state and its system of governance. This was most obviously the case for institutions such as the Church of England, which experienced a significant downturn in rates of attendance and was increasingly subjected to withering media scrutiny in this period.[25] The monarchy too was forced to adjust painfully to the shifting expectations associated with intense media scrutiny, experiencing a significant fall in popularity in the wake of the death of Princess Diana in 1997. Like other public institutions, it was affected by changes in the public mood, which were refracted through an increasingly competitive media, and had their roots in the more assertive and consumerist sense of individualism associated with the 1980s.[26] Both the NHS and the BBC, which for many represented the corner-stones of modern Britain, declined in popularity during these years.

Longer-range changes also appeared to have weakened the foundations of Britishness.[27] The abandonment of Empire had been conducted success-fully and without too much political fall-out in the decades after 1945, but had bequeathed nagging questions about what now were the causes and enter-prises for which the kingdom needed to be united. And as a greater genera-tional distance was established from the collective memory of the patriotic British moment associated with the Second World War, uncertainty about the purposes and international role of the UK made its way into the political mainstream.

Constitutional observer and Labour MP Tony Wright insisted that, from the vantage point of the turn of the century, Britain could and should now be seen as a 'historically contingent experience', rather than a nation-state which was in any sense exemplary or exceptional.[28] Like others, he declared that the 'traditional support systems of Britishness have all weakened'.[29] But, whereas those commentators on the left, working in the shadow of Tom Nairn's influ-ential analysis (which is assessed in Chapter 2), detected an unfillable void in the national identity of the English that was now exposed by the weakening of Britain's culture, Tony Wright was one of a small number who detected new pos-sibilities and opportunities in the waning of Britishness.[30] He was open-minded about the forms which a politics focused upon English national identity might take, offering a pointed contrast between the prospects of a regressive and grievance-fuelled appeals to the beleaguered English nation, on the one hand, and the possibility that the qualities which had shaped a pragmatic, liberal, and flexible sensibility among this people might come to the fore, on the other. The likely forms that English nationhood would assume were impos-sible to decipher, but it was certain that the old narratives that had defined the

British state, and its relations to the national communities it contained, were no longer viable.

Tony Wright's account reflected the development of a much more sceptical climate of opinion regarding Britain's historic achievements and future trajectory. This emerging mood fed off the weakening of the foundational assumption that Britain was an exceptional, and perhaps exemplary, nation-state, with a unique institutional architecture and political culture.[31] The various kinds of exceptionalism which had infused and sustained leading forms of national self-understanding were, in different ways, subjected to a range of telling criticisms during this decade, with only a handful of intellectuals and politicians attempting to mount a defence of Britain in the traditionalist terms that had, until recently, been axiomatic.[32] With the delegitimation of such thinking, the very notion of Britain as a natural and viable entity came increasingly to be seen as potentially problematic in political and intellectual circles. The decay of this once foundational axiom was a gradual and uneven process, and was sometimes overstated by contemporaries.[33] One of the various causes of its demise was the deliberate politicization of ideas about the British nation associated with the Conservative governments of the 1980s. It was the manner in which the Conservatives under Margaret Thatcher chose to mobilize a divisive and Anglo-centred notion of British nationalism, which was directed against a variety of internal and external enemies, that resulted in the profound unsettling of the forms of thinking about nationhood and state that had generally served as stable underpinnings for political life in the UK. Writing shortly before Labour's victory in 1997, Philip Dodd saw an intimate connection between the critique of the constitutional structure and system of territorial governance associated with the British state which Thatcherism engendered, and a new affirmation of English identity.[34] For so long used to being the actor at the heart of the British drama, the English were now coming to feel like 'specimens' under the microscope of a scientific community that no longer saw Britain as paradigmatic and the English as its natural guardians. Englishness, he concluded, was becoming a more resonant and 'organic' imagined community for many of the English.

Scepticism began to surface too about the main historical narratives that had bolstered the dominant tradition of liberal-constitutionalist thinking. The notion that Britain was exceptional in both its institutional characteristics and the national character of its majority population were foundational elements in the mode of historical understanding associated with leading forms of Anglo-British thought since the late nineteenth century. At times, this had sustained a strong sense of the exemplary virtue of people and state, notably within the Whiggish story of Britain's historical development, and the celebration of England's inherent moderation and love of liberty.

Exceptionalist thinking about Britain played a major role in public discourse until late into the twentieth century. Ian Buruma, for instance, has pointed to the important role played by 'white émigré' intellectual figures, such as Isaiah Berlin and Lewis Namier, in the middle years of the century in forging a new narrative within which Britain was presented as the home of pragmatic moderation, in contrast to the utopianism and totalitarianism which the ideological politics of Continental Europe encouraged.[35] The notion of Britain as a beacon of moderation, evading the evils associated with ideological excess, gave a new lease of life to the exceptionalist mentality that sustained the guardians of the British state. This relied above all upon a clearly defined contrast between the tolerant sense of moderation reflected in the self-image of the English and the nationalist doctrines identified with other peoples. As Ignatieff observed in 1994:

> Living on an island, having exercised imperial sovereignty over more excitable peoples, priding themselves on possessing the oldest continuous nation state in existence, the English have a sense of a unique dispensation from nationalist fervour.[36]

But the diminishing confidence of commentators, intellectuals, pundits, and politicians in the continuing viability of this kind of perspective during the 1990s created the space for a more open debate about the future of Britain and the contemporary purpose of the union. Within both the political and scholarly worlds, the notion that this self-congratulatory mind-set might not only represent a degree of historical distortion, but also stand in the way of long overdue forms of modernization, became an increasingly familiar refrain.

The core doctrines of the Westminster model of government had been challenged by nationalist movements outside England during the 1960s and 1970s. But there were signs too that they were losing their traction among the English prior to the turn of the century. A medley of different factors combined to dethrone the constitutional discourse associated with the British tradition. The perception that, in economic terms, Britain was caught in a spiral of relative decline, which burrowed its way into the political world from the late 1950s, combined with the continuing psychological and cultural fall-out of the abandonment of Empire. While Thatcherism rested upon the assertive declaration that it had answers to these declinist fears, Margaret Thatcher's own eviction from power, the recession of the early 1990s, the pronounced reaction against the project of European integration, and the crisis-ridden nature of the Major government after 1992, all combined to stimulate a new bout of fatalism in British politics, and this sense of national pessimism proved a fertile breeding-ground for the revival of Englishness.

The weakening of established forms of national and constitutional thought over time exerted an unsettling effect on long-standing orthodoxies about nationhood and constitution in British politics. The established myth of the virtuous nature of the gradual evolution of the British system of government and the ordered approach to liberty it had pioneered were still resonant into the last decades of the twentieth century, in part because the forms of thought from which they emerged had always prized the qualities of adaptability and an instinct for cautious modernization.[37] And in political circles, above all, the notion of the English as temperamentally inclined to express their nationhood in cultural terms, while diverting any desire for political recognition into the institutions and structures associated with Britain, was still influential. Until quite late in the twentieth century, some of the leading textbooks on British politics unselfconsciously mirrored such thinking, praising the osmosis between English and British identities that underpinned parliamentary government. This ambiguity about nomenclature was widely held to be an established virtue of the English people. Constitutional expert Richard Rose provided a pithy expression of this orthodoxy, arguing that being English represented, in constitutional terms, 'a state of mind, not a consciously organised political institution'.[38] The sense of identification with British institutions which he celebrated was closely associated with an affinity for the common ventures which political union with the Scots, Welsh, and Irish had enabled. Such thinking also reflected the enduring resonance of an unbroken lineage of Unionism within British politics, leading James Bryce to observe a century before Rose that: 'An Englishman has but one patriotism because England and the United Kingdom are to him practically the same thing.'[39] Such was the strength of such sentiments that when demands for Home Rule for the Irish emerged as a highly divisive issue within party politics in the late nineteenth century, the reformist argument for the provision of 'Home Rule all round' gained little traction. And yet, this broad seam of constitutional thinking, which undergirded the governing wisdom of the British state, was starting to lose its grasp upon some parts of popular consciousness in the last decades of the twentieth century. One of the most important arenas where its hold began to loosen was that associated with the telling of the national story: it was among professional historians that the delegitimation of liberal constitutionalism was first apparent.

AGAINST WHIGGISH HISTORY

The scepticism exhibited by many historians towards the leading forms of historical understanding associated with progressivist and Whiggish thinking can be traced back to developments in the last few decades of the twentieth century. One key source for a gathering chorus of criticism was the address that the historian J. G. A. Pocock gave to the New Zealand Historical Association in 1973—'British History: A Plea for a New Subject'.[40] In this he captured a growing sense that British historiography had, in essence, come to consist of the history of England, with the Scots, the Irish, and the Welsh increasingly inclined to develop their own separate subdisciplines. He called instead for the creation of a 'new subject' of British history, a development that was triggered also by his perception of the threat to Britain's future associated with Edward Heath's decision to take Britain into the European Economic Community in January 1973. The particular concern that a turn to Europe would sunder the historical ties between Britain and the Commonwealth prompted Pocock to envisage a British history which focused on the history of interaction and exchange between peoples and nations in what he called the 'Atlantic archipelago'. In this grand vision, British history would pay attention to the movement, formation, and interaction of a range of societies—Roman, English, Gaelic, and Scandinavian—within the archipelago and in Continental Europe, and it would also encompass British expansion and settlement in the Atlantic, Pacific, Africa, and India during the eighteenth and nineteenth centuries.

The challenging nature of this radical reconception of the parameters of the national past took some while to be assimilated by the historical profession. By the 1990s, a sense that a 'new British history' had come into being, which examined the kinds of interaction and exchange which linked together the inhabitants of England, Ireland, Scotland, and Wales, was widely acknowledged. The old Anglocentric narrative of the expansion of the English state was increasingly challenged by histories which stressed both integration and diversity.[41]

One of the first subsequent works to internalize Pocock's vision was Hugh Kearney's 'four-nations' approach to the history of the United Kingdom in his *The British Isles*.[42] Pulling away from the familiar assumptions guiding national history, he focused upon the interactions between the various major cultures found in the British Isles. This was an outward-facing approach that allowed him to portray the UK as a 'melting pot' in which 'various cultures struggled for supremacy or survival over a thousand years and more'.[43] Just like Pocock, Kearney undermined the Whiggish idea that England was the exceptional or privileged state within the British Isles. England was instead presented as merely one of the four nations that inhabited the Atlantic archipelago. By decentring familiar ways of telling Britain's story, he anticipated a richer account of the manner in which English nationhood itself had been framed and projected. Having for so long appeared stolid and unexciting, Englishness was itself becoming an object of curiosity. Increasingly, he concluded, it was impossible for his colleagues to accept the received view of previous historiographical generations that 'England, most fortunate of nations, had experienced a steady progress toward liberty over the centuries.'[44]

There were other signs too that ideas of nationhood and patriotism were being critically rethought in this period. In 1989 there appeared a landmark three-volume collection of essays (based upon a conference organized by the *History Workshop* journal in Oxford in 1984), under the editorship of historian and intellectual Raphael Samuel, in which leading socialist historians and thinkers engaged with the themes of patriotism and the past.[45] These authors displayed a common hostility to the Thatcher government's deployment of nationalist rhetoric during the Falkland Islands' conflict, but instead of recoiling against patriotism *tout court,* they displayed their determination to contest this right-wing vision of national identity by recovering those moments in the past when the language of patriotism had been appropriated by progressive and radical currents and figures, a stance that was bolstered by a number of historical studies that pointed to the close relationship between radicalism and patriotism in the eighteenth and early nineteenth centuries.[46]

More generally, many professional historians in these years displayed an increasingly pointed scepticism towards the assumptions and conclusions of the national histories that had been produced in earlier decades.[47] The Whiggish account of Britain's historical progress was increasingly depicted as hackneyed and unconvincing. And some of the underpinning assumptions and main story-lines about the national culture of Britain, and the success of its constitutional structures, were now regarded as self-serving mythologies, not the bases for stable historical understanding.[48] Some of the bedrock myths of Anglo-British identity were thus exposed to the choppy headwinds of critical reflection and dissent.[49] Some looked quizzically at the question of how the relationship between the English nation and British state ought to be understood in historical terms, and explored how and when the former had come into being. Each of these themes became the site of considerable and growing debate from the late 1980s onwards. Linda Colley's watershed account of the construction of British national identity was the centre-piece within this broader historiographical shift, and was flanked by other major historical statements, including: Norman Davies's restatement of the European dimension of British identity in his *The Isles*; Keith Robbins's rival account of the blended nature of British identity; and Laurence Brockliss and David Eastwood's major edited collection, *A Union of Multiple Identities,* which reflected upon the fragile hold of Britishness over most inhabitants of the British Isles during the nineteenth century.[50]

As these trends began to filter into public discourse, they generated a growing sense of uncertainty, on the part of politicians and intellectuals alike, about the viability of some of the fundamental features and axioms of the

British system of parliamentary government. A slightly different challenge to entrenched thinking about Britain's historical trajectory emerged from the community of political science in these years. There, an increasing emphasis upon the merits of the comparative method reflected a growing scepticism towards thinking associated with 'the British tradition'.[51] This imperative nurtured a bevy of sceptical studies about the limitations of the Westminster model of government. The Whiggish notion of Britain as a unique kind of unitary state was now displaced by an emphasis upon its status as a 'union state', in the words of Stein Rokkan.[52] This idea was subsequently challenged by James Mitchell's characterization of the UK as a contingently formed 'state of unions', which had bequeathed a complex and differentiated model of territorial management, with varying governance arrangements evolving across the different territories of the UK.[53] Other scholars agreed that the parameters established by earlier patterns of institutional development had established a developmental path which explained how the British state responded to territorially rooted pressures.[54] Devolution, on this view, was far from being a watershed in British historical development. It had merely grafted new legislative bodies onto already established patterns of territorially differentiated governance.

DEBATING BRITAIN

This growing climate of anti-Whiggish scepticism among historians and social scientists reflected and contributed to a distinct sense of national fatalism among the cultural and political elites.[55] And, increasingly, a wide-ranging debate about nationhood began to move to the forefront of the public culture. Books written for general audiences, plays, newspaper articles, and TV programmes, all devoted to exploring and celebrating the national past, suddenly became prominent. These typically achieved a reach beyond the more specialist debates consuming professional academics, even as they drew upon the insights and research of the latter. This considerable body of materials also instigated an extended debate within the mainstream media about the British past and the current identity of its peoples

At the heart of this, often anxious, public conversation were several high-profile television series which retold the history of the country and its leading institutions. These programmes inaugurated a new genre of programme, and enabled a handful of producers and commissioners—such as Head of the BBC's History Department Janice Hadlow—to challenge the deep scepticism among broadcasters about the prospects for historical programmes that could sustain popular interest.[56] The keynote series she produced, Simon Schama's *A History of Britain,* gained large viewing figures and critical plaudits. A new cadre of public historians—'the Trevelyans of our time'[57]—including Schama, David Starkey, Diarmaid MacCulloch, and Niall Ferguson, all achieved considerable prominence, fronting programmes that drew large audiences in these years. Starkey revealed that part of the mission of his series on *Monarchy*, which was aired by Channel 4 in 2004, was to redeem an avowedly English sense of identity from the carapace of Britishness, and to redirect attention towards England—'the country that dare not speak its name'.[58] All of these programmes displayed a sharp awareness of contemporary preoccupations and anxieties. As Cannadine has remarked of their appeal, 'some of it, of course, relates to debates about identity'.[59] Thus, well-known broadcaster and historian Michael Wood produced a popular book and subsequent TV series, *In Search of England*, which reflected the widely shared concern that the English were in danger of losing touch with their national story and identity.[60] 'We are post-industrial, post-modern, post-God, post-everything. Ours are children who have never seen an altar', he complained, anticipating a slew of subsequent anxieties that were channelled into the vernacular of injured Englishness.[61]

More generally, a growing interest in questions of national identity was palpable across the media. BBC Radio 4, for instance, commissioned a series of programmes on Britishness, presented by the musician and campaigner Billy Bragg whose pro-English convictions were becoming well known. And, in the wake of the rioting by a small group of far-right English football fans in Dublin in 1995, the left-wing magazine *New Statesman* produced a supplement on Englishness which elicited a wide range of responses from contributors.[62] Other related developments included an upsurge of interest more generally in historical programmes and topics within the media, a trend that linked the focus upon the national past with a wider turn towards the excavation of history—often for the most personal of reasons. The increasing public appetite for history and heritage reflected a broader interest in the idea of 'belonging in time and place'. The English, according to Tristram Hunt, were becoming 'a nation of history hunters'.[63]

Beyond history, well-known media figures such as Jeremy Paxman and Andrew Marr produced books on the English which were tailored to a wide audience. Both set out to shock their liberal readerships by asking for a more sympathetic appreciation of the emerging plight of this people.[64] Paxman focused on the absence of a clear and rooted sense of identity: 'the English have no national song, as they have no national dress'.[65] Drawing upon the familiar stew of representations of the national character of the last few centuries, he intoned that, while they lacked an identity, the English possessed enduring attributes. These included a proclivity for gloominess, a strongly held sense of privacy, and a well-established disposition to eschew nationalism.[66] His argument was more distinctive in its dissection of a gathering mood which connected disparate political discontents to a growing affiliation with England and its cultural heritage. As he put it, 'the belief that something has rotted in England is widely held'.[67] He not only observed a growing sense of nationally mediated disaffection, but, rather strikingly, indicated that the English were becoming fed up with their constitutional lot, and were right to feel dyspeptic on this score:

> This naturally retiring, unintrospective, pessimistic people cannot continue as they are for much longer. They find themselves governed by a party whose organizing principles come from across the Atlantic and whose leadership caucus comes from north of the border.[68]

NATIONHOOD IN POPULAR CULTURE

A recent study of pop music in these years also notes the marked upsurge of a media-fuelled desire to identify particular bands and singers as icons of Englishness. This interest was just as apparent in relation to other cultural arenas, most notably football, which was increasingly established as the primary theatre where the psychodramas of the nation were played out. Against expectations, the formerly working-class pastime was the focus of considerable cultural interest in these years as it became an increasing preoccupation for a more middle-class audience.[69] The Euro '96 football championships, held throughout England, were especially notable for the way in which English supporters manifested their allegiance. Suddenly, flags festooned with the Cross of St George became ubiquitous, and the Union Jack, the traditional symbol of national pride, all but disappeared from view. After 1996, each appearance by the English football team in a major tournament was accompanied by the display of this national insignia, and the same habit quickly spread to other sports. England's cricketing success in the Ashes series against Australia, in the summer of 2005, and victory at the Rugby World Cup of 2003, both provided opportunities for very public outpourings of pride and celebration that also resulted in the mass reappearance of this flag.

The growing trend to adopt the Cross of St George represented a striking change of habit which caught the attention of some commentators.[70] Journalist Simon Heffer, a self-confessed hater of football, has testified to its major impact upon him.[71] Writing in 2004, journalist Amelia Hill declared that the question of what it means to be English had been asked with increasing frequency and intensity in recent years, with a greater flurry of books and television programmes debating whether the English had lost their sense of common identity.[72] Like other commentators in these years, she was mesmerized by the notion that the English were increasingly culturally unified when it came to sport, while increasingly divided in other respects. She boldly claimed that 30 million flags of St George had been sold in the run-up to England's match against France in the European Championships of 2004, speculating that these would now be 'fluttering from every shade and model of car, driven by English men and women of every age, religion, culture and class'.[73]

Whether the flag represented the same thing for these different demographic groups, or was indeed taken up quite as universally as this hyperbole suggests, is a question I will consider in Chapter 3. Excitable speculation of this sort about the significance of national iconography has tended to attach an excessive amount of meaning to such staged moments of 'ecstatic nationalism', as Michael Skey puts it.[74] In fact, the increasingly familiar appearance of this iconography in the scenery of everyday life—on cars, taxis, and roadside cafés—has proved to be of more enduring significance. A key cause of its metamorphosis into the primary signifier for the English nation was economic. The Cross of St George quickly became a brand with considerable commercial potential as mugs, T-shirts, bumper stickers, children's toys, and football replica kits came to festoon the high street; and this symbol has since become one of the most ubiquitous and unremarkable forms of contemporary fashion.

More generally, St George and the feast day associated with him—23 April—became the focus of growing interest in this period. St George's Day greetings cards began to appear. The tabloid newspaper *The Sun* ran a campaign in 1997 urging its readers to cut out its half-page picture of the Cross of St George and place it in their window. In 1998 the English Tourist Board promoted a week-long set of events under the banner heading 'St George Invades Britain'. And in 1999, *The Sun* chose to mark this day with a four-page pull-out, titled '100 Reasons Why it's Great to Be English'.[75] Skey has observed the upsurge of media coverage of St George's Day since the early 2000s, and the tendency of some tabloid newspapers to frame these as signs of an 'awakening' of English national consciousness.[76]

An increasing cultural focus upon the rise of Englishness was closely accompanied by a mixture of anxiety and excitement about its potential ramifications. For many liberals, these shifts raised the fear that the 'civic' model of the nation, with which Britain was routinely identified, was giving way—at home, as elsewhere—to its aggressive and unpleasant ethnic cousin.[77] This worry connected with a broader progressive concern, that nationalism might more generally be reverting to its roots as an expression of ethnically focused tribalism.

THE DEATH OF BRITAIN FORETOLD?

This multi-faceted focus upon the themes of nationhood, Britain, and Englishness was intertwined with a deepening pessimism about the prospects for the UK, and a shared concern about the forces deemed to be undermining the cultural unity of its people. A number of commentators bemoaned or cheered the prospect of the death of Britain as the century drew to a close. Paxman pronounced that, with the demise of the props of empire and war, and the emergence of the European Union, all that was distinctive and purposeful about the United Kingdom was gone. Capturing a wider shift in conservative thinking he characterized the union as akin to 'an unnecessary woollen sweater on a warm summer's day, one layer of political clothing too many'.[78]

Other commentators agreed that Britishness was in terminal decay. Andrew Gamble stressed that the British state was an artefact based on the supremacy of England but offering other nations partnership within, or incorporation into, the greater political entity of the United Kingdom. What had held together this enterprise was a set of 'interests, values and institutions', including the monarchy, the Protestant religion, Empire, the armed forces, and the welfare state. Since the 1960s each of these props had begun to weaken.[79] Other studies reported on a growing body of polling evidence which appeared to show that Britishness was declining as an important or meaningful source of national identity for many citizens across the UK. Sociologists Frank Bechhofer and David McCrone noted a fairly significant decline in the numbers of those in England, as well as Wales and Scotland, who identified strongly with a sense of Britishness.[80] They concluded that 'even in England a British identity has now fallen behind an English identity'.[81] And, in a review of various surveys of attitudes towards national identity in the UK, Anthony Heath and Jane Roberts argued that a two-tier model of national identification was now established across the UK.[82] The data they reviewed pointed to 'quite substantial changes during the 1990s in all three territories, with a declining sense of Britishness and a rising sense of the separate national identities'.[83] Their analysis of the findings of the annual Eurobarometer surveys led them to conclude as well that there had been a diminution since the early 1990s in the depth of attachment to Britain across the UK. They reported that age was an increasingly important determinant of how ordinary people responded to these issues, with older cohorts more likely to evince an attachment to Britain than their younger counterparts.

DEVOLUTION AND ITS AFTERMATH

Within the political world, however, the Labour party was increasingly drawn towards the position of providing the most unambiguous case for the merits of the union, and the Conservatives were increasingly cast as reformers (as we shall see in more detail in Chapter 5). Faced with a rise in support for its nationalist political rival, the SNP, as well as the growth of nationalism in Wales, Labour had come under increasing pressure to formulate a programme of UK-wide reform that would address discontent outside England. This commitment was eventually turned into legislation following its victory of 1997, despite Prime Minister Tony Blair's lack of personal enthusiasm for these reforms.

The Labour party leadership's approach to devolution was undoubtedly informed by some of the broad currents of thinking identified earlier. Other, more directly political considerations also intruded, including the influence of the constitutional reforms demanded by the campaign group 'Charter '88', and the desire to head off advances made by nationalist forces in Scotland and Wales.[84] The government also undertook to return significant powers to London, which had been removed by the Conservatives in the 1980s, and proceed with plans to reform the structure of local government more generally. Some voices from outside the political arena, and a few within it, raised the question of why devolution was being introduced everywhere in the UK, and not in England, as these reforms produced a very apparent inconsistency in how the different territories of the UK were to be governed and politically represented. And, while the architects of these changes justified them as a further step in the evolution of the British system of government, the introduction of distinct and relatively powerful political centres throughout the UK generated a considerable strain upon established ways of thinking about constitution and state.[85] Devolution created a situation in which the obviously asymmetrical arrangements through which the union was now managed would increasingly require explanation and justification to English audiences whose compliance had hitherto been taken as a given. As will become clear in Chapter 5, the challenge of reconfiguring a governing orthodoxy for the era after devolution is one that the major political actors have, as yet, chosen to avoid rather than embrace.

The introduction of devolution did not itself generate doubt about the future of Britain, as some polemicists have claimed, but it did impact upon an already established set of debates, and gave further life to the anxieties and fears about the future of Britain that were already in circulation. By the arrival of the millennium, a markedly 'new politics of identity, culture and territory' was apparent among the English, according to the editors of one of several volumes devoted to the English question.[86] And, as we shall see in Chapter 4, a plethora of culturally rooted images and stories about who the English were, and what they might become, bubbled to the surface in the years that followed, generating a much more rounded and diverse set of arguments about English nationhood.

In government, Labour engaged to varying extents with the swirl of anxieties and debates associated with these shifts, but it did so with particular political imperatives in mind. It set out deliberately to wrap itself in the Union flag in part to establish its own centrist political credentials, and also to head off the traditional Conservative argument that it could not be trusted with the country's national interests. Lurking beneath these developments, and especially its hubristic attempt to 'rebrand Britain', was a continuing and deepening anxiety about the UK's standing in economic and geo-political terms, in the emerging world of the late twentieth century.[87] Labour's cohort of Scots and Welsh MPs entrenched the party's ideological hostility to nationalism, and further embedded its support for the union. But the version of Britishness which it assembled and sought to promote, in the wake of its election in 1997, was deliberately angled away from traditional forms of national thinking. Instead, Britain was declared to be a 'young country', which would not stand in the shadow of its former glories and could actively reinvent and promote itself within the international community.[88]

Labour's celebration of Britishness in these years generated little enthusiasm among the public at large. Indeed, in some parts of England quite the opposite appears to have happened. It was during these same years that a slow, but noticeable growth in the number of citizens identifying with English forms of identity became apparent, as we shall see in Chapter 3. The sense that Britishness was an artificial and state-orchestrated form of identification, which reflected the liberal strictures of public authorities, rather than the organic culture of the people, became an increasingly familiar refrain on the political right. Heffer became one of the first Conservative figures to identify strongly with this reactive mood, making the case for breaking apart the union on the grounds that it was holding back English interests.[89] His argument was an important harbinger of a shifting perception of Scotland and the union in Conservative circles.

From the late 1980s onwards, Labour had, under the influence of its leader Neil Kinnock, become the more enthusiastic of the two main parties in its attitude towards the other union to which Britain belonged—the European Union. Figures across the party increasingly came to see the model of labour-market regulation and social rights associated with it in positive terms. Labour also aligned itself with the promotion of an increasingly interdependent, unfettered international economy, and stressed the need to ready Britain's economy and citizenry for success within it.[90] Both the nation and the citizen needed to be equipped to compete in the new economic order that was now taking shape.[91]

CRISIS OVER BRITAIN?

For many critics, such debates were a sure sign that the long anticipated crisis of the British state and its accompanying form of nationality was now coming to a head, as a difficult set of questions were being asked of the English about who they were and wanted to be, in national terms. Kumar encapsulated this widely shared judgement:

> Bereft of empire, no longer a global economic or political power, confronted by secessionist movements without and by 'alien' cultures within—the English seem to have found it best to turn in on themselves. Never having had an identity as an ethnic group, never having needed one, they are now—like the Russians—in the process of inventing one. In doing so they have thrown up, perhaps for the first time in their history, a nationalist movement.[92]

A resurgent English nationalism was, on this view, a pathological reflex to a situation where the English were beginning to realize that they were left behind, trapped in the crumbling ruins of 'rump Britain', embarrassed and exposed by their inability to fall back upon a meaningful and modern sense of nationality. Yet the popular notion that the proliferation of English sentiment, culture, and reflection which began to emerge in these years was doomed to lack any kind of positive and substantive content has generated characterizations of contemporary English sentiment that are distorted and almost invariably hostile. England became an increasingly imagined community in these years, offering both a set of rhetorics and a point of reference for a variety of different arguments, not just a repository for grievance and anxiety. Far from being, in the words of McCrone, 'at the sharp end of this identity crisis', the English were actually beginning, in faltering and undramatic ways, to find their way towards new—and old—forms and expressions of their nationhood.[93]

It was not, therefore, just the Scots and Welsh who came to think about themselves in an increasingly hybrid fashion in this period, even if the split between the 'home' identity and an allegiance to Britain was far less clear-cut at this point in the English case. At the very moment when many commentators were declaring the English to be hopelessly confused about their identity, and unable to salvage a modern sense of nationhood from a historic allegiance to the pre-modern forms of the British state, a significant phase of national self-discovery and reassertion was getting under way.

The proposition that the English have only begun to ponder their own nationhood under duress reflects a considerable under-estimation of the enduring force of those forms of Englishness that were already familiar long before devolution, and which were typically connected to an outer shell of Britishness. Writing in the mid-1990s, sociologist Robin Cohen offered a perceptive dissection of the unity that could be forged from the different aspects of national identity that were folded into Anglo-British nationhood.[94] He argued that British identity represented a highly successful counterpoint to the many different forces leading towards fragmentation in the modern world, including differences arising from ethnic, religious, and cultural affiliations which intersected with one another in 'overlapping and complex circles of identity-construction and rejection'.[95] Vagueness and flexibility were necessary features of British identity, engendering a decidedly 'fuzzy' and porous frontier with English identity.

During the mid to late 1990s, however, the nature of the identification felt by many English people began to shift—often in small and unnoticed ways, but increasingly, as we shall see, in a more explicit fashion. Yet, this did not result in the kind of existential crisis anticipated by many commentators. For some, this shift created an opening for an avowedly nationalist sense of English entitlement and grievance to incubate. But, for a much larger group, as will be clear in Chapter 3, the emergence of a stronger sense of English, rather than British, identification resulted in a more gradual and evolutionary transition, so that a growing sense of attachment to, and affection for, England as the predominant community of the national imagination became palpable, but did not result in the wholesale rejection of Britain as a point of affiliation.

These nuances have, however, been occluded by a body of commentary that has become unduly wedded to the a priori assumption that national identity and state were both afflicted by a profound sense of 'crisis' in these years. This favoured progressivist trope has suffered from being both overstated and underspecified. I will suggest, to the contrary, that while a considerable amount of uncertainty, and some angst, were undoubtedly apparent in the debates of the 1990s, this was also a period when new, civic kinds of national identity began to re-emerge in all of the different national territories of the UK. In the English case, a gathering sense of uncertainty about the prospects facing Britain provided new opportunities for English sentiments to return to the fore, and become attractive to those seeking new, and old, forms of belonging and cultural commonality. Many people wore such an identity in a relatively light manner, experiencing no fundamental tension between it and a host of other loyalties and affiliations which Britain's cultural diversity made available to them.

Other features of this embryonic return to English identity are also worth noting. Unlike the 'moment' that Kumar identified in the late nineteenth century, which left little imprint upon formal political discourse, there are good reasons to think that this more recent bout of national self-assertion has left its mark upon some of the leading actors in British politics and the political system more generally. This is partly because, after devolution, parliament has itself become much more consumed by English issues and, arguably, more Anglicized in its cultural assumptions. But it is also because the shift towards a more pronounced sense of English identity has found its way into a political culture that is increasingly focused upon English audiences and concerns. In a context where Britishness and Britain were increasingly the focal points for anxiety and concern, a multi-faceted discourse of Englishness became the site where nationhood was increasingly explored and remade.

2

Interpreting Englishness
Views from Right, Left, and the British Centre

INTRODUCTION

The debates which came to prominence during the 1990s about the value of nationhood in general, and the prospects for Britain in particular, resulted in powerful new connections being established between a revived historical consciousness and the growing salience of the themes of belonging and nationhood among the English. Amidst the cornucopia of ideas, arguments, and stories which these themes attracted, several recurrent, politically resonant characterizations of the English past were especially prominent, spanning the concerns of academic scholarship and public discourse. These perspectives established alternative interpretations and arguments at a time when leading forms of constitutional and national thought were, as we saw in Chapter 1, beginning to wane.

In this chapter I focus upon these narratives and highlight the expectations, hopes, and fears which they have projected onto English identity. I also identify and critically evaluate some of the influential political claims about the nation which they have sustained. In order to elucidate and assess these broad and internally diverse patterns of argument, I refer to a number of landmark works and authors that are identified with them, and chart some of the debates that each has spawned. I also point to their precursors, suggesting that each drew upon long-established traditions of thinking and sentiment about England. Not only have they served as vehicles for the revival of long-standing, and in some cases, latterly forgotten, ideas about the English people and British state, they have also contributed to an increasingly marked disagreement about the historical character and political dimensions of Englishness. I argue, in particular, that while two of them have been advanced as alternatives to a weakening lineage of liberal constitutionalism—and one promises to reconfigure this lineage in today's fraught circumstances—they are all challenged, rather than reinforced, by the complex and fragmented nature of emerging English sensibilities. I caution therefore against the notion that any one of these narratives will, as their proponents claim, emerge as an alternative paradigm to the doctrines associated with the British tradition of governance.

I begin by considering the re-emergence of a historical and normative perspective that has proved enormously influential—that associated with the thinking of leading Scottish nationalist and New Left intellectual Tom Nairn. The eye-catching thesis which he first set out during the 1970s drew attention to the imminent and inexorable 'break-up' of Britain, and advanced an interpretation of English nationalism which stressed its stalled and pathological character, a view which has assumed the status of a near orthodoxy in progressive circles. I focus in particular upon his characterization of the English as a people who did not develop the consciousness or self-image of a democratic nation, and abjured the principle of popular sovereignty. Nairn's thinking, I will suggest, has been refined and built upon by later commentators, and most recently supplemented (and in some ways supplanted) by a major new historical analysis of the 'missionary' character of Anglo-British nationhood, provided by historical sociologist Krishan Kumar. Evaluating these ideas, I identify a number of historical and conceptual weaknesses at the root of Nairn's thinking about the English. This has relied too heavily upon an overly prescriptive conception of nationalism which has informed his dismissive response to nearly all concrete expressions and forms of English nationhood. Progressives have been too uncritical in their absorption of Nairnite thinking, and have, as a result, remained overly wary of, and distant from, recent shifts in national identification among the English people.

The second generic perspective which I evaluate invokes an utterly different kind of historical sensibility. This coheres around the claim that English nationhood is a much older and more durable lineage than is supposed either by progressive critics of the British state or by liberal-conservative constitutionalists. On this view, Englishness is a patrimonial lineage, not a newly created identity, and is best captured through an appreciation of unbroken ways of living and feeling, sentiments that are most likely to be cultivated through contact with a select band of traditions, customs, and places. The countryside has played an especially important role as a venue where the sense-experience of Englishness can be developed, on this view, and represents a refuge from a variety of threats associated with modern life. The conservative, but also radical, modes of thinking which this perspective prompts frame English nationhood in affective terms, evoking a powerful sense of nostalgia for a formerly great nation that is once again in danger. For some of its proponents, such as Roger Scruton (whose work is considered at some length below), an authentic English nationhood can only be felt and experienced, not stipulated and rationally debated. This mode of English sentiment has been advocated, in recent times, as the basis for an oppositional politics targeted at the dead hand of state bureaucracy and the instrumentalism of the market. But it is also beset by some powerful internal contradictions, and suffers from a fundamental uncertainty about the relationship it wants to promote between the English past and the present.

The third interpretation I consider emanates from a rich body of scholarship that has devoted itself to the historical study of the political thinking of elite-level actors and political parties, and takes its cue from leading intellectual proponents of the 'British tradition' such as philosopher Michael Oakeshott. It coheres around the notion that a rich seam of national thinking informed elite political discourse in the late nineteenth and twentieth centuries, and generated supple and broadly liberal understandings of both England and Britain. This perspective is considered in relation to the recent work of Arthur Aughey, and his subtle exploration of the Oakeshottian idea of an ongoing, encompassing 'big conversation' around state and nation which can be employed as a template for understanding the contemporary evolution of national sentiments and constitutional debate. I pay close attention to his contention that it has been the distinctive contribution of some of the leading traditions of Anglo-British thought to obviate the emergence of mass nationalism within England, generating more subtle and resonant accounts of nationhood than Nairnite criticism has tended to allow. In evaluating this perspective I conclude that some of its key assumptions and normative claims are so proximate to the core doctrines of the British tradition that it struggles to achieve any kind of critical purchase on the latter, and is therefore vulnerable to a growing imperative to separate more clearly the ideas and sentiments associated with England from those that were part of the Anglo-British inheritance.

THE BREAK-UP OF BRITAIN

In an interview with *The Economist* magazine in January 2012, the current leader of the Scottish National Party (SNP) and Scotland's First Minister, Alex Salmond, was asked what English public opinion would make of the prospect of Scottish independence. In reply he expressed the hope that the English people might also be liberated to 'craft a new modern identity without the "appendage of Britain"'.[1] Salmond has long been a keen, if somewhat mischievous, advocate of English nationalism, anticipating that its emergence would aid the goal of ensuring Scottish independence from the United Kingdom. His comments are also, however, indicative of the long shadow cast by a book published by an obscure left-wing press in 1977. Written by Tom Nairn, then a leading figure on the editorial board of the journal *New Left Review, The Break-up of Britain* has arguably exerted a greater influence than any other single work upon current thinking about Englishness.[2] Its core theses, and Nairn's subsequent analyses of the obfuscatory mystique fostered by the core institutions of the British state, have gradually become a template for subsequent progressive thinking. Here I explore some of the reasons for its appeal, and argue that Nairn's thesis has proved to be a mixed blessing for progressives seeking to come to understand developments in relation to national identities in the UK.

At the heart of his analysis lay an ambitious, theoretically informed account of the development of the state itself, and its relations with the territories it governed. It had grown, he maintained, out of what was in essence an ancient English state, and had, over the course of several centuries, expanded its hold over outlying areas, and peoples, ever since the Norman invasions, absorbing the many different peoples and cultures on the archipelago it dominated. But this goal had been pursued, in part, by giving a significant amount of latitude to the 'personality of the nations' under the rule of the English.[3] During the nineteenth century, the increasingly powerful British state had set itself on the course of overseas expansion based upon its naval pre-eminence and considerable advantage as the first power to experience industrialization. Nairn based his interpretation upon the controversial account of British historical development which he developed with his collaborator Perry Anderson.[4] Together they argued that the English middle class had buried its revolutionary ambitions, making peace with the landed gentry, rather than seeking to supplant it. The state form that emerged out of this historic compromise oversaw rapid industrial development and developed a sinuous statecraft motivated by the ambition to contain the threat of rising social forces. The working class was successfully incorporated into the political system, and its radical ambitions blunted. Nairn highlighted the role and importance of a particular kind of 'inter-class nationalism' that was deliberately promoted by the state in the nineteenth century, a suggestion that chimed with the major historical interpretation offered by Linda Colley in her watershed study *Britons*.[5]

The state-sponsored patriotism which encompassed the distinct nationalities and territories of the UK, and served to obscure the frozen nature of the class relationships over which the state presided, was, Nairn argued, on the point of extinction. The nationalist currents that were raising their heads in the 1970s were the first signs that the British 'state-way' was losing control. This gathering crisis could only be resolved in a moment of disruption 'at the level of the state, allowing the emergence of sharper antagonisms and a will to reform the old order root and branch'.[6] It was also increasingly clear, he suggested, that the underperforming British economy was being held back by the absence of a modern state system. The nationalisms that were pushing forward at the periphery, therefore, were early symptoms of a growing crisis of legitimacy. Nairn was adamant that the portfolio of reforms then circulating within the world of high politics—including ideas for devolution and greater autonomy for the English regions—amounted only to 'ways of preserving the old state—minor alternations to conserve the antique essence of English hegemony'—rather than representing meaningful attempts to grapple with the underlying situation.[7]

While the bulk of his book offered a historically rooted analysis of each of these resurgent nationalist movements, he also devoted considerable space to an assessment of the recent emergence of a particular form of English nationalism—that orchestrated by the Conservative politician Enoch Powell. The latter's politics were deemed to represent a 'comment on the absence of a normal nationalist sentiment, rather than an expression of nationalism'.[8] Much was to hang—here and elsewhere in his work—on his use of the term 'normal'. It referenced the kinds of modern, democratic nationalism that were more typical of other European states, and were harbingers of the kind of modern political order that he, and other socialists, yearned to see in Britain. Powellism, while deploying the rhetoric and syntax of nationalism, offered something different altogether—a further, morbid symptom of the continuing power of the *ancien régime* to divert and suppress the national will of the English. The racism and populism associated with Powell represented the most 'regressive possible side of an eventual English nationalism'.[9] The more the opportunity to express and inhabit a shared sense of popular nationhood was delayed, Nairn maintained, the more likely it was that resentment, grievance, and racist sentiment would emerge instead.

The distinction upon which this analysis hinged—between an ideal-typical form of modern nationalism on the one hand, and the 'cryptic' and pathological simulacrum that had taken root in England—was, however, much harder to sustain than was apparent from Nairn's fluent argument. Such was his commitment to the notion of a 'normal' model of nationalism that forms of national sentiment that departed from this template were implicitly regarded as deviant. In a judgement that has been endlessly echoed by progressives when faced with claims to the English *patria*, Nairn concluded that Powell's politics represented a kind of regressive fantasy, a 'conservative dream-world founded on an insular vein of English romanticism'.[10] This, he sneered, amounted to a 'Disney-like English world where the Saxon ploughs his fields and the sun sets to strains by Vaughn Williams'.[11] Powellism was a form of ersatz romantic nationalism which retained none of the authentic sentiments of either of these forces.

And yet, Nairn could never quite dismiss the Powellite enterprise entirely, nor did he convincingly wall it off from an ideological family—nationalism— that was much broader and more varying in its character than he cared to admit. For all his evident distaste for Powell's beliefs, Nairn did concede that the latter's thinking was referencing the sorts of questions that the English ought to be asking, and needed to be understood as a response to the absence of national-democratic options facing them:

> It is quite true that the English need to rediscover who and what they are, to rein-vent an identity of some sort better than the battered cliché-ridden hulk which the retreating tide of imperialism has left them—and true also...that the politics of the last 20 years have been entirely futile in this respect.[12]

This kind of sentiment spoke to the 'void' where popular nationalism ought to lie. The English seemed doomed to find solace in rural dreamscapes when it was, in truth, time for them to 'wake up' and realize their own sense of col-lective sovereignty, independently of the institutions and affiliation granted to them by the British state.[13] Only when the English forged a new national myth, Nairn insisted, could their democratic energies and collective will be realized.

This broad argument was refined further in a number of subsequent writ-ings. Following the devolution legislation introduced by Labour after 1997, Nairn penned a searing critique of what he regarded as its half-baked and half-hearted constitutional radicalism.[14] Although twenty years had now passed since his earlier doom-laden account of the British state, he continued to insist that the 'dissolution of the old multi-national state is indeed under way'.[15] Devolution represented a rearguard action disguised as a power-dispersing piece of modernization, but it would only delay the 'unitary end-game'.[16] What others hailed as a new constitutional dawn was really a 'dissolution by stages' which would take the form of 'the erosion and qualification of a once unified Sovereignty'.[17] Blair's project, he declared, amounted to the 'preservation of the world's oldest multinational state through cautious, negotiated reform con-trolled from the centre'.[18]

But, even as the union's dying breaths drew near, the English refused to wake up from the dreamscape conjured by this antiquated state and its core institutions.[19] The role that Powell had played in polluting the soil from which a genuine democratic nationalism should have emerged was now being filled by 'proto-nationalist mythologies' that were encouraging a rising tide of Euroscepticism.[20] The English, Nairn concluded, were in the most curious of positions. Having tended to take their hegemony over the archipelago they dominated for granted, and having not had to fight to assert their own sense of nationhood, they had consented to a political system which provided precious little space for their own collective identity. But, increasingly, Nairn saw signs that the asymmetrical character and consequences of devolution were starting to irk the English. It was, he suggested, increasingly likely that English nationalism would return, but, as with Powell, this would most likely take a populist guise:

> Blair's project makes it likely that England will return on the street corner, rather than via a maternity room with appropriate care and facilities. Croaking tabloids, saloon-bar resentment and back-bench populism are likely to attend the birth and have their say. Democracy is constitutional or nothing.[21]

Nairn's wide-ranging analysis has left its imprint upon a good deal of subsequent political commentary and thinking, in both England and Scotland. His contention that the antiquated structures and institutions of the British state prevented the development of a democratic national imagination among the English is a familiar theme within much progressive thinking. And so too is his assertion that, until the undemocratic structures of the British state are dismantled, expressions of English nationhood will invariably take the form of a reactionary form of nostalgic delusion for a vanishing past. He remains wedded to the notion that only a major break from the institutional architecture of the British state can release the democratic imagination of the English. In a blog post he authored in 2012, he reflected that his own earlier analyses of the power and function of the monarchy had underplayed the vital role it had played in diverting the English from 'standard-issue nationalism'.[22]

RE-EVALUATING NAIRN

Nairn's key arguments have not passed without challenge, as we shall see, yet they have rarely received extended critical engagement in progressive circles. One notable exception to this was the historian Edward Thompson's powerful riposte to the overarching thesis which Nairn and Anderson produced, and his rejection of their cosmopolitan dismissal of the merits and impact of English radicalism. Thompson successfully challenged a number of the grander claims made by Anderson and Nairn.[23] He also punched significant holes in Nairn's presumption that the substantive cultural and intellectual traditions that have shaped and contested the English imagination did not provide the basis for a modern form of nationhood. Nairn's writings were infused by the assumption that it is only when the English opt for those 'normal' forms of political representation and governance which are associated with other, unnamed modern polities that we can be assured that they have exercised their own collective national will. Equally, the possibility that the English may well have been, for the most part, content and willing to express their nationality in relation to institutions and structures that blurred the boundaries between the imagined communities of England and Britain is simply foreclosed by his argument, a historical judgement that betrays a revealingly prescriptive approach to the principle of national self-determination. As a result, his thinking and that of the many progressive commentators who have followed his lead, has been fatally alienated from the actual manifestations of English culture and identity, including those that might have provided rich resources for progressives.

Nairn's position has been sustained by an abiding sense of political frustration and disappointment with the English. His representation of a people who are all too easily seduced by the pomp and circumstance of the pre-modern state, and comprise a uniquely quiescent and passive nation, has reverberated widely throughout socialist and radical circles.[24] One further aspect of Nairn's analysis has also been transmitted much more widely. This stems from his depiction of the 'void' that supposedly lies at the heart of English national identity, the result of the blocked sense of aspiration associated with the delegation of sovereignty to the British state. The recessive promotion of a nostalgic, whimsical, and Arcadian Englishness offered little more than a simulacrum of nationhood, he maintained. Without a robust and democratic national 'myth', the English have returned again and again to a slew of pastoral fantasies. This underpinning conception of the English as a people defined by their lack of a collective identity has been referenced far and wide within political and cultural commentary in recent years. Leading progressive thinker David Marquand implicitly invoked it when he declared that the English lack a foundational myth that could supply the underpinning for a democratic sense of nationality.[25]

Yet this kind of sweeping dismissal overlooks the persistence and reappearance of a much more varied stock of national mythologies, a number of which have been of considerable resonance for the left—the freeborn Englishman, the Norman yoke, Magna Carta, and Robin Hood being some of a large number of examples. More generally, Nairn's historical account of the English trades upon a depiction of the lower orders as the conditioned objects of class forces and historical patterns, rather than, as Thompson supposed, actors who had both shaped their own sense of class consciousness and forced important concessions from the ruling class.[26] Thompson's scepticism was echoed in an important critical response to Nairn's 'break-up' thesis penned by Pocock. He insisted that Britain's history is better conceived as 'a pattern held together by its divisions and antagonisms'.[27] In Pocock's understanding, 'British history ... has been, and is, a game for a number of players, in which each player's self-image, and image of the game, must be taken into account'.[28]

Nairn's characterization of the break-up of Britain as a democratic imperative, Pocock suggested, represented an ultimately undemocratic attempt to end
the way in which this game is currently played, inviting each of the national
'players' to write the rules which they believe suit them best, independently of
others. Such thinking occluded the very real possibility that the English might
have good reasons to remain members of a political association that would
preserve their established inter-relations with the Scots, Welsh, and Northern
Irish. Nairn's position, by contrast, was fixed in its opposition to emergent
democratic arguments for the renegotiation of the arrangements for territorial
governance within the United Kingdom.[29] His thinking, Pocock noted, echoed
that of those on the political right who found it hard to believe that, if con-
sulted, the English would choose to be part of a multi-national entity. Nairn's
work, he shrewdly observed, was haunted by the possibility that reform of the
British state might actually prove popular and effective.

AFTER NAIRN

Nairn's arguments have cast a lengthy shadow over subsequent attempts to
understand the historical nature and contemporary significance of appeals
to, and constructions of, English identity. And this is due, in part, to its
rich combination of historical sweep and theoretical sophistication. But it
was also because Nairn rekindled a rich seam of progressive fears about
Englishness. For many on the left, his thinking represents the unavoidable
gateway to an understanding of the culture, character, and sensibilities of the
English. In an essay for the *Guardian* newspaper in 2009, Patrick Wright,
for instance, reminded his readers of the unrivalled importance of Nairn's
thinking, and particularly the latter's conviction that, lacking a 'coherent, sufficiently democratic myth of Englishness', the English lurched between their
worship for the 'semi-divine Constitution and the Mother of Parliaments',
on the one hand, and crude racism of the sort shown by the London dockers
who marched in support of Enoch Powell in 1968, on the other.[30] But this
writer was also, rather unusually, prepared to step outside the parameters
supplied by Nairn, and, in so doing, to open up a wider field of enquiry. He
noted the depth of the liberal suspicion that English nationalism represented
'an incorrigibly primitive beast best kept carefully locked up in its cave',[31] and
proceeded to develop a more balanced, if still critical, characterization of the
swelling chorus of English-rooted grievances than was typically offered in
these circles.

The entrenched liberal prejudice towards any actual manifestation of English nationalism, which Nairn's analysis has fuelled, illustrates one of the abiding limitations of his analysis. It has resulted in the significant neglect of other geographically and socially rooted forms of English identity, even though these had long represented alternatives to the leading images upon which Nairn focused his fire. Nairnite thinking has, in key respects, served to reinforce the tendency to see only the kinds of political and national thinking that were associated with elites based in London and the South East. Yet, a broader geographical compass and willingness to look at English identity from the 'bottom-up', as Robert Colls has illustrated, brings into view a range of other forms of Englishness.[32] And, as we shall see in Chapter 4, a number of distinct forms of English identity were rooted in the divides that had grown up around region and class since the nineteenth century, yet these remained absent from Nairn's reified picture of an archaic Englishry, frozen in aspic.

Such weaknesses have been forgiven or overlooked by those enticed by the prospect of the death-throes of the British state that Nairn conjured up. With the emergence of Scottish nationalism as a major political force in the last few years, and signs of a greater ambivalence towards the union among sections of English opinion (which are considered in more detail in Chapter 3), the dissolution he anticipated has finally become imaginable, generating a new wave of interest in his ideas. In an edited volume published in 2008, activist and campaigner Mark Perryman announced that this 'break-up' was already under way.[33] The waning of Britain had cleared the way for the reinvention of a progressive English patriotism. Perryman spoke for a small, but growing, number of leftists who supported the view that the English should slough off the more traditionalist aspects of their self-image, and recant the 'sour-faced jealousy' that supposedly typified their relations with the other nations of the UK.[34] An important element of this project involved learning lessons from other nationalist movements in the UK, an idea that also originated with Nairn.

One of the guiding assumptions of this, and other similar arguments, is that the atavistic aspects of the English nationalist imagination need to be contained for a progressive harvest to be yielded. In this instance it is the civilizing influences associated with developments in Scotland and Wales from which the English should be ready to learn, a stance that offered an inversion of the lingering sense of cultural superiority which dominant forms of Britishness had traditionally offered to the English. Here, the Nairnite model of 'normal' nationalism is transferred to currents that lie outside England within the UK. Yet, once again, the key question of why the peculiarities of the English need to be set aside, rather than cherished and built upon, remained unasked.

BEYOND NAIRN? KUMAR'S ENGLISH 'MOMENT'

A growing number of commentators have been struck by the diminished prospects for the English if they are left as sole occupants of 'rump Britain'. This is certainly one of the concerns evinced by Kumar, in his major study of English nationalism. Nairn's thinking forms an important backdrop to the interpretation of the history of English national identity he advanced in his *The Making of English National Identity*, and yet he also established within it an important point of departure from a Nairnite reading of the English past.[35]

At the start of his book, Kumar cited with approval Nairn's caustic meditation upon the varying nomenclature applied to the constitutional situation of the English:

> We live, says Tom Nairn, in a state 'with a variety of titles having different functions and nuances—the UK (or "Yookay" as Raymond Williams relabelled it), Great Britain (imperial robes), Britain (boring lounge-suit), England (poetic but troublesome), the British Isles (too geographical). "The country" (all-purposes within the Family), or "This small Country of Ours" (defensive Shakespearian).'[36]

But Kumar also examined, in some depth, a number of different historical periods in contrast to the panoramic historical overview that Nairn provided. Importantly, he also offered a rather different account of the relationship between British nationhood and the development of the British Empire to that offered by Nairn. Empire had been defined around the pursuit of two distinct goals: the management of the overseas dominions and the need to establish the basis for a stable settlement and sense of mutual purpose among the different nations within Britain. These twin imperatives ensured that the most sizeable national grouping within the state—the English—were required to suppress overt traces of their own ethnic and cultural lineage so that a leading form of nationhood, that could encompass other forms of national sentiment, might be forged.[37]

Kumar proposed, therefore, that English nationalism be understood as imperial in character, but in a different sense to that conveyed by Nairn. It resembled the restrained and culturally inclusive mode of state-focused nationalism which had historically been adopted by leading nations in multi-national empires. In crucial respects this represented a more capacious and civic form of nationality which extended beyond the core traditions and cultural assumptions of any single nation. Empires required the development of such an encompassing form of nationality in order to ensure the allegiance of the various national peoples within their borders. And they typically developed a sense of purpose that was couched in 'civilizational', rather than narrowly national, terms. There are parallels, therefore, Kumar suggested, between the

British and both the Ottoman and Habsburg Empires, and a particular resonance with the case of Russia.[38]

Kumar deployed these comparisons to highlight the development of a
leading national ideology which both enabled the hegemony of the ruling
bloc, which Nairn had emphasized, but also involved a deliberate attempt to
obscure the boundaries between English and British identity, and gave some
considerable scope to non-English peoples to identify with the nation's wider
goals.[39] Empire, in conjunction with Protestantism, supplied the key ingredients underpinning the national identity and constitutional thinking of the
English, at least until the end of the eighteenth century. This cocktail began
to wane somewhat in the nineteenth, when the Protestant faith ceased to play
such a salient role, following the annexation of Ireland and the emergence of
rival Protestant states abroad. The organizing idea of Britain as an association
defined by its opposition to the Catholic monarchies of Europe was no longer
sufficient to command the loyalty of its subjects. In the late nineteenth century,
therefore, a new case for the British state was needed, reflecting the imperatives and challenges generated by the industrial revolution, and the growing
emphasis upon the role of the state in providing social welfare across the various territories of Britain.

During this period, Kumar suggested, there began to develop a new, more
emphatic sense of English national consciousness. In his major book-length
study *The Making of English National Identity*, he reviewed a plethora of different interpretations of the history and genesis of a distinctly English sense
of nationhood, and concluded that it was only in the late nineteenth century
that the kinds of sentiments and patterns of thought that could be mean-
ingfully labelled 'nationalism' began to coalesce. This 'modernist' reading of
English nationalism has proved controversial among professional historians.
A number of scholars have contended that the secular and egalitarian model of
nationalism which Kumar projected back into the different periods he examined inhibited his ability to appreciate the national character of pre-modern
thinking.[40] Others have observed that his emphasis upon a singular, extended
'moment' when a national consciousness was supposedly born, misrepresents
the evolutionary and rooted nature of national thinking.[41] For Anthony Smith,
the notion that a discernible break from established ideas about Britain and
the Empire can be detected in this particular period is highly questionable.
And, likewise, for Colls, the idea of a single watershed when the notion of a
modern English nation was born, is belied by the reality that a great many different 'moments' affected the course and nature of English identity.[42]

But for Kumar it was only when sections of the British elite began to doubt
that it was their destiny, as the leading imperial power, to pursue the missionary
role associated with Empire that a more self-aware form of Anglo-nationhood

began to surface. This development was crucially informed by the growing influence of late nineteenth-century discourses on language, race, custom, and culture, which promoted the search for true expressions of the 'folk-spirit of the English race'.[43] His illuminating dissection of this 'moment' of English nationalism has done much to establish the importance and singularity of the upsurge of interest during the Edwardian era in the cultural reimagining of Englishness. He identified, in particular, a range of discrete, but connected, intellectual endeavours, including developments in the adjacent fields of languages, literature, folklore, fiction, and historiography, to illustrate his thesis about the coming of an English national consciousness in this period. This ferment was predominantly cultural in kind, never quite percolating into the arenas of high politics. As a result, the carapace of British constitutional thinking, rooted in the twin doctrines of parliamentary sovereignty and the Crown-in-Parliament, remained unthreatened. The nationalism which emerged during this moment was, he also suggested, highly Whiggish in its character, committed to extolling English liberty and pragmatism, and also given to flights of lyricism about the landscapes and inhabitants of the countryside. The latter was typically imagined, in Alun Howkins's suggestive phrase, as the 'south country'.[44] Ultimately, this 'moment' was diffused and contained by different factors that served to uphold the commitment of the English to the British state and its associated modes of thinking and governing.

ENGLISHNESS AS ABSENCE?

Kumar concluded his book by considering whether a new phase of English nationalism was once again imminent, at the dawn of the twenty-first century, and has explored this question in a number of subsequent writings. His assessment of the character of the various forms of English identity that appear to be re-emerging was notably ambivalent. Holding to the Nairnite notion of the absence of a substantive core to English identity, he approvingly cited other commentators who have also adhered to the 'absence thesis', including literary theorist Robert Young, for whom Englishness 'was never really here, it was always there, de-localised, somewhere else: by the end of the nineteenth century, England had been etherised, so that England and the English were spread across the boundless space of the globe'.[45] Yet Kumar also injected a more optimistic note into the appraisal of contemporary Englishness. Noting that the English possessed little history of nationalist celebration, he identified the possibility of the development of 'an open, expansive and diverse society' which welcomes 'new peoples, cultures and ideas'. England, he observed hopefully, had never been a homogeneous society, 'but has typically looked outward from itself to the world'.[46]

The notion of Englishness as an 'absence', which Kumar also evoked, signals the enduring influence of Nairn's thinking. The idea that English national identity necessarily lacks substantive content as a result of its subservience to the governing ideologies of the British state, has proved immensely attractive to progressively minded commentators and critics, disappointed and frustrated by the seemingly unshakable conservatism of the English. Kumar also considered that the leading cultural expressions of Englishness were still refracted through the sepia-tinted Edwardian 'moment' of a century ago. There persisted:

> scraps of cultural Englishness—a love of the countryside, an aversion to cities, a distrust of intellectuals—but much of this is nostalgic and backward-looking, heavily slanted towards the middle and upper-middle class outlook that has been so dominant in modern England. It excludes too many groups to make it very serviceable for a national identity, and as the basis of an English nationalism it is almost bound to be reactionary.[47]

Kumar concluded, in Nairnite fashion, that the crisis that first eventuated with the rise of nationalism in the 1970s now extended to the English who found themselves the last remaining inhabitants of 'rump Britain'. This expansive conception of a rupture slowly spreading though nations and state has become an increasingly ubiquitous trope, even though, until very recently, there have been few signs that Britain is anywhere near to breaking up.

Nairn's thinking, more generally, has become part of the unstated framework which many progressive commentators employ when called to speak on these issues. Writing in 2004, journalist Andrew Anthony referred to the sense of identity crisis associated with new developments in national consciousness as if these were established matters of fact:

> the flag has been, as they say, reappropriated, and everywhere you look the kind of people who would have once taken great care to avoid the matter now can't stop talking about the multi-layered meanings of Englishness...So much so, in fact, that you could argue that the defining characteristic of being English is to be in a state of confusion about what it means to be English. The modern English identity, we might conclude, is an identity crisis.[48]

And in the lecture that we encountered in the Introduction to this volume, O'Hagan recycled Nairn's picture of the passive and quiescent English:

> There is an aversion in England to organised or even personal resistance, a frightening bend towards compromise. There have always been good causes worth

fighting for, but seldom, in the modern era, has there been the common volition to fight for them…Usually, the ordinary people of England only have one word to say to authority, and that word is 'yes'.[49]

His lecture illustrates that Nairn's framework can be used to legitimate sweeping expressions of disappointment in, and even a thinly veiled contempt for, the English lower orders. O'Hagan talked of a 'vast and overwhelming numbness of England's working class'.[50] This grouping, he declaimed, had 'been docile and careless for years', and had lost a sense of itself as a social group with a common purpose.[51] Worse still, the only sense of commonality that could be discerned within its cultural life related to the ersatz form of 'national belonging' associated with the country's perpetually underperforming football team:

> Supporting the English team has long since become a synecdoche for patriotic allegiance. Fans are moved to paint their faces red and white not on election day, not even on Armistice Day, but on holiday in Majorca or at international fixtures where 22 men will struggle to score goals.

Nairn's strictures have had a strikingly prescriptive effect when applied to the proliferating signs of a growing national self-awareness among the English. His dismissal of the mythological, romantic, and Arcadian themes that crop up in expressions of English nationhood has rendered him, and those he has influenced, inattentive to the different ways in which Englishness has been recuperated and expressed. Equally, his commitment to the principle of national sovereignty is obviated by an unduly doctrinaire insistence on the kinds of constitutional and political choice that the English ought to be making.

BEFORE BRITAIN? RESUMING THE
ENGLISH PATHWAY

In a column he wrote for *The Spectator* in 2010, Matthew Parris reported a quiet epiphany on his part that England, not Britain, had—quietly and imperceptibly—become the country of his, and many of his fellows', imagination.[52] And this, he realized, did not feel like a radical break with a once cherished order, but constituted the resumption of a lineage that was familiar and comfortable. Englishness, he suggested, was returning, not emerging, in this period. Parris linked this mood to a new attitude at large—an abandonment of the stance of polite forbearance towards the Scots and others, and a heightened sense of indifference. This he labelled 'the collective shrug of English shoulders'.[53] While the major political parties were obsessed with the prospect of Scotland drifting away from the UK, it was in truth the English who were increasingly cutting themselves apart from the other nations of the islands they inhabited. His argument also signalled the slightly startled realization that the UK consisted of non-English peoples, whose existence had hitherto been obscured by the conflation of England and Britain.

Versions of this idea have been advanced by many pundits and campaigners, writing from various ideological vantage points. The notion that a long-standing form of nationhood is now coming back to life, casting off the different masks it has worn since the establishment of Britain, has sustained a powerful and resonant seam of thinking about England in public discourse and the communities of historical scholarship. A number of historians have, in recent years, insisted that the English were one of the first peoples to think of themselves in national terms, and that the current renewal of national awareness represents the reappearance of an older, established pattern. This was the eye-catching thesis advanced by historian Liah Greenfeld in 1993.[54] The English, she argued, were forerunners, not latecomers, in the development of a national consciousness. It was during the later medieval period that a distinctive sense of an English national community became prevalent, and this was orchestrated by Henry VIII for his project of state centralization and expansion. These trends were cemented during the Elizabethan period, when the state tapped into a rich vein of popular patriotism. These arguments were taken further in the scholarship of Adrian Hastings, who characterized England as a medieval nation, the oldest in Europe.[55]

Greenfeld's thesis, and others that focused upon the Tudor period, signalled a continuing debt to the influential thesis of leading historian and émigré intellectual Hans Kohn, who had made a powerful case, in a landmark essay published in 1940, for the unique genesis and character of English nationalism.[56] Whereas England had once been a poor, relatively backward country, under the twin influences of Henry VIII and the Reformation, he argued, it acquired a striking new sense of cultural confidence and self-belief, much of which was rooted in the influence of Protestant-inspired providentialism.[57] The English were increasingly receptive to notions of themselves as a 'people re-born', whose identity rested on a sense of religious mission. Such ideas, he and other later historians maintained, were central to the events leading up to the Civil War of the late seventeenth century.

Kohn's account has been of enduring significance, both in terms of its characterization of the exceptional content of English national sentiment, and his contention that the phlegmatic English mind remained unmoved by Continental nationalism in the late nineteenth century. The English could not recognize in themselves what they recoiled from in their rivals, he suggested, and while they increasingly turned away from the notion of nationalism, they were actually cementing their own unique form of it, one that was rooted in liberal patterns of thinking about liberty and constitutional government.

The notion that the national DNA of the English was set down in earlier centuries and, having been dormant during the period of British hegemony, is now steadily returning to the fore, has been very widely echoed in recent writing. It has figured in a number of popular, as well as scholarly, histories. Thus, newspaper columnist and chairman of the National Trust, Simon Jenkins, provided an accessible and largely unsentimental version of this narrative in his *A Short History of England,* published in 2011.[58] The uniqueness of the English was established in the centuries before the Reformation, and stemmed from the development of a common language and the mixed-form government that grew out of the juxtaposition of a Saxon adherence to the values of 'kith and kin', on the one hand, and the Norman commitment to the establishment of centralized authority, on the other.[59] This productive tension, he suggested, continued to define the fluid, but stable, way in which the English came to understand their relationship with their own state. By the nineteenth century, this pattern of thinking crystallized into the idea of a constitutional monarchy that would be subject to the rules and spirit of a parliamentary democracy, an outlook that undergirded the most stable polity in Europe.

While academic scrutiny tends to give short shrift to the claims advanced in such versions of the island story, Jenkins's and other similar accounts have played an important role in shaping and confirming the sensibilities of audiences that have been increasingly receptive to this kind of Whiggish retelling of the English story. His own people, Jenkins insisted, were no longer content to subsume their sense of nationality beneath the carapace of British citizenship, nor to subsume their culture and identity to a British statehood. The very notion of writing a history of England for the English was, he revealed, motivated by the idea that the people of his own nation were 'entitled to define themselves'.[60] The implication of his assertion—that the right to national self-determination had for many years been subtly denied to the English—is a close companion to the contemporary emphasis on the restoration of the English lineage. The notion that England had been quite deliberately 'occluded' by the British constitution became an increasingly familiar theme in public discourse after devolution.[61]

ROGER SCRUTON

One of the main architects of this restorative approach to Englishness in the current period has been the philosopher, writer, and campaigner Roger

Scruton. He emerged as a prominent opponent of the New Labour governments, becoming a leading campaigner against the banning of hunting with dogs which passed through parliament in 2004. Scruton located
his dislike of the metropolitan liberalism which he saw as the animating
impulse within the New Labour governments in a wider lament about the
imminent demise of institutional and cultural aspects of the English tradition. In his much discussed book, *Elegy for England,* he declared that 'things
had moved on so much that the whole concept of Britain had been thrown
into disarray. It had become quite apparent that there is no such cultural
entity any more.'[62] Instead, he turned his attention to the ideals, institutions, and landscapes that had prompted an Englishness which was now
on the verge of extinction.[63] In the Burkean compact between the living,
the dead, and the unborn, trust is placed in our collective inheritance, particularly in the form of those organizations, practices, and traditions that
had emerged out of the customs and cultures of the English past. A sense of
place and territorial loyalty, he argued, were central to the inner core of this
people. The endless, natural focal point for the expression of Englishness
was the countryside, the locus of a resonant sense of home and belonging,
and now the object of the expressed hostility of a powerful government. In
response, Scruton offered an elegy for this supposedly disappearing cultural
formation.

Yet, even at this late hour, he detected signs that all may not quite be lost: there
were still pockets of resistance to an alien British modernity: 'rumours of the
death of the countryside are exaggerated'.[64] While a good deal of Scruton's
account of England's law, customs, and ways of life borrowed from the store
of romantic ruralism which Kumar identified in the Edwardian era, his argument also contained some decidedly new elements, several of which proved to
be prescient of the shifting patterns of conservative sentiment. These included
a redoubtable critique of the contempt shown by the liberal political elite—
now fully empowered through the election of a Labour government—to the
heritage of England. New Labour, he opined, 'inherits from Old Labour an
anti-English stance', and this was symbolized by its ill-considered ban on
fox-hunting.[65] This, he contended, was seen by sections of the left as a way
of attacking the ancient English settlement which it so thoroughly despised.
Immigration recurred in his writings on England and the countryside, and in
the press articles he wrote in this period. It was invoked both as a symptom
and source of the forces that he saw as undermining the cherished soul of
England. The nostalgic-cum-elegiac tone was leavened with doses of populist
resentment and flecks of grievance. Scruton scoured the horizon for signs of
popular disaffection with the government over its stance towards the countryside and immigration policies. And he found some indications that the

English were on the verge of rediscovering their own nationhood, spurred to do so by recoil from the pieties of liberal Britain. As well as indicting current government policies, he also identified longer-range trends that were menacing the social and cultural settlement which had provided a crucible for the English tradition. Globalization and unplanned forms of urban development were, in tandem, digging at the roots of an established pattern of living which stretched back across many centuries, based upon the assumption that it was in the most intimate local communities that the rituals, customs, and rules of national affiliation were learnt. Some of the key institutional expressions of this order, such as the Church of England were seemingly in terminal decline. With the waning of Anglicanism went the trinitarian unity of nationality, religion, and language which had long underpinned a deep and common sense of Englishness. And, with its passing, a palpable sense of loss emerged among many of the English.

England, in his view, represented the cultural and ethnic soul within the body of Britain, constituting the authentic national tradition where the character of its people, language, culture, institutions, climate, and landscape were infused with, and sustained by, a pool of shared 'social feelings', which took the form 'not so much of respect for the community, as respect for the individuality of others'.[66] In this vision, a lived sense of national community provided the bedrock for the expression of liberty in private life, and an intuitive tolerance of difference within the public realm. Authentic English identity was, for Scruton, expressed and reproduced not in abstract ideals, nor in the dominant tradition's capacity to sustain dialogue with other ideas and emerging sensibilities. It was, instead, learnt and practised in specific places, through inculcation in forms of customary life and, more generally, by the experience of participating in the cultural practices that grounded these ideas of nation and liberty. In a separate homage to the virtues of fox-hunting, Scruton suggested that Englishness represented a return 'to the realm of ancestral freedoms', including the right to hunt.[67] This practice, he claimed, was a central part of the 'study, love and evaluation of the past', all of which are intrinsic to 'improved national self-understanding'.[68] Hunting constituted a 'living limb of Old England'.[69] Such sentiments formed the basis of a number of public interventions he made during these years, including a widely reported speech he delivered at the 'Endangered Exmoor' rally of 1999.

Scruton's elegiac characterization of an England at the mercy of the interlocking processes of globalization, immigration, and Europeanization, and increasingly unprotected by its political and economic leaders, spoke to an important shift in parts of the public mood during this period. His argument also anticipated the emergence of new strains of Conservative thinking that were increasingly removed from the venerated orthodoxies of British government. He detected a growing disquiet with the union itself, and its perceived capacity to protect the English from the new threats posed by the European Union and the global economy. While this represented a fairly unorthodox position at the point at which he proposed it, by the end of the subsequent decade such a notion had moved into the mainstream of Conservative discourse.

Other parts of his argument have proved harder for fellow Conservatives to swallow. His determined emphasis upon English separateness—in intellectual, cultural, and historical terms—is belied by his repeated references to figures, such as Edmund Burke and Oscar Wilde, whose assimilation to a delineated sense of Englishness, is, by definition, problematic. More generally, the kind of radical disentangling of the English and British lineages that he invoked, began to push Scruton away from the intellectual moorings of English conservative thought, towards a wholehearted, and rather unconservative, nationalism. In this he exemplified a growing disjuncture within conservative thinking, which has been noted by Aughey, between the perception of the English as a 'constitutional' people, on the one hand, and as a 'sovereign' nation on the other.[70] While the former sustained the idea of a people inclined to abide by the institutional and legal frameworks associated with Britain, the latter notion, increasingly favoured by Scruton, suggested that they should see themselves as a sovereign people. It is this latter vein of thinking that has sustained a swelling chorus of opinion on the political right in opposition to the two unions that are seen as infringing upon English rights and the national will—the United Kingdom and Europe.

Scruton was convinced that his conservative predilections were compatible with his militant defence of the English national tradition, but the latter has increasingly come to shade into the kind of nationalism that he himself once regarded as outside the bounds of Englishness.[71] Equally, his thinking left him adrift from, and mostly alienated by, the shifts in national sensibility that are documented in Chapter 3. For the institutions, social conditions, and cultural tradition which he saw as the crucible for this particular lineage had either vanished or were almost extinct by the millennium. And so, the proliferation of contemporary expressions of Englishness could not, by definition, bring him much comfort. As he put it in a blog post he wrote in 2007:

> The factors that shaped that identity in the past—the Anglican church and its non-conformist constellation, the empire, the common law, the monarchy and parliament—are all in a state of retrenchment or decline. For most people English literature survives only in TV adaptations, English music, whether folk or classical, is a closed book, and English art is represented by a few kitsch Gainsboroughs and a mound of offensive 'young British art'. There is a real question how one might build an English identity from such ruins.[72]

The notion that English nationhood was being remade in the conditions of the present, and might be appropriated for different kinds of political and social contention, was dismissed from view in this argument, leaving Scruton's idealized Englishness irredeemably detached from nearly all actual manifestations or expressions of English culture. And, beyond its sense of deep hostility to the incumbent government, his argument offered little in terms of political guidance to those who might be attracted to it.

Yet the underlying mode of argumentation that Scruton mined has echoed more widely in the recent period across the political spectrum. A concern for the prospects of Englishness not only led conservatives towards increasingly radical perspectives on the nature of the British political system and the union, but also led some radical minds towards a more conservatively inclined conviction that the progressive future lay in the fusion of patriotism and radicalism that had been characteristic of earlier moments in labour history.[73] This position was popularized by musician, song-writer, and campaigner, Billy Bragg. His widely discussed book *The Progressive Patriot*, published in 2007, interwove his own autobiography with selected, heroic moments from the history of the British left.[74] It offered a clarion call for progressives to set aside their prejudices towards Englishness, and reclaim the radical patriotism of the labour movement's past. Just as with Scruton's watershed text, Bragg's work provided a harbinger of a shifting political mood in the years following its publication. The contention that Englishness could be engaged in progressive terms, and might even, in some rather unspecified sense, 'belong' to the left, established an important reference point for a growing number of advocates of the merits of English patriotism.

Bragg's populist position chimed with an important shift in the academic historiography devoted to the British left in this period. The notion that a significant overlap between the languages of radicalism and patriotism had been an important ingredient within English socialism and the normative conviction that this synergy might once again be vital were widely debated.[75] Various historians showed how patriotic language had supplied both a powerful vehicle for expressing opposition to the class-based policies of the ruling elite, and a means of securing a foothold in working-class culture during the late nineteenth century, offering both a 'tool of opposition, and…a means of possessing the past'.[76] Hugh Cunningham's landmark contribution to the Samuel volumes told the story of how in the course of the nineteenth century the language of patriotism was transferred from the democratic left to the conservative right.[77]

New calls for a radical Anglo-patriotism were, as Aughey has observed, haunted by the recurrent fear that the high-minded patriotism which progressives favour would be washed away by the release of nationalist energies. The question of whether the people, in their national guise, could be trusted to pursue the values favoured by the left has remained an endemic worry. Bragg's text exhibited these concerns, even as he tried to find a positive and upbeat way of dissolving them through his commitment to the decency of the English who, 'when true to themselves', are inclined to the values of cooperation and tolerance.[78] But even in this most optimistic of activists, the gnawing fear that the English may well not always be faithful to their better national self could not be entirely expunged.

Despite these misgivings, a number of figures from the left have, over the last two decades, come to rethink the character and prospects of English nation-hood. Senior voices within the Labour party, including Ministers of State David Blunkett and John Denham, as well as backbench MP Jon Cruddas, chair of the Labour party's Policy Review under Ed Miliband's leadership, called for the party to reconnect with a proud lineage of specifically English socialism. Cruddas, and the wider 'Blue Labour' group with which he was associated in the aftermath of the party's election defeat of 2010, presented the idea of an imaginative reconnection with England as an integral part of a broader attempt to renew the party's ethical compass.[79]

In his widely discussed book *Patriots*, historian Richard Weight illustrated the insights and arguments that a progressively patriotic take upon British his-tory could yield.[80] He argued that English nationhood had been deliberately held in check after 1945 by a political establishment that was decidedly fear-ful of the implications of a growth in English national awareness. Like many other progressive commentators writing in this period, Weight regarded 1945 as the high-water mark of Britishness, after which it waned considerably and rapidly, despite the best efforts of the guardians of the state.[81] He argued too, in Nairnite vein, that only by rediscovering their authentic national identity, long denied to them by the archaic structures and culture of the state, would the English be able to constitute themselves as a collective actor, ready and will-ing to flex their democratic muscles. But his deep historical familiarity with England's popular culture also led him to inject a rather un-Nairnite note to this argument, specifically via his attention to the medley of cultural genres that had enabled the English to establish a sense of who they were, and forge an outward-looking and modern sense of nationality from the 1960s onwards.

In these different political incarnations, the argument for the restoration of an unbroken English lineage boosted the habit of imagining the English nation in broadly exceptionalist terms. These variously stressed the unique properties of place and topography, and the singular radical spirit and cultural forms that were said to be distinctive to the largest part of the British archipelago. The common, underlying rationale for such thinking was that the English could still see themselves as a nation in charge of its own destiny. But proponents of this kind of English traditionalism were divided on one major point. Whereas for Weight the past represented a vital resource from which contemporaries could learn, for Scruton and others—including writer and campaigner Paul Kingsnorth (whose writing is considered in more depth in Chapter 4)—a deep nostalgia for the English past was the key to national renewal in the present. Yet, while nostalgia has undoubtedly supplied an important, under-estimated resource in political argument, the Tory–radical celebration of it encountered some major challenges. The golden age evoked by these authors referred to practices and relationships that many contemporaries regarded as antedi-luvian and illiberal. And such a romanticized approach to the past bumped against other entrenched features of the re-emerging English imagination, not least a decidedly unromantic scepticism, and an intuitive sense of plural-ism. More generally still, the conviction that the character and implications of Englishness in the here and now could be rediscovered through a return to the past left its proponents at odds with most contemporary manifestations of English nationality.

ENGLAND AND BRITAIN: A CONTINUING DIALOGUE

A very different sense of why and how Englishness has returned to the fore in the last fifteen years is associated with the work of those who pointed to the enduring value of the governing British tradition, and stressed its potential capacity to respond to current English anxieties. While this idea has, for the most part, been elaborated in specialist intellectual circles, and lacks the wider appeal of the rival perspectives considered here, it tallies with the dominant assumptions of mainstream politics. It is associated with the work of a number of historians of ideas, including Aughey and Julia Stapleton, who have pointed to the merits of recalling earlier forms of national thinking in relation to con-temporary challenges over constitution and state.[82] Their work, and that of other historians, have supplied a robust normative challenge to the tendencies of progressive and conservative patriots to assume that the achievement of a more secure and stable sense of English nationhood is contingent upon the dissolution of the constitutional and political structures that have developed over the last few hundred years.

These figures have shed important light upon some of the main patterns of national thinking in British politics during the nineteenth and twentieth centuries. Stapleton stressed the complex and shifting nature of England and

Englishness as powerful themes within elite thinking, and identified their imbrication with liberal ideas of citizenship in the early twentieth century.[83] Mandler's study of the different ideas of the English character that pervaded political discourse from the eighteenth to the mid-twentieth centuries also provided an important counterpoint to the Nairnite contention that the English lack an animating democratic myth.[84] He stressed the impact of a 'civilizational' perspective upon leading ideas of the national character which served as a bulwark against the promotion of the idea of England as a nation defined through bloodlines and ethnicity. And Margaret Canovan pointed out how this kind of English patriotism was disseminated through various genres, including literature and poetry during the nineteenth century, and provided an important crucible for the promotion and inculcation of broadly liberal principles.[85] The authors of the works she considered typically had the heterogeneous roots of 'the English' at the front of their minds, and, accordingly, fastened onto the idea of providential purpose, rather than ethnic purity, as the basis for their depiction of this unique people. Moreover, the pattern of thinking charted by Mandler was central to the thinking of national liberals, such as Sir Ernest Barker, who stressed the combination of continuity and subtle change which was deemed central not just to the governing tradition, but also found echo in the character of the people. As Barker put it: 'this long slow movement of the character of England, has it not something enduring?' Conceived in this way, such an idea offered an attractive means of characterizing the liberal-conservative core of Englishness through the twentieth century. In his often cited depiction, Orwell characterized England as an 'everlasting animal stretching into the future and past, and, like all living things, having the power to change out of recognition and yet remains the same'.[86]

Aughey has distilled these insights in his important study, *The Politics of Englishness*. In this he charted the importance of the backdrop supplied by a supple and interwoven body of ideas about British nationhood, parliamentary sovereignty, and English culture, which he characterized, following philosopher Michael Oakeshott, as the governing tradition of the British polity.[87] On this view it is continuity, adaptability, and evolution that have been the hallmarks of the development of elite and popular forms of national identification among the English. Oakeshott placed emphasis upon the interwoven pattern of national and constitutional thought that underpinned leading ideas of nationhood, and decanted from these an idealized understanding of conversation as the hallmark and vehicle of the British tradition. In a recent, jointly authored introduction to a volume of essays on Englishness, Aughey has pursued the conversational metaphor derived from Oakeshott, opening up some fertile new avenues of enquiry.[88] Englishness ought to be understood not as a tradition with a fixed essence, but, in Oakeshottian terms, as: 'a national conversation, an imaginative rather than a purely functional engagement, about the country's history, culture and society, where what is being conversed about is the meaning of England itself'.[89]

This is a dialogue that takes its bearings from, and is made possible by, the established tradition that precedes it, and which, by definition, 'involves a plural notion of *these* Englands rather than the singular notion of this England'.[90] Oakeshott's conception of tradition as an ensemble made up of many contingent elements, without an ulterior rationale, is commended both as a methodological approach and as reflection of the main attributes of Englishness itself. Its deployment also allowed Aughey to underscore his account of the national paradigm as a multi-vocal entity, which is not fixed by any one claim or practice. This has been a flowing, living lineage which has brought together disparate, sometimes conflicting, ideas and impulses.

A good deal of the normative force associated with the conversational analogy stems from the presumption that it is available to those who possess a disposition to appreciate the intimations of the tradition which they are taught. This metaphor subtly promoted the contention that the ebb and flow of the dialogue is itself one of its enduring qualities of the British tradition. Suggestive as this account is, it faces the considerable difficulty that many of the English are increasingly unlikely to relate to their own sense of nationhood in this way. Whereas, in Oakeshottian terms, Englishness is a supple and adaptable conversation between a plurality of voices within a common tradition, the claims made in relation to Englishness are increasingly characterized by their loud, polemical, and vernacular qualities. The rather high-minded and rule-bound conception of national discourse which is envisaged here is confounded by the forms and variety of political arguments which a more assertive sense of English nationhood herald.

A further difficulty associated with the Oakeshottian perspective is that his own sense of the British tradition was indissolubly bound up with his commitment to the unique, non-nationalist disposition of the English people, a temperament that has 'made Britain not an abstract idea but a manner of living and a way of life'.[91] Yet it is exactly this manner of thinking about the character and disposition of the English that is increasingly being contested, in cultural and political terms, rendering this an increasingly difficult platform from which to interpret and engage English identity. Aughey himself is alive to a long-standing tension between self-conscious invocations of an avowedly Anglo sense of heritage and identity (as in Kumar's 'moment') and ideas of allegiance to a British system of governance. In recent years this divergence has become accentuated to the point where the underpinning liberal-constitutionalist paradigm, with which Oakeshott was closely associated, is itself coming under considerable pressure.

This development has historical roots as well as contemporary causes. The Unionist lineage has, as Iain McLean and Alistair McMillan have argued, shifted markedly during the last two centuries, from a primordial sense of identification to a more transactionally conceived relationship.[92] This gradual evolution in ideas of Britain and Britishness represents a vital backdrop to current developments, and raises questions about the viability of Oakeshottian-style emphases on the capacity of the British tradition to stretch across the major challenges of the modern period. Events such as the Second World War and the development of the welfare state undercut primordial Unionism by reframing Britain's strengths in terms of different endeavours and achievements, and contributed to the slow reconfiguration of the Unionist idea. As these authors observed, the deliberate attempt, from the eighteenth century, to intertwine the ideas of English and British identity, became, during the nineteenth, a matter of common habit: 'For three centuries, political leaders in England, like most other English intellectuals, have confused "national", "English" and "British".'[93] But in recent years, this habit has been increasingly open to challenge, as the English idea of Britain as the constitutional nation has given way to a stress upon England as the potentially sovereign nation.

Aughey has shown himself highly sensitive to these changes of perception and mood, and has provided an astute analysis of the different kinds of anxiety and grievance through which a reactive sense of English identity has been channelled in recent times.[94] And yet, while he has detected signs of the coalescence of a 'nationalist platform' among the English—'a sense of injustice, a feeling of powerlessness, the mood of exploitation and the occasion for righteous anger'[95]—he was unconvinced that this mood has yet been catalysed, and wary of talk of an incipient nationalism among the English.[96] At the same time, his commitment to the dialogic principle that is encoded within the British tradition has imparted to his interpretation of the contemporary forms and politics of English identity a subtly normative character. He has, accordingly, been concerned to bring to our attention the values, allegiances, and forms of national thinking that would, in all likelihood, disappear with the break-up of Britain, and implicitly called into question the capacity of conservative or radical accounts of Englishness to offer anything as sinuous and inclusive. His worries on this score are well founded. Yet his own analysis—by dint of his commitment to the evolutionary virtues of constitutional government and the blurring of English and British identity—is itself challenged by the tenor of new trends in English consciousness. The declining enthusiasm for the British model of government which is now palpable among the English contributes a major challenge to the paradigm he has tried to extend.

More generally, it has long been argued that Oakeshottian thinking leans too heavily upon an assumed sense of the merits and subtleties of the tradition it celebrates, and renders its adherents unduly inattentive to its contradictions and failings.[97] The civilized, comfortable dialogue that made sense in such venues as Westminster and Whitehall, where the 'national conversation of decency' has for the most part prevailed, now speaks to a significantly smaller pool of citizens than was the case twenty years ago. In a context where—especially after devolution—the need to secure legitimacy and popular assent is becoming increasingly fraught and vital, it now requires a leap of faith to assume that the British tradition, and the kind of political conversation it embodies, retains the capacity to underpin a stable territorial and state system in the UK.

CONCLUSIONS

These contrasting perspectives on the rebirth of English nationhood are each tied to particular forms of historical understanding, and each relates to different parts of the ideological spectrum. While I have evoked them here in relation to the work of a handful of specific authors and texts, they have resonated, and been expressed, much more widely in the recent period, and have sustained some of the main patterns of interpretation that Englishness has elicited.

Those operating in the shadow of Nairn's arguments have been wary of most actual expressions of Englishness, and are quick to see regressive and pathological implications within them, while simultaneously awaiting the termination of the asymmetrical and archaic constitutional order through which the British state has governed. For those of a restorative temper, by contrast, there has been an urgency, as well as hope, to be expressed about the prospects for a renewal of English national consciousness. This mode of thinking has involved a powerful mixture of historical idealization, cultural frustration—at the apparent unwillingness of the English to reconnect with their vanishing lineage—and a highly romanticized idea of the implications of such a retrieval of the national past. The third perspective considered above has, by contrast, been much more closely orientated to the existing constitutional settlement and the forms of thinking underpinning it. But it too has insisted upon the need to understand the challenges of the present through a historical appreciation of the forms of thinking underpinning the national tradition. From this vantage point, it remains unclear whether the increasingly febrile and sour mood of a growing portion of the English public will result in a wholly new kind of nationalist orientation. Politicians and intellectuals operating within the terms of this paradigm retain the hope that the wisdom accumulated within the British model of statecraft might yet point towards a way of reorganizing the furniture of government and representation in order to persuade the English that their future lies with the union.

While each of these narratives claims to be able to account for the revival of a sense of English identity, it is important to see that they have, in different respects, been upstaged, as much as reaffirmed, by the growing salience of English nationhood in this period. Specifically, each perspective finds itself alienated from the particular manifestations of this form of nationhood because of the highly idealized, and often prescriptive, character of the Englishness which they favour. All are doomed to misrepresent, rather than engage, the complex ways in which English identity is being developed and reinvented in the present. An appreciation of some of the empirical and normative weaknesses of these perspectives should not, however, detract from an understanding of their importance and influence. Each has been the source of significant forms of argument about Englishness, and they have done much to establish the terms upon which this phenomenon is debated and understood.

Their most abiding, common weakness is a tendency to underplay the degree of ideological and political competition that has developed in relation to the imagined community of England. In the remainder of this book I give particular emphasis to the variety of perspectives and political arguments that have been enabled by the reappropriation of English themes and ideas. And I suggest that different forms and ideas of Englishness are anchored by deeply rooted traditions, rather than representing brand-new inventions.

3

Englishness as a Mass Phenomenon
Evidence and Interpretation

INTRODUCTION

A good deal of the commentary devoted to the question of whether a growing sense of English pride is beginning to displace older forms of Britishness relies upon the well-worn axioms that the English are not interested in defining or promoting their national identity, and are largely indifferent to the constitutional system under which they live. But, in the wake of the introduction of devolution in the late 1990s, a very different notion gained ground—that a backlash against the asymmetrical character of these reforms was inevitable, and would result in the shattering of these habits. In this chapter I explore the adequacy of this account of English attitudes. I sift a body of available evidence, and argue that, while an avowedly English sense of identity has become more prominent in this period, this is expressed in very different ways and carries a variety of meanings for different groups of people. For most, a quietly growing sense of identification with England does not, as is often claimed, imply the abandonment of loyalty to Britain. But, while the expectations of nationalist campaigners have not been fulfilled, it is also becoming clearer that a strengthening sense of English national awareness is generating ever more significant political and constitutional reverberations.

This chapter focuses, therefore, upon what different kinds of social scientific research tell us about how the English feel about these issues. It also reflects on some of the guiding assumptions about English attitudes that figure in these communities of scholarship. I argue, in particular, that analysis of the English question needs to involve a more critical and reflexive approach towards the evidence than is routinely employed to support rival characterizations of the national 'mood'. In the course of this discussion I sift the plethora of polling data compiled during the last fifteen years, and ask what we can reasonably deduce from the multitude of opinion surveys that have tested public attitudes on questions of nationhood and constitutional preference. And I conclude by arguing that, while these generate vital insights, especially the time-series data supplied by some of the more rigorous attitudinal surveys, there are inherent dangers in an over-reliance upon such sources. An appreciation of the meanings and depth of national attachments necessarily requires an engagement with other kinds of evidence and research. And there is particular merit in adopting what social scientists term a 'mixed method' approach when studying a complex and multi-dimensional phenomenon such as Englishness, which acknowledges that both quantitative and qualitative sources are likely to enhance our understanding. Cross-referencing studies that employ both methodologies enables us to weed out some of the more extravagant claims that have been made about English nationalism, and achieve a better grasp of the micro- and macro-level dimensions of recent shifts in national consciousness.

I conclude by making the case for a more self-consciously interpretive approach to the study of public attitudes in relation to the English question. This emphasis is intended as a counter to the rather selective deployment of survey data associated with debates in this area. But it also arises from the argument I advanced in Chapter 2 about the merits of an enhanced awareness of the implications of the normative and analytical frameworks which commentators bring to bear upon these issues.

Throughout this discussion of available data on public attitudes towards Englishness I focus on two key questions: (i) what can we reasonably deduce from the array of available data and research about the strength and implications of national identity among the English?; and (ii) can we discern a relationship between shifting perceptions of nationality and attitudes towards political and constitutional issues? For politicians and campaigners this last issue is a pivotal concern. I tend to side with those advocating caution in the face of claims about the consequences of shifts in English nationhood. Too much political analysis assumes that constitutional issues are the primary shapers of national sentiment, an assumption that may well reflect the impact of the Scottish experience. But, if we confine our understanding of the political dimensions and implications of Englishness to the question of whether it signals a desire for national self-government along the lines enjoyed by the Scots and Welsh, there is every chance that we may neglect the different dynamics that have contributed to a re-emergent sense of English nationhood and its various political ramifications.

TRENDS IN ENGLISH NATIONAL IDENTITY,
1999–2007

The question of how to interpret changing patterns of national identity within the UK has drawn the attention of social scientists from various disciplinary backgrounds. This wide field of study is broadly divided between those who employ quantitative and qualitative methods in their work. A considerable body of polling data has been compiled and interpreted, while other researchers have employed questionnaires, focus groups, and face-to-face interviews. Only a handful of scholars have reflected on the nature and limitations of these different sources.[1]

The many different surveys conducted into how the English perceive their sense of identity and the constitutional structures through which they are governed, have generated very different, and sometimes conflicting, results across this period. These have occasionally been dramatic in kind, with some pointing to sudden upsurges of support for such options as an English parliament, which have been gleefully seized upon by parts of the media. Thus, a poll produced by ICM in April 2007 reported that 67 per cent of respondents indicated their support for an English parliament, when asked directly if they favoured such an outcome.[2] And yet, this result is significantly out of kilter with other surveys that include this as one of a menu of options, and pose the same questions on a regular basis, as is the practice of the annually conducted British Social Attitudes (BSA) survey. Support for this option has tended to be especially high when respondents are reminded that Scotland has a parliament but England does not, and much lower they are not so reminded.[3]

Without discounting 'one-off' polls entirely, I rely more heavily in this discussion upon longitudinal data such as those generated by the BSA's annual survey. The evidence supplied by polls in general need to be treated with considerable care, and regarded as suggestive and indicative, rather than objective and determinate, when it comes to both individual and collective identity. They tell us little about how strongly people feel about the issues in question, or about how a particular loyalty weighs against the other affiliations they possess. Those polls that do invite people to indicate their own personal priorities rarely find that issues such as the English question are more important than worries about the economy or public services (though it is worth noting that both immigration and the European Union, which have a strong national inflection, have become issues of much greater priority for many).[4]

Despite the warnings about the likelihood of an English 'backlash' that rang in the ears of the architects of devolution, the general consensus among psephologists is that no such trend became apparent in the first few years after its introduction. In their comparative study of popular attitudes towards national identity and constitutional change throughout the UK, Ross Bond and Michael Rosie concluded that English identity is unique in the UK because of the lack of correlation between strength of national pride and attitudes towards the constitution.[5] In Scotland, Northern Ireland, and Wales, by comparison, a sense of national pride was more likely to shape people's views on questions of sub-state autonomy.

There are, however, indications in a number of different analyses that less dramatic, but still significant, attitudinal shifts have been taking place. These include: the continuing decline of British nationhood as a primary form of national allegiance; the increased salience of an English identity for a large and growing number of English people; and the development of a more sceptical attitude towards current systems of politics and governance. An important, but difficult, question, to which I give some attention below, is whether these three trends are inter-related.

Psephologist John Curtice has provided some of the most dispassionate and insightful analysis of the available polling data on these issues. He observed a small rise, from the late 1990s, in the proportion of respondents who, when invited to respond to a 'forced choice' question about whether they feel more English than British, chose the former over the latter—31 per cent in 1992 compared to 41 per cent in 2008. More strikingly, he reported an 18 per cent fall in those who prioritized their sense of Britishness (63 per cent in 1992, 45 per cent in 2008) in the last two decades. This latter finding is an important one, and has been echoed in other studies. James Tilley and Anthony Heath charted a 'decline in British national pride' among all groups, in all areas of Britain in the last two decades: 'The average person in 2003 is clearly less proud of their Britishness than the average person in 1980.'[6] This decline, they suggested, was particularly marked among younger cohorts. The waning of British sentiment which these surveys report was, however, a relative, rather than an absolute phenomenon, as a significant majority of English respondents have continued to indicate that they identify with both English and British identities. Table 3.1 reveals a quite significant increase between 1997 and 1999 in the proportion of people who, when forced to choose, opted to identify as 'English' rather than 'British', rising from 33 to 44 per cent, and little change in the years that followed. During the late 1990s devolution was being extensively debated and covered in the media, and this appears to have had a galvanizing effect upon the national self-awareness of some of the English.

The BSA's annual surveys have also posed questions that allow respondents to indicate if they identify with more than one national affiliation. They employ the methodology developed during the 1980s by Spanish political

Table 3.1 Trends in 'forced choice' national identity,
England 1992–2009

	British	English
1992	63	31
1996	58	34
1997	55	33
1998	51	37
1999	44	44
2000	47	41
2001	44	43
2002	51	37
2003	48	38
2004	51	38
2005	48	40
2006	39	47
2007	47	39
2008	45	41
2009	46	41

Sources: British Election Study; British Social Attitudes Survey

scientist Luis Moreno, asking respondents to select from a menu of five combined or single national identities, and to indicate, in the case of dual identities, which affiliation they consider most important.[7] As Table 3.2 reveals, a
majority of respondents have continued to identify with both nationalities in
the decade after devolution.

These findings suggest that, in so far as there has been a rise in levels of identification with Englishness, this has not necessarily happened at the expense
of a sense of loyalty to Britain. They also indicate that the ingrained habit of
seeing England and Britain as interchangeable, which has long been the object
of critical commentary, has continued into the current period. Importantly,
the same broad pattern is apparent when respondents were given a completely
open choice about which national identities they wanted to select, as Table 3.3
reveals.

And yet, a number of pollsters have come to the conclusion that, despite these
broad indications of continuity, a growing sense of English self-consciousness
is also discernible. Up to 1998, for example, the proportion of respondents

Table 3.2 Trends in national identity, England 1997–2007

	1997	1999	2000	2001	2003	2007
English not British	7	17	18	17	17	19
More English than British	17	14	14	13	19	14
Equally English and British	45	37	34	42	31	31
More British than English	14	11	14	9	13	14
British not English	9	14	12	11	10	12

Note: These questions are based on the methodology employed by Luis Moreno
Sources: British Election Study; British Social Attitudes Survey

Table 3.3 Trends in 'free choice' national identity, England 1996–2007

	English	British	Both
1996	52	71	29
1997	54	76	36
1998	55	70	34
1999	65	71	44
2000	59	67	35
2001	63	67	39
2002	57	73	37
2003	59	70	38
2004	55	69	33
2005	60	70	38
2006	67	68	45
2007	57	68	34

Note: These percentages add up to more than 100 as respondents were able to select more than one option
Sources: British Election Study; British Social Attitudes Survey

saying that they felt English was never above 55 per cent. Since then, it has never fallen below that level. Curtice and Heath reported that the percentage of those who say they feel 'more English than British' rose from 24 per cent in 1997 to 33 per cent in 2008, while the number of those who felt 'more British than English' declined from 23 per cent to 17 per cent.[8]

Aside from issues of national self-definition, the BSA has also posed important questions about people's attitudes to constitutional issues. Table 3.4 tracks the popularity of the standard menu of constitutional options that have been mooted as potential responses to the English question during this period.

Faced with these alternatives, more than 50 per cent of respondents, until 2009, consistently indicated their support for the perpetuation of the current arrangements. There are no indications here of any kind of dramatic turn against devolution, and few signs that those who prioritized their own sense of English identity translated this into a demand for constitutional reform. John Curtice and Anthony Heath, writing in 2000, found little correlation between a commitment to English nationhood and support for the most obviously 'nationalist' option on offer.[9] As many as a half of those who defined themselves as English still supported the current constitutional arrangements. These authors also examined whether a preference for an English national identity was linked to support for the notion that England should become a fully independent country, but found little to support such a contention. These studies have done much to puncture exaggerated hopes and fears about an English backlash. Writing in 2010, Curtice argued trenchantly against the proposition that any linear trend towards Englishness, and away from Britishness, had occurred.[10] In this, and various other publications, he demonstrated how English irritation has become apparent on several specific issues, rather than being expressed in relation to demands for wholesale constitutional change. When asked directly about the anomalous arrangements for voting in the House of Commons associated with the West Lothian issue (which is considered in depth in Chapter 6), most respondents in England (and indeed Scotland) have tended to indicate that these are unfair, but there was no dramatic surge of disaffection on this issue, as Table 3.5 indicates.

However, on the question of how public expenditure is distributed within the union (an issue that is also considered in much greater detail in Chapter 6) Curtice reported a clearer sense of disaffection. When pollsters pointed out to their respondents that spending per head was some 20 per cent higher in Scotland than in England, the latter, fairly unsurprisingly, tended to say that this was unfair. But, in the absence of such prompting, only between a quarter and two-fifths indicated that Scotland received more than its fair share of public spending, as Table 3.6 shows.

Between 2000 and 2003, the proportion of respondents saying that Scotland secured more than its fair share of spending was consistently around 25 per cent. Rather strikingly, however, as economic storm clouds gathered in 2007, that proportion jumped to nearly a third. Figures for 2008 and 2009 show a further increase in the number of those holding this view. And the most recent polling shows that as many as 40 per cent of the English now feel that Scotland

Table 3.4 Constitutional preferences for England, 1999–2009. 'With all the changes going on in the way different parts of Great Britain are run, which of the following do you think would be best for England?'

	1999	2000	2001	2002	2003	2004	2005	2006	2007	2008	2009
England governed as it is now	62	54	57	56	50	53	54	54	57	51	49
Each region of England to have its own assembly	15	18	23	20	26	21	20	18	14	15	15
England as whole to have its own new parliament	18	19	16	17	18	21	18	21	17	26	29

Source: British Social Attitudes Survey

Table 3.5 Attitudes towards the 'West Lothian' question, 2000–2007: 'Scottish MPs should no longer be allowed to vote on English legislation'

	2000	2001	2003	2007
Strongly agree	18	19	22	25
Agree	45	38	38	36
Neither agree nor disagree	19	18	18	17
Disagree	8	12	10	9
Strongly disagree	1	2	1	1

Source: British Social Attitudes Survey

Table 3.6 Attitudes in England towards the financial relationship between England and Scotland, 2000–2009. 'Compared with other parts of the UK, Scotland's share of government spending is…'

	2000	2001	2002	2003	2007	2008	2009
Much more than its fair share	8	9	9	9	16	21	18
Little more than its fair share	13	15	15	13	16	20	22
Pretty much its fair share	42	44	44	45	38	33	30
Little less than its fair share	10	8	8	8	6	3	4
Much less than its fair share	1	1	1	1	1	*	*
Don't know	25	23	22	25	22	23	25

Source: British Social Attitudes Survey

receives more than its fair share of public expenditure; a figure that outnumbers all those who believe that Scotland either 'gets its fair share' or 'less than its fair share'.[11]

This issue aside, Curtice and other leading psephologists have tended to agree that English nationalism did not grow significantly in this period, and that national sentiments were not politicized. The abiding focus on a post-devolution backlash has given way in the political science community to the examination of why it is that those who identified increasingly with England as their primary source of national identification did not come to support the idea of English political institutions. For some commentators this was further proof that the established model of Englishness remained intact, and that its cultural expression remained disconnected from questions about statehood, sovereignty, and governance.[12]

A SEA-CHANGE IN ENGLISH OPINION?

Yet the picture of English attitudes established by this polling has, in recent years, begun to change. The bulk of the data informing the broad academic consensus that an English backlash had not materialized was collected between 1999 and 2007. Since that point, however, a number of different polls, including those produced for the BSA survey, have generated results which appear to indicate that the picture of English indifference to constitutional issues has begun to give way. Recent polling has identified a growing correlation between those who identify most strongly as English and attitudes on various issues associated with the governance of the union.[13] It also points out that the constitutional status quo is becoming a decreasingly attractive option for many of the English. In 2009 support for it fell below 50 per cent for the first time in the BSA series, and that for an English parliament continued to rise, in part due to the discrediting of the idea of regional government following the 'No' vote in the North East referendum held in 2004.

Other recent polling in this area appears to confirm these trends. Based on their review of a range of polls since devolution, Rosie, Bond, and Charlie Jeffery suggested that underneath the 'sweet reasonableness' of the English, a hardening resentment towards the position of Scotland was gathering pace.[14] Equally, a survey conducted by YouGov in 2011 showed a clear majority of English people in favour of Scottish independence.[15] And a qualitative, rather than survey-based, study, conducted by researchers at the Institute of Governance in Edinburgh during the early 2000s, reported that a large sample of interviewees, from Sussex and Manchester respectively, had become much more inclined to say that they felt English rather than British.[16]

The Future of England survey, conducted by YouGov in 2011 for a team of academics and researchers at the Institute for Public Policy Research (IPPR), employed a number of the BSA's questions, and also posed these to comparable publics across Europe. The results it generated pointed to an even greater sense of disaffection with England's position within the union.[17] Its authors revealed that when respondents were asked to choose between defining themselves as English or British, in response to a 'forced choice' question, a clear majority plumped for the former (49 per cent) rather than the latter (42 per cent). And this was the largest proportion of respondents reporting an English affiliation in response to this question since the BSA survey first began, as is clear from Table 3.7.

This study also reported a marked fall in the number of people identifying with Britishness, a trend that has been amplified by the publication of the most recent census data for England and Wales.[18] Englishness was included as an option in a new question about national identity that figured in this survey. In response, 70 per cent of respondents (from England) indicated that they considered themselves English, compared to 25 per cent who opted to identify as British.[19]

Even more importantly the Future of England survey replicated the question employed in the BSA survey which employs the polling methodology devised by Moreno. This offers a menu of combined, as well as single, national identity options, and is widely considered to provide a more robust and nuanced way of measuring national affiliations in multi-national states. The results generated by this question are set out in Table 3.8, and broken down by region. With the exception of London, where an orientation to Britain remains stronger, it would appear that such sentiments have advanced in all parts of England in a broadly uniform fashion.

In their most recent version of this survey, its authors found that, while the English continue to retain a dual sense of identity, they are increasingly likely to place more emphasis on their Englishness than their Britishness.[20] And they have provided a telling contrast, using the Moreno question they posed, between those groups who say that they are either exclusively English, or more English than British, on the one hand, and those who are exclusively British, or more British than English. Forty per cent of respondents prioritized their English over their British identity compared to 16 per cent who placed their British over their English identity affiliation.[21]

Unlike most other surveys, this polling has also shed a comparative light on the relative strength of Englishness. Its authors reported that being English was a much more strongly felt sense of affiliation than nearly all other national or regional identities across Central and Western Europe, with the exception of those found in Scotland and Catalonia, as Table 3.9 reveals.

Just as importantly, this survey asked respondents for their own views on the question of whether 'people in England have become more aware of their English national identity'. In response, 60 per cent stated that they felt that Englishness, as opposed to a sense of British affiliation, had increased in strength in recent years. It also demonstrated a new correlation between a growing identification with English nationhood and a sense of disaffection with the constitutional status quo. In response to a question about whether the UK government at Westminster could be trusted to serve the long-term interests of England (a foundational axiom of the Westminster model of British government), a majority of English

Table 3.7 Trends in 'forced choice' national identity, England 1992–2011

	1992	1996	1997	1998	1999	2000	2001	2002	2003	2004	2005	2006	2007	2008	2009	2011
British	63	58	55	51	44	47	44	51	48	51	48	39	47	45	46	42
English	31	34	33	37	44	41	43	37	38	38	40	47	39	41	41	49

Note: These results reflect an aggregation of the responses of those who feel only English or British, and those who feel more English than British, or vice versa.
Source: British Election Study; British Social Attitudes Survey; Future of England Survey

Table 3.8   National identity: Moreno results by region of England, 2011

	England	London	Midlands	North
English not British	17	13	17	17
More English than British	23	19	24	20
Equally English and British	34	25	36	39
More British than English	9	12	9	8
British not English	7	14	6	6

Source: Future of England Survey

Table 3.9 National and regional identity, Moreno results: England in comparative context

	Identify just with nation-region	Nation-region more important than state	Equally important	State more important than nation-region	Identify just with state
Scotland	19	41	26	4	7
Catalonia	16	29	37	6	6
England	17	23	34	9	7
Wales	11	29	33	10	15
Upper Austria	10	16	38	11	22
Bavaria	9	19	36	11	19
Thuringia	9	18	44	9	17
Salzburg	9	17	50	9	10
Vienna	7	14	38	15	19
Galicia	6	25	57	6	4
Lower Saxony	6	11	34	15	27
Brittany	2	23	50	15	9
Castilla La Mancha	2	4	52	18	20
Alsace	1	17	42	20	15
Île-de-France	1	7	30	42	12

Source: Future of England Survey

Table 3.10 Attitudes in England towards how England should be governed, 2011

For England to be governed as it is now with laws made by all MPs in the UK Parliament (status quo)	24
For England to be governed with laws made by English MPs in the UK Parliament	34
For England as a whole to have its own new English Parliament with law-making powers	20
For each region of England to have its own assembly	9
Don't know	14

Source: Future of England Survey

respondents (59 per cent) responded negatively. And a significant proportion favoured reforms that might grant a greater degree of national-democratic representation to the English. Table 3.10 sets out respondents' attitudes towards the familiar portfolio of answers to the English question.

This indicates that approximately one in five English are consistently in favour of an English parliament. And it shows too that the most popular current choice corresponds with the policy stance favoured by the Conservative party—an adjustment to the workings of the House of Commons to provide a system of 'English votes for English laws'. More generally, the survey reported a growing sense of irritation with devolution, as opposed to the indifference it had hitherto received. And, in terms of the West Lothian question, this survey reported a significant increase in the numbers of respondents from England registering an objection, as Table 3.11 illustrates.

The survey's authors argued that these findings signalled a marked rise in scepticism about whether parties within the political mainstream were able or willing to 'stand up for the interests of England'.[22] This result complements other recent polling which also points to a growth in the salience of Englishness among sections of the English public. More importantly still, this report raised the significant possibility that an embryonic notion of an Anglicized political community was bubbling to the surface of popular consciousness.

It remains unclear whether the sentiments charted in this polling are necessarily generated by constitutional issues themselves, as the report's authors acknowledge.[23] More plausibly, they reflect a broader sense of disaffection with the systems of governance and politics that the English encounter, and may well have other causes than devolution itself. But this survey, like other recent polling data, indicates that a growing sense of affiliation with England has begun to coalesce with an increasingly dyspeptic, pessimistic, and populist attitude towards current political arrangements.

Table 3.11 Attitudes towards the 'West Lothian' question, England 2000–2011
'Scottish MPs should not be allowed to vote on English matters'

	2000	2001	2003	2007	2011
Strongly agree	18	19	22	25	53
Agree	45	38	38	36	26
Neither agree nor disagree	19	18	18	17	15
Disagree	8	12	10	9	8
Strongly disagree	1	2	1	1	4

Source: British Social Attitudes Survey; Future of England Survey

EVERYDAY IDEAS OF 'THE NATION'

Caution is, therefore, required in determining whether the disenchantment tracked by recent polling is directly related to changes in the national gestalt, or if it reflects a short-lived response to a particular set of political and economic circumstances. This is a difficult question to answer using this kind of data alone. A number of recent studies that have employed qualitative approaches to national identity offer important, complementary insights, and shed particular light upon some of the issues that were more prominently connected with micro-level understandings of the nation. Several analyses of 'everyday' forms of English identity have pointed to the significant strengthening in recent years of a discourse of resentment directed at various 'others', including the perceived privileges of the Scots compared to the English, and the allegedly disproportionate influence of Scottish Ministers upon the British government.[24] These studies noted the many negative references to the prominence of Scottish Ministers in the Blair and Brown governments of this period. Pollsters also observed a hardening of English attitudes towards Scotland's position around this time. Curtice, for example, reported that 60 per cent of English people (and indeed 50 per cent of Scots) consistently indicated that they believed that Scottish MPs at Westminster should not vote on laws that had effect only in England, and 75 per cent of English respondents agreed that 'Scotland should pay for its services out of taxes collected in Scotland'.[25] The studies, using very different methodologies, unearthed signs that sections of the English public were starting to 'envisage a fuller demarcation of the government of Scotland from the government of England'.[26]

These sentiments also figured in Skey's extensive analysis of everyday under-standings of 'the nation' among working-class people in England.[27] These sit, he suggested, within a broader web of beliefs that cohere around a highly pes-simistic view of the nation's fortunes and the conviction that the state is unduly responsive to minority groups. This emergent outlook has been identified most recently in polling conducted by Conservative peer, Lord Ashcroft, in 2013.[28] This pointed to the development of a declinist and populist mentality among a significant minority of the electorate, which translates into an entrenched scepticism about politics and politicians, and a sense that England's traditions and heartlands are being deliberately marginalized by liberal public authori-ties. Since 2012, the beneficiary of this fluid and unpredictable mood has been the United Kingdom Independence Party (UKIP), though its recent emer-gence can be traced back to the final years of Labour's period in office.

English-focused sentiments offer the vernacular within which a range of grievances and complaints are aired in this context, invoking a national golden age against which the current state of the country is negatively measured. In this discourse the traditions and values of the nation are at the mercy of social elites and public authorities committed to the liberal and civic values associ-ated with British institutions.[29] The combination of gathering economic uncer-tainty, the decline in living standards experienced by middle and lower income groups from 2004 onwards, and the growing disillusion with a Labour govern-ment that was widely perceived as unsympathetic to the people's culture, laid down a pattern of populist-cum-nationalist sentiment within which an appeal to English culture and interests was central. Ashcroft concluded that the European issue is much more a symptom than a cause of this mood.[30] And the same may well be true of disgruntlement with the domestic union. One of the resonant themes linking up these various complaints was the contention that it was the national and ethnic majority—the English—who were the main los-ers in the arrangements associated with both. Sections of the media have done much to stoke the connection between a populist sense of discontent and a grievance-fuelled identification with Englishness. A content-analysis of cover-age of topics relating to English national identity in the tabloid and broadcast press, undertaken by Skey, revealed an upsurge of coverage in the middle of the 2000s, which sparked and reflected a gathering mood of disenchantment that has typically been expressed in the vernacular of injured Englishness.[31]

Two separate arguments in relation to the constitutional position of the English within the union are increasingly familiar as a result of this broad shift in national sensibility. These are, first, the contention that English interests are being jeopardized by current arrangements and, second, that England now needs to be more clearly delineated and protected within the system of rep-resentative democracy.[32] Both of these ideas enjoy considerable tacit, as well as overt, support at the popular level. Together, they point towards the emergence among sections of English opinion of a preference for some degree of national recognition in both political and institutional terms.

ENGLISHNESS AS ETHNIC-MAJORITY NATIONALISM?

There is considerable merit in broadening our perspective on these developments, and considering if constitutional anomie necessarily has roots in constitutional issues alone. One important, and largely under-examined, alternative possibility is that the emergence of an intertwined stream of nationalist and populist sentiment is a more generic trend, to which a disaffected mobilization of Englishness provides a local contribution. Certainly, various international opinion surveys have tracked a hardening of opinion against migration and migrants in this period across Europe.[33] This shifting attitude is apparent across all social groups, and appears to be linked to a deepening sense of cultural anxiety, much of which is animated by rising fears of the implications of a growing Muslim presence in Western societies.[34] These sentiments are also bound up with economic insecurity and falling living standards among indigenous working-class communities since the early 2000s. They have been widely debated in the context of the rise of new populist parties of the right in the mid to late 2000s, and a steady haemorrhage of electoral support from social democratic and centrist parties.

In the UK, both electoral and party systems have, for the most part, stymied the emergence of an equivalent populist party to those that have emerged elsewhere, although the United Kingdom Independence Party (UKIP) is currently surfing this mood with considerable success.[35] But, even though populist politics has not as yet achieved a breakthrough in elections to the UK parliament, it would be erroneous to assume that Britain has not been affected by these trends, as growing anxieties about cultural diversity and multiculturalism, debates about the declining social fabric, and a significant hardening of attitudes towards Europe and inward immigration have all become apparent.[36] These concerns have typically been expressed in populist terms through reference to the general will of the people and their organic shared culture, in stark contrast to the self-serving machinations of elites.[37] Such sentiments have incubated a markedly anti-political form of understanding and a growing impatience at the apparent incapacity of representative democracies to honour the social bargain forged in the years after 1945.[38]

Some theoretically minded accounts of the turn towards ethnic majority nationalism point to the emergence of new forms of cultural outlook which, far from undergirding the liberal and collectivist projects pursued by states in the late twentieth century, are increasingly eroding trust in representative democracy.[39] The academic literature on this phenomenon has identified the salience of 'the nation' within the ensemble of identities possessed by individuals, and an increasing turn towards an ethno-cultural manner of thinking among the indigenous majority. Some research has argued, in particular, that a new, subaltern sense of ethnic-majority nationalism has become a point of anchorage for many citizens, and is affecting many people's sense of political affiliation.

A report produced by the Searchlight Educational Trust in 2010 fleshed out the political alignments emerging from shifting patterns of collective identity in England, including the renewal of Englishness.[40] Its authors identified the emergence of 'a new political spectrum and dynamic that explain attitudes to culture, identity and nation, presaging a "new politics" that is grounded in notions of belonging and loss, and given expression in new ideas of "identity, culture and nationhood".[41] Specifically, they identified several identity 'tribes' which had coalesced within English opinion. These they termed 'confident multiculturalists' (estimated to comprise 8 per cent of the population), 'mainstream liberals' (16 per cent), 'identity ambivalents' (28 per cent), 'cultural integrationists' (24 per cent), 'latent hostiles' (10 per cent), and those displaying 'active enmity' towards various 'others' (13 per cent).[42] They argued that the most populated categories of 'identity ambivalents' and 'cultural integrationist' occupied the 'centre ground' of politics and were of particular importance to mainstream political parties.

While the suggestion that these categories have displaced more familiar allegiances, such as those associated with class position or age, may well represent an overstatement, the notion that a significant bloc of voters, drawn across different social classes and age cohorts, was—for a mix of cultural and economic reasons—increasingly responsive to the rhetorical appeal of populist forms of nationalism, echoes some of the findings outlined above. Certainly, the suggestion that these sentiments do not fit neatly with the political loyalties founded upon a left–right axis is born out in the English case. Contrary to the weight of received wisdom, there is little evidence to suggest that those who privilege an English national affiliation are significantly more likely to be politically conservative. In 2007, for instance, the proportion of those prioritizing Englishness in terms of their national identification who said that they identified with the Conservative party was, at 30 per cent, just four points higher than the equivalent figure amongst British identifiers. The most recent Future of England survey, meanwhile, suggests that voters inclined to support the Conservatives and UKIP are now most likely to identify with Englishness, but this is also the national preference of most Labour sympathizers.[43]

The authors of the Searchlight report found that a commitment to national identity represented the most important form of identification that people felt, with 64 per cent of their respondents seeing 'nationality, country of birth or country of residence' as the primary aspect of their identity.[44] And they observed that a sense of Englishness was most popular among groups they termed 'latent hostiles', conservative-minded 'cultural integrationists', and the more ideologically ambivalent 'identity ambivalents' to whom, they suggested, the three main parties needed to pay particular attention.[45] Viewing the renewal of English identity through the lens of these broadly defined cultural stances allows us to appreciate the political dimensions of the emergence of new forms of collective identity, and of deepening insecurities generated by such issues as immigration and globalization. The populist appeal to Englishness may well, in part, represent the domestic equivalent of this wider trend.

This focus illustrates that English identity has been expressed in divergent ways, with some of its more traditionalist overtones now being rivalled by newer populist notions. Far from establishing forms of unity and common-ality that span the divisions associated with class, geography, and ethnicity, Englishness is intimately tangled up with these cleavages. Nationalism of this sort has become a political and cultural weapon for different groups rather than a point of shared identification. Whether this diagnosis tells us the whole truth about the social character of English identity is a theme I will consider in more detail below.

SOCIAL AND DEMOGRAPHIC FEATURES OF ENGLISH NATIONHOOD

The idea of interpreting Englishness as, in part, an expression of ethnic-majority nationalism complements a developing academic and political debate in the UK about the fate and consciousness of the poorest sections of the working class, who are widely held to be the key audience for such ideas.[46] I subject this broad claim to critical evaluation and consider, more generally, which are the demographic and social groups to which Englishness most appeals. A more finely grained, disaggregated understanding of the social, and indeed geo-graphical, resonance of this form of nationhood is imperative, I suggest, if we are to understand whether English nationality really does remain the preserve of the indigenous majority, or if it has the potential to appeal to a wide range of social, ethnic, and demographic constituencies.

Here, I draw together a body of relevant polling data and call upon a number of recent qualitative studies to investigate if we can establish, in more concrete terms, which social strata and demographic groups are most inclined to identify with emerging forms of English nationhood. And, while there is considerable need for caution in this area, given the inconsistent and incompatible findings of a number of different polls, I also highlight the prevalence of an emerging and demonstrable set of social characteristics which are associated with English identity. The available evidence, I conclude, serves to confound, rather than support, some of the most familiar assumptions about the nature and appeal of this form of identification, and throws considerable doubt upon the proposition that Englishness represents the consciousness of the disaffected, white working class.

CLASS AND THE ENGLISH

A number of commentators have identified varying degrees of correlation between class background and strength of feeling about English identity. Curtice and Heath reported in 2009 that university graduates were least likely to see themselves as English.[47] In the BSA's survey of 2007, 28 per cent of those in receipt of a university degree said that they saw themselves primarily as English, compared with as many as 44 per cent of those without any qualifications.[48] Yet a more finely grained analysis of the socio-economic profiles of those who identify as English in different polls suggests that a more complex social profile has emerged in relation to this form of national identity. In 2007, for instance, ICM produced a much discussed poll showing high levels of support for the idea of an English parliament.[49] The social profile of those in favour of this idea broke down as follows: those at social grade AB (higher professional) 62 per cent; C1s (clerical and junior managerial) 68 per cent; C2s (skilled manual workers) 73 per cent; and DEs (semi-skilled and low income workers) 66 per cent. The pattern suggested here—in which skilled manual workers (C2s) are more inclined to identify with this cause, while those at the top and bottom of the social scale are somewhat less likely to do so—is repeated in other polling data. An ICM poll from 2006, for instance, posed the question 'Would you be in favour or against the establishment of an English Parliament within the UK, with similar powers to those currently enjoyed by the Scottish Parliament?' The social profile of those answering 'yes' to this question was as follows: ABs 63 per cent; C1s 72 per cent; C2s 67 per cent; DEs 70 per cent.[50] The polling conducted by the Future of England surveys of 2011 and 2012, meanwhile, found that more C2s were in favour of English, rather than British, identity than members of other groups.[51]

These results broadly replicate what scholars have identified as the most common pattern of response to nationalism among distinct social classes in modern societies. Affluent, professional groups are generally the least moved by it, and the skilled working classes and lower middle classes (who have come to be loosely labelled the 'squeezed middle' in current British political parlance) are more consistently amenable. Given that this broad social constituency is widely held to be unusually fickle in its political loyalty, and to have lost heavily in terms of disposable income and living standards since 2004, the possibility that a more grievance-tinged form of nationhood has become appealing in these quarters is a proposition that merits further investigation.[52]

There is an interesting parallel here with the social profile of the electoral support achieved by the far-right British National Party (BNP) in recent years. Contrary to the widespread assumption that the party's core vote is rooted in the cultures of the white working class, a number of analysts have suggested that its anti-political message and hard-edged nationalism are especially attractive to more affluent segments of the working class and the lower middle classes.[53] Roger Hewitt has identified a broad, cross-class 'white backlash'—of which BNP support is one manifestation—against policies associated with multiculturalism.[54] Equally, in their analysis of the 2004 mayoral elections and European elections in London, Cruddas *et al.* found that support for the BNP was highest among skilled manual workers (C2).[55] They concluded that, 'it is not the poorest groups who support far-right parties, but slightly more affluent groups outside the traditional middle-classes'.[56] And, following a ward-level analysis of the BNP vote in the 2003 local elections, the same authors stated that this particular party fared best where there was a large proportion of skilled manual workers.[57] While support for the BNP cannot be regarded as co-terminous with the populist-nationalist outlook under consideration here, there has clearly been some degree of overlap between these phenomena. These various findings point to the need for a more finely grained analysis of those drawn to resentful and populist forms of Englishness than is suggested by reference to 'the white working class'.

The relationship between class background and national identification is further complicated by the tendency for middle-class English citizens to distance themselves from overt displays of nationalist sentiment. Sociologist Steve Garner conducted an important qualitative study of the attitudes of groups of working- and middle-class residents in which he highlighted the particular sensitivity of the latter to the prospect of being too closely associated with views that might be deemed vulgar and chauvinistic.[58] This attribute, he argued, led to a marked difference in terms of tone and language when issues of identity and belonging were under discussion. Yet, he argued, if allowance is made for such rhetorical differences, it is the similarities in attitude—on, for instance, immigration and the EU—between different class cohorts that becomes most apparent, not their differences. Social class ought, therefore, to be seen as having a more ambiguous relationship with Englishness than is widely believed to be the case. If any pattern exists at all in relation to class position, it is one whereby upper segments of the skilled working classes and lower segments of the middle class appear to be most receptive to populist forms of English nationalism. Yet, overall, there is a less pronounced distinction between how middle- and working-class citizens relate to these sentiments than contemporary depictions of the 'white working class' tend to suggest.[59]

Some commentators have long maintained that it is more plausible to see age, not class, as the most important determinant of sentiments towards national affiliation in England. The contention here is that, as the familiar forms of British identity that were forged in the post-war decades have slipped out of the collective memory of citizens born more recently, it may well be that we should expect younger cohorts to be more enthusiastically drawn towards newly constituted ideas of English nationhood. Various polls produced by ICM contain some interesting data in relation to age. Support for the idea of an English parliament in 2007 broke down as follows: 18–24 year olds 58 per cent; 25–34 year olds 50 per cent; 35–64 year olds 53 per cent; and 65+ 28 per cent.[60] And in a poll it conducted a year earlier, on the West Lothian issue, it asked respondents if MPs representing Scottish seats should be stopped from voting on matters that affected only England. The age profile of those who said 'yes' was as follows: 18–24 year olds 48 per cent; 25–34 year olds 40 per cent; 35–64 year olds 31 per cent; and 65+ 28 per cent. And, finally, the affirmative responses elicited to a question in the same poll about an English parliament—which was favoured by 68 per cent of respondents overall—broke down as follows: 18–24 year olds 75 per cent; 25–34 year olds 74 per cent; 35–64 year olds 67 per cent; 65+ 63 per cent.

Taken in the round, these results appear to suggest that younger people are more inclined to be supportive of pro-English reforms than their elders. But caution is needed here too, for other polling data have painted a very different picture. In 2008, according to Curtice, the BSA annual survey reported that those over 55 were:

- more likely to be in favour of an English parliament—30 per cent compared with 26 per cent for 34–55 year olds, and 22 per cent for those under 35;
- much more likely to think that the Scots get more than their fair share of public expenditure in the UK—56 per cent compared with 38 per cent and 25 per cent respectively;
- somewhat less likely to think that the Scots get a fair share of public expenditure—28 per cent compared with 35 per cent and 35 per cent respectively;

• and markedly more likely to view themselves as English rather than British—50 per cent compared with 38 per cent and 35 per cent respectively.[61]

And if we compare answers to the BSA's 'forced choice' question about English and British identities given by different age groups over time, it becomes clear that a sense of attachment to Britishness is equally apparent among those aged between 25 and 34 and those over the age of 65. The notion that it is younger people who are consistently less inclined to identify with traditional ideas about Britain, and to contemplate radical changes in England's constitutional position, is far from convincing. Indeed the results of the most recent census provide a further reason for doubt. Seventy per cent of those aged over 60 identified their nationality as English only, compared to 56 per cent of those aged 30–59.[62]

These findings may also be affected by the different levels of awareness of, and engagement with, these constitutional questions that is apparent across different age cohorts. Various audits of socio-political participation in the UK have reported that people over the age of 55 are more connected to political debate, more likely to vote, and more exercised by constitutional issues than their younger counterparts.[63] It may well be that for those whose memories stretch furthest back into the period prior to devolution, there is both a stronger sense of interest in the constitutional changes introduced in 1999 and a heightened sense of discontent with the deal that England now receives.

ENGLISHNESS AND ETHNICITY

The other main social characteristic that has been strongly associated with a renewed focus upon English identity is ethnicity. At the heart of debates about English nationhood is the familiar contention that it is endemically lacking in appeal to those from minority backgrounds who feel excluded by its implied 'whiteness'. This is undoubtedly a key question, both in empirical and political terms. And there is an abundance of attitudinal data in this period indicating that, in general terms, citizens from ethnic minority backgrounds overwhelming see themselves as British, not English, regarding the former as a more capacious and neutral form of identification.

Yet, here too conventional wisdom is not entirely supported by the available evidence. There is certainly a good deal of survey data indicating that, at an aggregate level, most ethnic minority citizens are more inclined to identify in this way. And yet, a review of a large body of pertinent evidence and recent research on this question throws up some intriguing signs that this deeply embedded assumption is not entirely well founded. There are, specifically, indications that the broader shift towards a more avowedly English sense of nationality is being registered among members of these communities as well, if in more limited and gradual ways. And there is a body of research and anec-dotal evidence to support the proposition that younger cohorts are more likely to identity with England as their primary national community of attachment than their parents or grandparents were.[64]

Such a trend should not, however, be exaggerated. The conventional wisdom on this issue rests upon a strong body of evidence, and undoubtedly reflects an entrenched perception among minority communities about the ethnic charac-ter of Englishness. Curtice and Heath, for instance, reported that, among those who describe themselves as 'white', the proportion saying that they are English has been little different from the proportion claiming to be British since 1999, whereas amongst those from an ethnic minority, only a small number have consistently indicated that they feel predominantly English, with more than 50 per cent indicating that their preferred form of nationality is a British one.[65] Equally, as Table 3.12 shows, it is white respondents who account for the bulk of the increase in English identification over this period.

Curtice and Heath concluded that 'Englishness is not something with which many of those from an ethnic minority background feel much empa-thy'.[66] A separate report published in 2009 argued that 'ethnic minorities liv-ing in England find it hard to adopt an English identity'. It noted too that 'It is assumed that Englishness is a matter of lineage and bloodlines.'[67] As one respondent (a young male from Plymouth) put it, 'I think if you say you are English, most people would assume you are white.'[68]

And yet, while these macro-level findings have remained broadly consistent across this period, if we attempt to disaggregate the experiences and outlooks of different communities, a more complex and dynamic picture of patterns of national identification among England's minority communities begins to emerge. In a detailed analysis of data supplied by the BSA, Condor, Stephen

Table 3.12 Forced choice national identity by ethnic origin, England 1997–2007

	1997	1999	2003	2007
'White' favouring English	35	47	42	44
'White' favouring British	55	44	47	47
BEMs favouring English	5	15	7	5
BEMs favouring British	58	50	54	58

Sources: British Election Study; British Social Attitudes Survey

Gibson, and Jackie Abell pointed to a significant degree of variation in the manner in which people from different ethnic backgrounds responded to a 'forced choice' question about their national identity.[69] Participants from an Indian background were three times more likely to say that they think of themselves as English than black people of African origin.[70] They observed, as well, the different results that subtle differences in the wording of survey questions produced. Rates of 'feeling attached to England' were much higher among British Ethnic Minorities (BEMs) than rates of 'thinking of yourself as English', which appeared to represent an altogether more encompassing and problematic form of identification: 75 per cent of black Caribbeans and 85.6 per cent of Indian-Asians reported a sense of attachment to England.[71] And the results of the 2011 census confirmed the persistence of differences arising from ethnic background in determining attitudes towards both Englishness and Britishness. Thus, while this survey illustrated the trend for ethnic minorities to identify overwhelmingly with Britishness, this was much less true of those from a 'mixed race' background, 47 per cent of whom prioritized being English.[72] And, when broken down by religion, these results revealed that individuals from a Muslim background are significantly less likely to identify as English than other congregationists, notably Christians and Jews. Finally, in the Future of England survey, conducted in 2011, a larger proportion of BEM respondents indicated—in response to a Moreno-style question about identity—that they saw themselves as English and British rather than saw themselves solely as British, as Table 3.13 shows—though these figures reflect the views of a relatively small sample of voters.

Despite the small numbers involved, these results do point to the possibility that the views of ethnic minority citizens towards English identity may not be quite as fixed as is commonly supposed. The latest version of this survey,

Table 3.13 National identity, Moreno results by ethnicity, England 2011

	White British	BEM
English not British	18	9
More English than British	25	13
Equally English and British	36	23
More British than English	7	11
British not English	7	26
Other	5	9

Source: Future of England Survey

conducted in 2012, polled a much larger number of BEM citizens and found that only one in ten chose to identify as mainly or exclusively English.[73] Yet, when it came to identifying with England as a territorial entity, there was little aggregate-level difference between non-white and white respondents.[74] Indeed the notion that a precarious, but increasingly meaningful, sense of identification with England as a place—if not with Englishness as an identity imagined in relation to ancestry and ethnicity—was being forged in this period was echoed in other research. Condor, Gibson, and Abell observed the different ways in which young Pakistani men in Manchester framed their own sense of nationality.[75] This group was willing to adopt the tag 'English' as a description of their relation to the place in which they lived, and the state to which they belonged. But, when describing their own ethnic background and loyalties, they shied away from such a description. England, these commentators concluded, carried different meanings for ethnic minorities in various contexts, sometimes signalling a sense of belonging to a particular place, or implying a sense of identity which was only available to the indigenous, white population. But the possibility that a gradual shift towards a new accommodation with English nationality may be happening in some minority communities is one that merits further investigation.[76] In a deliberative workshop I held with a group of community stakeholders from a variety of cultural and religious backgrounds in Leicester in 2009, for instance, several middle-aged participants reported that their children appeared far more comfortable identifying with an English heritage than was typical of their own generation.[77]

Other observers have also noticed the emergence of a more fluid outlook in relation to nationhood among younger ethnic minority cohorts. Robin Mann identified a telling ambivalence in the ways in which the category 'English' is often employed, noting how it is often:

> treated as one of…many…ethnicities within a multi-ethnic national space…Thus the use of the term English to refer to white majority people is not, in itself, incompatible with multicultural political projects.[78]

And, based on his interviews with residents in an ethnically mixed area of South London, Charles Leddy-Owen concluded that, while Englishness represents a rather precarious and often fraught form of identity for those from non-white backgrounds, a sense of the need and the right to make claims upon it in some minority communities was also palpable.[79]

This trend has been aired by a number of high-profile commentators. Writing in 2010, columnist Gary Younge explained that he now felt able to identify with the English football team in the forthcoming World Cup tournament, and more generally with the imagined community of Englishness.[80] He described this shift as the outcome of a painful personal journey, beginning with his own experience of street-level racism in the 1970s. And, having come to the view, during the 1990s, that Britishness might provide the basis for a post-imperial accommodation of ethnic and cultural diversity, he now confessed to a wary embrace of England, as an affiliation to a place and a people. It is possible, he insisted, to 'find an accommodation between blackness and Englishness'.[81] Indeed, the prospects for a new settlement between multiculturalism and a shared national identity were more promising in England than elsewhere, given the levels of diversity characteristic of England's cities. More generally, he suggested that 'the apparently seamless link between Englishness and whiteness has long since been broken... From pop to politics, cuisine to music, fashion to business, the black experience is now intimately interwoven into the fabric of English daily life.'[82]

Other leading voices joined in this chorus. George Alagiah, a senior BBC journalist and newsreader, recorded a similar movement from alienation to identification with his adopted home country. And while he tended to reference Britain as well as England, he indicated that he and his family 'now call England home because this is the place where we grew up... and where we are now most comfortable'.[83] As Kumar has observed, the indication here is of an Englishness still, as of old, fused with Britishness but capable of widening and adapting itself to the changes of the last fifty years.[84]

Clearly the interconnected questions of whether ethnic minority citizens can and will, over time, come to identify primarily as English, and if the main forms of English identity are capable of broadening their cultural appeal, are vital to political debates about Englishness. The disparate forms of national identity which members of these communities have developed are subject to a considerable set of cross-cutting pressures. The sense of wary attachment and uncertainty that defines the relationship which many ethnic minority citizens have had with established forms of nationhood over the last thirty years remains palpable. It is nicely captured by the remark of Karim Amir, the hero of Hanif Kureishi's novel *The Buddha of Suburbia*: 'I am an Englishman born and bred, almost... '[85] Yet it is also becoming clear that established orthodoxies about the ethnically determined character of English nationality, and its congenital inability to provide an attractive or meaningful source of orientation for those from minority backgrounds, are in need of critical appraisal, not simple repetition. Very gradually, and often painfully, a new relationship with England as an imagined community is being forged in some communities. And, importantly, this trend appears to be symbiotically linked to the more frequent articulation and promotion of Englishness as an identity that is framed in multi-, not mono-, cultural terms. Just as importantly, this issue provides one particular illustration of the proposition of a number of recent ethnographic studies—that English identity is becoming a much more unstable compound, a simultaneous source of admiration and fear, and a point of identification that a wider range of English people are drawn to explore.

NATIONAL IDENTITY BEYOND THE POLLS

The plethora of surveys that have been conducted on these issues offer important, and sometimes contradictory, insights into the social characteristics of those drawn towards a sense of English identity. But polling data alone only offer a static, aggregate-level snapshot of a much more complex and fluid situation. And they tell us nothing about the various meanings that are attached to the assertion of Englishness, or about the variety of ways in which this sense of nationality is being expressed. Indeed an over-reliance on such data risks reducing a fluid and multi-faceted set of phenomena to a one-dimensional attitude, detached from the cultures, contexts, and wider beliefs within which they make sense. Asking people to supply answers that abstract from the many different situations in which they live and think, necessarily places limits on the value of this kind of data.

More generally, the underpinning approach to identity that is often employed by psephologists differs starkly from the predominant ways in which this category has come to be understood in large parts of the social science community. Pollsters necessarily record the cognitive responses that citizens offer to a particular question, and they frame these within the conventional terms associated with the wider public discourse. Yet, as a good deal of theorizing about the processes of identity formation and maintenance suggests, these forms of identification are typically lived, experienced, and intuited, rather than necessarily being the products of cognitive reflection and calculation.[86] Attempting to judge the rise and fall of English identity without attending to the question of what it signifies to people from different backgrounds is a necessarily limited, and potentially misleading, exercise. Analyses that rely upon survey data are sometimes inclined to regard the identity under examination, in this case nationality, as a kind of quantum, the rising or falling of which can be measured and charted in a determinate fashion. Yet such a notion negates the integral, qualitative dimensions of identity. The battery of survey evidence devoted to this particular topic tells us little about what giving a greater weight to an English sense of nationhood actually means to those who espouse, or indeed reject, it, and about how it fits with, and crowds out, other forms of identity.

There is an intrinsic value to cross-referencing quantitative with qualitative research in the analysis of a phenomenon like national identity. In particular, the more disaggregated approach employed above is helpfully amplified by research that offers micro-level analysis of the patterns and meaning of nationality. Studies that use qualitative methods tend to highlight the fluid and multi-dimensional character of national identity, emphasizing that individuals live and practise different facets of their identity in different social arenas.[87] At the same time, studies that rely upon such methodologies are themselves far from foolproof, and, as we shall see, particular methods that fall under this broad heading—such as interviews with individual participants—have generated interpretations that are also contestable. In the discussion that follows, I place particular stress on the prior assumptions about the nature of Englishness which have shaped some of the leading interpretations of its meanings and character generated from within the sociological community in particular. I argue too that much of this scholarship has focused upon the resentful and racialized dimensions of English identity, and has, as a result, obscured or ignored some of its other main facets.

IDEAS OF ENGLAND IN EVERYDAY LIFE

A slew of recent studies, exploring the provenance and implications of English symbols, practices, and cultural references in the textures of everyday life, offer vital insights into the meanings and salience of this form of identity.[88] As leading theorist of modern nationalism Michael Billig has famously argued, ideas of national identity are, for the most part, generated and reinforced through the banal rituals and practices of everyday culture, rather than the highly orchestrated points of 'ecstatic nationalism' associated with high-profile events and public celebrations.[89] His argument is an important one in relation to Englishness, given that public discourse about national identity in the UK has often chosen to read popular sentiments through the prism of international football matches and extravaganzas like the Olympics. Precious little analysis of the English question has involved a consideration of the various everyday settings and contexts in which nationhood is made meaningful. Recent academic commentary, by contrast, has drawn our attention to the *habitus* associated with social life that lies beyond the ken and control of policy-makers and politicians. In these settings, some particularly important shifts of habit and practice have happened in recent years, including the greater diffusion of English symbols and icons, the growing propensity for the popular celebration of English traditions, and the increasingly familiar articulation of the claim—noted by many different observers—that Englishness is both disapproved of, and deliberately marginalized by, a metropolitan and self-serving political elite.

None of these shifts are readily amenable to quantitative analysis, and each carries very particular meanings for the groups and individuals associated with them. In Chapter 4 I explore some of the distinct and overlapping strands of sentiment that inform recent cultural expressions and explorations of English nationhood. And I suggest that this has become a more readily available and culturally salient 'frame' through which a range of values and emotions can be expressed and explored. But the panoply of sentiments associated with Englishness is more diverse and mutually disputatious than has generally been assumed. They encompass a relatively confident sense of national self-understanding rooted in familiar traditions of liberal and conservative discourse as well as harder-edged forms of populist resentment.

A number of academic studies have linked the vernacular of English resentment to the declining position of the white working class.[90] Within this field of study a concern with how claims to Englishness reflect a defining and defensive sense of 'whiteness' has become widespread. In his recent work, Skey, for instance, has stressed the growing importance, in a culture dominated by the values of mobility and sociability, of the 'ontological security' associated with organic forms of nationhood, 'notably in terms of anchoring subjectivity'.[91] A rhetorical appeal to Englishness has come to play exactly this role, strengthening a sense of in-group membership which simultaneously gives various 'others' a more tenuous form of belonging. He also argues that debates around belonging in England 'continue to define certain "...ethnic" groups as more or less national, because they embody certain traits, practices or norms'.[92] Those who, in his terms, belong 'without question', are afforded a degree of symbolic security through reference to the national 'we', and this identification, and its attendant forms of exclusion, are 'underpinned through routine practices, symbolic forms and institutional arrangements'.[93]

In his recent study Skey argued that national identities are comprised of layers of sentiment and attachment, which contain a rich seam of complementary and contrasting inferences.[94] He gave particular emphasis to the forms of contestation and conflict that arise from rival attempts to give shape to a particular identity. And, like other scholars influenced by the work of Billig, he stressed how the 'routine habits, symbolic systems and familiar material environments' that constitute the *habitus* of everyday life consist of sedimented ideas of who 'we'—in national terms—are.[95] He detected in recent years a 'tentative, but noticeable, shift towards an English identity'.[96] And, like others, he identified a toxic mixture of grievance, resentment, and ethnicized sense of belonging at its heart, as well as deeply entrenched ideas about the entitlement of indigenous people when it came to the allocation of social goods such as jobs, council and social housing, and welfare benefits. Such indigenous characters, he has argued, are a

> group of people who articulate a more secure sense of belonging to the nation, which is defined in relation to ethnic minorities. Majoritarian belonging is bound up in narratives of ancestry, ethnicity and place and is in turn used to underpin powerful claims to key social, economic and cultural resources. In other words, there is a strong link between belonging and entitlement, so that 'I belong more than you' also means 'I deserve more than you'.[97]

Importantly, he has also suggested that the sense of entitlement that is prevalent is not just connected to tangible goods, such as housing, but is also related to a more diffuse set of cultural norms, concerning how people behave and the ability of 'others' to be understood. It is this shift in the sense of belonging experienced by many within the ethnic majority which lies behind the growing sensitivity and resentment attached to the question of immigration in particular.

Skey's interviewees were unmoved by debates about devolution and the union, and indeed by most conventional political issues. Many of the younger people he interviewed regarded their own national identification as a choice stimulated by the puzzlement and resentment generated by the perception that other national groupings were determinedly anti-English, or supposedly enjoyed a position of advantage in comparison with the English.[98] His research, and that of various other sociologists, illustrates the prevalence of an abiding sense of grievance among parts of the English public. His interviews with the organizers of St George's Day events, for instance, pointed to the ubiquity of the anxiety that 'other' nationalities were more self-confident and visible than the English.[99] As one of his interviewees put it, 'People are getting fed up with people flogging St Patrick's Day and St Andrew's Day and not allowing St George's Day. You put a St George's Day flag up and they call it racialist.'[100]

Numerous academic studies, and many different journalistic contributions, have taken as a given the notion that English nationalism serves as the form of consciousness through which the disaffection of the white working class is expressed. The very emergence of the term 'white working class' in public discourse, and an associated debate about the negative ways in which this grouping is often represented, reflects a longer-range process whereby the older language of class division has been displaced by that associated with ethno-cultural diversity. In this context, the emergence of the figure of the 'chav'—a pejorative embodiment of the venality, vulgarity, and criminality associated with the poorest strata of the working classes—has gained wide cultural traction.[101] References to English nationalism are endemic to cultural representations of chav culture. Thus media reportage often lingers upon a tattered flag of St George when white working-class estates are represented, providing a visual cue signifying the endemic chauvinism to which this grouping is supposedly inclined. In a public culture where the terminology of class has all but disappeared, the white working class is often framed as a beleaguered ethnic minority, 'stripped of its dignity, its self-worth, its culture and its hope'.[102] For some commentators, the cultural stereotyping of the chav is the latest episode in a much longer story of the attempts of the English bourgeoisie to distinguish itself from the working classes: 'an entire social and cultural system works to continue the constitution of white working-class people as entirely devoid of value and worth'.[103]

Attempts within the political and policy worlds to respond to the demonization of this social constituency, and a growing concern about the poor social outcomes associated with it, have proved highly controversial. Vron Ware has pointed to the development of a 'resentment discourse' among Labour politicians who, in a period of declining popularity, prior to 2010, declared themselves willing to listen more sympathetically to the frustrations and resentments of working-class people. She derided these efforts as a kind of government-sponsored therapy which implicitly accepted the populist claim that the real cause of a pervasive sense of class-based resentment was immigration.[104] Thus, in October 2009, Minister John Denham launched the Connecting Communities programme which sought to address perceived feelings of marginalization and resentment among the 'white working class'. And in 2011 Labour MP and Shadow Minister Ivan Lewis argued that the current resurgence of English identity was in part

> a cry of defiance from people who feel alienated from the mainstream political establishment. They write off politicians as being the same, are sceptical about progress and pessimistic about the future and feel their identity is being marginalised in their own country.[105]

His was one of a growing chorus of voices from within mainstream politics now arguing that the alienation of white working-class voters should be seen as a symptom of a deep-rooted sense of marginalization and exclusion. The guiding assumption of such thinking was that it was the structurally deteriorating position of this constituency which explained the growing appeal of resentful and populist Englishness, so that the injuries of class were being aired in the argot of disaffected nationhood.

The waning of the language of class from Britain's public culture has, on this view, enabled this grouping to be represented in derogatory ways, and seen as impoverished by its own cultural—and national—preferences, rather than by its economic situation: 'Theirs is also a cultural impoverishment, a poverty of identity based on outdated ways of thinking and being.'[106]

For Skey too, current forms of class-based contempt, as expressed through the archetype of the chav, have helped represent the inhabitants of white working-class communities as 'other', by dint of their vulgar cultural habits and low moral standards. As a result, these communities are deemed to lie beyond the accepted mores and norms of polite society, and their supposedly visceral and irrational attachment to English nationalism widely invoked as a symptom of their own willed estrangement from middle-class norms.[107] But in his wide-ranging critique, Chris Haylett suggests that the dual emphasis upon the 'whiteness' of this constituency and its deep attachment to exclusivist forms of nationhood which characterizes many sociological treatments of it, has undeservedly propelled the themes of racism and resentment to the forefront of current discussions of class: 'There is a resulting tendency for white working-class cultures to be cast as emblematically racist.'[108]

THE ENGLISH AND THEIR 'OTHERS'

It is certainly notable that in a slew of recent sociological studies, the analysis of contemporary forms of English nationalism involves a recurrent focus upon those practices, habits, and ways of speaking that reflect an exclusionary, and often chauvinist, idea of national community, and these are typically deemed to work through visceral forms of 'othering'. The national 'we', it is suggested, takes shape through its opposition to a derided, external 'they'. In the recent period the latter role is often allocated to incoming migrants, ethnic minorities, and other social groups deemed unworthy of the sense of entitlement associated with membership of the English nation.[109] This tendency has been stressed by a large body of academic commentary which is convinced that Englishness offers the discursive vehicle for the expression of a pronounced sense of ethno-cultural consciousness. On this view, the language and symbolism of the beleaguered national community, which is defined by its opposition to, and fear of, various externalized threats, provides a potent and regressive core to English nationalism. Not surprisingly, given these entrenched assumptions, the sociological study of Englishness is dominated by the themes of resentment and chauvinism directed at various non-white 'others'.

And yet, forms of 'otherness' rooted in internal differences within the English imagination have been just as integral to national thinking in this period as has a recoil against various perceived external threats. And these are reflective of differences arising from distinctions associated with regional geography, wealth, and class. These have been expressed most commonly in relation to the imaginary divide signalled by the duality between 'North' and 'South'. This deeply embedded antinomy continues to exert a significant hold over current expressions of the meaning, culture, and landscapes of Englishness, so that the national 'we' is routinely defined against a 'they' who are deemed to represent another kind of English sensibility and culture. The renewal and reinvention of a decidedly folk sensibility in the current era, which is examined in Chapter 4, has provided an important source and vehicle for a renewed expression of distaste for the power and wealth of London and the South East, which has itself become a recurrent feature of the English imagination. A powerful contrast between London, which is increasingly presented as a globalized cosmopolis, and organic forms of rooted Englishness, has become increasingly salient.[110] Among Londoners, pride in their polyglot city is intertwined with a culturally rooted sense of self-importance and, along with the extraordinary cultural diversity of the population who live there, has engendered a much weaker sense of attachment to the imagined community of England. Since the granting of significant powers of self-government, the capital has become closely identified with the culture and outlook of the political and economic elites that dominate it. None of the UK's other large cities have become as imaginatively disconnected from the rest of England as London has.

The continued presence of a variety of regionally rooted notions of Englishness, beyond the heartlands of South East England, has long been a vital, though overlooked, dimension of English cultural life. A range of particular places, iconic figures, and works of culture have, in the modern period, become readily identifiable with forms of English nationhood that are seen as alternatives to elite, Southern-inflected images. This pattern has been expressed in a recurrent contrast between representations of Northern Englishness, and their associated characteristics and values, and the dominant seam of Southern Arcadianism.[111] Often depicted as the haven of an industrial modernity which was the antithesis to the rural spirit of the nation, Northern regions have long been associated with very different forms of English character and culture. The distinctive pride and local tradition associated with many cities and towns outside the South East undergirded a number of distinctive expressions of English identity. These were celebrated in popular cultural forms such as the Northern music-hall tradition, and in more contemporary times through the development of distinctive city-based musical scenes. A rich tapestry of local forms of pride and identity, many of which sustained divergent claims about the 'real' culture of England informed different 'trajectories for thinking about English modernity itself from the industrial revolution onwards'.[112]

The various kinds of national culture rooted in local and regional differences were much more prominent in the thinking of leading intellectuals in earlier decades than is the case today. Both Orwell and Priestley made journeys to the North in part to explore these different modes of Englishness.[113] And, writing in the 1950s, anthropologist Geoffrey Gorer provided a sensitive analysis of the geographical distinctions and historical traditions integral to established ideas of the English character.[114] He observed that what was typically labelled 'English' often involved a covert attempt to naturalize Southern aesthetics and values, and to marginalize practices and ideas associated with what he termed the 'Northern temperament'.[115] Thus, the rural England that was 'rediscovered' in the nineteenth century was 'largely southern in its topographical connotations'.[116] As various observers have noted, a subtle hierarchy of forms of identity came into being, and were often experienced by those who subscribed to them as natural and unproblematic. Particular features and parts of the nation were 'made to stand—repeatedly, and in a multitude of contexts and associations—for the whole' within this layered hierarchy of national representations. And the domestic metaphor of the 'home counties' allotted to the South East hinterland a core symbolic position, buttressed by its geographic proximity to, and economic dependence on, London.[117]

The stark imaginative dualisms associated with regionally distinct archetypes of Englishness did not accurately reflect the complex nature of the inequalities that existed between, and within, the geographical areas associated with the categories of 'North' and 'South'. Yet they were sufficiently reflective of certain enduring social and economic realities to render these overarching cultural representations meaningful and appealing. And they have continued to figure prominently in contemporary projections of Englishness.

A related, but also somewhat distinct, contrast also continues to infuse expressions of English nationhood. This concerns those ingrained forms of alterity that are rooted in forms of class distinction. One of the most fertile accounts of English identity to have emerged from the academic community in the last two decades—supplied by the historian George Schöpflin—has identified social class as the fulcrum of shifting patterns of Englishness. In a major essay published in 2000, he argued that the predominant cultural images of the English nation were associated with the different classes that made it up, and were as much mutually reinforcing as rivalrous.[118] The class-endowed character of national sentiment imparted an unusual degree of inclusivity and permeability to Englishness because it pivoted upon the axis of class, not ethnicity or cultural background, as was more typically the case elsewhere.

Other historians have echoed this argument. Joanna Bourke supplied a telling discussion of the contrast between national identity as an idea propagated by elites, on the one hand, and as understood through the lived experiences of working-class people in East London during the twentieth century, on the other.[119] She pointed to a shifting and uneasy balance between a form of imagined classlessness which English patriotism was, on occasions, able to project, and an entrenched and enduring sense of nationhood rooted in the solidarity and familiarity of working-class life. She concluded that, in the arenas of family and intimate community, classlessness was more successfully imagined, but outside of these spaces—in public life or the media—the working classes were, for the most part, still constructed as 'a race apart'.[120]

Englishness has thus served both to express deeply rooted differences— of geography and social class—and also to project forms of imagined community whereby these might be transcended, and the tensions associated with them imaginatively dissolved. English identity has long been expressed through depictions of the national spirit that reproduce archetypical representations of the established social classes—a familiar motif of the novels of Elizabeth Gaskell and Charles Dickens and, in more kitsch fashion, of numerous TV dramas focusing upon the distinct worlds of masters and servants in country-house England.[121]

Projections of the character and culture of the upper, middle, and working classes have often been integral to leading accounts of the national character.[122] And the recurrence and evolution of these contrasting 'types' have served to bolster a sense of the enduring order and fixed hierarchy of Englishness itself. But Schöpflin also observed that the relationship between class and nation was, in many ways, mutually dependent. Englishness has long provided a rich idiom for expressing and making sense of the differences associated with distinct social interests within the wider political culture. And as class has disappeared from the language of mainstream politics in the last thirty years, it may well be that the language of nationhood has become more important as a carrier of anxieties and themes associated with class distinction. Commentators have thus noted the emergence of a growing polarity between representations of England as a point of retreat for the 'white working class' on the one hand, and the more expansive, post-national culture associated with sections of the middle class in England since the 1990s.[123] Whereas Englishness was once defined in the image of middle-class character, in the last few decades it has become increasingly projected as a pathological form of consciousness associated with economically declining segments of the working class.[124]

A number of recent studies have illustrated how this class-based contrast tends to work. There is an increasingly marked inclination among sections of the middle class to disavow any association with nationalism, and to establish a distance from the working classes by tarring the latter with the brush of atavistic and regressive forms of national chauvinism. That it is an unskilled, alienated, and uncouth 'white working class' that is seen as the standard bearer for Englishness (even if, as we have seen, this is a far from accurate empirical characterization) has done much to confirm established metropolitan prejudices about the dangers of nationalism in general, and Englishness in particular. Skey reported, for example, that in some of the middle-class groups he convened, areas where English flags were allegedly more prominent were casually dismissed as 'shit and chavvy'.[125]

Both of these entrenched and powerful imaginative contrasts—North against South, and working against middle class—are integral to contemporary expressions of English identity. However, in the last few decades a third internal axis of difference has become prevalent. This dates back to the 1960s when rising anxieties about immigration from the Commonwealth, and a growing sense of British decline, generated a new internal dynamic within ideas of the nation—one associated with ethnicity and cultural difference.[126] This development provided an important backdrop to the construction of a more assertive and Anglicized British nationalism during the Thatcher years. This has spread more broadly in recent years, and has been assiduously promoted by fringe parties keen to harness the alienation of the indigenous poor, framing this group as 'the last tribe of England', a residuum denied cultural recognition, respect, and socio-economic standing by a state that is assumed to treat other social and cultural groups more favourably.

The rival forms of Englishness shaped by these contrasts have been just as important in determining the contemporary English imagination as the exterior dynamics of otherness. And, as we shall see when we consider in more detail the principal narrative forms of English nationhood, these established imaginative dualisms have continued to generate some of the most salient images, themes, and points of reference within current expressions of Englishness.

FAIRNESS AND THE ENGLISH

An additional reason for wariness about the proposition that the themes of resentment and grievance are the defining motifs of this form of nationality is supplied by recent research which points to the recurrence of different normative ideas that remain intimately connected to English self-understanding. The work of Condor is especially important in this regard. Together with various collaborators, she has provided a more refined understanding of 'the ways in which ordinary social actors construct themselves as nationalised subjects' within England.[127] Her research has highlighted a range of meanings and discourses associated with the English imagination. She and her co-authors have given particular emphasis to the intimate relationship between personal biography and national identity, showing that Englishness is commonly understood as a source or object of discovery, rather than a simple matter of inheritance.[128] Several of her studies have stressed how the various meanings associated with this form of identification come to the fore in different social contexts, depending both on the subject under discussion and the respondent's own sense of identification with different categories of national membership. Condor has also done much to highlight the various rhetorical and behavioural mechanisms which individuals employ in order to avoid associating too directly with a sense of nationality that might carry chauvinistic implications. And she has noted how many English participants take the rhetorical position of the 'external voyeur' when invited to comment upon their own national background, as opposed to 'primary participant', a stance typically adopted by counterparts in Scotland.[129]

In methodological terms too, she has made some telling points about the limitations of qualitative research methods, such as survey questionnaires and structured interviews, with regard to the challenge of capturing people's thinking about their own national background. Her own research has displayed an unusual degree of reflexivity about the limits of such methods, and has highlighted the importance of the social etiquette which affects the ways in which participants talk about national identity. Echoing Orwell's emphasis upon the persistence of an unconscious sense of the *patria* beneath the surface of everyday life—which is endemically resistant to intellectual definition and classification—she concluded that contemporary 'white ethnic majority interview respondents in England are inclined to treat national identity as a taken-for-granted fact of life, rather than as a suitable topic for conversation'.[130] Very few of her large sample of respondents gave an entirely unambiguous account of their own national identity, and most took their 'ontological status as English as a conversational given' rather than a topic that they felt comfortable discussing.[131]

This is one reason, she suggested, why those researchers who have adopted the 'confessional' style of interview with research participants are more likely to conclude that the English do not have a clear sense of their own nationality. Yet the tendency to interpret denials and mitigations regarding national background as direct empirical evidence of the abnormalities—and possibly deficiencies—of English national identity, tells us more about academic analysts' cultural preconceptions than the phenomena under investigation. Condor's work has made a powerful case for greater interpretive attention to those ideas of 'the national' that are widely taken as given features of the social and cultural world, and are rarely the subject of reflective examination or conversation. And she has offered numerous insights into the ambivalent and fluid ways in which many of the English approach questions of nationhood, establishing an important counterpoint to the stress upon the regressive and exclusionary Englishness that is prominent in much sociological analysis. In specific terms she has recorded that many English respondents use the term 'British' to signal a loose but 'common in-group' in a more positive and deliberate fashion than much commentary has indicated. Rather than treating Northern Ireland, Scotland, and Wales as 'others' against which Englishness is negatively and competitively defined, the intuitive stance of many English respondents has been one of empathy, displaying recognition of the existence and sensitivities of these parts of the United Kingdom. For many of the English, national identity was frequently treated 'as an essentially private matter' which defined neither the boundaries of community nor the social networks within which people interacted.[132]

More recently, she has highlighted a persistent strand of normative thinking among the English which reflects a strongly proceduralist intuition regarding the right of the different countries of the UK to determine their own future.[133] What has widely been viewed as a sense of indifference or grudging resentment towards devolution is better understood as tacit support. The deeply rooted sense among many English people about the right of smaller nations not to be dominated by government based in London might be fruitfully extended to explain the sense of effrontery which is growing among the English at their own, apparently diminished, standing within the union. Such an interpretation tallies with the judgement of observers such as Curtice, who have long argued that expectations of an Anglo backlash are founded upon an under-estimation of English tolerance for devolution. Writing in 2006 he argued that the English 'appear to be sympathetic to Scotland and Wales having their own institutions while at the same time remaining part of the UK'.[134]

A good many social scientists continue to work with the assumption that Englishness is broadly analogous to other forms of mass nationalism, and that it gains its appeal and force from the resentful and fearful alterity at its heart. Yet such an approach has tended to erase an appreciation of forms of nationhood that have evolved from older, established traditions and beliefs, some of which have been positive and enabling, rather than divisive and resentful. The notion of English nationalism as a crucible for grievance remains a close cousin of the absence thesis, discussed in Chapter 1. On this view, Englishness is defined by its sour, resentful, and inward-looking character. But this perspective significantly under-estimates the plurality of meanings associated with English nationhood in the current period. There are, and indeed always have been, different versions of what it means to be English in circulation, and an accompanying diversity of ideas about who belongs to the imagined community it invokes. And while these often converge upon a familiar set of national myths, stories, and icons, they diverge markedly in terms of the political and cultural sensibilities that they promote. Thus, while some current expressions of Englishness do indeed intersect with the broader nationalist-populist turn in European culture, it is distorting to reduce this form of nationality to this particular expression. Other rival ideas and notions of Englishness have continued to figure within, and shape, the national imagination.

CONTEMPORARY POLITICAL EXPRESSIONS OF ENGLISHNESS

So far, I have stressed the need to appreciate the plural character of current forms of English identity, and challenged those interpretations that reduce Englishness to a single stream of cultural and political sentiment. Here, I provide a more detailed indication of the leading narrative forms which expressions of Englishness have taken in this period. While the typology that I present is far from being exhaustive in its representation of the range of ideas and sentiments associated with this form of identity, it seeks to reflect some of the main patterns into which those characterizations of English nationhood that have accrued a political resonance have tended to fall. Specifically, I delineate: a rising, hard-edged sense of populist nationalism; a distinct, everyday kind of conservative Englishness; and a disparate body of ideas and endeavours that seek to reframe England in liberal terms. Below I flesh out some of the main lines of thinking within these very broadly drawn perspectives, and highlight some of the internal differences within them. In each case I give weight to some of the leading expressions of these ideas, and highlight their increasingly important political implications.

POPULIST-NATIONALISM ASCENDANT

The notion that a reconstituted English nationalism has become an important vehicle for the expression of a growing sense of resentment directed at various ethnic and national 'others' has been widely aired in recent years. One feature of this outlook, which has been underplayed in public discourse, is the hostility to the political system in general, and the major political parties within it, which lies at the heart of populist appeals to the beleaguered English nation.

The increasingly familiar proposition that a 'political class' has now come to the fore is itself a sign of the steady diffusion of populist assumptions about politics.[135] And while proponents of anti-political populism are not always nationalists, and themselves come from various political backgrounds, the growing alignment between populism of this sort and nationalist rhetoric is an important aspect of the current retrieval of the idiom of Englishness. These impulses are often connected through the proposition that the national culture and traditions of the people are being deliberately marginalized by a political establishment which holds to forms of 'political correct' orthodoxy and views expressions of English pride as inherently suspect.

This trope has a lengthy pedigree in English culture. It was central to the 'Little Englander' intellectual current of the early twentieth century, and associated with conservative proponents of Englishness in the inter-war years, such as Arthur Bryant.[136] The historical pedigree of this lineage is symbolized by the ubiquitous references to G. K. Chesterton's poem *The Secret People*, and his ominous reference to a populace that is quietly seething, waiting for its chance to break from the condescension of the political elite: 'Smile at us, pay us, pass us; but do not quite forget; For we are the people of England, that never have spoken yet.'[137] These lines have been cited again and again by campaigners and polemicists in recent years.[138] Indeed for many observers, populist resentment is the inevitable destination of English nationalism, and may even be latent within the English character.[139] In the current period, new targets for nationalist resentment have become prominent. The European Union, as Wellings observed, has been particularly important in helping spark a reactive kind of nationalism.[140] But the latter has fed off other sources too, not least a rapid rise in disenchantment with politics and politicians more generally. Over the course of the past fifteen years a range of different threats to the soul of the beleaguered nation have been identified, with inward migrants and welfare scroungers especially prominent in the demonology assembled by nationalists. In this vein, populist forms of Englishness signify a sullen, two-fingered response to the political establishment and its values, as well as affording a rhetorically rich framework for expressing a form of collective self-understanding which is now presented as trumping older allegiances founded upon party politics, geography, or class.

But populist Anglo nationalism is a more internally differentiated outlook than is sometimes supposed. It spans, at one end, those drawn to the street politics of groups like the English Defence League (EDL), and also encompasses more moderately inclined voters who are recruited by the heady mix of social pessimism and national declinism which it promotes. These sentiments have been mined by a number of different parties of protest, most notably UKIP, since the advent of the Coalition between Conservatives and

Lib Dems in 2010.[141] One important, long-range shift which has abetted this trend is the steady decline of the kinds of social deference upon which both the Conservative and Labour parties were previously able to call, and which acted as a significant restraint upon populist and nationalist impulses among the English.[142]

Populist manifestations of English nationalism are steeped in assumptions about, and images of, class difference. As we have already seen, the language of nation has supplied a resonant medium through which such distinctions have been projected within English culture. Increasingly, 'vulgar' forms of nationalist identification have come to be viewed as distorted expressions of a resentful class consciousness, and closely associated with an ever more reviled, white working class.[143] But, as various studies suggest, the contention that it is primarily among this constituency that the forms of 'whiteness' associated with English nationalism have gained their appeal is a mistaken one.[144]

And yet, there are indications to suggest that there is a class dimension to perspectives on nationhood in England. Curtice and Heath noted in 2009 that respondents opting for 'English' rather than 'British' identification tended to hold a more ethnic than civic conception of belonging.[145] Britishness, various studies suggest, has, for many working-class respondents, become a more separate and remote layer of belonging than Englishness, and the latter has also become 'whiter' in terms of its ethno-cultural resonance, Garner has shown.[146] In an important recent study, Steve Fenton and Robin Mann explored the appearance of two linked, and opposed, archetypes—'resentful nationalists' and 'liberal cosmopolitans'.[147] The interplay and rivalry between these types, they argued, has become one of the major forms of identification through which class distinctions are lived in England. Those whose outlook broadly conforms to the first commonly refer to a decline in civility in the neighbourhood or locality, typically look upon the presence of immigrants with suspicion, and are very likely to regard political and economic elites as having failed the working classes. And in diametrical contrast, the second perspective conveys a decidedly trans-national orientation, especially among those from professional backgrounds. For many of the latter, an unashamed sense of pride in the nation is implicitly identified as a marker of belonging to the lower echelons of society. In this analysis, populist English nationalism is rooted in the experiences of a class that feels itself to be moving downwards, while an upward sense of trajectory is more likely to appeal to an 'open', liberal, and positive view of the social order.[148]

This stark contrast which Fenton and Mann propose between the Englishness associated with working-class 'whites' and the metropolitan defence of the multicultural is a powerful and challenging one, and is echoed in other research. There is a danger in such characterizations, however, that they overstate the coherence and stability of the manner in which the national community is imagined.[149] In some of its manifestations, populist Englishness assumes that its core constituency is made up of respectable working-class people from indigenous stock. In others, the imagined community of the national heartland is assumed to include members of ethnic minority groups who are united against the presence of a particular set of 'others', for instance Muslims. Many of Garner's respondents saw their ethnic minority neighbours as 'English', but distinguished these from more recently arrived groups, including those classed as 'white', such as the Poles who arrived in great numbers after their country's accession to the EU.[150] And as a recent analysis of the census results of 2011 illustrated, those from a mixed-race and Afro-Caribbean backgrounds are much more likely to identify as English than are other ethnic minorities.[151] The trend to view the white working class and the rise of populist nationalism as integrally interconnected can result in a debilitating inattention to other, very different forms of national thinking in relation to England, and runs the risk of caricaturing the kinds of subjectivity and political resonance associated with Englishness. It also risks reinforcing forms of representation of working-class citizens that border upon caricature. Polling data tend to suggest that approximately one in five voters in England align consistently with nationalism of this sort, though a larger group of working- and middle-class citizens remain open to its appeal. In fact, the tendency to assume that this perspective is the primary expression of an ascendant English nationalism is most revealing about the fears which Englishness continues to evoke among liberal-minded commentators. Other strands of sentiment have contested the English national identity as well, and these have often drawn upon the same reservoir of national myths, images, and ideas to which populists lay claim.

EVERYDAY ENGLISH CONSERVATISM

The main counterpart to populist expressions of national resentment is a rich and sinuous seam of pragmatic, adaptive, and conservative English sentiment. This has been most fully elaborated and celebrated in the realms of high politics and thought, notably in the treatment of the merits of a governing national tradition produced by philosopher Michael Oakeshott and other exponents of the unique qualities of the British constitution and English character.[152] This often overlooked tradition has in recent years become central to contemporary expressions of national identity among the English. And, while it was for a lengthy period identified with the dominant lineage of thinking about the

British state and the union, there are new signs of its gradual decoupling from long-standing patterns of constitutional thought.

This perspective coheres in broad terms around the inclination to favour the values and ways of living associated with established forms of community, allied to the intuitive disposition to show a degree of tolerance towards those with different values and backgrounds. It has long been anchored within idealized visions of the countryside as the crucible for the spirit and temperament that make the English unique.[153] This association dates back to the proliferation of Arcadian images of Englishness that emerged during the period of national consciousness which Kumar has identified.[154] At that time a medley of authors, poets, and artists characterized English nationhood as a sensibility that was best attained and preserved through contact with the topography and customs of the pre-industrial village. These conservative and pre-industrial images of the national character flowed into a modern conservative idiom during the last century, and were expressed in the form of a powerful movement for countryside conservation, as well as a distinct ambivalence about the values and norms associated with cities.[155] As James Fenton put it: 'When the English reach for an image of the quintessential England it is almost always to the countryside that we turn—to the villages or small towns rather than the cities, to the parish churches rather than the cathedrals, to the woods and fields rather than the great urban vistas.'[156]

Since the late nineteenth century, such sentiments have been harnessed to a range of different political visions and arguments. It was through recourse to such idealized accounts of the English past, Raymond Williams observed, that some of the most penetrating critiques of industrial capitalism were advanced prior to the First World War.[157] During the inter-war years conservative intellectuals became more at home with this tradition, promoting whimsical and nostalgic versions of the English past that were designed to anchor contemporary conservative arguments against the expansion of state direction in both economic and social life.[158] It was during this period that some of the most enduring forms of folk wisdom about the everyday consciousness of the English were established, not least the axiom that this is, by inclination, a people who prefer the concrete and the pragmatic over the abstract and theoretical, and possess an intuitive sense of proportion and moderation in relation to political and social issues.[159]

One of the most iconic statements of the proposition that political conservatism was a natural companion to the English character was supplied in Prime Minster Stanley Baldwin's frequently quoted speech to the Royal Society of St George in 1926.[160] The supposedly timeless rural scene he conjured up became a stock reference for later commentators on this topic: 'The tinkle of the hammer on the anvil in the country smithy, the corncrake on a dewy morning, the sound of the scythe against the whetstone, and the sight of a plough team coming over the brow of a hill.'[161] This carefully crafted, bucolic vision was cannily designed to appeal to a growing middle-class audience in the expanding suburbs of England's largest cities. Baldwin's vision was utterly anachronistic, bearing no relation to the harsh realities of farming in the mid-1920s, when the agricultural depression was having a damaging effect upon living standards and conditions in many rural areas. Yet the kind of conservative modernity that Baldwin advanced reflected a keen political antenna and familiarity with the ordinary and everyday—as well as Arcadian—manner in which Englishness was intuitively understood by large parts of the population.

This pattern of national sentiment continued to inform subsequent ideas about the English character. During the 1960s and 1970s, however, critics from both left and right increasingly began to argue that this was the embedded national culture that needed to be torn down if Britain was once more to prosper.[162] Yet this form of national sentiment continued to cast a considerable cultural shadow despite the efforts of its critics. Shifting patterns of leisure and changes in cultural taste gave it a new lease of life, in popular terms, towards the end of the twentieth century. The emergence of the 'heritage industry' during the 1980s, as socialist historian Samuel observed, reflected both a growing sense of interest in the themes of belonging and nationhood, and also signalled an increasingly consumerist and individualistic approach to the historical past.[163] For a growing number of middle-class citizens, the rural retreat was now incorporated within weekend leisure choices, as more and more stately homes and heritage museums were opened to the public, and membership of organizations such as the National Trust and English Heritage rocketed. These redoubtable bodies were quick to badge visits to their properties as safe and pleasurable journeys into a sanitized English past.

References to the English countryside have continued to serve as a potent signifier for the conservative values of stability and continuity. The notion that there was, until the recent period, a not-too-distant past when the English lived in a stable social order has provided a recurrent and appealing vision for those opposed to various kinds of progressive reform. The quiet renewal of this broad discourse in the last years of the last century and the early years of the twenty-first represents an important response to the transformations associated with the transition from an industrial to a post industrial order in Britain. As well as the new-found popularity of bodies like the National Trust, other indications of the power of such sentiments include the commercial success of a number of publications that fetishize the aesthetics of the Edwardian era, including periodicals such as *This England, Country Life,* and *Country Living.* The notion of England's tradition as defined in relation to a vanishing rural idyll has become ever more appealing despite the myriad of changes that have impacted upon the life and habitats of the English countryside.[164] In his critical dissection of the revival of the heritage industry during the years of Conservative government in the 1980s, Patrick Wright observed the enduring power of some of the sentimental and affective qualities generated by the recurring imagery of 'deep England' at moments of socio-economic change.[165]

A host of recent academic studies have identified the regressive and socially exclusionary implications of this form of the English imagination, as ethnic minorities, women, and the working classes are airbrushed out of the reimagined nation of yesteryear. Many commentators have been sceptical about whether it can possibly sustain a meaningful sense among the increasingly confused English of who they are, in the complex, interdependent world they now inhabit. But such criticisms have, importantly, tended to understate the complexity and balance of the relationship between past and present that informs modern English consciousness. A better appreciation of the dialogic interplay between the reimagined past and contemporary sensibilities brings to light some of the pragmatic, as well as retrospective, features of the conservative English imagination. The flip side to an abiding sense of nostalgia is a striking sense of Englishness as practically minded, moderate, and adaptive in kind. Equally, the pleasure taken in the escapism and whimsy associated with the rural past has not prevented a clear-headed sense of its potential inadequacies as a means of representing the diverse, socially fractured, and morally plural nation that England has become.

The bundle of sentiments which writer Julian Baggini reported as prevalent within the English suburbs in his account of the everyday conservative philosophy he encountered there, illustrated how a quiet sense of patriotism is sustained both by a familiar set of national images and a bundle of underpinning beliefs.[166] The latter, he suggested, are broadly Burkean in spirit, taking shape around a shared belief in the values of 'stability, community and continuity', a preference for change when it is incremental in kind, and an entrenched commitment to procedural forms of fairness.[167] Baggini noted that, for those who held to these values, the presence of 'others' from various different cultures was, for the most part, neither a development to be welcomed nor one that necessarily provoked resentment. This rough sense of 'live and let live' persisted alongside a commitment to the preservation of a stable social order which reflected the shared values of the nation, within which liberty, fairness, and community were especially prominent. This pragmatic, but not unbounded, sense of toleration was, he suggested, deeply embedded in the English mind-set, and reflected a commitment to providing people who often held 'incompatible ideals about how society should be run' the space to rub along together.[168]

This vein of commonsensical, everyday Englishness has long been observed by commentators from left and right. Orwell regarded it as a characteristic that stemmed from the essential decency, as well as privacy, of the English. As Mandler has shown, at the heart of Orwell's characterization was a reworking of the 'little man' English archetype of the inter-war period.[169] Recent authors have also noted the continuation of this seam of Englishness. Tony Wright termed this a tradition of 'quiet patriotism and undemonstrative decency', citing Orwell's reference to 'the England that is just beneath the surface'.[170] And on his travels around contemporary England, Kingsnorth noted a 'solid, quiet Englishness that had nothing to do with pained intellectual definitions and everything to do with belonging to the historical landscape they were part of'.[171]

This form of national understanding has often been overlooked within academic and media commentary, in part because of its habitual character, and also due to its close imbrication with lived experience and entrenched patterns of 'common sense'. But its persistence and strength have been significantly under-estimated by radical critics of the constitutional order, convinced as they often are that Englishness is an identity defined by its lack of content. Such a judgement misses the solidity and adaptability that shape forms of Englishness that are expressed and practised in a very different register to populist and radical kinds of nationalism. This seam of English nationhood has provided a home for the antinomian images of the rival classes stressed by Schöpflin, and has been able to accommodate some of the regionally and socially rooted images that have shaped the English imagination.[172] It is on the basis of these contrasting ways of thinking about the nation that the English have for the most part, he argued, disavowed ethnically charged forms of nationalism.

Highlighting the prevalence of this seam of conservative Englishness provides an important counter-weight to Nairn's insistence that the British class structure and its ancient state have inhibited the development of a substantive and modern sense of English nationality. Indeed, the residual presence of conservative Englishness may well help explain why, despite the diffusion of the populist mentality outlined above, England has for the most part remained an inhospitable venue for the kinds of ethno-cultural populism that have made significant inroads into the political systems of other Western states.

LIBERAL NATIONALISM REBORN: TOWARDS A MULTICULTURAL ENGLISHNESS?

This evolving seam of conservative national sentiment has provided the cornerstone for ideas of English nationhood since the late nineteenth century.

Its core values span the conventional demarcation between conservative and liberal thought. And in important respects this tradition has served as a carrier for an embedded, indigenous strain of liberalism, a lineage that is far removed from the kinds of meta-ethical and cosmopolitan theories that have increasingly found favour among Anglophone theorists in the last few decades.[173]

The presence of liberal elements within conventional expressions of Englishness has provided an important point of growth for a distinct cultural-cum-political narrative in recent years, which seeks to construct a more plural and multicultural sense of English identity. This is the third broad pattern of national sentiment which has become embedded within contemporary English culture. It is currently the least noticed of all, and is regularly overlooked by most cultural and political commentary devoted to Englishness. Yet, it carries considerable implications not least because of the conviction of some commentators that the English intelligentsia has histori-cally recoiled from engaging with, and leading the people's sense of national identity. Scottish commentator Neal Ascherson, for instance, has pointed to the tendency of 'university educated liberals' to prefer Britishness and to reject Englishness:

> I believe it was the huge expansion of higher education in the 1960s, rather than the nationalist surges in Scotland and Wales during the 1970s, which encour-aged it. The English began to use the term 'British' to describe not only the other inhabitants of the multinational state—but themselves... the term 'English' began to acquire a vaguely improper, even negative flavour to English ears. It implied not only obtuseness to the sensibilities of others, but a right wing nationalist self-assertion ('There'll always be an England!') which was best left to football hooligans or Prom audiences.[174]

The picture painted by Ascherson is, however, increasingly belied by recent developments. There have emerged a variety of attempts to promote a more cosmopolitan and culturally diverse kind of Englishness. These efforts have secured the support of a small, but growing, number of thinkers, and a band of politicians and commentators eager to make the case for the liberal rec-lamation of this identity. Thus, the argument for constructing a multicul-tural sense of national belonging, which would in turn be reflective of the realities of life in many of its cities, has become a prominent feature of con-temporary debate. And some have connected the case for the diversification of the English imagination to the goal of challenging England's insularity, seeking to reinvent an outward-facing, culturally expansive form of nation-ality. Sociologist Christopher Bryant has termed this the renewal of a cos-mopolitan sense of Englishness.[175] Its appeal is most obviously directed to workers in the knowledge economy, young professionals, and members of ethnic minority groups. And while its forms of common sense and distinctive mythologies—about, for instance, the English as an inherently hybrid nation in ethnic terms—are less deeply embedded than those of its rivals, they have become increasingly prominent and attractive.

Attempts to identify the ethnic and cultural diversity of England's urban populations as the basis for a reconfigured national self-image have their roots in earlier liberal accounts of England's character and culture. As Mandler has shown, references to the ethnic and cultural eclecticism of the English figured prominently in nineteenth-century political thought. Depictions of the English as a polyglot, mixed people have been a recurring feature of recent media and cultural commentary. Writing in *The Spectator* in 1996, Anthony Everitt mused that 'Now the Empire has gone—or rather, it has come and settled here. Communities from former colonies in Asia, Africa and the Caribbean have become part of the fabric of daily life.'[176] But, rather than citing these developments as the source of the crisis of identity afflicting the British, as many of his readers might have expected him to do, he reached for the mythology of the English as a hybrid people: 'In fact this is nothing new. From the days of the Romans, wave after wave of immigrants have flooded our shores. We have never been sure who we are.'[177] Other leading writers on Englishness also did much to undercut the prevalent idea that the English and the multicultural were mutually opposed categories. In the conclusion to his major study of the English imagination, Ackroyd argued that: 'Englishness is the principle of diversity itself. In English literature, music and painting, heterogeneity becomes the form and type of art. This condition reflects both a mixed language comprised of different races.'[178] In this argument, the adaptive and assimilative capacities of the English imagination, which explain the centrality of the themes of continuity and evolution to the national consciousness it has sustained, are reflective of a mixed culture which has been forged by the movement and interplay of many different races.[179]

This ancient ideal was revived in the most recent period in the self-conscious efforts of several public figures to reclaim a sense of nationhood rooted in the cultural diversity of contemporary England. In a speech on this issue, delivered in 2009, Archbishop of York John Sentamu declared that a significant shift of attitude towards English symbols was under way within some ethnic communities:

> As is often the case with cultural revolutions the change came not through a directive from the top, but from those at the bottom of the economic hierarchy. In the city of Birmingham, where a good number of private taxi cabs are operated by Asian, often Muslim, men, the flag of St George became an addition to every

cab. The commercialisation of the flag and its linking with a national hope which sought inclusive celebration, led to its adoption by those for whom it was previously used as an exclusionary symbol.[180]

A stream of pundits declared an affiliation with the English cause on a similar basis. Columnist Suzanne Moore pitched her cultural tent on English, not British, soil, arguing that ideas of England were being powerfully reshaped by trends rooted in contemporary urban culture:

> The scuppering of Englishness as any kind of ethnically pure or white identity is happening: listen to the way kids talk....But where I live, where I hear so many tongues and see so many faces, where many worlds collide, where I may be a citizen and as awkward as I like, is actually England.[181]

Commentators in the media have played a key role in promoting this perspective, and, indeed, the other narratives outlined here. Their attraction to this theme and role in promoting ideas about the nation is revealing in that these figures are typically located at the interface of mainstream politics and high culture, and have tended to be more sensitized to the vibrations emanating from cultural trends than politicians. They have also done much to ventilate debates about English identity within the public culture. Thus, Madeleine Bunting, writing in the *Guardian* in May 2011, broke new ground with her left-leaning readership by presenting the entrenched liberal suspicion of Englishness as a subject for enquiry, rather than simply repeating its familiar tunes.[182] Such arguments also challenged the established consensus of many leftists that the only acceptable patriotism was that associated with a civic account of Britain, a stance popularized by Jonathan Freedland's *Bring Home the Revolution*.[183] The idea of England as the quintessential immigrant nation which might refind its soul in forging a common culture rooted in its internal diversity became an important alternative to the forms of trans- or post-national thinking that were prominent in liberal circles during the 1990s. Indeed, the very notion of a cosmopolitan Englishness reprised older forms of national-liberal thinking which accorded to England the role of an exemplary liberal nation, showing other countries the way towards a more civilized and peaceful future. In the early years of the last century, for instance, Ernest Barker presented England as the particular embodiment of a universal, civilizing ethical ideal.[184] For him, the realization of the national principle was closely entwined with the achievement of a modern civic order, a balance that was most perfectly realized in the case of England, and which shaped a character that transcended the limits of ethnicity, tradition, and communalism.[185]

This enduring vision of a nation that could, at its best, rise above the prejudices and limits associated with differences rooted in class and ethnicity, remained haunted by the fear that when nationalism—as opposed to liberal nationality—gains traction at the mass level, it results in xenophobia and chauvinism. The abiding wariness of the national consciousness of 'the people' exhibited by many liberals has also acted as a spur for the reanimation of a different strand of progressive Englishness in the current period. This stems from a concerted effort to refind the mix of patriotic and radical ideas which lay at the heart of the development of English socialism in the nineteenth century.[186] The idea of reimagining the left's contemporary political mission by claiming a decidedly English stream of radicalism was aired by several political figures during the years of Labour government, including Ministers David Blunkett and John Denham, and MP Jon Cruddas. They, and others, questioned the fixation with British patriotism associated with these administrations. They also contributed to a wider current of opinion on the left which was moving towards the argument that it was time for the English to be encouraged to develop their own version of the civic nationalism that had flourished in Scotland and Wales.

The notion of renewing a patriotic outlook as a crucible for progressive politics has taken a number of different forms in recent years. For some, it has arisen from a sociological reflection upon the extent and nature of the cultural pluralism and ethnic diversity associated with England's towns and cities; and for others, the old dream of a nationhood that provided a source of unity, beyond the corporate perspectives and cultures associated with the groups populating English society, has been most important.

Yet, in its different guises, progressive patriotism has been haunted by the thought that English nationality still carries within it the mentality of Empire, and is most likely to find expression in xenophobic, rather than civic, terms. In this period, these issues have been engaged and debated to an almost unparalleled extent in liberal circles, and a serving Labour leader delivered a speech in 2012 on the importance of Englishness, an event of some historical importance given the depth and nature of Labour's Unionist affiliations.[187] At the same time, while these various progressive narratives have occupied a less secure position within the wider culture than their rivals, they have nevertheless provided a vital alternative contribution to a growing debate about the identity and culture of the English.

CONCLUSIONS

I have highlighted three of the most prevalent and internally diverse patterns of English sentiment that have come to the fore during this recent period. Their political dimensions do not, I have suggested, translate neatly into the alignments associated with party politics though I have stressed their close relationship with patterns of thought that have been integral to British politics. Each of these strands of thinking is engaged in an increasingly tense competition to establish itself as the leading expression of the English imagination. And an appreciation of their appeal offers an alternative to standard characterizations of English nationalism—as, for instance, a distorted expression of class-based resentment. Indeed, if we hold at bay the familiar claim that Englishness serves only to divide and exclude—driven by its purported hostility to various 'others'—it is easier to see the internal symbolic contrasts which are marshalled and reproduced by this form of consciousness.

More generally, the various debates about methodology, evidence, and interpretation I have navigated in this chapter form the academic infrastructure around which the main interpretations and characterizations of English national identity have developed. I have sought to illustrate the importance of some entrenched normative expectations about English nationalism which have done much to shape the emphasis upon an anticipated backlash against devolution among political analysts, and the recurrent focus upon the resentful and ethnically charged nature of Englishness among sociologists. I have chosen to bring debates about method and definition to the front of the stage to illustrate that our understanding of English nationhood is unavoidably connected to expectations and assumptions that underpin the frameworks through which it is viewed. I have also sought to demonstrate that differences of judgement about whether Englishness is increasingly taking the form of ethnic majority nationalism, depend, to a considerable degree, on differences rooted in interpretative approach, definition, and evidence. Engendering a greater awareness of these important issues is a necessary step towards the inculcation of a more reflexive debate in which categorical, and often tendentious, assertions about 'what the English want' are received more sceptically. In addition, the propensity to characterize English national identity as a one-dimensional entity that is readily amenable to quantitative measurement has resulted in the neglect of the qualitative questions of meaning and context that are integral to its interpretation.

These cautionary notes aside, I also contend that much can be learnt from taking a holistic approach to the various kinds of data and research relevant to this question, rather than sticking to the findings and methods associated with any one particular approach or school of interpretation. Drawing upon this wide array of sources, I suggest that, as various forms of Englishness have become more salient, available, and appealing, Britishness has, in relative terms, become a less prominent and more distant point of identification. And this suggests that we have entered a new phase in the history of national identity within the UK. As Kumar has noted, 'we find ourselves in a historic moment when the English have a clear conception about the distinction between England and Britain, Britishness and Englishness.'[188] It is also, I contend, reasonable to deduce from the available body of data and research that some of the underlying causal dynamics that have brought new forms of English self-consciousness to the fore relate to factors other than devolution itself.

Equally—and contrary to a good deal of received wisdom—there is no easy correlation between the re-emergence of these forms of Englishness and existing patterns of political allegiance. The familiar assumption that Englishness is simply a crucible for regressive forms of populism, or a vehicle for Conservatism, are inadequate as characterizations of the political dimensions of English nationhood. This is not to suggest that socially conservative and grievance-fuelled sentiments are absent from projections of Englishness. But an abiding sense of ambiguity, and indeed contestability, needs to be restored to its interpretation. As Curtice and Heath have pointed out, 'There is nothing inevitable about the association of Englishness with a more exclusive, ethnic conception of identity.'[189]

One further implication of the analysis offered here is that the current intellectual fashion to characterize an identity through (certain forms of) difference, and to interpret the construction of nationalism as constituted by negative forms of ethnic and national 'othering', has tended to obscure the nature and operation of some of the leading ideas and representations of English identity. These are shaped by a well-worn set of internal imaginative contrasts, including rivalries rooted in regional geography and class. In more recent times, the emergence of an idea of England as a fortress to which the indigenous majority can retreat has generated a significant degree of cultural concern and political tension. But to define Englishness, as has often been attempted, around the poles associated with one of these contrasting sets of images is to miss the sense of identity generated by the continuing interaction and rivalry between them. In scholarly terms, there is considerable further scope for enquiry into why these different imaginaries have taken root in the ways they have, and how and why they continue to appeal.

This emphasis is not intended to obscure the role played by English patriotism in supplying forms of imagined commonality and cross-class unity, especially at moments of national crisis. Nor is it to contend that Englishness is unique in carrying class-based associations, unlike its counterparts elsewhere in the UK. But it is to argue that national expressions and sentiments have been much more integral to English culture than has often been appreciated. And, unlike the 'moment' of Englishness that Kumar identified a century ago, the national culture defined around these axes of difference is leeching into the arenas and assumptions of high politics.

4

The Cultural Politics of Englishness

INTRODUCTION

The versions of Englishness that have become prominent in recent years are more varied in their political connotations, multi-layered in their composition, and eclectic in terms of the range of artefacts, places, and objects with which they been associated, than is usually suggested. I have observed at several points already that it was in the realms of art, cultural practice, and everyday life, rather than high politics and public policy, that these sensibilities were forged and experienced. In this chapter I illuminate this claim, and draw attention to different ways in which English nationhood has been imagined and asserted, and its political significance explored, in a variety of cultural and artistic arenas. I suggest, in particular, that a multiplicity of different texts and works have played an important and largely unheralded role in negotiating the fears, hopes, and dreams associated with England as an imagined community. Taken together, these developments can be seen as sustaining an unusual, creative period of national renewal, a trend that is in stark contrast to the limited and often timid manner in which politicians and policy-makers have engaged with 'the English question' in these years.

Below I consider the various ways in which the English imagination has been stimulated and challenged within different cultural genres. A cornucopia of novels, non-fiction books, plays, poems, pieces of visual art, TV and radio programmes, newspaper articles, and a great number of blogs have taken as their focus the question of what an English identity involves, where it is to be found, and what counts as its authentic manifestations.[1] One of the main threads running through this multitude of texts is the notion that the spirit of the nation can be recreated by establishing new connections with the landscapes and artefacts that have a special place within the English imagination and the customs and traditions of earlier eras.

A rounded assessment of current forms of English nationhood, therefore, needs to step across the established intellectual wall that divides the study of the cultural from the political. Those who have been waiting expectantly for an English nationalism to emerge in the form of a political backlash against devolution have, for the most part, been looking in the wrong direction. Those interested in the political dimensions of a renewed sense of English nationality would do well to consider sources and materials that rarely figure in current debates. Representations of the nation have been extensively studied in the fields of cultural studies, sociology, literary studies, and anthropology, but these analyses have, for the most part, ignored the importance and implications of conventional political dynamics and issues in their characterizations of English identity. In contrast I draw upon insights from a range of literatures in order to develop a richer understanding of the cultural politics associated with contemporary English identity. The materials I consider can be seen as symptoms of, and responses to, growing uncertainties about who the English are, and also as a stimulus to the development of new ideas and feelings about this form of identity. My aim is to offer an interpretation of the major themes contained in some of these works, rather than provide a comprehensive account of the many different cultural expressions of nationhood in this period.

The lack of critical attention to what has been an extraordinarily fertile period in terms of English cultural expression reflects the intellectual divide that I identify above. It also stems from a well-worn progressive reticence, noted at various points in this book, which stipulates that the English, unlike other nations, lack the stock of foundational national myths to sustain a modern, democratic sense of nationhood.[2] One of the main effects of this shibboleth has been to warn generations of leftists and liberals away from any contact with the English folk tradition, on the grounds that it invariably harbours the kind of reactionary dream of a return to the imagined lifeworld of pre-industrial England which progressives need to disavow.

Yet one of the main impulses within the recent renewal of English cultural expression has been a desire to derive contemporary meanings from a rich stock of mythologies, fables, and folklore, and to harvest established kinds of national nostalgia for various contemporary political ends. This imperative has generated reflexive and self-conscious attempts to establish connections between a meaningful sense of nationality in the present and those traditions, places, and figures deemed central to the national past. This desire to find roots for current expressions of Englishness has been central to the national-cultural revival that is documented here. These sensibilities are thoughtfully captured in remarks made in an interview by Kazuo Ishiguro, author of the prize-winning novel *Remains of the Day*:

> What I'm trying to do here...is to actually rework a particular myth about a certain kind of England. I think there is this very strong idea that exists in England at the moment, about an England where people lived in the not-so-distant past that conformed to various stereotypical images. That is to say an England with sleepy, beautiful villages with very polite people and butlers and people taking tea on the lawn...Now at the moment, particularly in Britain, there is an enormous nostalgia industry going on...trying to recapture this kind of old England. The mythical landscape of this sort of England, to a large degree, is harmless nostalgia...The other side of this, however, is that it is used as a political tool.[3]

These comments suggest a keen awareness that the impulse to reconnect with the national past is invariably informed by contemporary concerns, and that heritage and folk can be appropriated for different political ends. They also point towards an anxiety about a closely related, but distinct, impulse that has also been palpable in the recent period. This sets out to rediscover the 'real England', and insists that the current inhabitants of England need an unmediated contact with the practices or customs that signify the authentic national past to stimulate and guide their patriotism now. In the account that follows, I place considerable emphasis upon the manifestations of these impulses, and, accordingly, make the revival of folk art and aesthetics a central part of my discussion of the wider English cultural revival. The space I give to the return of folkish themes and the revival of folk arts in recent years also serves as a corrective to their neglect in most analyses of English identity.

THE FOLK AESTHETIC

The place and role of myths and folk culture in modern forms of national consciousness has, more generally, become a subject of considerable interest and debate among scholars of nationalism. Arguments about the importance of these elements to the historical memory and cultural sensibility that inform contemporary forms of identity have become particularly prominent over the last decade.[4] A leading school of interpretation insists that myths and fables should not be dismissed as forms of deception and manipulation, nor as excrescences of the pre-modern past that do not the pass the tests set by rationalism. They in fact represent universal and necessary features of established human communities which have an ingrained need to tell stories about where they came from, and where they are going.[5] All communities devise self-referential narratives about their own past, and myths are an integral part of the sub-structure of beliefs upon which these forms of historical memory rely, establishing a sense of continuity and rationale for the living.[6] According to Schöpflin, myths offer an important medium through which national groups strive to establish 'the foundations of their own being, their own systems of morality and values'.[7] They are among the exemplary narratives that reinforce and justify the norms of a particular community. The question of whether these background beliefs are historically accurate is not primarily relevant to their function as elements that can be employed to promote 'a common thought-world'.[8] They also provide a sense of order for the scattered fragments of the national memory, helping to draw attention to iconic moments and key developments within it—the enclosure movement, or the industrial revolution, for instance, in the English case.

A broad shift towards a more rounded appreciation of the 'pre-modern, local and regional, and traditional elements of national cultures, which are often reviled by cultural elites', has become discernible within the appraisal of modern nationalism in recent years.[9] As part of this process, some commentators have returned to the insights contained in the writings of one of the major theoreticians of national cultures and their political dimensions—Italian Marxist Antonio Gramsci.[10] In his thinking, mythical references, fables, and folk-tales were all vital and resonant elements that needed to be recuperated by those seeking to shape the 'national-popular'—the leading patterns of national consciousness in modern society. Viewed against this intellectual backdrop, the recurrence of mythic and folkish elements within recent English art and culture, and the recessive emphasis on the recovery of an authentic England, can be understood as integral features of the emerging imperative to reconstitute and explore a modern English consciousness. Just as importantly, there was a much greater receptivity for such materials and themes among audiences in this period.

PLACES AND LANDSCAPES IN MODERN ENGLISHNESS: FINDING THE 'REAL ENGLAND'

The contemporary analysis of nationalism gives considerable emphasis to the normative importance of places and landscapes, more generally, as these 'come to stand as icons of continuity, the product of land worked over and produced, etched with the past, so that "history runs through geography" '.[11] Such references provide vital 'symbols of continuity', enabling the purveyors of a particular understanding of the national consciousness to endow their argument with a sense of authenticity and rootedness. It is in the light of these observations that an additional theme within the current national-cultural revival can be understood: the recurrent focus upon place and landscape.

One of the most notable aspects of the current revival of English awareness, therefore, is the resurgence of travel writing, a genre that has long provided a vehicle for ventilating different ideas about, and geographically rooted images of, the nation. Reflections upon the English soul arose during epic journeys across different parts of England, as for instance in A. V. Morton's *In Search of England*.[12] The iconic *Shell Guides* to Britain included reflections on the cultures and landscapes of the English counties by a host of leading inter-war intellectual figures, including John Betjeman, John Piper, and Paul Nash.[13] Featherstone has noted of these earlier waves of travel writing that:

> The act of travelling in England during the first half of the twentieth century provided a means of describing the nation to itself in a popular literary genre that emphasised haphazard revelation and identity defined through rural, Southern landscapes and communities.[14]

And in the current period too, the imperative to re-encounter the particular places associated with the 'real England' has acquired considerable cultural significance. It has resulted in the publication of a host of books exploring the history and topography of different parts of the country, and many different parts of the landscape. Writers such as Robert Macfarlane produced popular works that brought forgotten locales and practices back to the attention of contemporaries and fed a growing appetite for non-fiction writing devoted to England's historic places.[15]

The intense value placed upon the idea of rootedness, and of achieving a sense of attachment to, and deriving meaning from, particular places, objects, and landscapes, has been central to the renewal of Englishness. As Baucom has demonstrated, this way of conceiving the nation reprises an important, earlier lineage of national sentiment.[16] He observed that an emphasis upon the normative value of distinct localities was integral to leading ideas of the English character in the eighteenth century. These were subsequently displaced by the imperative to find the English ideal reflected in the newly acquired colonies associated with the era of imperial expansion, a development that divided the national imagination between a global, outward-facing, civilizing liberalism—suited to the purposes of Empire—and a sense of England as located in its most intimate and particular places and customs. The profound sense of dislocation that resulted from a sense of nationhood that was identified both in imperial and universalist terms, on the one hand, and as a sensibility that grew from first-hand experience of the traditions and customs of the land, on the other, became a defining, insurmountable paradox. Englishness, Baucom suggested,

remained bifurcated by these opposing tendencies, reflecting the consciousness of a nation destined to lose itself either in grandiose geo-political adventures, or in the desire to return to a genteel and parochial 'little England'.

Baucom's suggestive argument offers some important clues about the connotations that place, landscape, and locality carry in English national thought.
In the current context, these sentiments are widespread, and accompany the
fear that the national spirit itself is endangered by the tendency to forget, or
overlook, these locations and landscapes. His account also offered an important insight into why the search for the English ideal has so often taken the
form of a quest to find a mythical golden age, and identified very particular
locations as the crucible of the English spirit. A significant body of writing and
artistic work has appeared in recent years, motivated by the idea of exploring
places and practices that express an aspect of the national past and are deemed
to have been neglected or endangered.

A highly particularistic outlook is apparent in many of these texts which
often cast the character and culture of the English as fundamentally antithetical to the universalist imperatives of modernity—typically conceived as either
the triumph of the free market or the bureaucratic rationality of the modern
state. Such sentiments are especially pronounced, for instance, in the work of
the architects of the Common Ground project, associated with campaigners
Sue Clifford and Angela King.[17] This initiative set out to catalogue the plethora of artefacts, traditions, and habits that make up the rich tapestry of life
throughout the localities of England. Its authors took their cue from conser-
vationist Richard Mabey's indictment of the impact of industrialized systems
of agricultural production upon the ecology of framing practices in England.[18]
In their recent guide, *England in Particular*, Clifford and King documented
the enormous quantity of habits, pastimes, and idiosyncrasies that exist within
England. Their project was defined in terms of their love of the particular,
and an abiding commitment to the intrinsic value of rediscovering artefacts
and practices that have been marginalized or forgotten in contemporary culture. They called too for a significant perspectival shift, urging their readers to
adopt the view from below, and to refind their connections with the histories
and textures that have long made up the lifeworld of their localities.

This very particularistic take on the nation's heritage is replicated within
other recent attempts to recall an authentic England that has latterly been
betrayed by the country's economic and political rulers. This kind of narrative
is favoured both by self-styled conservatives and insurgent radicals, and by a
growing number of contemporary figures who see themselves as both.[19] In his
much discussed denunciation of the erasure of the most distinctive traditions
and hallmarks of English life, for instance, campaigner Paul Kingsnorth invited
his readers on a journey in search of the 'real England' which is vanishing

before our eyes.[20] His book signalled a wide range of intellectual debts, including the agrarian radicalism of William Cobbett and George Orwell's feel for the practices and artefacts endowed with significance in English culture. And it offered a repeated, emphatic contrast between authentic English artefacts and practices—including traditional farming, rural pubs, and small shops—and the forces of progress determined to obliterate them in the name of profit and consumerism. His argument also mined the Edwardian Arcadianism that Kumar identified as central to the moment of Englishness of the early twentieth century.[21] And, like these forebears, his lament for an endangered nation gained considerable resonance in a period of bewildering economic transformation and extensive cultural change. This is an especially important contextual consideration for this particular book and the broader genre to which it has contributed.[22] It is in such periods that the sociologically implausible, but affectively powerful, idea of renewing national consciousness in the image of an idealized rural heritage has tended to gain most traction.

Nostalgia for the rural idyll has been harnessed to a variety of different political arguments and visions in recent years.[23] Kingsnorth's nostalgic reimagining of England spoke to a broad constituency, spanning social conservatives, political radicals, and countryside preservationists, all united in believing that the country's heritage was imperilled by an indifferent, metropolitan government, huge corporations, and rapacious developers. As well as nodding towards Cobbett and Orwell, Kingsnorth drew upon writings from the middle years of the twentieth century, including inter-war conservationism and the critiques of modernized farming and new trends in urban planning that emerged in the post-war decades. Writers such as Mabey and Ian Nairn had questioned the approach to planning associated with a new phase of suburban development and the establishment of new towns during the 1950s and 1960s.[24] And they too called upon England, not Britain, to signal the ancient realm they wished to defend. The impulse to plan, Nairn complained, represented the antithesis of the organic and individualistic spirit of the English.[25]

While Nairn was writing from the political margins, addressing a predominantly conservative set of audiences, the interest elicited by Kingsnorth's argument illustrated that broadly similar sentiments were becoming much more mainstream in political terms, lending themselves to populist expression. His book also showed how the leftist argot associated with anti-globalization and environmentalist politics was cross-fertilizing with the sentiments of conservationists and shire Tories.[26] His account spoke to a widely shared set of anxieties about the rapidity and scale of the changes affecting many towns and villages in these years, the displacement of local shops by supermarket giants, and the lack of accountability felt by many communities about planning decisions which affected them profoundly. And, most strikingly of all, the author wrapped all of these issues within an assertive sense of English nationalism, a sensibility that he acknowledged was a heterodox one in progressive circles. England, he declared, 'is a nation, Britain is a convenience.'[27]

The central contrast in Kingsnorth's argument was between the plasticity and fluidity of contemporary culture, on the one hand, and the redemption associated with the authentic activities, institutions, and places that embodied 'real England'. The rhetorical contention that it was only through a certain kind of unmediated cultural experience that the nation could be refound, is itself a very familiar one within English culture, but was now put to a novel political use. That he was able to develop a broadly leftist political programme from these ideas would not have surprised Williams, who, in his landmark work *The Country and the City*, had pointed to the variety of political ideas and ambitions that the ruralist and conservative mind-set could engender.[28] The image of an unchanging, timeless English countryside represented a potent weapon for ideological contention, one of a stock of mythologies that had animated earlier moments of radical-patriotic politics.[29] On the political left, it had enabled the celebration of craft production, the dignity of labour, and the value of locally constituted communities. And, among conservatives, the imagery of Englishness as defined by its rural heritage had long sustained the belief that the hierarchies and social relationships with which it was associated reflected the natural social order.

Yet, many critics remained convinced that such a nostalgic depiction of the English past was the antithesis of a modern, democratic idea of nationhood. They observed that the lineages to which Kingsnorth, and others returned, were saturated with assumptions about class, race, and gender, and served to reinforce the symbolic construction of England as a place where the hierarchies that had disfigured English society were reaffirmed and celebrated.[30] Backward-looking evocations of the English spirit have long been seen as parochial and shallow by liberal-minded intellectuals, yet Williams shrewdly countered that such references offered resources for those engaged in the very modern endeavours of national reimagining and ideological contestation. The stock of emotions, stories, and mythologies that were bound up in familiar evocations of old England were more open, he argued, to competitive political appropriation than progressive critics cared to imagine.

Many commentators have been similarly wary about the revival of interest in the aesthetics and traditions associated with English folk culture which has been an increasingly prominent motif in the cultural life of the last decade. Its salience was apparent, for instance, in the proliferation of books, and radio and television programmes devoted to retrieving English food, manners, humour, and leisure.[31] In an argument that replicated the rhetorical structure employed by Kingsnorth, David Crystal offered an entertaining survey of the multitude of accents and dialects shaping the English tongue in his brief history of the English language,

and pointed to the gradual erasure of these differences as a result of the stand-
ardization associated with today's media culture. Once again, organic forms of
Englishness were being cast aside by the standardizing imperative of modernity.[32]

An interest in folk aesthetics arose both from the growing imperative to
rediscover authentic parts of the English cultural past, and the accompanying
worry that finding them in the present might no longer be possible. But, as
Williams astutely observed—and as contemporary critics have tended to forget—the folk idiom has always offered a terrain upon which different kinds of
political and social understanding could be developed. In some hands, it has
enabled the reactionary fantasy of a nation cleansed of the divisions and differences associated with contemporary England. But, more commonly, ruralist
nostalgia has been donned in a more ironic or critical sense, underpinning
sceptical reflections on present-day developments.[33] Kingsnorth's writings
veer between these different forms of argument, leaving some critics concerned about whether such a nostalgic approach to heritage can in any sense
be progressive. Patrick Wright pointedly noted that it can amount to an 'exotic
anthology of almost lost causes',[34] and observed that such arguments exhibit a
selective vagueness about why certain objects and practices, and not others,
should be deemed to be of particular value in the present. His worries about
the 'decidedly unpleasant undercurrent' sometimes associated with this strain
of Englishness reflect the fear that such a sensibility betrays a yearning for a
world prior to the diversity and dynamics associated with modern life.[35] But
such criticism can obscure the possibility, identified by Williams, that the retrospective impulse may well also be a tool to be employed in the construction
of contemporary-focused forms of thought and identity.

This kind of critique has led to a significant under-estimation of the different ways in which the rural ideal can be invoked in the present, and the subtly
mutating character of this idiom. There has, for instance, recently emerged a
body of writing that has applied this nostalgic ethos to the city, rather than the
country. Urban communities and particular districts have been presented as
mortally imperilled by a combination of indifferent planners and corporate
greed. Writers such as Rachel Lichtenstein, in her account of the changing
communities that inhabited Brick Lane, and Iain Sinclair have explored hidden or neglected features of London, locating the residues and fragments of
earlier patterns of settlement, and of particular communities and the ways of
living associated with them.[36] These had typically grown up in an unplanned,
higgledy-piggledy fashion, and were increasingly on the wrong side of
unsympathetic planning departments, development corporations, and public
authorities. In a number of his writings, Sinclair provided striking insights
into the occult geography of London and its many ancient sites, presenting
the city as 'imbued with mythology, both archaic and modern'.[37] Other writers,

meanwhile, returned to the tradition of English pastoral, but deliberately pushed beyond its established parameters, and adopted a more reflexive and questioning stance to its assumptions. Bunting offered a beguiling mixture of travelogue, family memoir, and national reflection in *The Plot*, which appeared in 2009.[38] The places she evoked were utterly unlike the genteel Southern landscapes idealized by the enduring Edwardian tradition. Instead, she pondered the personal and cultural associations of a wild, uncultivated piece of land purchased by her father, exploring its subsequent role within her own biography and family relationships. Bunting's meditation upon the value and nature of place, and the relationships that were actively forged in relation to it, sustained some thoughtful and unsentimental reflections on the nature of the 'home' that a sense of place and nation can supply.[39] She argued that the kind of belonging and security associated with the quest for a homeland has become ever more prominent in a society in which fluidity, change, and consumerism are the key motifs: 'We live in times when relationship and identity are subjected to increasingly anxious interrogation, but we ignore an equally urgent need to know our place, know where home is and where we belong.'[40]

The kind of nationhood that has, in the recent period, emerged from the many different texts which have explored and recalled the rural past has been more multi-layered and diverse than is typically supposed. For some historians, this has always been a characteristic of Englishness, properly understood.[41] Considering the great variety of ideas and visions of England that have been developed across the social and geographical diversity of the country, Colls concluded that English national identity 'draws on a vast underground network of historical discourses draining into one another as the occasion demands'.[42] Condor too has identified the 'subtle and varied ways in which people understand English national identity'.[43]

Below, I follow these authors' lead and draw attention to some of the different ways in which Englishness has been imagined and contested in various artistic and cultural quarters. A number of these works provide evidence of a growing interest in folkloric traditions, enabling the dispersal of mythologies and fables to a range of different audiences, and a growing ideological competition over their ramifications.

RECUPERATING THE ENGLISH 'FOLK'

Given the wariness with which folk traditions are viewed in many intellectual circles, it is perhaps not surprising that relatively little attention has been paid to the cornucopia of folkish references that have been central to the artistic reclamation of Englishness in recent years. Yet, this has arguably resulted in the neglect of motifs and materials which have been integral to the renewal of current ideas of English nationhood. This genre needs also to be set in historical context, for it constitutes the latest in a number of phases in the history of the revivalist impulse that is integral to folk. Importantly, the most momentous points in that history have coincided with periods of profound social and economic transformation.

I draw attention, as well, to some of the distinguishing features of the contemporary revival, including a reflexive wariness of the political dangers associated with folk-based nationalism, and a commitment to envisioning the folk aesthetic as a prompt, rather than a template, for the rejuvenation of national sentiment in the present. The golden-ageist and whimsical aspects of the English folk tradition have in recent times been cross-cut by a different, more modern, outlook. At the same time, folk aesthetics continue to appeal to those with right-wing political ambitions, though a growing sense of ideological competition around the meanings of this particular genre has also become apparent. I identify, therefore, a range of political arguments and ideas that have been thrown up by the folk revival of recent years. And in order to make sense of these, I borrow insights from those theorists who point to the polysemic character of 'cultic' and folkloric elements within modern national consciousness.[44] The return to, and recirculation of, ancient myths about the English—including such familiar motifs as the 'freeborn Englishman' or the Robin Hood-style outlaw—have afforded a culturally resonant means of expressing the aspirations and anxieties associated with national identity in the present. And this deeply rooted impulse to turn back to the themes and aesthetics identified with folk has generated a wider reverberation throughout English culture.

The normative and political limitations of the folk tradition—including its ahistorical conception of the seamless transmission of the organic culture of the people from the pre-industrial village to the modern era, and its essentialist, and often elitist, conception of the authentic culture of the nation—have been repeatedly observed by its critics. But the inclination to dismiss folkish impulses as the residues of pre-modern forms of sentiment that need to be expunged from modern consciousness has contributed to an under-estimation of the various forms of national understanding which their recollection enables. These 'cultic' elements survive because they are recuperated and endowed with new meanings as part of the process of forging modern, and rooted, national identities. They represent forms of knowledge that are regarded as having been suppressed by an alien jurisdiction, yet can offer useful ingredients for the shaping of alternative kinds of national understanding in the present.[45]

The renewal of a number of well-worn English mythologies has not passed unnoticed in this period. Labour MP and historian Gordon Marsden identified the power of a recurrent set of fables that the English have chosen to tell themselves, observing how these assist the articulation of a number of contemporary claims within contemporary politics.[46] The most prominent of these myths included: the notion that the country has not been invaded since its ancient past; the suggestion that the English are an exceptional people due in part to the early development of their state, and their status as the first people to experience the industrial revolution; and the idea the English identity has been unusually open to new arrivals and cultural influences because of the polyglot make-up of the English people. Marsden sensed the malleability and protean character of each of these mythologies: Englishness is 'far from the robust, no-nonsense fixed identity that the *Telegraph* reader might imagine it to have been'.[47]

The extended bout of national self-questioning that arose from debates about Britain's diminishing prospects—which I discussed in Chapter 1—quietly gave way to the emergence of new kinds of national-cultural reflection and discourse among various English publics. One of the key features of this latter trend was a disposition to reimagine country and people at some remove from the familiar categories and identities associated with Britain. The excavation and exploration of English traditions, artefacts, and places was one of the primary forms which this impulse took. And this focus can be detected across a wide variety of genres, encompassing music, the visual arts, literature, drama, film, and poetry.

REVIVING ENGLISH MUSIC

Folk song occupies a small niche within the totality of contemporary popular music, yet it retains a highly symbolic aura in relation to the folk arts more generally.[48] It is through this genre that the ethos of renewing contact with a golden age of pre-industrial Englishness has been advanced since the late nineteenth century. A consideration of folk music in the recent period is especially revealing because of the growing interest in its aesthetics and forms shown by musicians and audiences outside its boundaries. And this trend is paralleled by a growing willingness among a new generation of folk performers to reach out to a wider set of constituencies. One consequence of this greater receptivity has been that English folk music gained a more prominent place within the music industry, a situation that would have been almost impossible to foresee during the 1980s and early 1990s.[49] In July 2008, for instance, BBC Radio 3 hosted the BBC Proms Folk Day concerts in the Royal Albert Hall, with a selection of English folk music ranging from orchestral works by Vaughan Williams to performances by contemporary folk artists. And in 2008, another key figure on the folk scene, Tim Van Eyken, played the role of 'The Songman' in the National Theatre's production of Michael Morpurgo's *War Horse*.[50] A succession of folk artists has been nominated for the prestigious Mercury Music Awards. And the media profile of folk has shifted too, as it has gained much greater media visibility within arts and cultural programming (such as BBC2's *The Culture Show*) and popular entertainment shows.[51] The absorption of folk into the standard programming of concert halls across England is a tangible sign of its growing cultural respectability.

The presence and recognition of folk music has also engendered a new pattern of interchange whereby established artists have borrowed extensively from this tradition, and a younger group of folk performers have become much more widely known and commercially successful, in part by blending folkish songs with contemporary musical styles. These trends have opened up some considerable tensions in the folk world, generating fissures in a community where traditionalism is a central motif, and a lingering hostility to the introduction of other musical styles and techniques is still pervasive.

A further, distinct set of tensions have arisen as a result of a new focus upon the merits of a specifically English tradition of songs and performance. A growing interest in contesting the established hegemony of Irish and Scottish songs and styles has swept through large parts of the English folk community. The influence upon this trend of changes in the political environment, including devolution, has been documented by academics Trish Winter and Simon Keegan-Phipps.[52] These authors observed that the desire to carve out a distinctive English folk lineage has been enabled and legitimated by the simultaneous attempt to recast folk as an English contribution to 'world music'. At the same time, the impulse to retrieve and replay traditional English music stemmed from a widely felt sense that this national tradition had been unduly marginalized within the wider folk community. The tensions and debates resulting from this trend have been revealing. For some in this community, any move to reclaim an English heritage carries an unacceptably nativist aura.[53] But, rather strikingly, for the majority of progressively minded figures in this scene, this idea has proved highly appealing.

Along with this newer emphasis, some of the foundational mythologies of the folk arts continued to figure in this community, including the notion that that today's performers and audiences can reach back to an unbroken tradition of musical performance which, through the work of various collectors, returns to the world before the industrial revolution. A hallowed status is, thus, accorded to Victorian folklorist and collector Cecil Sharp in particular.[54] In the most recent period, however, his role and the political character of his, and other collectors', work have been subjected to sustained historical scrutiny, and several major studies of the English folk revival have generated arguments with major repercussions for this community. One effect of this critical literature has been to undermine the self-image of folk as a cultural community set apart from the concerns and motivations associated with modern politics and society. This understanding has been extensively challenged in recent years as the political resonances and implications of the renewal of Englishness have come to bear down upon this musical sub-culture. In the section that follows, I consider some of the principal claims about the character and role of English folk music that have been advanced by several high-profile historical studies in recent years, and consider their implications for an appreciation of the relationship between English national consciousness and the folk arts. I give most emphasis here to the connections between folk music and the notion of an English heritage associated with the pre-industrial past and the countryside, even though the folk scene also encompasses a very different heritage—associated with the industrial working class and radical political protest during the mid-twentieth century.[55]

THE POLITICS OF ENGLISH FOLK: LESSONS FROM HISTORY?

In his widely discussed account of the English folk tradition, *Electric Eden*, published in 2010, Rob Young argued that, far from being conservative or marginal, folk music expressed the defining mythology within English culture—the notion that the nation's spirit lay in its countryside.[56] Folk became attractive to a wide array of musical performers in the three decades after the Second World War. And, contrary to this community's self-perception, the strength of this musical idiom lay in its adaptability and capacity to fuse with other musical styles. Young stressed the utopian, rather than conservative, character of the impulse to escape from the limits and inauthenticity of industrial society which underpinned the enduring popularity of the folk idiom. And he stressed its affinity with the various currents of mysticism and occultism that were integral to the aesthetics of the 1960s and 1970s. The imaginative displacement associated with the search for Eden carried 'futurative dimensions', as well as conservative ones, offering escape from the mental confines and conventions of the present, and providing the ground for 'alternative speculations'.[57] English music, he maintained, had gone back to its folk roots again and again in order to tap into the powerful charge associated with the search for the lost estate, away from the confines and corruption of the urban present. Young was also at pains to point to the radical political credentials associated with the modern folk aesthetic, a stance which, as we shall see, has been challenged by other historical treatments of English folk music in this period.

Importantly, his account pointed to the broad cultural resonance of folk sensibility, arguing that this had travelled in recent decades beyond the folk music community itself. This genre was important because it offered a way of joining up the two contrasting impulses of the Edwardian age, both of which lay at the heart of the English 'moment' identified by Kumar—an almost despairing sense of conservatism in the face of the dislocation generated by the emergence of industrial society, and a renewed sense of radical possibility associated with the regaining of the moral order and social harmony of ancient England.

Young's celebratory study of the aesthetics of folk music was in stark counterpoint to the other major account of this lineage to have emerged in recent years—an important critical book written by musicologist Georgina Boyes.[58] Despite its detailed, academic treatment of the history of the folk revival, *The Imagined Village* has become a major point of reference among practitioners and participants in the folk community. It has acquired this status primarily by dint of its author's willingness to tackle the conservative and regressive political associations which English folk music has acquired, and also due to her readiness to deconstruct the reputations of some of its iconic figures. The revivalist impulse which informed the work of Sharp and his fellow collectors, she argued, was sustained by the desire to restore the organic community that was thought to have been lost in the modern, industrialized world. According to the author of the book's preface, Peter Martin, English national identity was represented as a 'fantasised rural community, an imagined village of sturdy, smiling—and suitably deferential—country folk'.[59] Boyes insisted that the endeavours of this first generation of folklorists reflected this regressive national mythology, which was ultimately hostile to the worth of industrial labour and laced with dubious ideas about race, class, and gender.

Boyes leavened her critique with a determined attempt to rescue the contribution of lesser known performers whose roles had been obscured by the dominant, heroic narrative associated with the idealization of Sharp as the 'father-figure' of English folk. She therefore stressed the role of some of his contemporaries, notably Mary Neal, whose attempts to promote a less rigid and patriarchal understanding of folk practice were deliberately marginalized by him.[60] The development of a bitter rivalry between Sharp and Neal, the founder of the Esperance Society, formed a pivotal moment within her account. Neal's emphasis upon the spontaneity and freedom that should be the hallmark of English folk dance, and the potential it offered for promoting independence and self-respect in working-class communities, especially for young women, pointed to a very different kind of social order and political message to that which Sharp favoured. Boyes's conclusion that his victory represented a watershed in the developing character of the English folk tradition has been echoed by other commentators too. Featherstone has noted how various styles of folk performance, especially those associated with Northern cities, were systematically downgraded by the English Folk Dance Society, and dismissed as 'degenerate'.[61]

Like Young, Boyes identified the enduring influence of European romanticism in this scene's elevation of the rural above the urban, and its recessive focus upon the cheery peasant as opposed to the unfit industrial worker. She showed how the Edwardian reclamation and performance of supposedly authentic songs from earlier eras typically involved hidden processes of selection and geographical bias, as well as the alteration of lyrics to suit bourgeois tastes, and the quiet omission of elements deemed unsuitable for contemporary audiences. Her clear-sighted targeting of some of the more conservative and reactionary ventures with which the revivalist impulse has been associated contributed significantly to the wariness with which the current folkish revival has been viewed in some quarters, and also worked its way into the consciousness of the folk scene itself, as we shall see below. In various respects her argument builds upon a controversial and polemical volume *Fakesong*, published in 1985.[62] But while Boyes's argument left room for a sense of the contested character of folk, and inspired new developments within this musical community, Dave Harker offered a blanket critique of the entire lineage. In his view, Sharp was tied to the sensibilities of the 'Little Englander' movement, and the revivalist impulse he promoted was dismissed for its irreducibly racialist character. Harker condemned the self-serving falsity that underscored the notion of recovering a supposedly authentic lineage of pre-industrial folk song. And he set out to demolish the mythologies associated with the collection of songs, registering telling criticisms of the geographical selectiveness and urban bias of Sharp's endeavours.[63]

Harker's and Boyes's arguments have not gone unchallenged, and have opened up an extended debate in musicological circles about the folk lineage. In contrast, therefore, David Gregory has pointed to the exaggerated nature of many of their historical claims, and proposed the merits of a respectful, not dewy-eyed, assessment of the revivalist tradition.[64] He spoke for many other folk practitioners and supporters when noting that folk has remained far more counter-cultural than such critiques implied, failing to elicit the approval of public authorities for the bulk of the twentieth century. Sharp has, indeed, remained a difficult figure for the cultural establishment. The Arts Council declined to fund the English Folk Dance and Song Society, based at Cecil Sharp house, until the first years of the current century.[65]

THE POLITICS OF CONTEMPORARY FOLK

These various historical arguments have all contributed to a growing disagreement about the status and meaning of the English folk arts. They have also filtered into its core communities an enhanced awareness of some of the political anxieties long associated with this genre. The recognition that it was, in different respects, replete with political significance grew significantly too as a result of attempts by leading figures from the far right to identify themselves with this increasingly popular genre. Leader of the British National Party Nick Griffin, for instance, expressed his admiration for English folk music, praising the work of folk performer Eliza Carthy in 2000—a compliment she did not return.[66] And in 2008 the folk-cum-acoustic duo Show of Hands produced a popular song, *Roots*, which called upon the English to reconnect with their own form of nationhood. To their dismay, the British National Party (BNP) pounced upon its catchy chorus, giving it a prominent place on its website.[67] This appropriation was also rebuffed, in this case through legal action. These, and other, claims upon this increasing popular genre helped trigger a lively counter-campaign in the shape of Folk against Fascism.[68]

Meanwhile, the title, as well as spirit, of Boyes's book gave life to one of the most innovative endeavours associated with the folk music scene in these years—the establishment of the musical collective The Imagined Village in 2004. This set out to blend folk with a number of other musical genres, and brought together folk performers, Asian musicians, and well-known commercial artists, including the dub poet Benjamin Zephaniah. It developed around the notion that a specifically English folk tradition needed to be reclaimed in the name of cultural and musical diversity. And while it paid due homage to Sharp and the original revivalists, Boyes's critique of the illusion and dangers of authenticity were also given pride of place. As the group's founder, Simon Emmerson, put it:

> It's not about authenticity, it's about identity. I'm not interested in people listening to this record searching for authenticity. But there's a lot of identity there. That's what multiculturalism is about—not losing your identity in some beige soup, but standing up and saying...'This is what I am, I'm rooted and I'm English.'[69]

The notion that a distinctively English musical heritage was being reclaimed in this period reverberated far and wide, within and beyond the folk community. As the description of a new collection of old English music put it, a major revival of interest in 'indigenous music' had been under way since the 1990s, as 'The English tradition fought back.'[70] This rejuvenated lineage could be safely reclaimed in part because of its new location within the cosmopolitan stew of 'world music'. This meant that it could be framed as the local version of the quest for belonging associated with the revival of national, regional, and tribal cultures across the globe: 'Surely if others could be proud of and fascinated by their own roots and culture, then so could we?'[71] Both the heightened interest in nationhood and belonging, and the notion of reclaiming English cultural traditions, established important points of connection between folk artists and the wider culture. And while folk remained relatively marginal within the ecology of contemporary music in these years, a more diverse set of audiences was introduced to its musical styles and iconic songs. The number of folk festivals held throughout England began to multiply significantly and drew greater numbers by the year.[72] And folk diversified its appeal considerably as it spawned a new cohort of cross-over performers and became a more familiar presence in the musical landscape, and also as a new generation of song-writers and musicians sought inspiration in it. Folk dance too has experienced a minor revival in recent years, becoming a largely middle-class pastime in towns and villages throughout England, and spawning troupes such as the popular The Belles of London City.[73]

The two guiding motivations behind the contemporary folk revival have been the impulse to find roots for current national sensibilities, and the dream of escaping from the inauthentic and unsatisfying confines of modernity. These sentiments often overlapped, but also pointed in different directions. The interest in folk as a medium that could supply various forms of imagined rootedness, proved compatible with the production of music that was aimed at a broader set of audiences, and was consonant with efforts to recast Englishness as a living tradition threatened by the monochrome and banal nature of contemporary popular culture. But the quest for authenticity, on the other hand, promised the illusion that the past could be regained in the present, and that Englishness could be located in the Arcadian retreat. It has, for the most part, been the first of these sentiments that has shaped the manner in which folk has been reclaimed and re-energized in recent years.

FOLK CROSSES OVER

As a result of this newly found appetite for avowedly English cultural forms and traditions, various opportunities arose for a number of younger folk artists to reach wider audiences, often by blending traditional songs and styles with contemporary musical styles. Artists such as Carthy, Jim Moray, and the Unthank sisters hailed from families and communities where folk music remained a strong presence, notably in the South West and North East of England. They and other performers identified strongly with the argument that an English musical lineage had been unduly marginalized, and deserved the respect accorded to other national musical cultures. According to folk musician Steve Cox:

> Englishness is important, and becoming more so in the aftermath of devolution. Previously we didn't tend to question identity but now we're starting to think more about what is important to celebrate about England in an international context. It depresses me that we can't celebrate Englishness without people going down the UKIP/BNP route. To be able to recognise other cultures you have to celebrate your own culture.[74]

Moray became perhaps the best known of this cohort of artists, his profile secured by his best-selling album of modern arrangements of English folk songs, *Sweet England*.[75] This revelled in the sentimentality, mythologizing, and romantic yearning at the heart of the folk revival, with songs that were performed using a range of musical styles. Moray has publicly identified himself as a 'new breed of Englishman', unafraid to proclaim and celebrate his own national pride, just as other national and ethnic communities in the UK now feel able to do.[76] He has been a forceful proponent of the view that English traditional music needs to be more assertive about its own virtues: 'Folk music in this country seems to be hidden away. It's somehow shameful to assert your Englishness and sing about it and celebrate it. Irish music and Scottish music and even Welsh music don't have this problem.'[77] For commentator John Mullen, the popularity of figures like Moray and Carthy, and the unexpected emergence into the mainstream of a number of traditional folk bands, such as Bellowhead, illustrated a growing thirst for cultural idioms that addressed the decline of Britishness and a growing interest in rootedness.[78] Similarly singer Frank Turner, whose profile was considerably boosted by his solo performance at the opening ceremony of the London Olympics, produced a highly successful acoustic-cum-folk album, *England Keep My Bones*, which drew heavily upon English folk references and mythology. His own journey towards folk, following his initial background in punk, offers a further illustration of its magnetic pull for those keen to explore the national dimensions of identity. Turner expressed a growing need to 'say something positive about the English', and identified English cultural traditions as the source of an identity that might fill the void left by the waning of Britishness: 'It's a fact that as a race the English are ignorant about our roots, and that's a major hole in the national psyche. As a people the English are floundering; we have trouble establishing our identity and recognising our culture.'[79]

But an abiding wariness, and critical distance, informed his, and other artists', relationship with English traditions. Identifying too directly or strongly with notions of English pride and tradition still carries a degree of risk for performers aspiring to commercial success. And while the folk idiom enabled some artists and audiences to explore new, and old, forms of nationhood, other audiences remained suspicious of its connotations.

FOLKISHNESS BEYOND FOLK

These kinds of sentiments were not confined to this particular musical genre.[80] While pop music has, by definition, been a far more eclectic and commercialized genre than folk, a growing interest in identifying an English sound and sensibility was discernible from the 1990s onwards. Nabeel Zuberi has suggested that it provided an important and ambiguous arena within which some of the pressures and anxieties associated with the national question could be aired. The musical culture of these years 'reveals a much wider, more variegated terrain of popular memory, national belonging and identification than the apparently singular theme-park nation'.[81] He and other observers also noted the salience of the ethos of 'authenticity'—in this case associated with groups and songs that embodied folkish ideals. Other critics pointed out that attempts to promote and sell different ideas of England have been prominent within the music industry over the last few decades. And while these have varied in content and style, most have been associated with a handful of white, male performers.[82] Critic Martin Cloonan has noted that while the phenomenon of pop musicians being hailed as exemplars of Englishness can be dated back, at least, to the 1960s, there was a notable upsurge in such claims towards the century's close. According to musician and performer Damon Albarn, a new cultural space opened up at that time, which expressions of, and ideas about, England's culture began to fill.[83] One striking illustration of this trend was the critical success and cultural impact of the 2011 album *Let England Shake*, by P. J. Harvey, which blended romantic English sounds and themes with an angry anti-war message.[84]

As well as percolating into the consciousness and practice of pop in this period, the appetite for music that related directly to themes of nationhood and belonging was also apparent in the world of classical music. Here too a growing interest in the role that folk had played in stimulating a national music became prominent. Sharp's work, and the aesthetics of folk songs more generally, had famously inspired a generation of English classical composers, including Ralph Vaughan Williams, George Butterworth, Frederick Delius, and Gustav Holst.[85] Vaughan Williams himself was a prominent collector of folk songs, scattered folkish themes and poetry throughout his compositions, and wrote an opera that was suffused with the themes and songs of the English folk revival—*Hugh the Drover*.[86] His work, in turn, became a focal point for the subsequent development of a self-consciously invented tradition of English classical music, and helped ensure that folk achieved a greater respectability, in cultural terms, during the early years of the twentieth century.

Vaughan Williams's compositions have elicited renewed interest in their own right in the recent period. In his biographical account, Simon Heffer argued that one of the defining threads of his subject's career was the ambition 'to manufacture a distinctly English musical voice, as no one had in modern times, and take English music back to its roots.'[87] Heffer documented how, in addition to his compositional work, Vaughan Williams also became a leading national intellectual, devoted to promoting the role and value of music in the creation of a modern national consciousness, and lecturing and writing extensively on this subject. He was associated, above all, with the folkish idea that English music did not need to be created anew, but was already immanent within its traditions and historical lineage, and offered a vital source of ethical and cultural replenishment. The ancient folk songs of England were, Heffer felt, distinguished by their 'strain of heroic melancholy and profound peace that is religiose without being religious; it is an evocation of the ancient rhythms of the English countryside and English life, stripped of sentiment and romanticism'.[88] Folk song was only one of the traditions that coursed through the English musical revival of the early twentieth century, and which become prominent at its end. Vaughan Williams and some of his contemporaries derived considerable inspiration from the revival of interest in the polyphonic music associated with the Renaissance, with Henry Purcell's work generating particular interest. Vaughan Williams was himself a leading member of the Purcell Society. In recent years this tradition has once again become prominent, as the significant growth of interest in 'early music' has provided an important stimulus for a resurgence of interest in the nation's musical lineage.[89] And the centenary of the birth of the enormously popular and influential composer Benjamin Britten, in 2013, provided the occasion for a sustained reappraisal of the local and national influences upon his compositions.[90]

The revival of English music has attracted the interest of various political champions of Englishness. Writing in 2008, Scruton declared that: 'We need the English music that the Arts Council hates.'[91] In his rather selective account, the indigenous musical tradition, which was 'gentle, nostalgic, an organic growth from a deeply settled landscape where many generations had been quietly at home', was now re-emerging beyond the parameters of elite influence.[92] And English music, he claimed, 'speaks to us not merely of a beloved landscape and rediscovered legends but of the distinctively English way of life'.[93] Borrowing the language normally deployed to characterize the folk tradition, he argued that there was 'a living heritage of English classical music' which needed to be vigorously defended against its foes, notably the Arts Council and its allies in the cultural establishment, who have 'our cultural annihilation as their hidden goal'.[94] Scruton's populist contention was, in fact, rapidly overtaken by events. Only a few years later, English music was in huge demand, figuring prominently on many concert-hall schedules and publishers' portfolios, and being given considerable air-time on the main classical music radio stations. The centenary of Britten's birthday provided the opportunity for the extended celebration of a figure who has been vaunted as England's finest modern composer.

LITERARY REFLECTIONS ON ENGLAND

No other artistic genre is as closely identified with ideas about the state of the nation and the character of its people as the English novel, with many commentators seeing these as its defining preoccupations. In his major historical overview of this genre, Patrick Parrinder argued that fiction had been the source of important and influential ideas about national belonging and identity throughout the modern period.[95] In the decades after 1945, as Britain's geo-political role and self-understanding were significantly reshaped by the renunciation of Empire, the diminished standing of the British economy, and the development of a more internally divided culture, the novel became one of the primary arenas where these changes were registered. One of the leading motifs of post-war British fiction was an increasingly critical representation of models and figures associated with a formerly dominant sense of Englishness, among whom was the perennial figure of the country gentleman.

For some critics, the English novel, and the sensibilities it evoked, was indissolubly tainted by a lingering association with the imperial mind-set. This was the conclusion reached by Simon Gikandi who presented the national imagination as paralysed by the tensions between centre and periphery that had developed during the high period of Empire.[96] Yet, some of the leading literary figures of the late twentieth century offered more subtle and introspective reflections upon the national culture and past than were encompassed in

Gikandi's critique. These included the poet Geoffrey Hill, whose anti-bucolic conception of the English heritage was anchored in a rich sense of the myths and legends of the pre-Christian world.[97]

More generally, from the late 1970s onwards, much English fiction was attuned to the crises and conflicts animating politics and public life, and the themes of decline, the free market, and cultural fragmentation were all increasingly familiar.[98] The complexities and dislocation of the immigrant experience, and the wider effects of geographical mobility and British decline, were prominent themes in the work of a cohort of high-profile authors from non-English backgrounds, including Salman Rushdie, Monica Ali, Hanif Kureishi, and Zadie Smith. In her acclaimed novel *White Teeth,* Smith provided a very distinctive representation of a nation that was increasingly balkanized in cultural terms, and in which multiculturalism was adopted and rejected to varying degrees.[99] But she skilfully blurred conventional representations of 'the English' as white, and the non-English multiculture as its 'other', suggesting instead that a more complex mosaic of ethnic and national identities was coming into being. Unlike many other recent novelists, Smith intimated that the new kinds of Anglo identity which she explored were contiguous with, rather than a break from, older forms of Englishness. Hers was one of a spate of novels that considered how immigrants had dealt with the dislocating, and often traumatizing, experience of coming to England.[100] The national culture that these authors depicted was for the most part seen as suffused with inequalities rooted in Empire and class, and hostile and insular in equal measure. But some authors took another view, sensing that Englishness itself was an increasingly open-ended and uncertain category. As Caryl Phillips put it:

> this is rapidly rendering archaic the old view of Englishness as an ethnic club, and we now begin to recognize that we are in the middle of a cultural struggle to reinterpret exactly what Englishness and Britishness mean, who has the right to say what we are, and towards what we should be sympathetic.[101]

Similar sentiments echoed in other fictional works in these years, which cumulatively called into question the very notion that Englishness might itself be a stable and coherent form of identity. Novelist Andrea Levy, writing in the *Guardian* in 2000, reflected that 'Englishness must never be allowed to attach itself to ethnicity'.[102]

The more folkish themes—of place, roots, and locality—considered above were also present in recent fiction. In *Ulverton* Adam Thorpe returned to the much heralded landscapes of Southern England.[103] But in a reversal of convention, he focused attention on the violence upon which the rural idyll at the heart of the English imagination was predicated, while simultaneously promoting the idea of an England that was endangered as its landscapes were under threat. In his subsequent novel, *Still,* he explored the sensibilities and resonances associated with Edwardian strains of Englishness.[104] What Baucom termed the 'melancholy discourse of nostalgia', which Thorpe extensively mined, has remained a crucial medium for reflecting upon English nationality.[105] In this Thorpe was far from alone, with many other novelists also being concerned, in Hill's suggestive phrase, to 'draw the graph of nostalgia'—an endeavour he subtly distinguished from the unreflective employment of this emotion and its forms of affect.[106] A lingering fascination with the power and implications of nationally rooted melancholy was central to some of the leading works of fiction in this period, including Ian McEwan's *Atonement* and Julian Barnes's *Arthur and George.*[107] Such was the ubiquity of novels that were both historical in their focus and tuned in to current anxieties about the nation that the historical novel began to disappear as a clearly demarcated subset within fiction. As Parrinder observed, an increasingly self-consciously Anglo-centric fiction 'was back in fashion' in these years.[108]

The nostalgic ethos which much fiction indulged was increasingly out of kilter with the discordant and dystopian notes struck by a number of novels addressed to a supposedly post-traditional England. The notion of a 'post-English' country was central to some of the works produced by J. G. Ballard, notably his *Kingdom Come.*[109] This was now a country that had slipped from being perpetually in thrall to a past it could not reclaim or redeem, to one that was cut adrift from the tides of historical memory altogether. In similar vein, two other recent novels—Rupert Thomson's *Divided Kingdom* and James Hawes's *Speak for England,* both from 2005—offered dystopian visions of a contemporary England that had lost its sense of identity and was almost devoid of a collective will.[110] *Divided Kingdom* speculated on a post-devolution future, sketching a scenario of four new sovereign states in the UK that had to be restrained from pursuing their deepening desire for separation from each other.

Other authors reflected critically upon the relationship of the English to the historical memory that mediated their relationship with the national past. This was a central concern of Barnes's satirical novel, *England England,* which was published to critical acclaim in 1998.[111] Its main target was the folkish sentiment associated with the national heritage movement that had grown up since the 1980s.[112] He characterized its claims upon the past as a quest for authenticity that veiled the pursuit of less high-minded, commercial, and personal interests.[113] Any attempt to locate the essence of Englishness in its past was doomed to fail, he implied, because a nation's identity is subject to continual change, and its history is, in turn, continually reinvented as its identity shifts. Barnes also poked fun at the familiar notion of the English as a people obsessed with revisiting the past who liked to believe that heritage was a gateway to their own identity. His comic critique provided a safe harbour for the sceptical sensibilities of his liberal readers.

The critical distance from the English 'national-popular' which Barnes and other novelists sought, was, however, firmly rejected by an emerging school of literary criticism in these years.[114] This eagerly promoted the notion that contemporary forms of Englishness harbour a new, post-colonial consciousness, rejecting the constitutional patriotism which was held to be the defining axiom of the literary-critical tradition. Thus, Hywel Dix spied an English equivalent of the process of 'writing back' against the imperial culture which began to gain ground around the time of devolution.[115] This involved the attempt to identify points of connection and tradition that were prior, in both cultural and chronological terms, to the era of British imperial power and union. Dix gave as an example Graham Swift's novel *Last Orders,* in which the present-day equivalents to Chaucer's protagonists rediscovered the places and characters of England that had been occluded during the period of Britain's imperial and military adventures.[116]

The notion Dix advanced—which was echoed by other critics, including Andrea Westell and Michael Gardiner—that Englishness should be understood as a post-colonial form of nationhood represents a striking, though conceptually underdeveloped, claim. In her astute essay on these trends, Christine Berberich interpreted these arguments as elements of a broader shift of perspective towards the recognition that the conflation of British and English identities that had been a feature of national discourse since the eighteenth century needed to be unpicked if the English were to refind themselves as a sovereign and modern people.[117] This progressive-nationalist perspective represents an important departure both from the familiar traditions of English literary criticism and from the main critical schools that had set out to deconstruct Englishness entirely. And it offers an interesting example of a trend that is discernible across many different cultural genres in the recent period—the appropriation of the imagery of a reborn England now breaking free of the suffocating embrace of British institutions and governance.

Within the neighbouring genre of poetry, the topic of Englishness was a familiar, but largely subdued, theme. Though it was rarely explicitly examined, the identity and sensibilities of the English were routinely evoked, lamented, and variously embodied in the decades after 1945. The themes of belonging, nationhood, and the national past were found in the work of leading figures Philip Larkin, Ted Hughes, and Geoffrey Hill, all of who, in different ways, conceived of Englishness as a kind of imagined solitude, an outlook that was depicted as contingent upon key features of its history, cultural development, and topography. In the work of Tony Harrison, a more politicized and radical sense of Englishness, rooted in the radicalism and anger of declining Northern industrial towns, was given vigorous expression. In his remarkable film-poem *Prometheus*, he offered challenging reflections on the decline of a class-based sense of the nation in the conditions of the late twentieth century.[118]

More recently Englishness has become an explicit focus of interest. In 2012 laureate Andrew Motion was one of a group of poets involved in a project devoted to the reclamation of English iconography.[119] These figures set out to write a new liturgy for St George, exploring his wider significance in relation to debates about the English nation. This work was performed by the Royal Shakespeare Company at Coventry Cathedral. Much of the publicity it elicited focused upon these authors' commitment to move onto territory which politicians were wary of exploring. Titled *Redcrosse*, the project was inspired by the knight of that name in Edmund Spenser's updating of the myth of St George in *The Faerie Queene*.[120] This innovative attempt to draft an alternative, modern liturgy for the English spanned the divide between culture and politics. It also touched upon several major questions—What does it mean to be English now? How do the meanings of current forms of nationality relate to earlier incarnations? What kinds of common bond might Englishness now promote?—which were increasingly familiar in cultural circles.

In his thoughtful reflections on these themes, Hungarian-born poet George Szirtes echoed his national predecessor, Nikolaus Pevsner, in posing the question 'what makes English poetry so English?'[121] In fact, genre-specific versions of this question were tabled in a number of cultural and artistic arenas in these years, a telling sign of a growing impulse to consider the possibility of a more delineated sense of English culture. Thus, Simon Trussler reported on a project established at Goldsmiths' College during the 1990s, which set out to explore the ways in which 'the quality of "Englishness"' was rendered on the English stage.[122] And in the Leslie Stephen lecture he delivered at Cambridge in 1993, Ackroyd reflected upon 'The Englishness of English literature'.[123] In this he gave an early airing to a number of the arguments with which he became closely identified. A decidedly English tradition of writing, he declared, had grown up around a distinctive and rich national sensibility which was expressed within a number of overlapping genres, ranging from romanticism to gothic. His designation of an authentic, broadly Catholic heritage was deliberately contrasted against those characterizations of the nation's culture that defined it in terms of post Reformation 'secular Protestantism'.[124]

Ackroyd showed an acute awareness of the suspicion which a celebration of English cultural tradition tended to elicit within the arts and academe. The shallow internationalism which he discerned as increasingly voguish in the 1990s was in danger of forgetting that a universal culture and literature need to be 'imbued with a powerful local presence'.[125] His own large portfolio of writings has made an important contribution to a shift in this climate.

In his ambitious study of the 'origins of the English imagination', *Albion*, he provided a fuller account of the virtues and importance of its constitutive ingredients, including Catholicism, esotericism, and romanticism.[126] The heroes and exemplars upon whom he lingered were typically isolated individuals, struggling against the grain of post-Reformation culture. In his novels *Hawksmoor* and *The House of Doctor Dee*, he identified the genius of solitary figures who were conversant with the traditions of mysticism, esotericism, and occultism.[127] The Englishness which they embodied was less akin to a sense of imagined community and more an immanent sense of consciousness which flowed across the limitations of time and space. This decidedly pre-modern view found echoes in other writings on English culture in this period. In his study of the major impact of neo-romanticism, for instance, Peter Woodcock connected the enduring stream of mysticism to the unique nature of the English landscape: 'In our art, literature, poetry and music, the landscape continuously evokes an atmosphere and often mystical presence.'[128]

THE VISUAL ARTS

Similar themes and ideas were bubbling up in other artistic genres around this time. In the case of the fine arts, the themes of belonging and home were prominent in these years and, as Alexandra Harris has suggested, reactivated long-standing debates about the vexed relationship between modernism and the national tradition.[129] These themes had been major concerns of leading English artists like Paul Nash, John Piper, Eric Ravilious, and Edward Bawden in the 1940s. In their work, and in the reflections offered by Pevsner in his iconic lectures on English art in 1955, modernism was replanted in indigenous soil.[130] The stark antagonisms between the cosmopolitan and the parochial, and the romantic and the modern, were dissolved in favour of a conception of the national culture as the locus for new ideas about, and expressions of, an English modernity. In her assessment of the various writings on these issues produced by figures such as Michael Ayrton, Robin Ironside, John Piper, and Pevsner, Sophie Aymes noted how these typically sought to surpass the standard contrast between the integrity of experience and emotions, associated with English romanticism, and the formalism and abstraction of Continental European art.[131]

More recently a number of major exhibitions exploring 'the English eye' of these iconic figures have been mounted, including major retrospectives devoted to the work of Piper, Graham Sutherland, Cecil Beaton, Angus McBean, and William Orpen. And a growing number of galleries across the country showcased the contribution of artists connected with different regions and localities—for instance the Fry Gallery in Saffron Walden and the collections housed at the Tate St Ives, Cornwall.[132] These developments reflected and fuelled a significant renewal of interest in earlier phases in the history and nature of English art. Writing in *The Spectator* magazine in July 2011, critic Niru Ratnam joined an emerging debate about why the English tradition was so routinely packaged as British.[133] For this habit he blamed the ingrained fear of the artistic establishment that engaging with Englishness required surrender to the basest prejudices of nationalism. The prevailing assumption, Ratnam observed, was that the indigenous lineage was backward-looking and twee. The modernism that occupied the high grounds of European culture was seen as essentially alien to it. This duality was replayed in the debates that broke out over the Victoria and Albert Museum's 'Modernism' exhibition in 2006, and in ongoing arguments about the impact of modernist architecture on England's cities.[134]

A growing number of individual artists were drawn towards the themes of Englishness, place, landscape, and locality. Cathy Lomax, for instance, mounted a series of exhibitions that explored the national resonances of various iconic locations.[135] In 2005 she curated 'Eng-er-land', a show at London's Gallery 102, which explored and satirized the icons, artefacts, and traditions associated with the nation's popular culture, past and present.[136] And in 2007 she put on an exhibition, at the Transition Gallery, exploring the kinds of escape associated with seaside towns, inspired by Lindsay Anderson's film, *O Dreamland*.[137] In March 2012 Patrick Keiller completed the first Tate Britain Commission, 'The Robinson Institute', compiling 'a montage of paintings, artifacts, books, films, songs and industrial relics', all of which signalled different facets of the development of capitalism and its relationship with the English landscape.[138] This work grew out of an innovative research collaboration, involving Patrick Wright and cultural geographer Doreen Massey, titled 'The Future of Landscape and the Moving Image'. This was established to explore 'received ideas about mobility, belonging and displacement, and their relationship with landscape and images of landscape, in a context of economic and environmental crisis'.[139] And in 2010 conceptual artist Simon English revisited seventy-five places represented by the points on each letter of the word 'ENGLAND' which he had projected onto a map of the country. He had toured all of these in 1971, for his project 'England Revisited', and now supplied a thoughtful set of reflections on the relationship between changes in the physical landscape and shifting perspectives upon English nationhood.[140]

Cinema has also mined the themes of nationhood, place, and historical memory during the last two decades, although these were already established concerns for many of its leading practitioners. But new kinds of reflection also emerged, including a spate of films that explored the nexus of class, race, and nationhood in both present and past.[141] Among these were several that reflected on the divisions associated with class and regional geography, themes that were central to the work of directors Mike Leigh and Ken Loach.[142] The 2006 film, *This is England*, written and directed by Shane Meadows, offered an extended examination of the themes of belonging and Englishness.[143] Set in a Northern, working-class community during the early 1980s, it explored the kinds of belonging afforded by the skinhead sub-culture of that decade. It identified a determined shift within sections of the white working class towards a shriller and resentful form of nationalist consciousness, with ethnic minorities increasingly identified as threats and rivals. Meadows's film offered a portrait of white, urban youth that was some way from the caricatures familiar in much of the mainstream media. The sense of belonging and protection which membership of the gang evoked offered a subtle metaphor for the growing appeal of discourses of the nation for alienated working-class youngsters. Such was the cultural nerve it struck that Channel 4 commissioned Meadows to make a series for television, charting the lives of the film's key characters throughout the 2000s.

Steve Blandford has pointed to a number of films that adopted a more exploratory approach to the identities and conflicts bound up with English nationhood in these years. In the cinematic version of Graham Swift's novel *Last Orders*, the familiar trope of the English journey was reworked to illustrate how different kinds of connection with the past could shape new ways of thinking and feeling in the present:[144] 'the overall picture is not simply of the end of something, but of fluidity, of new inflections of identity opening up and of nationalism being only one dimension within the complexity of the way we choose to live'.[145] Even within the increasingly prominent, and often predictable, genre of heritage cinema, the stock motifs of nostalgia and melancholia could generate surprising and challenging ideas about the present. As Andrew Higson put it, 'Heritage is not simply an elite version of the national past; the past can be and has been appropriated in all sorts of ways.'[146] He suggested too that the impulse to recollect the practices, places, and images which it signified might itself supply an integral dynamic to the reimagining of the nation. Historian of conservationism David Lowenthal likewise rejected the tendency to dismiss heritage as a redoubt for reactionary visions of the nation, drawing attention to the different kinds of modernization developed in its name during the inter-war years.[147]

Debates about whether the growing interest in heritage represented a source of creativity and self-expression, or a pathological and regressive nostalgia, continued to rumble on throughout this period. Over time, the leading progressive reflex of the early 1990s, which was intuitively critical of heritage, gave way to a more mixed response. A number of commentators suggested that the return to the imagined past was integral to the development of meaningful forms of imagined community in the present.[148] Higson, for instance, pointed to the pastiche and subversive character of the national sensibility served up in the proliferation of costume dramas in these years.[149] Assessing their historical accuracy or authenticity was less important, he suggested, than identifying the meanings and resonances that they prompted among their audiences.

This example illustrates that even in those arenas where metropolitan sensibilities might be expected to prevail, the broad theme of nationhood, and the particular question of what being English now meant, were increasingly pressing concerns. This was true even of an unlikely genre such as fashion. Both in the much discussed work of leading British designers in these years, and in a burgeoning academic commentary on the history of fashion, a recurrent focus on what an English style might comprise became apparent.[150] Academic interest in this question informed various enquiries into the contents and stylistic forms associated with English dress.[151] For some commentators it was self-evident that Englishness represented a retro-focused sense of style associated with the 'classic' apparel of the aristocracy, now translated into modern clothing that appealed to a rising middle-class interest in outdoor leisure pursuits. Others commentators disagreed, noting that such ideas were themselves reflections of invented traditions that were being challenged, and subverted, by younger British designers.[152]

STAGING THE ENGLISH REVIVAL

A recent overview of the main trends within British theatre identified a marked interest in English, as opposed to British, identity as one of its major concerns.[153] According to Sierz, the desire to separate out these categories and to probe the racialized character of Englishness were prominent themes in some of the leading theatrical productions of these years.[154] Examples include *The Christ of Coldharbour Lane* by Oladipo Agboluaje and *Elmina's Kitchen* by Kwame Kwei-Armah.[155] The latter was among a number of productions staged at the National Theatre, during Nicholas Hytner's lengthy stint as its director, in which the themes of national identity and cultural conflict were prominent.

Other established playwrights also gravitated towards these themes. In his *Playing with Fire* (also staged at the National) David Edgar contrasted competing ideas of the nation through reference to conflicts within the governing Labour party and street-level clashes between young people from different ethnic backgrounds in a fractured Northern city.[156] And Sarah Kane penned several works that included searing critiques of Anglo-British nationalism, not least the highly controversial *Blasted*.[157]

These and other plays reflected established liberal worries about the perils of nationalism, and treated this topic with a familiar mixture of wariness, guilt, and embarrassment. Many playwrights took a pervasive sense of national decline as a given.[158] But some works also helped broaden the range and nature of the stories that were told about the English in this period, and contributed to a wider sense that 'national identity in the 2000s was incredibly fluid, dynamic and changeable.'[159]

So far I have focused upon the breadth and range of genres and artists drawn to the themes of nationhood and belonging. Here I offer a more detailed assessment of works that came to assume an iconic place in relation to debates about Englishness, and identify elements within them that appear to have resonated most powerfully. I begin with the play *Jerusalem*, which has assumed an iconic place within cultural discourse on English nationhood. Written by Jez Butterworth, this has become an artistic phenomenon in its own right, eliciting an unusual amount of debate and interest, much of it from political, as well as cultural, commentators.[160] The play's importance lay both in its 'state of the nation' commentary and its suggestive exploration of the importance of folklore and myth to contemporary national sensibilities. It invited audiences to sympathize with the plight of poor, white country-dwellers, an unusual stance for a work addressed to metropolitan audiences. For some commentators, its significance stemmed from this willingness to provide a voice for constituencies and sentiments that were rarely heard in such quarters. For others, the play came perilously close to endorsing the rhetorical disaffection it evoked:

> this is a state-of-the-nation drama with an incendiary difference. It speaks about a nation that has almost forgotten it is a nation—England. And it homes in on a section of the population that might be described as the 'silent majority', those living outside the metropolitan centres whose unglamorous existences have pushed them to the margins. The characters are, to a man, woman and 15-year-old fairy queen, all white.[161]

Jerusalem began its run at the Royal Court Theatre in 2009 and subsequently transferred to the Apollo Theatre in 2010. It was performed on Broadway during 2011, where it won a nomination for a Tony Award. Following its return to London it again played to full houses and drew a wider cultural interest.[162] Its central character is Johnny ('Rooster') Byron, a middle-aged traveller living on the outskirts of a small country town, and the occupant of a piece of scrubland that is under threat from the local authority's Planning Department. Children from the town hang around with him and are happily led astray as he fills their heads with a mythical vision of a wild and free England. The play referenced the rich heritage of romantic invocations of the English countryside, while simultaneously undercutting easy forms of nostalgia. Here, 'the rural' was far from being an Edenic retreat, constituting a contested zone at the margins of a hostile consumer culture, inhabited by a figure who becomes the focal point for the negative projections and fears of the society he cheerfully shuns. Byron is shaman, monster, and national prophet rolled into one.[163] The play's significance lay in part in its dramatic evocation of some of the major themes of the current folk revival, and their connection to powerful anxieties about the state of England. Byron's speeches are replete with mythological tales and folk references, all intermingled with his own propensity for wilful exaggeration. He channels the spirit of England's ancient mythologies, spitting out references to Wayland the Smith, Woden, the god of the slain, Thunor, Frigg, Balder, and Ing. In the programme notes he supplied for the London production, Kingsnorth celebrated the reappearance of these folk legends, depicting them as 'the small stories, the culture that grows from season and place'.[164] They were part of a tapestry of national myth that had been forgotten by the inhabitants of contemporary England.

For the play's author, Butterworth, a meaningful sense of English identity will only be discovered when we 'unearth the mythic hoard that has lain hidden in the landscape of the English psyche and allow it to stir up truths about what it means to be English'.[165] The notion that the clues to the recreation of a meaningful sense of nationality lay in stories and sentiments that harked back to England's pre-Christian era has been widely aired. In his personal reflections upon the waning of organized religion, writer Cole Moreton pointed to the revival of pagan sentiments in English culture, seeing these as repositories of an untainted, and still vibrant, sense of independence and dissent.[166] Today's inhabitants of England are, on this view, legitimate heirs to a rich skein of folklore that has grown up around the landscapes, forests, and villages of ancient England. In *Jerusalem*, Byron's trailer is located near to Stonehenge and other sites that date from a time when druids and magic were ubiquitous. References to traditional folklore pepper the casual conversation of his band of followers, whose cultural life is otherwise dominated by the twin forces of a rampant commercialism and social indifference. In the teeth of these threats, the soul of England—which is anchored in its ancient, fabled connections to the land—is deemed to be in peril.

What one critic termed the 'stirring sense of place' at the core of the play stemmed from the jumble of whimsicality, mythology, and social observation that Butterworth assembles.[167] The interplay of these elements, as well as the focus upon the state of England and the stunted consciousness of its people, transfixed audiences and intrigued commentators. As one critic put it, 'to watch this play is to experience a kind of reawakening: a rekindling, if not of nationalism, then certainly of a sense of belonging; to see it, to understand it, feels as if Butterworth has struck the ore of our national identity'.[168] Marr saw it as symptomatic of a re-emerging sense of English independence: 'Whether we are talking about arguments over traveller encampments, Europe or the City, there is a stroppier mood about.'[169] For others, it was the portrait or a crumbling social fabric that resonated. The prevailing mood is bleak disappointment, made bearable by a wry sense of humour: 'Mother, what is this dark place?', Byron was supposed to have asked his mother upon his birth, and to which she replied: "Tis England, my boy. England.'[170]

Journalist Michael Goldfarb argued that it should be seen as one of a number of cultural works that have pursued the questions 'Who are the English?', and 'How will they rediscover a sense of commonality?'[171] He highlighted too the operatic production *Dr Dee*, which was performed in Manchester in 2011, and in London during the Cultural Olympiad of 2012.[172] This work achieved a considerable profile in part because its score was written and performed by Damon Albarn, but also because of the centrality it gave to issues of English identity. Dee was represented within the piece as an avatar of the Anglo-Britishness that culminated in the folly of Empire.[173] Living at a moment of considerable political and religious turmoil, he was charged with orchestrating England's shift away from its Catholic lineage, following the Pope's declaration of hostility to the Queen of England. But, more than this, he was depicted as a figure who operated at the interface of science and mysticism.[174] It was Dee's involvement with these forces that brought him to the attention of the government of the day—he became an adviser to Queen Elizabeth on astrology and calendar reform—and which also led to his ultimate downfall.

The director of *Dr Dee*, Rufus Norris, made clear his sense that the piece was, in part, designed to refract a re-emerging contemporary sense of Englishness:

We are now a nation in decline. Nobody can argue with that. The whole of Europe is in decline at the moment. Also, our sense of connection with nature and the spiritual has been demonised and we're now in a culture of a million gods, most of them capitalist. But go into any of our great cathedrals or even a small parish church and you get a sense of peace and wonder which you can't get anywhere else. It feels inherently English. This is quite a magical land and as we shrink back down it feels like an apposite moment to be looking at that.[175]

Dee was in some respects a curious figure to select as a vehicle for such themes, not least as he was born in Wales. But he has sparked recent interest, in part, because of his invention of the idea of a British Empire, and also since he helped establish the terms upon which colonialism would come to be justified. The relationship between the imagined English nation and the imperial course upon which Britain was to be set—in part because of Dee's thinking—has connected the piece to wider developments in national identity. Englishness, Norris observed, was now a more readily available and meaningful identity, yet was still in need of reclamation from 'the ultranationalists'.[176] For Albarn meanwhile, reappraising Dee established a crucial point of reconnection with the traditions of mysticism, occultist practice, and folklore, which were now once more to the fore.[177]

CELEBRATING THE NATION: ST GEORGE'S DAY

The folkish motifs to which I have drawn attention were not confined to these artistic ventures, but were discernible too within the arenas of lived experience. One of the most profound shifts associated with the cultural exploration and expression of English nationhood in these years has been the relatively rapid emergence of St George's Day as a focal point for popular celebration. In Chapter 1 I observed the upsurge of interest in the iconography associated with St George during the 1990s, and the widely made claim that its reclamation was a telling reflection of shifting national sensibilities among the English. In the years immediately after the millennium, this symbol became established as the prime signifier of English nationhood, a change that was almost entirely unforeseeable a few years previously. Within a decade, this emblem had become such a familiar part of the wallpaper of cultural life in England that its ubiquitous appearance ceased to elicit comment or surprise. An important, related development involved a heightened interest in promoting the birthday of St George as a day of national celebration. The idea of publicly commemorating this date stemmed from a self-conscious desire to emulate the informal, but established, practice of celebrating the national days associated with the Scots, Welsh, and Irish. The case for commemorating St George's Day often carried an envious, and sometimes grievance-tinged, resonance. As Skey reported, such a focus became 'an increasingly accessible framing device through which English discontent in relation to issues such as multiculturalism, political correctness and devolution may be expressed'.[178] In 2008, the social media site Facebook hosted a large campaign (the second largest it had hosted until that date) calling for 23 April to be turned into a bank holiday in England, a plea that received over 100,000 electronic signatures. And in 2005 an alliance of nationalist campaigners and English brewers collected over 600,000 signatures for a petition calling for it to become a national holiday. Polling conducted for the Future of England survey in 2012 reported that 70 per cent of respondents favoured making this an official public holiday.[179]

The growing profile of St George's Day has not passed unnoticed in political circles, and a growing band of politicians have called for the granting of a bank holiday on this date as an overdue form of recognition for the English. Senior Lib Dem figures Chris Huhne and Simon Hughes, as well as Conservatives such as David Davis, Boris Johnson, and other backbenchers, have all associated themselves with this idea.[180] Labour figures too have gone out of their way to identify with this cause.[181] Other high-profile public figures have also caught this mood. Campaigner Peter Tatchell argued for commemoration on the grounds that St George was an early human rights advocate.[182] The rich mythology attached to a figure who emanated from the Middle East, and has been claimed as a national icon by various other nations, has itself become a subject of increasing interest in recent years.[183] In 2009 Archbishop of York John Sentamu delivered a widely reported address in which he argued for the overdue reclamation of St George from a resurgent British National Party, and the potential for converting him into an icon for a multicultural Englishness.[184]

In practical terms, the idea of according this day some kind of official recognition raises a number of difficulties, most obviously because it would require a standardized form of provision for the different national days that are celebrated across the UK. In the final months of the Brown administration, the idea of moving in this direction was strongly advanced by Minister for Communities and Local Government, John Denham MP, who tried, unsuccessfully, to persuade Brown and his advisers of the merits of this idea.[185]

Beyond the arena of party politics, 23 April has quickly become a fixture on the cultural calendars of many towns, villages, neighbourhoods, and high streets across England. Like the adoption of the flag itself, its profile was significantly boosted by the leisure and drinks industries as it provided a significant new source of commercial opportunity. The relatively rapid growth of activities commemorating this day was mirrored by a rise in the appearance of St George's Day memorabilia. Public bodies and institutions have proved increasingly responsive to this trend. Schools put on themed lunches, villages flew the English flag, and many local councils moved to incorporate St George's Day into their schedules, laying on a variety of activities, including festivals and concerts. These were designed by a range of urban local authorities as efforts to reach out to indigenous residents and incorporate them within their schedule of multicultural festivals. Southwark and Leicester City Council, for example both developed extended programmes of celebration for this date.[186]

An important conduit for this growing interest was the increasing focus upon this day within the print and broadcast media, though press coverage often framed this trend within the vernacular of populist grievance. Stories about the banning of the English flag were a familiar theme within tabloid coverage. Yet, for the most part, the nature of its celebration, which has been easily assimilated into familiar patterns of leisure activity, has confirmed a form of nationality that is more quietly conservative than populist and angry.[187] The celebration of St George's Day carries a variety of different meanings. Thus, a survey of students conducted at the University of Huddersfield in 2009 reported that it elicited both the kind of distancing reflex that Condor has identified as a hallmark of many English respondents, as well as a more whole-hearted assertion about the right of the English to celebrate their own national day.[188]

And yet, important as it has been, the rapid diffusion of the iconography associated with St George, which has provoked so much media commentary in these years, is easy to over-read. In many respects, the absorption of this insignia into the interstices of everyday life signals how unchallenging in its implications has been the adoption of a new English icon. What had once been a symbol associated with right-wing extremism and eccentric nationalism was quickly absorbed within the cultural mainstream, and transformed with considerable rapidity into the kind of empty signifier that Michael Billig has identified as the epitome of banal nationalism.[189] In a study of what flying the flag meant to English football supporters, Abell and Condor found few respondents who regarded its adoption in political or nationalist terms.[190] While the media have been very quick to inflate the significance of this iconography, there are good reasons to suggest that it is the easy assimilation of St George into the English cultural landscape that is most notable. More generally, the much discussed study of the everyday behavioural norms favoured by the English, which was authored by anthropologist Kate Fox, pointed to the continuing prevalence of a sense of nationality that was, to a considerable degree, reflected in everyday forms of cultural expression, rather than the display of national emblems.[191] In her eyes Englishness represents an ingrained behavioural grammar, reflecting a set of unspoken assumptions, habits, and notions that are 'not a matter of race or birth or colour or creed'.[192]

At the same time, however, her study has also contributed to a rising sense of national self-awareness among the English, and has, ironically, helped ensure that the unselfconsciousness to which she draws attention may well be giving way to a more reflexive sense of nationhood. Indeed, the many texts and works

considered here have, in different ways, engendered a much greater appreciation of what being English might, and might not, mean.

THE ENGLISH AND THEIR FORMS

This trend can be illustrated with reference to a specific institutional domain
that has been widely invoked in public discourse in the last two decades: the
lack of an opportunity for English people to identify as English, rather than
British, on official forms. A rather telling sense of disquiet about this seemingly
trivial issue has come to a head in recent years. Its salience reflects a combination of unease and frustration occasioned by the dearth of opportunities for
recognition afforded to the English. It is this lack which has invested this issue
with an inflated degree of symbolic significance. As a participant in a community stakeholder group in the London borough of Barking and Dagenham put
it: 'they've taken English off the forms—it says white British—I always cross it
out and put English—we've lost our culture'.[193] Various researchers have noted
how the lack of an option to self-identify in this way is routinely cited in the
course of references to the perceived marginalization of the English nation.[194]
Garner, for instance, reported that the absence of such an option on equalities
monitoring forms elicited angry criticisms from respondents who interpreted
the categories employed as signalling that the relevant authority went out of
its way to recognize 'minorities' of various kinds, but was indifferent or disap-
proving towards the English.[195] This issue provided a redolent symbol of the
apparent lack of permission granted by the state to the English people to affirm
their own sense of nationhood.

Following an extended public consultation, which elicited a number of
vociferous complaints from a small number of nationalist campaigners, the
question of whether an English sense of nationality ought to be made available
in the census of 2011 (along with Scottish, Welsh, Northern Irish, and British
options) was addressed in the White Paper published by the government in
December 2008.[196] This provided guidelines for the questions that the census
would pose, and put forward the proposal that the section devoted to national
identity should, for the first time, include an 'English' option. This amendment did not satisfy everyone. Critics noted that the new question options
did not permit individuals to indicate that they saw themselves as members
of an ethnic minority category and as English, an oversight which said much
about liberal assumptions in this area.[197] But, in making England available in
this way, the Office for National Statistics put itself some way ahead of other

organizations and authorities in the public sector, a large number of which still do not offer respondents the opportunity to register their nationality as English when completing official forms.

CONCLUSIONS

In this chapter I have set out to draw attention to some of the texts and practices that are rarely considered within political and constitutional analyses of the English question. And I have suggested that the themes of belonging, nationhood, and Englishness have been much more prominent within a range of cultural and artistic arenas in the last two decades than has generally been acknowledged. This is not to suggest that these were the only, or primary, themes in the cultural life of this period, nor that this focus has been welcomed in all of the genres in which these works appeared. Indeed, the renewal of a sense of English nationhood has not always been characterized in positive terms, often being presented as a symptom of a nostalgic and regressive mind-set. Yet, across these disparate cultural milieux, a growing interest in these issues, and the implications of folk aesthetics and motifs in particular, is discernible during this period. And a significant shift in the national gestalt was aided and shaped by these endeavours.

Two other features of this broader renaissance of English cultural expression deserve attention. The first is the sense of creativity and energy associated with these themes, in marked contrast to the rather tepid and technocratic policy debate which they elicited within the arenas of high politics. The second is that this growing interest in national expression and exploration among the English appears to have been happening simultaneously within the worlds of everyday life and artistic practice.[198] Across the various social contexts and cultural arenas where Englishness has been affirmed and contested, a range of overlapping and conflicting meanings has become attached to this form of nationality.

More generally the renewal of folkish themes has been integral to two different kinds of argument about England. On the one hand, the restless search for authenticity, signalled by the injunction to rediscover the real England, has animated the contention that the nation needs to find its way back to the traditions and trajectory associated with different points in its past. This contention is associated with conservative and radical forms of opposition to liberal and individualistic values. On the other, a desire to establish an anchorage and set of roots for current national sentiments has become apparent, and this sensibility has been appropriated for a wide range of cultural and political purposes. Folk has also been important in enabling new, imaginative connections between cultural elements that tend to be framed as opposites within the English imagination—present and past, countryside and city, working and middle class—and stimulating forms of national thinking that cut across these seemingly entrenched divides. The stories and myths associated with the folk tradition have played a more important and integral role in relation to contemporary national sentiments than is generally appreciated.

The rich medley of writings, plays, art, and music to which I have drawn attention ought to be given greater consideration by those interested in contemporary expressions of English nationhood. This largely unheralded cultural revival has resulted in the generation of ideas and sensibilities outside the direct influence of the state and its associated institutions. This emphasis upon the cultural sources of many current forms and ideas of English nationhood cuts across the emphasis of progressive commentators upon the lack of democratic myths available to the English. In contrast, I have highlighted the variety of different ways in which a fairly stock repertoire of English fables, archetypes, and folkloric references have been recalled and reworked in recent years. These elements have played an integral role in anchoring and shaping the imaginative contours of English nationhood in this period. More generally, the proliferation of cultural works that have taken Englishness as a central motif is both a cause and sign of a growing receptivity to these themes among a diverse set of audiences.

This new 'moment' of Englishness had its origins, I suggest, in the anxiety about British decline that characterized the early to mid-1990s. The repeated attempts by successive Labour governments after 1997 to promote and codify an official form of British nationhood may also have played an inadvertent role in catalysing a reactive current of national sentiment. Writing in 2007, for example, Minister of State Liam Byrne used the occasion of St George's Day to argue—seemingly without irony—that the English should 'rise up' in favour of the union.[199] Such sentiments were clearly out of kilter with the underlying dynamics of national consciousness in this period. In fact, art and culture increasingly reflected the desire to achieve a greater degree of disentanglement between a reconstituted Englishness and established notions of Britishness. As the editors of a recent collection on this topic rightly observe, 'the common slippage between Englishness and Britishness seems increasingly unsafe at the turn of the century'.[200]

One small example from within the domain of popular culture encapsulates this very gradual, but potentially paradigmatic, shift. In an appraisal of the film *Skyfall*, that broke box office records at cinemas during 2012, *The Economist*'s reviewer devoted nearly the entirety of her piece to the confused and inconsistent way in which England and Britain were referenced in the film.[201] The author's recognition that English audiences were far less likely to show tolerance for the familiar habit of interchanging these national references said much about the shift in cultural gestalt that was quietly under way in England. But, while it has become increasingly apparent that the English have fostered forms of nationality that sit at a greater distance from older forms of Britishness, it is far less clear whether this represents the first stage on a longer journey, or is, in fact, the new destination for English national consciousness.

5

Answering 'the English Question'

Party Politics, Public Policy, and the Nationalist Fringe

INTRODUCTION

One of the most intriguing questions raised by the devolution legislation introduced by Tony Blair's first government was whether the English would take umbrage at being denied an equivalent form of constrained self-government to that enjoyed by other territories within the UK. A considerable amount of expert commentary has reflected the expectation and fear that the English would be prompted to discover the principle of national sovereignty, or, as some nationalists put it, rediscover the historic idea of England as a political nation. But the excitement generated by the possibility of such a backlash has gradually been replaced by the more sober realization that such a development has not happened, and that English nationalism, as a mass phenomenon, is still notable by its absence.

Among political scientists in particular, the English question was increasingly considered in relation to the perennial puzzle of why exactly the English were still so unwilling to develop their own national-democratic ambitions. And, among the various explanations that were forthcoming, the familiar insistence upon the debilitating void at the heart of English nationhood has been prominent. Others, however, argued that, in order to understand the acquiescence of the English to arrangements that might, at first blush, appear to work to the advantage of smaller nations within the union, we should consider the continuing hold of the dominant narrative of parliamentary government upon the constitutional and national thinking of the English. Tony Wright encapsulated this as a conviction about the unique qualities associated with the peaceful adaptation and gradual evolution of a political system which, though it 'felt the force of battles over nationhood, rights, freedom, democracy, and class', was also able to avoid 'an experience of decisive rupture'.[1] The English had not therefore been required to remake their institutions, or write down their constitution, or deliberate about what kind of state they wanted to have. Instead, the state 'just went on being what it was, more or less'.[2] The visible continuity of the institutional landscape in the UK came to represent an intrinsic virtue of this asymmetrical and idiosyncratic system of government, and it appeared that the lop-sided nature of the devolution settlement had not forced the English to reconsider their loyalty to it.

It has long been argued that this tradition of strong, centralized government is interwoven with the unique, non-nationalist temper of the English people.[3] Such arguments reflect the dominant values of a state that had established a form of centralized control over its territory at an earlier point than any of its European counterparts. Since the Glorious Revolution of 1688, monarchs had come to govern with the consent of parliament, a qualification that evolved over time into a 'Crown-in-Parliament' arrangement.[4] The sense of a governing tradition that flowed from this history of gradual adaptation, rather than one that was reinvented following the experience of revolutionary rupture or defeat in warfare, spanned the eras of monarchical government and mass democracy. This dominant national-cum-constitutional lineage was, as Mandler has shown, closely interwoven with leading ideas about the national character of a people who were assumed to have tacitly conferred legitimacy upon a political system that was characterized by its anomalies and constitutional oddities.[5] As Benjamin Disraeli famously quipped, 'England is not governed by logic; she is governed by Parliament.'[6] This entrenched manner of thinking sustained the idea that the anomalies generated by devolution were unlikely to offend the English whose capacity and willingness to identify with the 'fifth nation' of the United Kingdom would ensure that they did not respond to its implementation in 'narrow' national terms. However, this mode of national reflection has, as we have seen already, come under growing strain in recent years, and various indications of changes in popular expectations of the British system of government have become apparent. Equally, leading actors within the political system have themselves become increasingly sensitive to this shifting mood, and appear less confident that the established pattern of constitutional thinking provides a secure platform from which to address the English question. As leading ideas about the British system of government, at both popular and elite levels, have begun to wane, the question of whether the English remain content to overlook the question of their own national-democratic representation is, I argue, becoming increasingly unavoidable. A growing weight of opinion now supports the notion that, if English irritation is left to fester, a more radical, and unBritish, response to England's constitutional position may well loom into view.

Debates about devolution, which stretch back to the nineteenth century, in the context of arguments about Home Rule for Ireland, have long been accompanied by the suggestion of an equivalent devolution process for England.[7] While for most of the previous century this was confidently regarded as a fringe concern, this notion has gradually acquired a degree of respectability in recent years, and has moved into the mainstream of political life. This chapter explores the tenor and substance of the debates associated with this shift, and assesses the various policy ideas that have been advanced in relation to this issue since devolution. I argue, in particular, that the main political parties have reluctantly begun to move towards the realization that the English question signals an interlocking set of issues— about nationhood, representation, and governance—that are now unlikely to disappear from view. But I also point to an increasingly marked dissensus within high political circles about how best to deal with some of the issues where the tensions and strains associated with devolution are starting to become apparent. These are expressed in relation to two iconic questions— about the manner in which public expenditure is distributed throughout the UK, and the anomaly associated with the West Lothian issue, both of which are considered in detail in Chapter 6. As a report produced by the House of Commons Justice Committee in 2009 put it, 'The governance of England is seen by many as the "unfinished business" of devolution, but this perception is not accompanied by any widespread agreement on what should be done.'[8]

The policy debates that have developed in relation to these issues are underscored by some notable assumptions and anxieties among politicians and policy-makers about how the English feel about their own national identity and how they have come to regard the union. The spectre of a rising tide of English resentment, triggered by the devolution settlement, haunts the debates about governance and democracy that have become more prominent, even if fears about a putative English backlash have been considerably overstated. Many within the political world worry that the English have, as Tony Wright put it, become 'silent and uninvited guests at the devolution feast', imbued with a combination of resentment and dissatisfaction that will ultimately lead towards the break-up of the union itself.[9] They would do better, I suggest, to consider some of the more specific forms of disaffection and disenchantment that sections of the English public increasingly feel towards the manner in which they are governed and politically represented.

DEVOLUTION AND THE ENGLISH QUESTION

In Chapter 3 I argued against the proposition that devolution itself has been the cause and trigger of a renewed sense of national self-awareness among the English. Yet it is also important to recognize that this significant set of reforms has accentuated an unpredictable set of political dynamics throughout the UK, and has, over time, helped bring to the surface questions about the position of England within the union. In this chapter I focus particularly upon how politicians have responded to arguments about the implications of the devolution reforms introduced in the late 1990s for England's constitutional position and system of governance. These policy debates have tended to treat the English question within these specific parameters, and have not, until very recently, reflected the connections to which I have pointed in this book between shifting patterns of national identity among the English and attitudes towards a wider set of issues, including the EU and inward immigration into the UK.

One leading academic authority on devolution suggests that while these measures were designed to stabilize the United Kingdom outside England, through the offer of limited degrees and varied forms of self-government, the devolution process has set in train a growing sense of diversification among the four separate political communities that are now established within the UK:

> Wales is now on its third variant of devolution, with yet another reform commission preparing the ground for variant number four. Scotland has just acquired new powers under the Scotland Bill and faces the possibility of more profound change. England now has a commission to explore the consequences for it of devolution.[10]

A process of ongoing, ratchet-like reform has been set in motion in part because the architects of devolution failed to develop and entrench a coherent, overarching vision for the United Kingdom, and did not develop a common framework spelling out the rights and entitlements associated with citizenship as a counter-weight to devolution:

> Labour did not think systematically: it treated the Scottish, Welsh and Northern Irish reforms discretely and never had much of an idea about what to do with England. Because there was never a UK-wide rationale for devolution there was no institutional design that might have harnessed devolved powers to address not only local needs but also common UK-wide interests.[11]

Devolution served to establish increasingly separate spheres of action for both the UK government and the devolved administrations, and was financed by the allocation of block grants that did not include any requirement for a compensatory UK-wide focus or provision. Relatively little attention was paid to establishing the 'structures of routinised and formalised intergovernmental coordination that in other countries both resolve differences and create shared purpose'.[12]

Scotland has, since 1999, been governed by its own parliament, and may well be allocated further responsibilities for domestic legislation, including some control over taxation, if it votes against independence in 2014. Meanwhile, the Welsh National Assembly was initially given more limited powers than its Scottish counterpart, but, following a referendum held in March 2011, has now been granted powers over primary legislation. And in Northern Ireland, after the long period of 'direct rule' that was instituted in 1972, a system of devolved government has been restored as part of the wider peace process. One consequence of these different reforms is that the government of the UK is now increasingly the *de facto* government for England in a number of areas of domestic legislation, including health and education. In many respects Westminster has become a parliament whose writ runs primarily in England and Wales, though, importantly, decisions it takes continue to carry implications for the other territories of the UK, and it retains state-wide sovereignty over foreign policy, security, and defence. As an unintended consequence of devolution, therefore, an increasingly Anglicized polity has quietly 'emerged as an incubus at the heart of the UK state', and yet this development remains largely unspoken within mainstream political discourse.[13] These trends have generated a growing sense of strain within British political culture as the dissonance between the altered territorial remit of various branches of central government and the established culture whereby departments operate primarily in functional, not territorial, terms, has become palpable. No concerted, cross-departmental attempt has been made to address this growing disjuncture within the central state.[14] Equally, the question of what these changes should mean for the nature of state organization and policy formulation within England—now widely acknowledged to be one of the most centrally administered territories in Europe—has gradually made its way towards the heart of political debate.

The working out of the unpredictable dynamics that devolution set in train has also resulted in a renewal of interest in one of the notable idiosyncrasies of the British parliament, whereby MPs representing constituencies in territories that have long had variable systems of devolved governmental autonomy continue to have the right to vote on matters affecting other parts of the union. This issue, conventionally known as 'the West Lothian question', has attracted growing political interest in recent years. It reflects an ingrained, historic anomaly, which long predates devolution, arising as it does from the development of differential governing arrangements in relation to the non-English territories of the UK. It came back to life with a vengeance on several controversial occasions when the Blair governments passed contentious pieces of legislation that applied to England alone by calling upon the support of Scottish MPs. As more areas of domestic policy have, over time, been delegated to the Scottish Parliament, the Welsh Assembly, and Stormont, interest in the question of who ought to vote on legislation that affects only certain territories—be it England, or England and Wales—has spilled beyond the bounds of parliament, and become a focal point for a proclaimed sense of English grievance. A commitment to set up an independent commission to consider the effects of devolution on the workings of the House of Commons was included in the agreement reached by the parties involved in the Coalition government established after the General Election of May 2010. The McKay Commission set out various proposals for reform to the way in which English-only Bills might be handled in parliament, in March 2013.[15] Its ideas, and other proposed models for reform, will be considered in Chapter 6.

As various commentators have observed, however, such are the complexities associated with this issue, and such has been the tacit consent of most of the English for a system of government that protects the position of the smaller territories in the UK, that a public debate about devolution has been slow to take hold.[16] Equally, while Scotland is widely viewed as a growing source of English irritation, the very different positions of Northern Ireland and Wales have been rather overlooked in constitutional debate. Wales retains a degree of entanglement with England, in legislative terms, which puts it in a very different situation to Scotland and Northern Ireland.[17] The boundary between the law and legislation that applies to England and Wales remains complex and opaque, though the granting of primary legislative powers to the Welsh Assembly may lead to greater clarity and some degree of disentangling. In strict terms there are very few occasions when legislation is introduced that applies to, or affects, England alone. Yet, despite the complex and opaque nature of these arrangements, it is striking, as we shall see in Chapter 6, that the West Lothian issue has increasingly served as a magnet for a nascent sense of disaffection and inequity, and has come to acquire an increasingly symbolic role within debates about the British state and the future of the union.

These arrangements are increasingly vulnerable to the populist contention that the other nations of the UK have been given the right and autonomy to develop their own divergent approaches to important questions about public service provision and funding, cushioned by the generosity of the English taxpayer. Thus, decisions taken by the Scottish Parliament to maintain existing levels of public provision in relation to social care for the elderly, and to avoid passing charges for prescriptions to the taxpayer, have become a totem for a growing set of concerns among segments of the English public. And these complaints are increasingly meshed with a broader sense of disenchantment towards the political system. In this increasingly febrile context, some commentators have detected the re-emergence of the idea of the English reconstituting themselves as a political, rather than purely cultural, nation, as they are no longer willing to be 'left-over people' or 'the last stateless nation' of the British state.[18] These sentiments have emerged, quite tellingly, across the political spectrum, with the English cast by some progressive pundits as the last victims of the British state. 'England, that great colonising land, has become a colony', intoned environmentalist campaigner George Monbiot.[19]

But a focus upon how the English have responded to devolution captures only one aspect of the politics of nationhood in these years. An interlocking set of national questions have, in the last few years, moved onto the centre stage of British politics, making questions of nationhood, identity, and sovereignty keynote themes, even in the wake of the financial crisis and economic downturn that began in 2007. These issues have become yet more acute following the election of a Coalition government at Westminster, which is led by a party which has barely any representatives outside England, and also by the election of an SNP administration in Edinburgh in May 2010. Since these events, there has followed the establishment of: a Scottish referendum on independence, scheduled for 2014; the Silk Commission examining the finances and powers of the Welsh Government and National Assembly; and a Commission under the chairmanship of Lord McKay, which reported on the impact of devolution on the business of the House of Commons in March 2013. The combination and temporal proximity of these developments mean that questions about nationhood and territory are becoming increasingly prominent in British political life. This accumulation of events, in conjunction with a more volatile mood among parts of the English public towards the European Union in particular, and the UK's systems of politics and governance more generally, has raised questions about the viability of the governing expectation at Westminster that the national question will not become a major concern for the English.[20] The devolution settlement looks to be in too uncertain a position for this stance to be plausibly maintained, and it may well be that seeking different kinds of answers to England's position in the union comes, in the next few years, to be seen as unavoidable, from a Unionist, as well as nationalist, perspective.

The gradual politicization of national issues marks a quite considerable change from the period of New Labour government when, devolution aside, constitutional issues remained in the margins of politics. And yet, there are reasons to think that, even then, the conventional assumption that the English are temperamentally indifferent to questions of democratic representation, governance, and sovereignty, was a misleading one. The intense interest of sections of English opinion in such issues as Europe, immigration, and the countryside suggests that issues which touch upon, and come to symbolize, the English question, broadly understood, have been gaining increasing resonance since the mid-1990s.

ANSWERING THE ENGLISH QUESTION? THE
IMPACT OF ELECTORAL BIFURCATION

The questions of whether and how the English question ought to be addressed, in policy terms, have generated a variety of rival answers at Westminster. Some of these have dropped out of favour over time—notably the idea of self-government for the English regions—and some that were once regarded as maverick have come to assume a degree of respectability, for instance the notion of a separate parliament for the English. The two main political parties have been increasingly drawn to articulate a response to this issue, sceptical as they have mostly been about the need to do so. Both have developed their thinking mainly within the broad parameters established by their long-standing commitment to the union and familiar ideas about the ethos and remit of British government. But this official mind-set is increasingly streaked by a sense of uncertainty engendered by the impact of one of the most irreversible and powerful political trends of this period: the striking pattern of geographical bifurcation that characterizes the rival electoral bases of the two main parties.

In his powerful riposte to those, like Nairn, who foresaw the imminent 'break-up of Britain', political scientist Richard Rose pointed out, in an important work published in the 1970s, that the party system was itself one of the most significant forces achieving integration in the UK.[21] In his judgement, the main political parties played a key role in converting a host of disparate, regional, and national concerns into the common, functional language of British politics. As a result, some of the most acute, territorially rooted divisions and rivalries were successfully nullified and rendered marginal.[22]

Yet, in recent years, an ever sharper geographical polarization has arisen from the pattern of parliamentary representation secured by both parties, and the opposite outcome to that envisaged by Rose has now come about. Both parties are increasingly reliant upon electoral support that is highly territorially concentrated, a trend that is in part the result of the 'first-past-the-post' electoral system used for elections to the Westminster parliament, since the party with the most support in different parts of the UK tends to be disproportionately rewarded by it. Thus, the Conservatives have, in the last thirty years, become much less successful at securing seats in Scotland and, to a lesser extent, Wales. At the same time, their historic strength in large parts of England, outside the inner areas of its largest cities, has become even more pronounced in terms of electoral representation. In 1997, the Tory party failed to win a seat in either Wales or Scotland, and, following the General Election of 2005, 98 per cent of Tory seats in the House of Commons were held by English MPs. Not surprisingly, members of its overwhelming English parliamentary party have proved to be increasingly attuned to Anglo sensibilities.

For Labour, the landslide victory achieved in 1997, which ensured that it won seats in parts of England that were typically beyond its reach, has proved to be the exception illustrating the norm that the party tends to win seats in areas where the Conservatives are weak. Thus, Labour's share of votes and seats has declined significantly across large parts of England since 2001, with a notable weakening of its electoral performance in the South, South East, East of England, and the Midlands. The party has been forced back, in terms of its parliamentary representation, to places that represent the bedrock of its historic support: Scotland, Wales, the cities of Northern England, and a handful of other urban seats in the Midlands and South. These do not, by themselves, offer a sufficient numerical return to secure an outright majority, engendering an acute sensitivity to a number of 'swing' seats in the Midlands and parts of the South of England.[23] And, as we shall see, the geographical pattern of its representatives in the Commons has exercised considerable impact upon Labour's understanding of England's position and role in the union.

Neither of these electoral trends originated in this period, but they have been considerably accentuated in the past two decades. One of their consequences has been to render less important a long-standing debate about the merits of reducing the numbers of seats in non-English territories as a compensatory mechanism when these areas are given powers of self-government. Such reforms have come to acquire a partisan dimension as they are likely to cause a disproportionate amount of damage to Labour, not the Conservatives.[24] At the same time, the Tories have become increasingly sceptical about the equity of the allocation of seats within England, which, due to a combination of birth-rates and population movement into cities, has resulted in an entrenched advantage for Labour in electoral terms.[25] A further consequence of this bifurcated geographical pattern of territorial representation at Westminster has been to make Labour, following the elections of 2001 and 2005, increasingly reliant upon Scottish MPs to secure majorities for its legislative programme. At the same time, the Conservatives have come to look like an overwhelmingly English party within the Lower House at the very moment when the ability to secure legitimacy across the different territorial units of the UK has become more pressing, in the wake of the election of an SNP administration in Scotland. While by no means the only political factors to play a part in bringing the English question onto the main stage of politics, these trends have acted as significant sources of destabilization.

A further underlying, often imperceptible, shift in this period has also had an effect upon the salience of this issue. This arises from the growing sense of separation which, various studies suggest, is a hallmark of the political culture associated with both the Scottish Parliament and Welsh Asembly, and the correlative Anglicization of politics at Westminster.[26] This latter trend reflects both the growing volume of parliamentary business that is devoted predominantly, or entirely, to England, and the—hitherto unacknowledged—Anglocentric framework adoped by all the main political parties.[27] It also reflects other, less tangible, cultural changes, including the increasingly prevalent assumption among Westminster politicians that the primary audiences for political debate are English, as well as the emergence within the Westminster parliament of an increasingly Anglo-focused set of political debates and priorities in this period.[28] The parties have become increasingly animated by very English preoccupations and themes—with debates about class, regional inequalities, the position of the City of London, and reforms in the delivery and organization of public services—coming to the fore in the last decade, and especially since the financial crisis of 2007–8.[29] The growing divergence of the political cultures and priorities of the different political centres within the UK is most apparent in terms of the different approaches to public service provision and funding that have become apparent within them. Jeffery, for instance, has argued that a distinctly English approach to the relationship of market and state has become embedded at Westminster across the last two decades.[30]

These interlocking developments have increasingly come to undercut some of the established conventions and assumptions associated with British parliamentary government, and the growing interest in the English question can, in part, be understood as symptoms of the waning of the latter. In combination, these trends have come to endow devolution and constitutional reform with a much greater degree of political salience and uncertainty.

THE CONSERVATIVES

The Labour government's devolution legislation prompted an extended debate in the ranks of its main opponent, the Conservative party. For the most part these discussions took place within the framework associated with its Unionist inheritance, yet fissures within its established position soon began to appear.

The parliamentary party's initial intuition that it ought to oppose the devolution referenda in Scotland and Wales reflected the widely held view that these reforms might well put the union in jeopardy by providing arenas where nationalist sentiments and parties could flourish. Apocalyptic warnings about the possible consequences of these changes abounded in Conservative circles.[31] One commonly expressed concern was that the genie of English nationalism was about to be unwittingly released, and the majority roused by the affront to its democratic sensibilities which devolution represented. Seasoned observers on the right began to express fears about the appeal of English nationalism following devolution in Scotland and Wales.[32]

The Tory party leadership rapidly came to the view that, once devolution was introduced, it was almost politically impossible, and self-defeating, to sustain a stance of outright opposition to it. Other parts of the party wondered if a growth in English indignation might work to its advantage. Right-wing MP Teresa Gorman tabled a Private Member's Bill calling for a referendum on the idea of an English Parliament, four months after the successful referenda establishing devolution in Scotland and Wales.[33] A prominent Eurosceptic who had lost the party's whip in 1995 over the issue of the UK's financial contribution to the EU, she now argued that the English merited fair and equal treatment, and noted pointedly that nine of the twenty Ministers in Blair's Cabinet represented Scottish or Welsh constituencies. She was, however, in a minority at Westminster in identifying with English grievances in this fashion. Most Conservative parliamentarians stuck to the familiar script about the sovereignty of the Crown-in-Parliament, and argued that British institutions needed to be reinforced in anticipation of the nationalist pressures that devolution would unleash.[34] But the party was also caught in some powerful crosswinds on this issue. Initially, it distanced itself from any hint of English nationalism. Yet, during the last months of 1997 and early in 1998, its leadership looked hard at whether it should propose a further, compensatory round of devolution—this time for the English. In his speech to the annual conference of 1998, leader William Hague canvassed several different possible ways of addressing England's asymmetrical constitutional position, and publicly identified the Tories with the goal of developing a devolution 'offer' for the English.[35]

Hague's intervention created considerable political difficulties, in part because his own position as leader was not entirely secure. Several Shadow Ministers quickly indicated their opposition to the notion of promoting English representation in a way that might endanger the union, forcing him into an inelegant retreat. And yet, viewed with the advantage of hindsight, his speeches in this period appear far more prescient and considered than was apparent in the pressurized context in which they were delivered. In several interventions he thoughtfully set out the main options that have, over time, come to define the debate animating nationalist and constitutional campaigners, mainstream politicians, and political commentators, and identified a specifically conservative rationale for further reform.[36] Hague made the case for a prudential rebalancing of the asymmetrical model of devolution in order to head off the prospect of an irritation festering into a hardened form of nationalist sentiment, a position that foreshadowed the consensus on which many later MPs and policy-makers have settled.[37] Addressing the Centre for Policy Studies in 1999, he indicated that his favoured solution was some version of 'English votes on English matters', and rejected other possible measures such as an English parliament or new system of regional government.[38] In the wake of devolution he detected the 'first stirrings of the sleeping dragon of English nationalism'.[39] In response, he suggested, policy-makers needed to find 'sensible political outlets for a new-found English consciousness', and to ensure that these were made compatible with 'our open, multi-ethnic British identity'.[40] In short, greater engagement with, and more recognition for, Englishness were, in the long run, likely to bolster, not damage, the union.

Despite the considerable attention he devoted to this issue, Hague and other senior Conservatives resolved not to make this a central theme in their opposition to Labour, a decision the party's leadership stuck to throughout the following decade, even after the anointing of a Scottish MP, Gordon Brown, as Prime Minister in 2007. But it did not entirely eschew traditional English themes or forms of rhetoric, especially when these enabled it to mobilize opposition to parts of Labour's legislative programme. The Conservatives were resolutely against the government's plans for the greater devolution of powers to the English regions, a policy that was widely viewed as aiding the goal of promoting a 'Europe of the regions' at the expense of the national integrity and traditions of England. Scruton's polemical declaration that such an approach would most likely mean the 'abolition' of England spoke to a broad cross-section of conservative sentiment.[41]

Yet, beneath the surface of the party's various policy pronouncements, there were some important signs during these years that its ingrained sense of 'primordial Unionism' was weakening.[42] Viewing the reforms of 1998 as largely motivated by Labour's reliance upon its Scottish and Welsh MPs, a number of backbench Conservatives increasingly moved towards the reformist proposition that further adjustments were now required to achieve an appropriate balance between the demands of territorial justice and the need to protect and renew the union. Writing in 2000, David Davis MP argued that devolution had generated considerable pressures upon the UK, and put the English in a precarious and unsustainable position. He identified a latent sense of Anglo-patriotism:

> Nobody should doubt that the English feel as passionately about their country as do the Scots or Welsh. The willingness of the English to subordinate their

'Englishness' to the greater interests of the Union is a measure of the strength of their commitment to that Union, not of any weakness in their love of their own country.[43]

Labour, he suggested, was guilty of reckless vandalism by introducing into British politics an unpredictable, and potentially incendiary, dynamic. Davis directed particular fire at its 'attempts to provide supposed "fairness" with regional councils'. These were 'soulless regional bureaucracies; bleak outstations of Brussels'.[44] And, going further than many of his colleagues were prepared to do at this time, he concluded that: 'If each of the other nations of the United Kingdom is going to have its own parliament, then England's choice should be no less.'[45] The principle of equal treatment for the English ought also to be extended to the question of a fairer system of financial provision across the union, an issue which, as we shall see, has gradually moved into the forefront of political debate in these years. While Davis's broad support for the principle of a separate English parliament remained a minority preference within the parliamentary party in this period, his trenchant critique of devolution and the unfair system of governance it bequeathed was an increasingly mainstream view within it. A survey of prospective parliamentary candidates before the 2010 General Election revealed that most were convinced of the need to make alterations to England's constitutional position, with a clear majority favouring the introduction of a version of 'English Votes for English Laws' within the House of Commons.[46] The party that had enshrined the conviction that the British model of parliamentary government needed to be protected from the reforming impulses of its enemies, was, by 2010, magnetically drawn towards the belief that a significant form of constitutional modification was now required in the wake of devolution.

LABOUR

During its long years in government, Labour's response to arguments about the English question was typically more defensive and ambivalent than its Conservative counterparts. This was both a product of its perception that those expressing concerns about this issue were rarely on the political left, and also due to the party's disinclination to consider devolution in UK-wide terms. This mind-set resulted too in an approach to the question of the reform of different tiers of government in England that was divested of any wider consideration of national-democratic principle in the context of the English. Instead there developed a considerable and largely unresolved disagreement, in policy terms,

between those favouring the idea of introducing a new layer of regional government to England and those advocating a programme of locally rooted devolution. These different perspectives were routinely aired as indirect responses to
the English question. But there also began to emerge an alternative argument,
expressing unease about the evasive and technocratic character of Labour's
response to the national-democratic and cultural aspects of this issue.

In broad historical terms, national questions in the UK have always generated considerable dilemmas for Labour, given its strengths in Wales and
Scotland, and sensitivity to nationalist sentiments in these territories, on the
one hand, and the abiding commitment to the goals of economic distribution
and inter-regional equity, both of which it associated with the central British
state. As historian Colin Kidd has put it:

> Labour's primary focus on class and the redistribution of wealth across the UK
> as a whole has led it to pay scant attention to the multinational union-state itself,
> except insofar as that state functions as an instrument of social and economic
> policy.[47]

In more recent years, Labour's electoral strengths in Scotland and Wales, and
some of the largest industrial and urban centres in England, have served to
reinforce its self-image as a party that is wholeheartedly committed to the
union and the tradition of parliamentary sovereignty which underpins it. It
was on the basis of this conviction that the party developed its plans for differential forms of devolution—in Scotland, Wales, and London—after 1997,
seeing these proposals as an alternative to the federalist or nationalist ambitions of its opponents.[48]

This stance also helped deal, if indirectly, with the political problems
posed by its growing reliance upon MPs from Scotland and Wales. At the
2005 General Election, sixty-nine Labour MPs were elected in these territories compared to only four Conservatives. Labour was highly sensitive to the
rise of nationalist politics in both of these contexts, retaining the memory of
the painful and divisive experience of attempting to bring forward its own
measures for devolution during the last months of the Callaghan administration. But, as it embarked upon the process of bringing varying degrees of
self-government to Scotland and Wales, the question of why the principles
underpinning devolution did not apply to the largest and most heavily populated territory of the United Kingdom hung in the political air, especially
among its Northern constituency parties where scepticism about devolution had been most pronounced. Labour was especially keen to ensure that
its reforms were not seen as reflecting the principle of representation based
upon national-popular sovereignty, a concession that would have drawn
attention to the absence of England from the devolution programme. It

argued vociferously that these changes would promote forms of governance that were more effective, decentralized, and accountable. A similar justification was provided for the granting of powers to a reconstituted London-wide authority. But this important reform generated a further set of difficult questions about its more limited approach to the delegation of powers to local government in other large cities and towns in England.

When its devolution legislation was being debated and introduced, Labour's response to questions about its asymmetrical character was dismissive. For Jack Straw, Secretary of State for Justice, writing in 2007, such thinking meant pandering to 'Little England', and represented a 'sure means of destroying the union'.[49] He had already paraded his conviction that English nationalism represented the dark side of the national character, as he discussed its 'propensity to violence' and 'history of subjugating other peoples'.[50] Following the disorder that accompanied English supporters' presence at the World Cup of 1998 and the Euro 2000 football tournament, he was equally condemnatory blaming the xenophobia of some English fans on 'the global baggage of empire'.[51] And in an intervention which reflected the underlying tribalism that shaped Labour's thinking on these issues, MP Michael Wills declared in 1999 that: 'The so-called "English question" is one which does not exist until the Conservative Party asks it, an issue which is not a problem until they try to whip it into one'.[52]

But the party's response to arguments for devolution to England was not entirely negative. Labour set out to identify itself with the notion of introducing various forms of administrative and political devolution within England and directed considerable energy to developing policy ideas in this area. And it prioritized the aim of passing significant governing powers to the regions of England. This goal was championed enthusiastically by the party in opposition, and was widely presented as the basis for an equivalent devolution to what was offered in Scotland and Wales, given the size and population of many of the English regions. Its supporters maintained that passing political powers to areas outside London and the South East represented a robust and democratic answer to a different English question—how to remedy the stark inequalities associated with England's divided economic geography.

LABOUR'S PLANS FOR REGIONAL GOVERNMENT

The regionalist focus which came to the fore in Labour's thinking during the 1990s represented a return to a much older lineage that had long hymned the praises of regional government—the 'Municipalisation by Provinces' as a

Fabian pamphlet of 1905 rather inelegantly put it.[53] In the 1990s, the notion that stronger institutional structures and coordinated planning, in housing and transport especially, were needed at this level to boost economic development in some of England's most deprived areas gained considerable ground. These economic ambitions were at the heart of the administrative forms of regional devolution that the party set in motion during its early years in office. They were justified also by the argument that a regional tier of government would provide a much needed counter-weight to the highly centralized system of governance which prevailed in England.

These two different rationales for regional government—resting upon the case for democratic accountability and a more geographically balanced form of development, respectively—were typically championed by most proponents of this vision. Yet, in policy terms they proved far more difficult to align with each other than was widely anticipated as Labour prepared for government during the 1990s. Labour's ambitions were set out in a consultation paper commissioned by party leader Tony Blair, and authored by Shadow Minister Jack Straw in 1995: *A Choice for England*. This provided the basis for its 1996 *A New Voice for English Regions*.[54] This document argued for the gradual passing of key powers from central government to regional bodies. Its core ambition was the development of a new administrative tier in the guise of grand-sounding regional chambers. These would be complemented in time, Straw's report suggested, by the introduction of directly elected regional assemblies. The notion of promoting a more balanced pattern of economic development was developed in a separate part of the party's policy thinking. In 1995 John Prescott established a Regional Policy Commission for the party, and appointed former EU Commissioner Bruce Millan to act as its chair. His 1996 report, *Renewing the Regions*, recommended that a Regional Development Agency (RDA) be established for every English region, modelled on the Scottish and Welsh Agencies.[55]

The different arguments set out in these documents remained walled off from each other in the run-up to the General Election of 1997, with little sustained attempt to integrate them, so that the key ideas associated with each cropped up in separate chapters of the party's manifesto. Once in government, the party moved cautiously and uncertainly towards the implementation of aspects of these ideas.[56] It was not until 2000 that it developed plans for the establishment of Regional Chambers. Its stately approach in this area reflected continuing disagreement among senior figures about the merits of regional devolution, and a growing awareness that public opinion was largely indifferent, and potentially hostile, to such reforms.[57] According to the BSA survey of 2001, 16.6 per cent of people in England supported the notion of an Assembly in their region, with only 15 per cent being in favour in 1999.[58]

It was not until it won a second term in office in 2001 that Labour felt able to pick up the threads of its regionalist rhetoric and act with greater purpose in this area. In 2002 it published a White Paper, *Your Region, Your Choice*, in which it offered its most concrete indication of the process for ensuring public consultation about the introduction of Regional Assemblies, and sought to find a way around the formidable obstacles represented by the variable levels of enthusiasm for regional government in different parts of the country.[59] Some areas, it declared, could opt to pursue a faster route towards devolution and take steps to set up elected regional assemblies. Those that were less keen might opt for a slightly enhanced version of existing powers. This document also proposed converting Regional Chambers into elected assemblies with responsibilities for planning and housing, as well as some areas of economic policy. The government's stated preference was for eight regional assemblies outside London, with their members serving four-year terms. These bodies would have some strategic planning powers and limited means of generating their own revenues, primarily through the addition of a levy to current rates of council tax and the award of limited borrowing powers.[60]

The government chose to hold the first of these referenda in the North East, where support for the idea of devolved government was relatively high, and a strong sense of regional identity appeared to be established. But, faced by a well-organized and funded 'No' campaign, and hampered by a lingering sense of disappointment about the limited nature of the powers that would be delegated, the referendum was overwhelmingly defeated in 2004.[61] Following this result, the project of creating a new tier of regional government fell away with remarkable speed in Labour circles. The disappearance of this agenda left a gaping hole in the party's thinking about the distribution of authority and balance of power among the different tiers of the system through which England was governed. Increasingly, the city-region came to be seen as a more suitable territorial scale at which to promote economic development, and the 2006 Local Government White Paper endorsed the principle through the mechanism of Multi-Area Agreements.[62]

But the economic policy objectives associated with developing a regional tier of administration continued to figure in governmental thinking during these years. And, once the Treasury under Gordon Brown signalled its conversion to the idea of building up coordinating powers at regional level in order to address long-standing socio-economic spatial inequities within England, this became a more salient theme within its macro-economic strategy.[63] Between 2004 and 2010 successive Labour governments continued to locate important coordinating powers over economic development, planning, and housing within the RDAs. They also appointed Regional

Ministers and tried to establish Regional Select Committees in 2007, though these were stymied by the refusal of the opposition parties to participate in them. Even though these developments clearly signalled the continuation of a circumscribed and centrally directed form of administrative devolution, the notion that the further development of this tier of government might constitute an important element of Labour's response to the English question continued to circulate in government circles, despite the palpable lack of popular awareness of these bodies, and the absence of accountability mechanisms attached to them.

Yet, the notion that tinkering with the cluster of agencies, quangos, and non-governmental organizations that had sprung up at this level of administration might signal a transition to a new tier of government was fanciful on various grounds. As Vernon Bogdanor has observed, the opaque nature of the relationships that had mushroomed between the various bodies and quangos which had emerged at this level, and the lack of clarity about which bodies were responsible for particular decisions, inhibited the establishment of a coherent or legitimate 'regional layer of government'.[64] In key policy areas, such as housing and transport, the government's ingrained preference for passing functions to non-departmental public bodies, many of which had different, and sometimes overlapping, territorial jurisdictions, rendered this tier of administration bewildering and offputting in equal measure.[65] The only social constituencies that were consistently successful in penetrating these policy arenas were local business elites and powerful city-wide local authorities that tended to view them as vehicles for the pursuit of their own interests.

The gap between the grandiosity of the democratic claims that were made on behalf of regional government and the opaque complexity of the administrative system associated with it did much to confirm Labour's reputation as a party that was indelibly wedded to an unresponsive and top-down form of governance. A good deal of energy during Labour's second and third terms in government was devoted to the technical challenges of attempting to join up this mosaic of bodies and functions, while avoiding functional duplication.[66]

LABOUR'S 'NEW LOCALISM'

The abiding limitations of these attempts to pass off an incrementally developed system of regional administration as an answer to the question of whether devolving powers within England was both democratically and economically imperative engendered an appetite for a very different approach during Labour's years in government. This involved a commitment to the idea of delegating powers to local authorities rather than the quangos and appointed bodies associated with the regions. A significant strand of support for this kind of 'localism' emerged within the Blair governments and found favour with leading Ministers and advisers.[67] Proponents of the 'new localism' tended to combine this ambition with the advocacy of major reforms to local government. Some figures, such as Minister for Communities and Local Government David Miliband, went further still, arguing for a deeper devolving impulse, with decision-making powers passed to communities and neighbourhoods.[68]

This seam of thinking encompassed, rather than challenged, the leadership's entrenched wariness towards local government, a stance reflected in the array of targets it introduced to assess local authority performance, and its refusal to countenance the idea of passing any significant degree of financial control to councils.[69] In key respects Labour approached local government with the same mixture of suspicion and frustration as its Conservative predecessors. The ambitions to loosen the hold of local political elites and establish clearer forms of executive authority fed into the Local Government Act of 2000. This legislation resulted in the abolition of the 'Committee system' used by town halls, and the introduction of a standardized, executive-led model of administration. The Act also included proposals for local referenda on the introduction of directly elected mayors. These proposals encountered considerable opposition, however, in all of the political parties, including Labour itself. Yet, the government refrained from setting out a strong public case for the mayoral model, or promoting a national debate about its merits.[70] As a result, most of the referenda that were held elicited little interest, while local parties often led the opposition to this idea. Only a handful of these ballots were consequently won by campaigners for the mayoral model.[71] The vision of a remodelled and greatly empowered system of local government, led by a visible and accountable leader, was therefore implemented in a handful of places, and hardly any major cities outside London. The Greater London Authority Act of 1999, by contrast, introduced to London a directly elected assembly and mayor, and passed a raft of new powers to the city's reconstituted government. This reform was implemented following a referendum held at the same time as London borough elections in May 2000. Nearly three-quarters of those voting backed this plan, though the idea itself evoked indifference, with only a third of potential electors choosing to vote at all.

But senior localists in the Labour party continued to champion an alternative form of democratic renewal and a less top-down model of governance to that associated with regionalism. An increasingly vocal argument for the delegation of powers to a tranche of consolidated, city-wide authorities, known as 'city-regions', became especially influential.[72] And some Labour figures saw in city-based localism the glimmerings of a very different kind of answer to the English question. Sheffield MP and Labour Minister David Blunkett identified the importance of reanimating 'English civic cultures' in various cities and localities outside London, and drew attention to one particular variant of the Northern Englishness that had become a major part of the Labour tradition in the late nineteenth century.[73] He argued for a focus upon locality as the bedrock for a reflowering of the cultures that had developed in England's great cities in the Victorian era. His position remained a maverick one under the Blair and Brown administrations, both of which tended to give pride of place to Britishness, and ignored or rejected the idea of a greater focus upon English national identity. But it has, to some extent, been given a new lease of life, more recently, by the Hannah Mitchell Foundation, which has been campaigning to some effect for Northern devolution.[74]

The idea of regional government palpably failed to resonate at a popular level, and its assertion became increasingly doctrinaire in nature.[75] Michael Wills MP, Minister for Constitutional Affairs during the Gordon Brown government, advanced the similarly implausible claim that Britishness was being renewed in these years as an organic national identity among the English.[76] Brown's insistently Whiggish retelling of the British story involved reappropriating as 'British' texts, figures, and episodes that were, more accurately, regarded as English in terms of their historical origins and cultural significance.[77] And the suspicion expressed by critics that this reflected a deliberate attempt to efface an English lineage, in cultural and political terms, was confirmed when Brown set out an ambitious portfolio for constitutional reform in the early days of his premiership, in his much trumpeted Green Paper *The Governance of Britain*.[78] In this major document, which set out the various constitutional issues that the government was determined to tackle, no space could be found for mention of the English question, and the largest nation itself was notable by its absence. Nor was this the only occasion when Brown opted not to mention the largest nation when discussing the UK and its constitution. In a pamphlet he co-authored with Scottish MP Douglas Alexander, on the importance of the union in 2007, England also failed to appear.[79]

Once Labour returned to opposition in 2010, and with the disappearance of the endemic rivalry between Prime Minister Blair and his successor Brown, the rather artificial competition between localists and regionalists diminished significantly. New leader Ed Miliband increasingly gave a hearing to figures such as Jon Cruddas MP whose interest in Englishness had been deemed maverick during the New Labour years. He argued for the revival of a latterly forgotten strand of Labour's heritage, the blending of radical and patriotic thinking that had been a major intellectual influence when the Labour move-ment was founded.[80] And, as the Labour leader himself acknowledged in a key-note speech about Englishness which he delivered in 2012, for the majority of citizens in the UK, patriotism was most likely to be focused upon England, in addition to the other kinds of affiliation and community that were held dear.[81] This apparently new departure in Labour's thinking has yet to be matched by any serious reconsideration of its policy positions in this area. Above all, the question of whether Labour accepts—as its Conservative rivals have come to do—that England's position within the union may need to be addressed, remains far from clear.[82]

POPULIST AND NATIONALIST RESPONSES TO THE ENGLISH QUESTION

While Labour focused for the most part on the question of how to devolve power and authority to lower levels within England, a rumbling of discon-tent about whether some form of national-democratic representation was now needed for the English gradually moved into the political mainstream dur-ing the 2000s. This assertion was buoyed by a rising sense of disenchantment with politicians and the political system, which was sharply accentuated by the MPs' expenses scandal of 2009. In this increasingly anti-political atmos-phere, the language of populism—in which 'the political class' was depicted as self-serving, out of touch, and monochrome in its thinking—provided an increasingly resonant and self-reinforcing vernacular.[83] This form of thinking found ready expression in various demands for the introduction of a more symmetrical system of devolution within the UK. These were aired by a num-ber of different parties and organizations located on the fringes of the party system. In this section I consider the fate and contribution of those groups that either mobilized on the specific question of England's constitutional position or identified, more generally, with the Anglo-nationalist cause in this period.

Nearly all of these endeavours have remained outside, or at the margins of, the Westminster political system, and, in combination, have helped project a broadly nationalist sensibility into the wider political culture. None have suc-ceeded in fermenting a significant mobilization outside parliament, or per-suaded any of the leading parties to change tack on these issues. I consider various possible explanations for the inability of these groups to catalyse a wider nationalist movement. And I point to the possibility that, even in the most recent period, when scepticism about politicians has been particularly acute, mainstream politics possesses an under-estimated resilience in the UK, and this is based in part upon a rather overlooked capacity to absorb shifting patterns of sentiments among the English populace. I argue also for greater acknowledgement of the contribution that this current has made to one of the most important developments in contemporary politics: the opening of a nationalist-populist space to the right of the Conservative party, which is very different in kind from the model of far-right politics of previous decades.[84]

THE CAMPAIGN FOR AN ENGLISH PARLIAMENT

The most important addition to the ecology of established political organizations which a growing concern with the English question has brought into being is the Campaign for an English Parliament (CEP). Aside from the Conservative party's brief liaison with this idea under the leadership of Hague, only a small number of MPs have spoken out in favour of the notion of introducing an equivalent assembly for the English to that which has been granted to the Scots and Welsh. A handful of mainly Conservative MPs and right-wing pundits have associated themselves with this idea. These figures have tended to argue that the recreation of an English parliament constitutes the best way of defending the principle of an uncodified constitution that would reflect the virtues of a smaller state and individual liberty, a view that was forcefully presented by Heffer in 1999.[85] In this view, the values and identity of an independent England would prove remarkably similar to those associated with right-wing sections of the Conservative party.

Such voices aside, support for an English Parliament remains anathema at Westminster, and it has been left to outsider figures and groups to promote this proposal. The CEP is the main organization associated with this idea. It formed as a non-denominational lobbying group devoted to making the case for an equivalent referendum to that which presaged devolution in Scotland and Wales. And it has sustained itself as a fringe lobbying group rather than becoming a grass-roots campaign, though its fairly small activist base is belied by its high visibility on the political blogosphere.[86] While the Campaign's official position has been that the English should also have an equal right to the exercise of national sovereignty to rectify the profound imbalances created by devolution, it has never fully shaken off the charge that some of its supporters see this as a stepping-stone to the dissolution of the UK. For the most part, the CEP has presented itself as a single-issue campaign, seeking to stand apart from English nationalist currents, and proclaiming its commitment to a civic, rather than ethnic, conception of the English nation. It has never had a large formal membership. One commentator estimated that it had approximately 1,000 members during the 2000s, with most coming from Southern England and London.[87] The Campaign has been run with very little funding and, lacking the support of wealthy donors, has relied heavily upon the efforts of volunteers.

The CEP grew out of the tiny English Parliament Movement (EPM) that existed prior to devolution. The idea of a more broadly focused campaign was discussed at a meeting held in June 1998 which was attended by a handful of activists long associated with this cause, and the CEP was formed later that year. At its first major national conference, in November 2003, it called for 'political, constitutional and cultural equality between the three countries of the island of Britain within the Union', and demanded that the government introduce a form of devolution for England on the same basis as that held in Scotland.

Its members were inveterately opposed to the Labour government's support for regional government, and invested considerable energy in its early years to opposing these reforms. The CEP's most significant intervention arose from its role in the launch of the English Constitutional Convention in 2004. The Convention idea fizzled out quickly, however, partly because of the organizational strain which this venture placed upon the CEP and, more fundamentally, due to its apparent failure to achieve a wider popular resonance.[88]

THE ENGLISH DEMOCRATS

Competitor organizations also sprang up in this period, seeking to exploit the possibility of a growing sense of English grievance, while paying less attention to the constitutional questions animating the CEP. These have also, however, struggled to prompt and sustain a wider nationalist mobilization. The English Democrats (ED) came into existence as a political party in 1997. With a small formal membership and an even smaller activist core, it has campaigned in nakedly populist terms for recognition of the cultural and historical distinctiveness of the English. The party supports an English Parliament, but frames this demand within a broader agenda, including a call for stricter immigration controls, a referendum on the UK's future within the European Union, and protests against the allegedly anti-English bias of institutions such as the BBC.

ED's decision to stand candidates in elections during the 2000s helped raise its national profile quite considerably.[89] It ran in twenty-four constituencies in the 2005 General Election, winning approximately 15,000 votes. Its most notable triumph was the election of one of its candidates, Peter Davies, to the position of directly elected mayor of Doncaster in 2009, though he resigned from the party in 2013, giving as his principal reason the growing influx of refugees from the British National Party (BNP) into its ranks.[90] Robin Tilbrook a former Conservative party member, founded ED's predecessor, the English National Party in 1997, and relaunched it as ED in 2002, with the call for an English Parliament its main campaigning focus.[91] He remains the dominant presence within this party, serving as its nominating officer and treasurer, and standing as a candidate in local, parliamentary, and European elections. Apart from sporadic successes in local and European elections, the party has performed poorly in General Elections, and been unable to establish itself as the pre-eminent populist party outside the political mainstream.

In the wake of the recent downturn experienced by the BNP, ED is reported to have become the home to a number of former BNP activists, and to have positioned itself as an alternative for disenchanted voters who had previously supported the BNP in local and European elections.[92] At present, its prospects of becoming the leading force on the populist right are significantly dented by the growing prominence and appeal of the United Kingdom Independence Party (UKIP).

THE ENGLISH DEFENCE LEAGUE

While both the CEP and ED have sought to secure leverage within the current party system, a very different kind of organization, the English Defence League (EDL), has emerged during this period, mobilizing a looser and more inchoate sense of British nationalism, while expressing little interest in the constitutional dimensions of the English question. It has contributed importantly to the shifting ecology of nationalist and populist politics in this period.[93] The EDL has focused almost entirely upon street-level politics, organizing a large number of symbolic marches and protests that typically seek to dramatize its opposition to the presence and influence of Muslim populations in various multi-racial towns and cities. Its rhetorical appeal to a once great nation, that is now desperately in need of vigorous defence from below, taps into the growing mood of English-focused grievance, as does its keen identification with the language and icons of disaffected nationhood.[94] The EDL is not formally committed to English nationalism, and its political appeal is designed to operate at two separate levels. In its public statements it identifies proudly with British traditions and institutions, and parades its commitment to Britain as a liberal and multicultural nation. But liberal democracy is now, it declares, threatened by the 'enemy within', and this is defined in terms of the presence of radical forms of Islam. The second, distinct level at which its political appeal is pitched is apparent when the EDL 'performs' its brand of nationalism at demonstrations and marches. At these, visceral forms of ethnic chauvinism directed at Muslims and other minority groups are widely reported.[95]

This unusual mobilization developed from a set of networks that were previously associated with football hooliganism and far-right activism. The EDL first appeared in 2009, growing out of a group calling itself the United People of Luton, and was formed after a handful of radical Islamists protested against the return of the Royal Anglican Regiments from Afghanistan during a homecoming parade. A small, militant group of far-right supporters already existed in Luton. Following the March 2009 incident, it became more organized, and turned itself into the United People of Luton. Its first protests were typically small and disorganized, but the group mushroomed rapidly during the following year, as it gained a considerable amount of media exposure, and subsequently adopted a more organized structure.

During the later months of 2009, the numbers attending EDL marches grew dramatically. In a short period of time it turned into a significant street-level protest movement, capable of mobilizing over 1,000 protesters for demonstrations in major cities. In January 2010, the EDL boasted on its Twitter website that it had 8,013 followers on its official forum, and 12,038 people affiliated to its Facebook page.[96] Its profile rests upon the dramatic, and often violent, character of its public performances of working-class alienation. This offers a style of politics in marked contrast to the increasingly electoral focus being adopted by the established party of the far-right, the British National Party.[97] At the protest it organized in Birmingham in September 2009, for instance, ninety arrests were made, as EDL supporters clashed with the police and local Asian youths in a series of running battles in and around the city centre.

The EDL's primary constituency has been among white working-class youth though, as one recent study shows, its activists are, for the most part, recruited from established communities of football hooligans.[98] The most concrete political aim associated with its polemical rhetoric is to dramatize the need for traditional forms of Anglo-British patriotism to be vigorously protected, in part because of the indifference and contempt for national traditions associated with the political elite. Its more concrete tactical ambition is to foment tension between young white men involved in, or on the fringes of, football hooligan networks, and Muslim youth in cities and towns across England and Wales.

One recent study of the online activities associated with the EDL suggested that its appeal went beyond those who actively appear on its marches and demonstrations.[99] This traced a significant, wider community of latent affiliation which is drawn to the contention that the liberal values and multicultural character of the British inheritance are threatened by the Muslim population. The organization went to considerable lengths to found Jewish and gay wings to symbolize these commitments.[100] This study also estimated the size of the online community that engages with the EDL to comprise 25,000–30,000 people.[101] And it found that only 30 per cent of its online participants had been educated to university or college level, an overwhelming proportion were male (81%), and a disproportionately high number unemployed. Its authors concluded that that most EDL sympathizers see their own views as quite distinct from those of the older far-right. Most profess their strong support for democratic principles, and an overwhelming majority invoke immigration as the main concern leading them towards the EDL. Forty-two per cent suggested that it is one of the top two issues facing the country, while a 'love of England'—signalling a 'commitment to preserving traditional national and cultural values, and a belief in representing the interests of "real" countrymen'—was the second most common reason given for identifying with it.[102]

By early 2011, the EDL had held over fifty demonstrations across England, with most eliciting considerable local and national media coverage. Since that point its fortunes have ebbed, leading to a growing debate within its ranks about whether it ought to fight elections in order to develop a more sustainable and legitimate political presence.

The broader significance of this new kind of street-cum-online protest politics has been much debated, with some commentators regarding the EDL as the harbinger of a rising tide of anti-political and anti-migrant populism of the sort that has made significant headway in other European states.[103] Yet the kinds of political mobilization of this sort that have happened so spectacularly in other political systems have not been paralleled in the UK, in part because the right-wing populist space exploited by parties elsewhere has proved much harder for any single group or party to command in a polity that retains a clear bias towards larger, well-funded, and organized parties. The EDL's lack of enduring political impact might also be explained by the presence of the largest and best-known far-right party, the BNP.

THE BRITISH NATIONAL PARTY

The marked recent decline of the British National Party (BNP) followed a period of considerable success for it. During the early and middle years of the 2000s it garnered increasing levels of support when it stood candidates

in elections, and received an unprecedented amount of media coverage following the election of a number of its candidates to council elections in parts
of London, the Midlands, and the North West. In 2006, the party came very
close to winning overall control of Barking Council, a high-water mark in its
impact upon mainstream politics. And yet, despite these various successes, the
BNP has been riven with internal divisions, and a new, modernizing leadership under Nick Griffin has come under considerable internal pressure following its relatively poor performance in the General Election of 2010. Recent
research has also suggested that the party's lingering associations with fascism
have placed a ceiling upon its capacity to move beyond an established core
vote, located predominantly in white working-class communities in London,
the Midlands, and the North West.[104] The extent to which the BNP's support
is confined to the 'white working class', however, has been the subject of quite
considerable debate, with some commentary suggesting that it has attracted
cross-class support to a degree that has been under-estimated.[105]

The BNP has been significantly affected by the growing sense of awareness of English identity in this period. And a lively internal debate about the
pro-British stance that has historically informed the party's outlook has broken out in recent years. In an essay published in its internal magazine *Identity*
in 2007, Deputy Treasurer David Hannan argued that, while the BNP had
been hostile to devolution on the grounds that it would accentuate divisons
within the Anglo-British nation, now that English nationalism was growing, it
was time to think afresh.[106] Hannan spied a considerable opportunity for the
BNP, but worried that the party's hesitation about the implications of English
nationalism—even though it had adopted support for an English Parliament
as part of its policy platform in 2006—was inhibiting its ability to capitalize.[107]
In the vernacular characteristic of internal BNP discourse, he declared that
English nationalism amounted to 'Ethnic English Nationalism' and declared
that 'the term English is a refuge for the racially aware voter.[108] This is our
territory!'[109] It was England that now offered a meaningful symbolic refuge
from the multicultural idea, with the latter being increasingly associated with
Britain and Britishness:

> the rise of English ethnic consciousness is now well under way, primarily as a
> natural reaction to the ruthlessly propagated fiction that all the hundreds of dif-
> ferent racial groups who have come to our shores since 1948 are now 'British'.[110]

Hannan noted that these issues were potentially 'awkward' for a party that had
historically identified itself as a British nationalist one, and which retained
bases of support in Wales and Scotland. And, while the BNP did, in these years,
begin to employ the iconography of English nationhood more extensively, the

party has not, as yet, made a public break with its British heritage, and has remained wary of identifying too strongly with this particular cause.

THE UK INDEPENDENCE PARTY

The constitutional and political dimensions of English nationalism have largely been incidental to the political appeal of the EDL and BNP during these years. The only real sign that debates about sovereignty and nationhood within the UK might gain traction at the popular level concerned the rise and strength of Eurosceptic sentiments. Wellings, as we have seen, has maintained that the resistance to the project of further European integration that swelled in the early 1990s incubated a renewed sense of English nationalism, suggesting that this took the form of the defence of the principle of British sovereignty, allied to the conviction that a people's referendum on Europe was now imperative.[111] More generally, various commentators have noted a correlation between Euroscepticism and the inclination to prioritize English identity. Thus, recent polling has found that those who self-identified as English tended to be more hostile to the UK's membership of the European Union than those who saw themselves as British, first and foremost.[112] According to psephologist Peter Kellner, 'What distinguishes people who call themselves "English" is a passion for keeping other countries at arm's length.'[113]

In this context, the rising popularity of the United Kingdom Independence Party (UKIP) in recent years and the fusion of Europhobic and Anglo-focused nationalism which it has promoted are of particular significance. The electoral fortunes of UKIP have fluctuated quite markedly in the last decade.[114] And, until recently, despite its considerable success in successive European elections, it struggled to have an effect in either local or national elections. It has, however, steadily increased its vote share, and—importantly—begun to appeal to a cross-class range of voters, while gaining acceptance as an increasingly legitimate and mainstream voice within political debate.[115] In the last few years in particular, the party has settled on a broad-ranging kind of right-wing populism, and has gained a hearing on issues other than Europe, while adhering to a traditionalist form of (highly Anglicized) British patriotism. And it has increasingly sought to wrap references to the unfair treatment of the English in its broader critique of the inequities of the political system.[116] This strategy has begun to pay off, securing the party a respectable third place in two successive by-elections in 2012, and an impressive second place—ahead of the Tory party—in the Eastleigh by-election of March 2013. It is currently enjoying a buoyant position within the opinion polls, and achieved a spectacular result in the council elections of May 2013, winning 26 per cent of the vote in England.

One recent analysis of its appeal has insisted that Europe is not itself a major dynamic attracting voters to UKIP.[117] Rather, it is its capacity to express a more generalized sense of disaffection and a mood of national decline—sentiments that are often linked to a stronger sense of English identification—that have made the party a home for those keen to register a protest against the political system as a whole.[118] Polling commissioned in 2013 by Conservative peer Lord Michael Ashcroft revealed that UKIP appeals most strongly to those with a broad sense of disquiet about the direction that the country is taking, and are most inclined to identify with the populist and nationalist sensibility that we considered in Chapter 4:

> schools, they say, can't hold nativity plays or harvest festivals any more; you can't fly a flag of St George any more; you can't call Christmas Christmas any more; you won't be promoted in the police force unless you're from a minority; you can't wear an England shirt on the bus; you won't get social housing unless you're an immigrant; you can't speak up about these things because you'll be called a racist; you can't even smack your children.[119]

The perception that, unlike its mainstream counterparts, UKIP will 'say things that need to be said but others are scared to say' is, Ashcroft concluded, a more important attractor for those inclined to think in this way than the party's particular stance on the EU or immigration policy.[120] According to the recent Future of England survey, conducted in 2012, UKIP is seen by the largest number of English people (21 per cent) as most likely to 'stand up for England's interests'.[121] The level of support it has received in response to this question has more than doubled in just two years.[122] The formal policy positions espoused by UKIP on such issues as the English question are, this analysis suggests, less important than the generalized mood that it has sought to mobilize. An appeal to an injured and disavowed sense of Englishness figures as an important theme within this wider discourse of complaint. But the party has also increasingly come under pressure to address England's constitutional position in more programmatic terms and to engage with rising currents of English nationalism, towards which its current leadership remains wary. In 1997 a working group was formed within the party calling for an English Parliament.[123] Bolstered by an influx of activists from ED, most of UKIP's leadership, including current leader Nigel Farage, have drifted towards a more favourable stance regarding an English Parliament. In 2011 UKIP declared its support for this measure, accepting a proposal advanced by the party's MEP Paul Nuttall at its annual conference.[124] This called for the creation of a legislature that would include representatives elected to seats modelled upon county borders, and topped up by additional members, and also argued for the establishment of an English-only executive authority within the UK state. But this stance encountered significant resistance from Welsh, anti-devolutionist members and also from those whose highly traditional sense of Britishness precludes an engagement with English nationalism. Other leading figures remain wary of a cause that might obscure UKIP's signature anti-European stance.[125] Yet, as recent polling has pointed to a very strong correlation between those who feel most strongly about their English identity and a proclivity to vote for UKIP, it may well be that the latter's leadership will be drawn towards a more wholehearted engagement with populist forms of Englishness, not least because of its weak electoral position outside England.[126]

CONCLUSIONS: ENGLISHNESS POLITICIZED OR THE ANGLICIZATION OF BRITISH POLITICS?

None of the organizations and groups considered here have succeeded in galvanizing the consciousness of the English public about the national question on anything more than a fleeting basis. And the most successful of them, UKIP, has identified more strongly associated with the issues of Europe and immigration than the English question, though this is an issue which it may come to address more fully. It could be that the inability of these organizations to mobilize a populist, subaltern English patriotism bears out Wellings's contention—that for many of the English, an incipient sense of nationalism has, paradoxically, been expressed through a renewed sense of affiliation to traditional ideas of British sovereignty. But another possibility is also worth considering: that the development of other, rival expressions of English nationhood may have worked to offset the appeal of a demotic and populist sense of Englishness. It is certainly striking that, despite the recurrent fears of politicians and commentators that resentful Englishness may become the vehicle for the wider expression of disaffection with the political system, these groups have not been able to catalyse a wider nationalist movement. A politicized English nationalism, which is the antithesis of established forms of Britishness, has not taken root as a mass phenomenon in the last fifteen years. And, while I have emphasized the uncertainties and difficulties which an interlocking set of national questions are posing for mainstream politicians, it is also clear that the kinds of resentment, alienation, and populism that have at times been associated with the English cause, have not been mobilized to any significant or long-lasting effect on the far-right of British politics.

More generally, neither of the two main perspectives upon English attitudes since devolution offers an entirely satisfactory account of the political and policy dimensions of English nationhood in these years. The insistence, on the one hand, that devolution has unleashed a nascent nationalism, and, on the other, the notion that Englishness is forever 'merely cultural', do not do justice to the political resonances and ramifications of debates about the English question in this period. As we shall see in Chapter 6, several questions about the treatment of England within the post-devolved union have attracted growing interest in recent years. At the same time, it is clear that in so far as many of the English have become more aware of, and proud about, their own sense of nationality, this has not primarily happened as a result of devolution-envy. Rather, the gradual diffusion of a sense of irritation as England's interests and identity are seen as being unduly marginalized is tangled up with the intuitive perception that various kinds of unfairness arise from the systems of governance and political representation that now prevail.[127] At the same time, a sense of injured national interest has been offset by grievances rooted in perceptions of inter-English inequity. Different parts of England, particularly its Northern regions, have become increasingly aware of, and assertive about, their own diminished collective interests in comparison with London, on the one hand, and Scotland on the other.[128] This growing sense of regionally rooted resentment has both cut across and fractured common expressions and understandings of English interest in this period.

Within the arenas of politics, considerable debate has been aired about the appropriate policy response to the English question, as we have seen, and this has mostly been determined by the partisan stances of both main parties. An anonymous survey of MPs conducted in 2009 revealed a clear cross-party consensus in favour of the notion that the constitutional position of the English now needed to be addressed.[129] It also found, however, that on some iconic questions—notably the issue of the Barnett formula and whether English identity should be given greater public recognition—MPs have far more varied views than is suggested by the official positions adopted by their parties. A majority, including many Labour MPs, indicated their conviction that the current public funding settlement across the territories of the UK was in need of alteration.[130] These findings would appear to indicate that—contrary to the assumptions of many campaigners and commentators—there is broad agreement spanning the divide between politicians and public opinion that the business of devolution remains unfinished in relation to the English.

And yet, the political risks and policy difficulties associated with the tasks of devolving governance and authority within England remain quite considerable. As Aughey has wryly noted, there is in British politics an abiding sense that politicians are 'damned if they do and damned if they don't', when it comes to this issue, a perception that has done much to inhibit the promotion of a democratic and forward-looking agenda in relation to the union.[131] But the development of a more reflexive and explicit sense of English identity is beginning to exert some quiet, but real, political effects. These are most apparent, as we shall see in Chapter 6, in relation to several touchstone issues that act as conduits for a more generalized sense of disquiet about how England is being governed. And politicians are now beginning—if in faltering and reactive, rather than reasoned and proactive, ways—to respond to these trends. The language and assumptions of party politics at Westminster have become more aligned with English cultural priorities and debates in this period. Indeed, this unspoken responsiveness, in combination with the resilience of the party system itself, may well help explain why a rising sense of English grievance has not translated into anything more than fleeting support for nationalist and populist causes.

It is in the Conservative party that the will and ability to act on these questions are most apparent. Yet, being a pro-Unionist party that is increasingly reliant upon English support, in representative terms, leaves it facing an awkward balancing act between 'an English temptation and a Unionist vocation', and these impulses are likely to pull further apart over time.[132] The party's leadership is faced by a difficult set of cross-currents generated by the coincidence of a number of different, loosely related, pressures, including: a renewed focus upon the UK's membership of the European Union and the rise of UKIP; the forthcoming referendum on whether Scotland should leave the UK; and the proposals for reform of the House of Commons set out in the report produced by the McKay Commission in 2013.

And, for its part, Labour's consistent denial that England needed or desired the kind of devolution that was introduced elsewhere in the UK has become decreasingly credible.[133] The party's inability, during its long years in office, to settle upon a convincing model of devolution for England, has left it vulnerable to the accusation that it is unable to respond authentically to either the national or democratic dimensions of the English question, primarily because of its dependence upon Scottish and Welsh MPs. Since it has been in opposition since 2010, a more open debate about these issues has broken out, but the party remains fundamentally unsure whether it should engage with this issue, or continue to hope that the demands and claims associated with it will disappear. The suspicion remains that Labour is decidedly uncomfortable on this terrain, and clings to the belief that redistribution and stability delivered through the long arms of the British state will win back the hearts and minds of the English people, despite the likelihood that popular disenchantment is in part directed at the systems of governance and politics which prevail within England. As Ascherson shrewdly observed:

> In general terms Labour continues to suffer from a major reputational problem in this area, which makes it generally inclined to avoid, rather than explore, these issues. A growing section of the English public came to believe, in the middle of the noughties, that the party depends disproportionately upon Scottish MPs, and that it still does not understand Southern English values or culture. This is perhaps not surprising given that the party has generally been united in this period by its wariness towards Englishness which it has dismissed as inherently regressive and chauvinist in character.[134]

As it becomes ever clearer that devolution is more like a slowly turning ratchet, rather than a stable settlement, and as the Westminster parliament is gradually evolving into an English-focused one, both of the main parties may well find themselves forced to engage more proactively and imaginatively with these national and constitutional issues. Indeed, even if Scotland votes against independence in 2014, the likely scenario that it is granted additional powers, including a greater degree of fiscal autonomy, will inadvertently make the question of whether Scottish MPs can still be returned to Westminster on the same basis as their English counterparts a contentious one.

More generally, while various different threats to the union have been considered at length in both political and academic commentary in recent years, more attention needs to be paid to the implications of changes in the forms and character of English national identity in relation to them. The guiding assumption of the architects of devolution that a backlash among the English was unlikely because of their abiding attachment to the structures and conventions of parliamentary government, has slowly crumbled, and been replaced in political circles by an anxiety about where the febrile and unpredictable mood of the English might lead. This anxiety ought to be understood in the context of a longer-range crisis of purpose affecting British politics and governance since the middle decades of the last century, as the various common enterprises in relation to which Britain was understood—ranging from Empire to warfare and, more recently, welfare—have waned in popular appeal. Their gradual fading provides a key background factor shaping the re-emergence of a sharpened sense of English identity.[135] Equally, the appearance of the question of European integration as a major point of contention in British politics, and the provision of devolution for other parts of the UK, have provided important, subsequent factors.

Despite the weak, short-term incentives that exist for politicians to engage with these issues, greater attention to them will soon be unavoidable. At the very least, a reconstituted vision of the case for the union, and a clearer account of what ought to be the various powers and entitlements associated with UK citizenship, in contrast to the different levels of autonomy enjoyed by the various political centres within it, will become imperative.[136] Such a focus may well go some way towards addressing the palpable sense of hurt among many of the English at the slight they perceive to their own sense of national-democratic right—an idea that is explored in greater depth in Chapter 6. Prime Minister Cameron's intimation in 2012 that, should the Scottish people vote against independence in 2014, further phases of devolution ought to take place within a UK-wide framework, pointed in this direction. Whether it also signalled that a broader democratic conversation about what ought to be the content of the entitlements and rights associated with UK-wide citizenship, and what might legitimately be provided differentially in the various territories of the UK, will ensue, remains to be seen.[137] Ultimately it is only such a wide-ranging debate that will enable a renewal of the legitimacy and sense of common purpose which the union is likely to require. It may well be that the current phase of devolution—which can be characterized as the cautious and incremental passing of limited powers to the UK's peripheries—may soon be superseded by a new phase in which the position of the dominant nation within a devolved United Kingdom becomes the focus for concerted political attention and policy debate.

6

Political Intimations of English Grievance

West Lothian and the Barnett Formula

INTRODUCTION

We saw in Chapter 5 how debates about the prospect of some form of devolution within England developed at Westminster during the 2000s. In this chapter I focus in more depth upon two of the specific issues that have become intimately associated with the English question in political discourse, even though each has deep historical roots and predates the introduction of devolution. I argue that it is in relation to these thorny problems, in particular, that a palpable sense of grievance among parts of the English public has welled up. I also chart the major debates that have developed on these themes, and assess the gathering momentum behind arguments for reform in both cases. And I tease out the underpinning constitutional and democratic principles that are increasingly at stake in relation to them. These have for too long been obscured by the ingrained habit of approaching these questions within the normative parameters associated with the Westminster model of governance. I conclude by suggesting that a growing sense of English disaffection in relation to West Lothian and the distribution of public expenditure across the UK should be understood as a sign that a deeply held sense of procedural fairness has been violated, rather than dismissed as a species of the 'sour me too-ism' which much commentary continues to identify as the core of English national consciousness.[1]

UNDERSTANDING DEVOLUTION, UK STYLE

In order to grasp the significance of rising public concern and intensifying policy debates about these particular questions, it is imperative to consider some of the main institutional and normative characteristics of the British model of territorial politics, and the nature and democratic implications of the devolution legislation introduced by Labour in the late 1990s. A comparative perspective upon the territorial dimension of the British system of governance serves to bring some of the main characteristics of the latter into particular relief. Various commentators have noted that Britain has been highly unusual in not attending to the establishment of institutional structures and intergovernmental forms of coordination, and in not generating new statements of common entitlement as accompaniments to the granting of greater legislative autonomy to its peripheries.[2] In other states devolution has generally involved both a centrifugal dynamic, wherein powers are granted to territories at some distance from the centre, and an accompanying focus upon compensatory forms of integration and coordination.[3] Jeffery and Wincott have pointed to the decidedly 'understated quality of intergovernmental relationships' in the UK's case.[4] The generation of any counter-balancing dynamic to the centrifugal processes unleashed by these reforms have been given little consideration, unlike in federal states where the centre itself has been extensively remodelled in the wake of significant programmes of national and regional devolution.

But in the UK the lack of any sustained focus on the need to bolster the institutional and civic components of what some have called 'the fifth nation', may well have supplied one further cause of the depletion of the substantive quality of Britishness in this period.[5] The lack of any clear delineation of the UK-wide remit of the core institutions of the state in the wake of the introduction of devolution has resulted in a deepening confusion about the entitlements and rights that citizens living in any of its territories possess. In this context, there has been little to counter the misleading impression, stoked by sections of the media, that the English are subsidizing the political autonomy of the other territories within the UK.

And, in institutional terms, awareness has grown that England is, for the most part, governed by the highly centralized departments at the heart of the British state. Numerous commentators have declared that this form of governance is both insufficiently accountable, and overly distant from the diverse local conditions and needs that affect the delivery of a range of public services.[6] Thus, the House of Commons Justice Committee identified the 'missing centre' at the heart of this new system of constrained self-government as a major problem in its fifth report on the workings of devolution.[7] It went on to highlight the lack of attention paid in Whitehall to the establishment of mechanisms and institutions designed to ensure coordination between the newly established layers of government, and stressed the importance of ensuring that UK-wide purposes were still being served. The variable territorial remit of Whitehall departments, and the significant increase in the degree to which most of the domestic Ministries have come to focus predominantly on England since 1999, have indeed begun to have unforeseen effects on public perceptions of the country's governance. And yet, politicians and parties have remained disinclined to speak in clear terms about the manner in which England is governed, or to debate the increasingly apparent dysfunctions associated with administering a territory the size of England from Whitehall. The rising sense of disenchantment and inequity which is outlined here is, as a result, addressed mainly by populist critics and tabloid newspapers rather than by voices from the political mainstream.

In seeking to explain the incremental and piecemeal nature of the UK's approach to devolution, some commentators have identified the 'path dependent' manner in which devolution was introduced in the UK, stressing the historically established pattern whereby the state had instituted special arrangements for the governance of its most far-flung territories.[8] The UK, it has recently been argued, should be seen as a 'state of unions', rather than a unitary or union state, contrary to the established understanding of its guardians.[9] The systems and institutions of British governance have, on this view, developed through the historically contingent agreements reached between the English-dominated state and the peoples of Scotland, Wales, and Ireland.[10] The development of an expanded legislature which protected the dominant values of English constitutionalism and parliamentary practice was accompanied by the granting of various degrees of legislative autonomy to these different peoples.[11] Thus, while the English parliament ceased formally to exist in 1707, in practice it expanded after union with Scotland, and absorbed territories from other parts of Britain, becoming the legislature of the whole of the kingdom. But, securing the hegemony of the state within this expanded territory was premised upon the recognition that significant concessions in terms of the manner in which the non-English territories were governed would need to be granted on an *ad hoc* basis, and adjusted to offset the potential intensification of nationalist sentiment.

Viewed in this way, devolution can be seen as the continuation of an ingrained habit of Anglo-British statecraft, reflecting the imperative to secure democratic legitimacy for a system of variable territorial governance. The devolution package introduced by Labour in the late 1990s was not, therefore, the decisive break from the tradition of unitary sovereignty which it has often been assumed to represent.[12] This perspective goes some way to explaining the lack of attention paid to the organization and remit of the central state itself, as devolution was devised and implemented. And, accordingly, intergovernmental relations have developed in a largely haphazard and uncoordinated fashion. As a result, the British system of representative government has become even more lopsided in a period when states throughout the Western world are finding the task of governing in the face of the rising expectations of their citizens increasingly challenging, and when many of Britain's European counterparts have found it expedient to delegate powers to subnational tiers of government.

In the UK the referendum now scheduled on Scottish independence, due to be held in 2014, has instigated a rare moment of sustained public debate about the rationale for, and future of, the union, bringing to the surface foundational questions about state organization and capacity, and what British citizenship should mean. A recent volume reflecting on the experience of devolution has proposed the case for a thicker model of shared social citizenship across the UK in order to provide a bulwark against the inexorable process of 'ever loosening Union'.[13] As Aughey has also observed, since devolution:

> Bargaining between the territories is more visible than the multinational solidarity that makes such bargaining possible in the first place. As a consequence, the English question has become England's British question, and the question is to what extent devolution has undermined English patriotic identification with the UK.[14]

Denied a separate legal identity within the system of parliamentary government, England has gradually come to acquire a distinctive and identifiable set of governing institutions, though as an unintended result of these reforms rather than by purposeful design.[15] This underlying drift was only thinly veiled by the proclamation of Britishness associated with New Labour's years in government, and with Chancellor and Prime Minister Brown in particular. As one critic put it: his notion of ' "the British way" negated the idea of England as a political community', and 'created a postcode lottery in citizenship and accountability' across the UK.[16]

Despite Brown's best efforts, this period witnessed the fragile blooming of a new set of ideas about the actual and potential separation of Britain and England, in political and institutional terms. Rather than stemming from any sudden upsurge in English nationalism, however, this was mainly instigated by the uncertainty generated by the weakening hold of long-established forms of national and constitutional thinking. Other shifts in public attitude may also have played a part in generating a more dyspeptic attitude among the English towards their governing institutions, not least the sharp increase in scepticism towards the political system and politicians, and the marked decline of deference that has been a hallmark of its culture since the late 1980s. The current period may well therefore mark a sea-change in terms of popular and elite thinking about England's position in the union. For, while the notion of devolving powers within England gained support in both the Liberal and Labour parties in the early decades of the twentieth century, the idea of introducing forms of representation or a system of government that recognized England as in some ways a separated polity—which had long been delegitimized by the Westminster view of governance—has been inching back towards political respectability in recent years. This drift is reflected in the increasing propensity for thinkers and politicians to observe the impossibility of preserving the fiction of England's non-existence, in both legal and constitutional terms. Thus, Henry McLeish, former First Minister for Scotland, suggested in his evidence to the Calman Commission in 2008 that the English needed a voice, and the current system of asymmetrical devolution could no longer be sustained: 'We must move towards a balanced, quasi-federal framework of which we can make sense rather than the English feeling aggrieved and their grief and anger spilling over on to us.'[17]

There is also a growing body of evidence that a large number of English people see a fundamental inequity when they turn to consider how it is that English-only issues can be determined by MPs representing non-English seats, and also in relation to how much public funding England receives in comparison with some of the other territories of the UK. As Jim Gallagher has put it:

> So far, the English have been pretty tolerant about the Scottish variation, but increasingly two issues concern them: money and representation. Does Scotland do unfairly well in the distribution of common resources, and do Scottish Westminster representatives have too much say on English questions?[18]

The first real signs of a heightened public interest in the question of representation was the loud chorus of complaint that arose following several notable occasions when the Labour governments led by Tony Blair relied upon the votes of Scottish and Welsh MPs to pass controversial pieces of legislation that applied primarily to England.[19] As Labour's majority was eroded at the General Elections of 2001 and 2005 (its English majority in the House of Commons dropped from 117 in 2001 to 43 in 2005), it became ever more reliant upon MPs representing seats outside England. The first occasion when Scottish MPs secured the Labour government a majority on an English-focused issue was the controversial question of the banning of hunting with dogs. Following devolution, this was no longer an issue applicable to Scotland. Conservative MP David Lidington emphasized this territorial anomaly when he called upon all non-English MPs to desist from voting in 1999.

This was merely a foretaste of what became a familiar concern as Labour's majority shrank after 2001, and the propensity of its backbenchers to rebel increased.[20] Thereafter, the government was even more reliant upon the votes of its generally loyal Scottish MPs. To pass the legislation introducing Foundation Hospitals within the health service in 2003, and the Higher Education Bill of 2004, which introduced 'top-up' fees for students—both contentious pieces of legislation that applied mainly to England—the government needed the votes of Scottish MPs to secure its majority. The territorial composition of Labour's parliamentary majority figured prominently in media coverage of, and public discourse upon, these pieces of legislation. Conservative MP Tim Yeo denounced the 'constitutional outrage' which this represented.[21] His sentiment was shared by a considerable portion of the English public. Various studies identified an upsurge in concern about West Lothian in the subsequent period. According to Curtice and Rachel Ormston, for instance, public opinion in England 'consistently expresses some disquiet at the apparent inequity of the WLQ [West Lothian question]'.[22] This clamour was expressed in terms of an intuitive sense of the right of any particular nation within the union to be protected from legislation that conflicts with the wishes of a majority of its parliamentary representatives. This, after all, had been one of the guiding dynamics informing the introduction of devolution elsewhere in the UK. Increasingly, the same principle was invoked in the popular mind in relation to the position of England.

There were considerable complaints too following the appointment in 2003 of Scottish MP John Reid to the post of Minister of State for Health, a department whose business was, after devolution, almost entirely devoted to England.[23] And, in the run-up to Brown's accession to the position of Prime Minister, the question of whether a Scottish MP could now enjoy the legitimacy in the eyes of the English, given that the Scottish Parliament was responsible for a large swathe of its own domestic legislation, was publicly aired.[24] As more powers have gradually been passed to both Scotland and Wales, and others are likely to follow in the wake of the Silk Commission and the Scottish Referendum of 2014, this shift in the territorial balance of the UK's system of governance is an issue attracting heightened public interest.

The question of what, if anything, the political parties should do in response, is considered in some detail in the remainder of this chapter. While I point to signs that for many English people these issues represent intuitive violations of a deeply held sense of procedural justice, it may well be that any putative reform emerges from a more familiar normative source—the kind of benign adaptability which has long been a hallmark of Britain's governing culture, and which may well encourage the introduction of modest adjustments designed to siphon off the emergence of popular resentment. It is in this spirit that the most likely reform of England's constitutional position—the introduction of 'English votes for English laws' (hereafter EVEL)—is advocated by the Conservative party.

THE WEST LOTHIAN QUESTION: PROPOSALS
FOR REFORM

The West Lothian question describes one of the best-known quirks associated with the British system of parliamentary government. It was given this particular name as a result of the anti-devolutionist case mounted by Labour MP Tam Dalyell during the heated debates on the subject that broke out during the 1970s. Dalyell famously expressed his reservations about the implications of a reform that would mean that he, as the elected representative for the constituents of West Lothian, could vote on matters affecting English electors, while English MPs might not be able to do so in return.[25] This issue had cropped up repeatedly, long before Dalyell's intervention, and figured prominently in debates about the implications of Home Rule for Ireland during Gladstone's premiership. But, following the devolving of significant powers to the Scottish Parliament, a much brighter light was shone upon this anomaly, and a chorus of complaint about it could be heard within, and outside, the political system. By the end of the period under consideration here, the prospect of reforms being introduced to address this issue increased considerably.

In the aftermath of Hague's brief flirtation with the idea of symmetrical devolution (which was discussed in Chapter 5), senior Conservatives, including former Minister Kenneth Baker, and MPs Michael Forsyth and David Davis, argued that the party should champion the demand to reform procedures in the Commons in relation to those Bills that applied solely to England. This proposal was endorsed by Hague in 1999, and the party's support for the idea of 'English votes on English matters' figured in its 2001 manifesto.[26]

But this issue was not solely a concern on the political right. The report published by the House of Commons Procedure Committee in 1999 set out the case for a process whereby the Speaker's office could be charged with demarcating the territorial remit of Bills, and individual clauses within them, in order to identify those that were of relevance only to England. It also proposed that one of the four stages of the life of these Bills should be considered at their Second Reading by a committee composed solely of English MPs. Moreover, a number of parliamentarians from other parties associated themselves with the case for reform in this area. In 2000 Labour MP Frank Field tabled a Private Member's Bill which proposed to restrict the rights of Scottish and Northern Irish MPs to vote on English legislation.[27] His declaration that 'England is in a resentful mood', and that this issue was 'becoming one of the festering sores of British politics' were not widely shared when he made them, but have gradually become more mainstream sentiments.[28] More generally, when former Minister Kenneth Baker introduced a Private Member's Bill in 2006 calling for measures to be introduced to ensure that English MPs voted on legislation affecting England only, it was sympathetically received not only by many Tory MPs, but also by some senior Liberal Democrats, including Menzies Campbell and Simon Hughes.

However, it was in Tory circles at Westminster that the most developed and serious thinking about putative solutions to West Lothian were apparent. This issue was given prominence in the report provided by the Commission to Strengthen Parliament, chaired by Conservative peer and constitutional expert Lord Norton, in July 2000. This proposed that Bills pertaining only to England should, at their Third Reading, be heard only by English MPs.[29] But it was the suggestion of former Secretary of State for Scotland, Sir Malcolm Rifkind, for the creation of an English Grand Committee that instigated a more serious engagement with this issue among the Conservative party leadership.[30] The idea of such a Committee (and, when necessary, an English and Welsh Grand Committee) built upon the practice of organizing regular meetings of Scottish and Welsh Committees of MPs. Introducing such a mechanism for English-related matters was intended as a failsafe, designed to prevent governments passing legislation that was fundamentally objectionable to English MPs, who would have a right of veto at a Bill's Second Reading, and to force any prospective government to negotiate in detail on amendments at committee stage on these pieces of legislation. Rifkind's proposal received extensive media coverage, and gave the issue it addressed a much higher profile within the party and beyond. On his model a committee to handle Bills that applied solely to England should be constituted according to the relative numerical strengths of the parties in England. This proposal was justified as a procedural adjustment that would rectify an unwise imbalance unwittingly created by Labour, rather than as a radical measure designed to provide some form of recognition for English aspirations to national sovereignty. The Rifkind plan was widely seen in the parliamentary party, and certainly by the leadership, as an improvement upon stronger versions of EVEL.[31]

Unlike many of his fellow Conservatives, Rifkind was also against one of the associated reforms that have been regularly aired in the context of West Lothian—the idea of reducing the number of MPs from outside England in order to diminish their demographic over-representation in the Commons. In his view, given that a significant portion of the business of the House was still focused upon issues of shared concern across the UK, reducing the number of these representatives might solve the iniquitous position of the English at the expense of creating a new inequity for the Scots and Welsh, whose voices on many UK-wide issues would be under-represented.[32] His proposal was also designed to head off the most familiar and deeply rooted objection to schemes for reform in this area—the cherished convention that all MPs should be able to vote on any legislation passing through the House.

His proposal provided the basis for the recommendations made by the party's Democracy Taskforce, which was established by David Cameron and chaired by senior MP Kenneth Clarke, before the 2010 election.[33] The Commission published a specific statement on West Lothian, setting out a refined version of his proposal.[34] It was similarly framed as 'a sensible constitutional change' designed to 'nip that [English nationalism] in the bud' and to complete the unfinished business of devolution.[35] In the paper he submitted to the Justice Committee of the House of Commons, Rifkind signalled that he was broadly happy with the Clarke proposal, which he thought would achieve:

> some of the purpose of EVEL without ultimately threatening the right of Government to use its majority in support of its legislative programme, unless a Bill has been so greatly amended in the Grand Committee or on Report that it no longer merits the Government's purposes.[36]

The taskforce proposed that those Bills which applied only to England should be considered by English MPs only at their committee and report stages, after which the whole House would review and vote on them at their Third Reading. It departed from Rifkind in proposing the adoption of a convention stipulating that no further amendments could be tabled at this stage, thus limiting the right of non-English MPs to amend legislation. The House as a whole would therefore be faced with a straightforward 'accept or reject' option at this point in the passage of a Bill, with the detailed work of revising and questioning being done by English MPs beforehand. Such a process, it was emphasized, would prevent the kind of situation that had come to pass during Labour's years in office, whereby legislation that a majority of English MPs found unacceptable was passed by the votes of non-English MPs.

Just as important as the detailed procedural recommendations which the taskforce advanced were the terms in which they were justified. The primary rationale for this reform was a prudential one. If the anomaly generated by the asymmetrical character of devolution was not addressed, 'the resulting sense of grievance on the part of the Union's largest nation, the English, could undermine the current constitutional settlement'.[37] In a subsequent interview Clarke elaborated on this rationale:

> There is a slight English Question, and there is some English feeling, that is being fed by an anomaly which it seems to me could be solved by comparatively straightforward changes which needn't undermine the authority of a future British government, or become too party political in their impact.[38]

This measure was advanced in the spirit of evolutionary, adaptive conservatism, rectifying an anomaly in order to preserve the value of the system as a whole. As he put it, 'For the unionist parties the whole point is to have a little sensitivity and make sure you don't feed all these odd attitudes.'[39] The idea of leaving this wrinkle alone, which was the abiding temptation for constitutional conservatives, was now no longer an option: 'Arguments from the past are flawed; this was under a very different constitutional settlement.'[40] The report made much of the spectre of a potential rise in English resentment, though it provided no concrete evidence for this. At the same time, it played down the extent of the change it would involve, noting correctly that only a small number of Bills would be affected by this new procedure. This watered-down version of 'English votes on English matters' figured in the party's manifesto of 2010.

The Labour party remained doggedly conservative about the settlement it had put in place after devolution, recycling well-worn axioms about the virtuous character of the anomalies and quirks of the Westminster model. Minister Charles Falconer argued at the time of devolution that Labour's proposals were designed to guarantee the rights of the non-English nations and, accordingly, strengthen the union. The government, he insisted, was not concerned about the question of 'constitutional symmetry' but was committed to the practical accommodation of 'difference and rough edges.'[41] While remaining forthright in its opposition to arguments for a more symmetrical system of devolution, Labour's defensiveness on this score was clear from its greater receptivity to arguments for a parallel reform—a reduction in the number of seats outside England in order to diminish the potential impact of the 'over-representation' of the non-English territories in the Westminster parliament. For many MPs in this period, this constituted a more egregious quirk than the West Lothian issue, the resolution of which might well mean that the anomalies associated with the latter became rarer. Scotland and Wales (though not, after 1972, Northern Ireland) had for many years returned more MPs to Westminster than was proportionate with the size of their electorates. As a consequence, there were fewer English MPs than the size of its electorate might suggest. With the introduction of devolution the familiar argument for this systematic over-representation—which traditionally invoked the separate systems of legal and educational provision in Scotland, and the tradition of independent governance in Wales—were fatally weakened. It was widely assumed that Scottish over-representation was dealt with in the Scotland Act 1998, which reduced Scotland's representation from seventy-two to fifty-nine MPs, from the 2005 election onwards. Wales has remained over-represented in numerical terms, though the current government at Westminster is planning to bring forward proposals to reduce its number of MPs from forty to thirty. But these changes have done little to dislodge the entrenched idea in parts of the public mind that the Labour government's lack of sensitivity to the culture and interests of the English is connected to its reliance upon non-English MPs.

A heightened sense of the disadvantages visited upon England during the years of Labour government figured prominently in Conservative discourse, but was simultaneously held in check by the party's continuing adherence to established forms of constitutional thinking. Its leader from 2005, David Cameron, offered repeated praise for the United Kingdom as a multi-national state buttressed by institutional structures and representative conventions that had evolved over time.[42] He steered away from a full-blooded articulation of English grievance and, in the run-up to the 2010 General Election, delivered a series of keynote speeches setting out his commitment both to the devolution settlement and its abiding implication that different political parties ought to be able to cooperate while holding power in different parts of the UK.[43]

The agreement between the Conservatives and Lib Dems that underpinned the Coalition government formed in May 2010 included a commitment to appoint an independent commission to reconsider 'the West Lothian question'.[44] For a growing number of Conservative MPs, and many of its members, this has become an issue of greater interest since devolution, and may well provide an occasion for the expression of a growing mood of assertiveness on the party's right wing. In September 2011 backbencher Harriett Baldwin submitted a Private Member's Bill demanding that the territorial reach of all legislation be more clearly demarcated.[45] And while she was unsuccessful in securing support for her Bill, her justification for introducing it was revealing about the mood of parts of her own party. It was motivated both by her strong commitment to the union and belief that the English are currently dealt a poor hand within it.

An important, additional context that now forms part of the backdrop to this issue has been identified by several observers.[46] Had the negotiations that followed the General Election of 2010 resulted in the formation of a UK-wide government led by Labour, the Lib Dems, and other smaller parties from outside England—as looked possible at one stage of the frenzied discussions that took place after the election—an administration would have come into being that did not hold a majority of seats in England. Quite what this would have meant, in the context of the need to address the major economic crisis confronting Britain at this point in time, was a question that was not raised by any of the actors involved in these negotiations.[47] Bogdanor was certainly convinced that the formation of such an administration 'would have resurrected the West Lothian Question with a vengeance'.[48] Given the possibility of a recurrence of such a scenario in the near future, it may well be that all of the main parties come to give the kinds of proposals aired by the McKay Commission fuller consideration.

There are some signs of movement in Labour's thinking on this issue, though for the most part the party appears entrenched in its unwillingness to engage with it, refusing to make a submission or offer a response to the McKay Commission. But in 2012 the influential centre-left think-tank the Institute for Public Policy Research (IPPR) published a paper which directly challenged Labour's thinking on this issue.[49] In it, former civil servant Gallagher advanced the case for parliament developing a clearer English dimension to its deliberations and legislative procedures, and proposed a distinct version of EVEL. Rejecting the argument that the Speaker ought to be responsible for determining the territorial allocation of particular Bills, he maintained that the least bad option in this area would be to ask the government of the day to determine the territorial remit of Bills. He also proposed that the reporting stage of a Bill should be undertaken by an English Grand Committee, and its Third Reading heard on the floor of the Commons, with all MPs present. Such a procedure offered an appropriate balance, he argued, between the two key principles at stake in this issue—the right of the UK government to govern its largest territory and the democratic need for the balance of representation within England to be reflected in the making of policy decisions that apply to it.[50]

The appearance of a serious proposal of this kind from an influential source of progressive political opinion is indicative of the gradually shifting balance of the argument on this question over the last fifteen years. A further indication of change is the number of senior establishment figures who have begun to argue that reform of this sort may increasingly be unavoidable in order to preserve the essentials of the union. Thus, Sir Roger Sands, Clerk to the House of Commons from 2003 to 2006, pointed out in his submission to the McKay Commission that:

> there have been, and no doubt still are, politicians who have claimed that there is no problem about the role of Scottish (or Welsh or Northern Irish) MPs in the current constitutional settlement. I do not share that view. It is true that our approach to constitutional development in the UK has normally been one of cautious and pragmatic change, and it has generally served us well not to apply the laws of exact logic or considerations of neat symmetry. Nonetheless the present situation does entail the elected representatives of the devolved jurisdictions having their cake and eating it to an extent which is manifestly inequitable and which I do not believe will be sustainable in the long term, particularly if current constitutional discussions in Scotland result in a significant increase in the legislative powers of the Scottish Parliament short of independence.[51]

There has been a gradual shift in perception, over the last fifteen years, that this is no longer an issue of interest solely for constitutional experts and campaigners, but, in its broad outlines, also attracts wider public interest. One consequence and manifestation of this change has been the articulation of unfamiliar democratic principles regarding constitutional government and national representation in relation to the English. Below I step back from the technicalities of the proposals that have been put forward in relation to EVEL and review the justificatory arguments that have been advanced for and against such a reform. I distinguish between two different kinds of normative position that have become prevalent in these debates. The first, most commonly employed, form of discourse is consequentialist in kind. There is in particular a growing consensus within mainstream politics that inaction on this front may well pose more dangers to the union than modest reform. And the second kind of argument to which I draw attention is made in the language of popular sovereignty, a principle that sits rather awkwardly with the main tenets of British parliamentary democracy. But this kind of perspective is increasingly immanent within English consciousness.

AGAINST EVEL

The case against reform typically references a number of practical objections, and is only rarely made at the level of democratic principle. Important concerns that have been raised on this score include the difficulties associated with delineating the territorial remit of Bills and their individual clauses. Such an enterprise, it is often suggested, is obviated by the many indirect consequences that legislation affecting specified territories can have for other parts of the UK. Thus, the legislation that introduced tuition fees in England in 2004 also included clauses that applied to Scotland.[52] Bills that carry financial implications have indirect, spill-over effects upon other territories, and create a potential anomaly for any process that seeks to identify different legislation that applies only to England. And, as various experts have noted, even after devolution, there are only a small number of Bills that apply to England alone. Introducing a complex, and contentious, set of conventions into the House of Commons may well, therefore, represent an unwieldy and counter-productive sledge-hammer designed for the occasional nut. An analysis of Bills passing through parliament in 2006 found that, of the fifty-five public Acts that were passed, some twenty-nine were UK-wide in their extent, eighteen were assigned as primarily applying to England or Wales (though ten of these had some Scottish content), and only eight had no visible Scottish content but might have reasonably been deemed to be pieces of legislation in which Scottish MPs have a legitimate interest. Only one Act in this period could have been deemed to apply to England alone.[53]

The relative scarcity of instances of pieces of legislation that apply solely to England without generating indirect, spill-over effects for other territories is confirmed by Bogdanor, who has insisted that one of the core axioms of Britain's system of parliamentary government has been the notion that any issue involving public expenditure is of concern to all parts of UK.[54] Due to the workings of the calculus used to adjust levels of public spending outside England (the so-called Barnett formula which is discussed elsewhere in this chapter), any Bill that has fiscal implications will indirectly affect the size of the block grants allocated to Scotland and Wales. The scale of these funds is calculated in relation to levels of expenditure in England on matters that are also devolved. Each line item of a central government department's expenditure is assessed in terms of how far it is devolved, and a devolution proportion assigned to it. This weighting is used to generate a payment known as the Barnett 'consequential'. English-only legislation will, therefore, have the consequence of altering the resources available to the Welsh, Scottish, and Northern Irish government in cases where a budgetary decision has either caused the need for legislation or is consequent upon it. Some analysts therefore think the desire of a growing number of Conservatives to develop a procedure in the House of Commons to handle English-only legislation signals the abandonment of an underpinning principle of a system that is premised upon the interwoven and inter-related nature of governance of its constituent territories.[55]

Some commentators have focused upon a different consequentialist objection, pointing out that any procedure which relies upon the Speaker to delineate the territorial remit of Bills will necessarily lead to the undue politicization of an office that has come under increasing pressure in recent years.[56] An additional, long-standing objection arises from the observation that employing differing voting arrangements for different clauses of a single Bill is simply unworkable, constituting a kind of legislative 'hokey-cokey'.[57] Gladstone's famous conclusion, that 'it passed the wit of man to frame any distinct, thorough-going, universal severance between the one class of subject and the other', has been routinely invoked as the last word on this issue.[58] One further, much repeated worry is that the introduction of an EVEL procedure would essentially constitute a major step towards the establishment of an English Parliament, giving fuel to the nationalist movement in Scotland, and engendering a destructive competition between the different nations of the UK.[59]

For many experts and political practitioners, it is axiomatic that such a reform represents a cure that may well cause more harm than the malady it seeks to address. This scepticism has been bolstered by two more principled objections. The first of these is that any restriction of the voting rights of particular groups of MPs would involve the creation of distinctive classes of representatives, an alteration that would signal a major break from a core convention at the heart of the Westminster system. This was the favoured line of defence employed by the Blair governments in response to arguments for EVEL. A second, weighty objection concerns the possibility of a scenario whereby a UK-wide government does not enjoy a majority of support in England, and in which a majority of England's MPs might possess the power of veto over the legislative ambitions of the UK-wide administration. In such a circumstance, a significant constitutional crisis would ensue, it has been suggested. Bogdanor has argued that such a situation would result in a bifurcation of governmental authority, with members of the UK government being replaced by backbench MPs when English legislation was being considered, and vice versa. This would be fundamentally antithetical to the constitutive principle of strong and coherent executive-led government.[60]

A common thread linking these disparate objections is the presumption that the British system of parliamentary government has evolved conventions, principles, and processes which, together, underpin its stability and success.[61] Constitutional expert Robert Hazell, for instance, has outlined the constitutional status quo in exactly these terms:

> the UK has always been an asymmetrical state, a political Union in which the different nations are embedded in the State in different ways. The English are part of the Union tradition, which may help to explain why they are so relaxed about Scottish devolution. They are famously pragmatic and will not seek uniformity for uniformity's sake.[62]

The defence of the anomalies associated with the West Lothian issue typically rest upon assumptions about the merits and viability of the core components of the British tradition and the system of government it has bequeathed. While some of the arguments in favour of reform have been advanced, as we shall see, within the parameters of this mode of argument, what increasingly distinguishes the current phase of debate about this issue is a sense that this liberal-conservative constitutional disposition may itself no longer represent the most appropriate normative ground upon which to understand the nature and implications of the parliamentary system of government.

IN FAVOUR OF EVEL

These various objections to EVEL have provided a solid bedrock of scepticism, and have readily prevailed over the reformist argument during the course of the last century. However, in recent years the political context in which these debates are aired has changed markedly. It is the Labour party that is readiest to employ these arguments, primarily to suit its own political conviction that EVEL would result in a semi-permanent Conservative majority in England. This fear represents a powerful, if rarely spoken, folk-myth on the left.

As well as reflecting a striking degree of pessimism about the party's prospects of winning seats in many parts of England, this partisan view rests upon a poor grasp of parliamentary history. As Iain McLean has shown, England in political terms 'is not as Tory as some commentators believe'.[63] There have been three occasions when the Conservatives have won an outright majority of seats in England since the late nineteenth century: 1955, 2005, and 2010. In the sixty years from 1945 to 2005, only three General Elections (out of a total of fifteen) produced a result where the territorial distribution of the vote meant that a UK-wide government (run by Labour) was faced by a majority of Tory MPs in England. And in only two of these cases did Labour's majority depend upon the support of Scottish MPs.

The ingrained mythology of a perpetual Tory majority in England offers one illustration of the degree to which perceptions of party interest infuse debates about EVEL. A growing body of argument and opinion has begun to counter each of the objections that have for so long been offered to EVEL.

The emergence in the last few years of the practice of demarcating the territorial application of different Bills in the Commons has gone some way to demonstrating that, however complex such a process may be, it is not impossible to undertake. A report produced by the Justice Committee of the House of Commons in 2009 noted that since devolution there has been 'an improvement in the demarcation of the territorial extent of legislation', and Hansard now routinely provides a list of the territorial extent of Bills introduced in each parliamentary session.[64] A number of experts have therefore called for legislation to be more clearly territorially demarcated as a prelude to the establishment of a greater English dimension to parliamentary procedure.[65]

In response to the objection that nearly all legislation passed at Westminster tends to have some kind of effect upon other territories, reformers suggest a clearer distinction be made between the financial implications of individual Acts of Parliament and the overall budget which is voted for by the House of Commons. A Bill that requires additional spending on, for instance, the health service in England, might typically result in savings being found in some other aspect of NHS funding, or from shifting priorities in other areas of expenditure, and these are issues on which all MPs have had the chance to vote. The prospect of an unbreakable sequence of indirect effects for devolved territories from English-only legislation has been exaggerated in much conventional constitutional commentary.

The remaining consequentialist objections have also been subjected to critical evaluation. The scenario of constitutional gridlock which has been especially prominent in these debates ignores the likelihood that the introduction of EVEL would itself require a shift of ethos within central government away from the exercise of untrammelled executive power, towards a culture of negotiation and deal-making. This reform, it is suggested, would place greater emphasis upon collaboration and negotiation, and put a premium upon the achievement of a non-antagonistic relationship between the UK-wide executive and the body reflecting the wishes of English representatives. Michael Keating has rejected the contention that the eventuality whereby a party might have a majority in the English parliament, but not be part of the UK government, would inevitably lead to a breakdown in the British model of government.[66] In such a situation, the government would be formed in the normal way—based upon the number of MPs elected across the UK—and in devolved matters affecting England it would have to adapt its programme accordingly, forming alliances to pass specific legislation and engaging in bargaining across the England–union frontier. Gerald Holtham has also agreed that any prospective government that did not command a majority of English MPs would have to work within the parameters of such a situation.[67] In devolved matters affecting England, it would need to adapt its programme accordingly, brokering alliances to pass specific pieces of legislation, and make deals with the representatives of the largest party in England. As Holtham put it, 'that is the sort of untidiness with which politics is supposed to deal'.[68]

What, for some, looks like constitutional disaster is therefore seen by others as the source of new kinds of challenge that would stimulate novel political conventions and shift the culture of British government in a positive direction. As Peter Behrens has pointed out, such processes have grown up in many other federal political systems: 'if only because it is not always possible to determine with absolute clarity in whose competence a particular matter falls'.[69] In his judgement, the key characteristic of the West Lothian problem is 'the extreme way in which the asymmetrical situation in the United Kingdom has been allowed to develop', rather than the willingness of most parliamentarians to contemplate changes to conventions in the Lower Chamber. This is, he concluded, a problem that is bound to become more acute, as devolutionary processes continue within the UK, 'and the chasm between the competences enjoyed by Scotland and the situation in England deepens'.[70] In such a situation, he contended, inaction represents the riskiest option for those who wish to preserve the fundamentals of the existing system.

The case for EVEL is not, however, solely dependent upon an assessment of its potential consequences for established parliamentary practices. It appeals too as an answer to a normative question that is immanent within recent shifts

in public consciousness: is the current system perpetuating a systemic unfairness that is infringing the democratic rights of the English? Such a question
fits awkwardly within the normative logic of the Westminster model of government which locates sovereignty within the government that is formed at
the behest of the monarch by the elected representatives in parliament. But its
increasing salience registers a growing willingness to consider the representation of the English through the lens of popular sovereignty, a trend that has
gained significant ground since devolution. Such an approach suggests a very
different normative perspective upon current constitutional arrangements,
one that implicitly posits the English as a collective actor in possession of
national-democratic rights on a par with those of other national communities
within the multi-national state. It is increasingly employed by those arguing
for a more substantive form of EVEL. Arguments in this vein, as we shall see,
increasingly run alongside, and move some way beyond, the consequentialist
discourse that has, until now, shaped debates about West Lothian. This shift
in normative sensibility is partially registered in the report published by the
McKay Commission, which argued for the extension of a principle that has
been implicitly applied to the non-English peoples of the UK to the English.
This was described as the idea that decisions taken at the UK level which have
a '*separate and distinct* effect for a component part of the United Kingdom
should *normally* be taken only with the consent of a majority of the elected
representatives for that part of the United Kingdom'.[71]

The emergence of relatively novel kinds of democratic argument within
debates about British government and representation constitutes an important
new stage in the evolution of governance in the UK, even if, as yet, the status
and traction of these ideas remain uncertain. There is certainly a growing consensus that whether the English do perceive the union and the British model
of government as unfair is an increasingly important political consideration.
As Adam Tomkins has noted, the extent to which Scots felt that their government was illegitimate in the 1980s and 1990s was a vital precondition for the
introduction of devolution in 1998.

But the growing number of Conservatives who support EVEL do so mainly
for different reasons, subscribing to an older tradition of adaptive pragmatism which sees reform of this kind as an adjustment designed to head off a
potentially significant threat to the entire constitutional system. This mode
of thinking has injected into current debates a precautionary note, reflecting
the growing concern at Westminster that, if English grievances about West
Lothian and Barnett are not addressed, there may well be 'further seismic
shifts in our constitutional arrangements, as significant for England (and the
union) as was the arrival in 1999 of devolution for Scotland (and the union)'.[72]
For many who hold to this view, it is clear that some form of EVEL represents

a prudential reform that aims to nip in the bud the possibility that the English become unduly resentful and sour towards devolution, rather than a measure designed to accommodate newly emerging democratic ideas. As Clarke, chair of the influential Conservative party Democracy Taskforce, put it:

> If there is, in the middle of what I regard as a load of silly attitudes, a genuinely slightly niggling point that has substance, then remove it, because there is always a risk that something dramatic might happen when something very unpopular is imposed on the English by a parliament in which the majority of English MPs voted against it.[73]

As the implications of the process of 'ever loosening union' have percolated throughout the party system, and awareness of the extent of English disaffection has grown, the realization has dawned in political circles that the reconfigured union needs to be explained and justified to an increasingly jaundiced English public. In this context, the case for EVEL as a kind of procedural lock, which guarantees that legislation for England is not passed against the clear wishes of a majority of English representatives, has quietly moved into the political mainstream. At the same time, it may well be that once the UK is so justified, and if reforms such as EVEL are introduced, further bouts of constitutional reform may become unavoidable. If such a reform was introduced to the Lower House, for instance, the anomalous position of the House of Lords in territorial terms would immediately come into focus, and most likely necessitate reforms to the Second Chamber that might in turn catalyse a further phase of debate about its membership and role. Indeed, for some leading commentators in this area, the lack of focus upon the Lords sabotages any viable prospect of resolving the West Lothian question. As Peter Riddell trenchantly puts it: 'It would be bizarre and anomalous if English only procedures were adopted in the Commons, but Scottish, Welsh and Northern Ireland peers, if they could be so defined, could vote on such bills in the House of Lords.'[74]

And yet, while the prospect of an extended bout of constitutional reform remains unappetizing to many, the defence of the status quo is becoming increasingly difficult as long as established modes of thinking about both constitution and government are waning in force, and proving decreasingly effective at ensuring the legitimacy of the political system among publics that are increasingly responsive to the language of national identity and popular sovereignty. Viewed against the backdrop of these slow shifts of intellectual gestalt, the rather arcane matter of how the Lower Chamber rejigs its procedures for handling English-only legislation carries a totemic, rather than practical, significance. It has come to stand for the larger question of whether the guardians of the British state are willing and able to move out beyond the parameters of established constitutional orthodoxy, if only to make adjustments that preserve the integrity and value of the system as a whole. While it is undoubt-edly important, therefore, to note how rarely West Lothian-type problems actually arise, a profound sense of symbolism has come to infuse this issue, and has imparted to it an inflated degree of significance. This question serves, above all, as an important conduit to a much broader debate about whether the English believe they require a more delineated form of political community.[75]

THE BARNETT FORMULA

The other issue that has surfaced most consistently in relation to complaints about England's position within the current system of British government con-cerns the distribution of public spending to its constituent territories. Here, the widely held belief that some parts of England have been poorly treated in rela-tion to Scotland, in particular, has become a source of growing concern within the mainstream party system. This issue is typically identified with the opaque workings of the Barnett formula, the calculus that has been employed since the late 1970s to determine the size of the block grants allocated to Scotland, Wales, and Northern Ireland once levels of expenditure in England have been established.

Although discussion of the territorial pattern of public spending in the UK is often elided with the workings of devolution, it is important to appreciate that this particular funding allocation mechanism has been in operation for several decades. While the anomalies generated by this formula have elicited criticism from all parts of the United Kingdom, the incentives for the parties at Westminster to engage in the painful process of replacing or reforming it are very small. And yet, like West Lothian, this has become an increasingly totemic focus for nationalist and populist grievance.

The Barnett formula was devised in response to growing concerns at Westminster about the revival of nationalism in Wales, Scotland, and Northern Ireland in the late 1960s and early 1970s.[76] The question of how levels of public expenditure across the UK would be determined, if some form of devolved government was introduced, was a major theme in the policy debates of that era. In the late 1970s the Treasury was commissioned to quantify the various 'needs' of each of the constituent territories of the UK against a notional aver-age benchmark, and produced an analysis showing that Scotland's spending was running some way ahead of its needs, while the opposite situation pre-vailed in Wales. The Treasury responded to this report by developing a for-mula (devised while Joel Barnett was Chief Secretary) which reflected the aim of containing any putative English backlash against devolution.[77] McLean and McMillan contend that this mechanism offered an apparently neutral way of achieving the potentially incendiary goal of gradually reducing levels of spending in Scotland relative to those in England, and was designed to do so in an incremental fashion.[78] It was intended, more generally, to address the challenge facing all regionally and nationally diverse polities—to allocate different levels of funding to populations that have varying levels of need.

Its existence was deliberately kept out of the public domain until 1980. And, while it has latterly fallen into disrepute, the Barnett formula was undoubtedly effective at providing a short-term answer to these vexatious issues. Above all, it removed the need to hold potentially inflammatory annual rounds of bargaining over spending levels, with a system based upon the objective determination of a single block grant. One technical difficulty that has beset its employment, ever since its introduction, concerns the accuracy of the data informing the calculation of the ratios determining the needs of the different territories of the UK. The needs assessment provided by the Treasury was ignored by Barnett who apportioned annual increases to the block grants according to a population ratio that gradually exacerbated England's poor position in relation to Scotland, given actual population levels in both countries. This ratio was in use until the 1990s, when it was finally adjusted in the wake of the fall in the Scottish population and the rise in England's.

The formula itself was designed both to calculate a proportionate share of any increase (or decrease) in comparable spending in England and to add it to the core funding received by the other territories of the UK. The size of the block grants which it determined for Scotland, Wales, and Northern Ireland in the period 1979–92 were set at levels higher than equivalent *per capita* spending in England, and have been adjusted incrementally ever since.

Increasingly, within England this mechanism has come to symbolize the state's purported bias towards Scotland. And this complaint has grown in volume since devolution which has refocused attention upon who receives what within the UK, primarily as a result of the impact of significant policy variations within the different legislatures which it established. Increasingly, the Barnett formula has become a totem for those arguing that the conventions and processes at the heart of the British state are systemically generating unfair outcomes for the English. Labour voices from the North of England, who have long complained about the financial advantages enjoyed by Scotland in comparison with their own regions, have been among its most vociferous critics. Prior to devolution it was often argued that successive Secretaries of State for Scotland had been highly adept at exploiting the centre's fears of nationalism to engender favourable financial settlement for Scotland. And this was one of the concerns that motivated the introduction by a group of Northern Labour

MPs of the Amendment to the Devolution Bill that passed before parliament in 1976. They insisted on a 40 per cent threshold for the devolution referenda in Wales and Scotland, dealing a fatal blow to the chances of this reform being enacted in this period.[79]

More recently, a wider range of political voices have expressed disgruntlement at the apparent advantage which this formula conveys upon the Scots, including Tory and Labour MPs representing constituencies in the South and South East, the region that receives the lowest overall proportion of public expenditure in relation to the amount of tax revenue it contributes. More generally, as McLean has pointed out, the separation which devolution entrenched between the lack of responsibility that the governments of Scotland, Wales, and Northern Ireland retain over the generation of their tax revenues, on the one hand, and their relatively unfettered ability to increase capital and current spending once block grants are allocated, on the other, represents a further, additional reason for making the English cast envious eyes across their borders.[80]

Yet the growing inclination to make comparisons between England and other national territories in the UK on the issue of public spending is cross-cut by a heightened sensitivity to differences in spending levels between the different English regions—which are not determined by the Barnett mechanism. At their extremes, these divergences are just as marked as those between England and Scotland, and have also figured prominently in political discourse in these years. Various commentators point to the growing perception among citizens living in the more prosperous regions in the South and South East that the wealth they generate is undergirding the higher levels of public spending that were transferred to other parts of England during the 1990s and 2000s.

But, while the increasing propensity to think in comparative regional terms about spending has become a marked feature of public discourse, complaints about the Barnett formula have served to bolster a simplistic and divisive, if not entirely inaccurate, form of national comparison. Table 6.1 provides an illustration of the continuing pattern of differential levels of public expenditure that underpin these complaints.

As awareness of these issues has become more palpable, disquiet about the Barnett formula has entered the political mainstream at Westminster. One recent study found that, based upon the years 2007–8 (and exempting payments for social protection and agricultural subsidies), Scotland's *per capita* average spending of £5,678 per head was 25.5 per cent higher than England's, at £4,523 per head. A growing interest in these comparative outcomes has helped confirm the populist intuition that English taxpayers are suffering a double disadvantage in relation to their Celtic neighbours—by subsidizing their greater political autonomy, and, as a result, having to put up with inferior

Table 6.1 Index of identifiable spending per head, minus social protection, across the nations of the UK, 2003/04 to 2008/09

	03/04	04/05	05/06	06/07	07/08	08/09
England	94	97	96	96	96	97
Scotland	121	116	121	124	123	120
Wales	113	109	110	111	110	110
Northern Ireland	132	131	129	125	127	122

Source: Institute for Public Policy Research, 2009

levels of publicly funded provision themselves. Polling certainly suggests that, over time, English public opinion has become increasingly aware of, and irritated by, this issue, though some commentators are unconvinced that this has grown significantly.[81] The belief that Scotland obtains more than its fair share of public spending has increased markedly in recent years. Up to 2003 no more than one in four held this view, while in 2007 this figure rose to one-third, and from 2008 onwards, the proportion has consistently been around some two in five of those polled.[82]

The Barnett formula and the wider system of distributing spending of which it is a part have very few public defenders in British politics. The report produced by the Justice Committee of the House of Commons in 2009 concluded very bluntly that the formula was no longer 'fit for purpose'.[83] And yet the political costs associated with the process of developing an alternative funding model, with the high likelihood that this would generate new classes of loser, and open up a slew of potentially incendiary issues, continue to sap the political will required to replace Barnett with a more robust or equitable procedure. And, until the Scottish referendum vote of 2014 has passed, there is very little likelihood that this issue will be addressed by the parties at Westminster.

However, less direct ways of alleviating the dysfunctions associated with Barnett are beginning to emerge. The allocation of greater autonomy over taxes to the Scottish Parliament, recommended by the Calman Commission established by the opposition parties in the Scottish Parliament in 2007, elicited widespread support in Scotland and Westminster. This is a popular idea with both Scottish and English public opinion more generally, and would also help tackle the lack of fiscal responsibility which current arrangements afford the devolved administrations. More generally, in parallel with the trajectory of debates about West Lothian, there is a growing constituency for the view that the retention of this particular anomaly is likely to prove more dangerous and destabilizing for the union than the risks associated with reform.[84]

CONCLUSIONS: PRINCIPLES AND POLICIES

In a general sense, the debates that have grown up around two of the most entrenched anomalies in the British system of government need to be set in the context of the considerable evidence that a heightened sense of national awareness among the English has been developing since the 1990s. One important consequence of this trend, I have suggested, has been the emergence of normative ideas rooted in notions of popular sovereignty and national right that do not take their bearings from the well-worn lineage of Anglo-British constitutionalism.

In addition, a challenging set of questions about how England figures within the British systems of governance and politics has quietly been released into the political ether by devolution and the continuing erosion of faith in the axioms and assumptions of the Westminster model of government. And these queries are likely to require fuller and more persuasive responses from the custodians of the state. Sir Brian Barder has suggested, for instance, that the West Lothian problem throws into relief the two distinct and increasingly incompatible roles which the House of Commons is being required to play, and which are increasingly hard to reconcile.[85] On the one hand, it constitutes a quasi-federal legislative body for the whole of the United Kingdom, dealing with all subjects not devolved to Scotland, Wales, and Northern Ireland, such as foreign affairs, defence, and other all-UK matters. But, on the other, it is gradually turning into a parliament that deals preponderantly with English matters, including subjects such as education and crime that have been devolved to Scotland, Wales, and Northern Ireland, but not to England. Since the members of the House of Commons are elected from all four home nations, parliament's membership makes it an increasingly unsuitable vehicle for this second role. For many advocates of reform, this anomaly can only be addressed through a much clearer separation of these increasingly different functions, a stance that appears to point towards a more federal model for the UK. Barder's contention that the anomaly reflected in the West Lothian question can only be resolved in this way may well come to acquire increasing resonance. Federalist responses, like nationalist ones, still remain at the fringes of these debates, but are increasingly likely to gain a hearing in a context where the intellectual platform upon which the existing system of governance rests is beginning to sag.

Popular opinion has certainly moved more markedly on both of these issues than on almost any other policy question in the last decade. Support for the principle of EVEL, as reported by a number of different surveys, has begun to grow quite considerably in recent years. The BSA's survey of 2007 found that 61 per cent of respondents in England believed that Scottish MPs should no longer be able to vote on laws that apply only to the English. Previous surveys, conducted in 2000 and 2003, also showed clear majority support for this idea, with 64 and 60 per cent respectively of respondents in favour.[86] And, as Curtice and Ormston have similarly indicated, ever since the advent of devolution, approximately three-fifths of the English public has agreed that Scottish MPs should no longer be able to vote on laws that only affect England.[87] There has, they pointed out, been a gradual, but consistent, increase in the proportion who 'strongly agree' rather than simply 'agree' with the proposition—rising from 18 per cent in 2000 to 31 per cent in 2010, and suggesting that this sentiment has also intensified. They compared this figure with the two-fifths of the English public who indicated disquiet about the territorial basis of public spending.[88] The most recent polling on these issues, undertaken for the Future of England survey in 2012, reported that: 52 per cent of English respondents indicated that Scotland gets more than fair share of public funding, compared to 45 per cent in 2011; 49 per cent thought that the Scots should pay for services from taxes raised in Scotland, compared to 42 per cent in 2011; and 55 per cent 'strongly agreed' that Scottish MPs should not vote on English laws, in comparison with 53 per cent in 2011.[89]

Yet, it is also the case that the groundswell of opinion in favour of the notion that an English dimension needs to be introduced into the existing system of British governance is unlikely to be satiated by the procedural adjustments associated with EVEL, or by the modest proposals advanced by the McKay Commission. This is because the asymmetrical character of devolution and perceived inequities in the distribution of public expenditure are not themselves the driving forces of growing disaffection among sections of the English public. Rather, they are issues towards which this dyspeptic mood has begun to gravitate. These aspects of 'the English question' have become tangled up with some of the other drivers of contemporary disenchantment, such as immigration and the European Union, a development which renders implausible the proposition that parliamentary reform will, on its own, dissipate this febrile mood. Yet the emergence of a more disenchanted mood towards the union among a significant portion of the English public stems from a separate normative dynamic as well. This arises from a growing conviction that a set of arrangements designed to protect the smaller territories of the UK have, over time, become unfair to the majority national community which is simultaneously developing a stronger sense of its own interests and identity.

The notion that significant numbers of the English are starting to see their national interests in more delineated terms is given particular emphasis in the report produced by the McKay Commission in 2013. Drawing heavily upon the polling conducted for the Future of England surveys of 2011 and 2012, this maintained that there is incontrovertible evidence that a 'significant level of grievance' now exists in England, 'sparked by the perception that Scotland enjoys advantages relative to England under current governing arrangements, particularly in the distribution of public spending and economic benefit.'[90] The Commission's report interpreted this polling to signal that 'respondents want a significant response to their concerns—a voice for England'.[91] It therefore proposed a menu of different amendments to current procedures for the handling of English-focused legislation in the House of Commons. Its recommendations were mindful of the objections considered in this chapter, and accepted the legitimacy of the objection to the possibility of English MPs vetoing the proposals of a government. It therefore proposed measures to ensure that MPs from England (or England and Wales) have new and additional ways to assert their interests—in the form of a new stage of pre-legislative scrutiny—but would not be entitled to vote down legislation emanating from the government of the UK. The changes it proposed involved the creation of an equivalent to a legislative consent motion (LCM) (currently used for legislation applying to non-English territories) being considered by an English Grand Committee before the Second Reading of a Bill, and a specially constituted Public Bill Committee reflecting the balance of English MPs. There would also be an opportunity at report stage for amendments to be made to a Bill to implement compromises between the Committee's amendments and the views of the UK-wide government. The report also proposed the establishment of a Devolution Committee in the House of Commons, and the introduction of a new system of 'double-counting', so that the voting patterns of English MPs would be routinely reported along with those of the House as a whole.[92] These proposals were intended to steer around the political controversy that would undoubtedly arise from a more full-blooded attempt to introduce EVEL at Westminster, and they reflected the case made by proponents of parliamentary government for a sole, uncontested source of executive authority.

Whether these proposals are agreed and acted upon by the main political parties will depend upon a host of different political considerations, but the prospects for the implementation of such reforms are undoubtedly more propitious now than at any point since devolution. The larger challenge facing contemporary reformers is whether the core assumption of the Commission's report that the English accept that their national voice will be strengthened through reforms to the working of parliament—remains viable in the context of the pronounced mood of political disenchantment that has developed in the last decade. There is, as we have seen, a strengthening, but often unacknowledged, linkage between disaffection with the manner in which England is governed and the belief that current arrangements are in some ways unfair to England, on the one hand, and a growing identification with Englishness, on the other. It is, therefore, increasingly likely that a deeper questioning of the principles that have underwritten the relationships and systems of governance at the heart of the union may well be needed. In policy terms, responding to these sentiments may well require a much wider and deeper set of reforms than mainstream politicians have been ready to envisage. And, to succeed, these may well need to contemplate the English question not just through the calculus of perceptions of national interest, but also through the less familiar lenses of national-democratic right and cultural recognition.

Conclusions
Reconfiguring the Politics of English Nationhood

It has long been regarded as an unquestionable truth in British politics that England constitutes the stable and secure heartland of the United Kingdom, in constitutional terms, and is the place where the struggles over legitimacy and nationhood that have affected its other territories have not come about. Yet, as the argument laid out in this book makes clear, this axiomatic assumption no longer holds. In some important and striking respects a quite profound reversal has taken place. The English are now increasingly viewed within the worlds of high politics and political commentary as a people who are worryingly disenchanted with the political system under which they live, and the two multi-national unions of which their country is a member. Various analysts have, as we have seen, detected a more nationalistic outlook among the English, although the extent, nature, and implications of this trend remain highly contested.

Northern Ireland, by contrast, has enjoyed a period of relative stability for the last fifteen years, primarily due to the successful establishment of a system of power-sharing and devolution, and the cessation of the armed struggle pursued by the Irish Republican Army. Wales continues to evolve an increasingly distinct sense of its own identity and culture, and has grown to accept the legislative institutions it acquired in the late 1990s. And in Scotland, the referendum that will take place in 2014 on whether the country should remain part of the United Kingdom currently appears likely to reflect an increasingly settled majority view which desires greater autonomy within the UK, rather than separation from it. And while debate about the merits and implications of these different options gathers pace, the national question in Scotland—at least as expressed in relation to the referendum—does not appear to be generating the passions and deep divisions that it once did.

And so, with no small dose of irony, it is in England that issues of national identity and sovereignty are generating the greatest sense of political uncertainty. At the same time, the sorts of constitutional question that have been foundational to nationalist currents elsewhere in the UK have, I have argued, been more epiphenomenal than foundational in relation to the gathering sense of English nationhood. The entanglement of a re-emerging sense of Englishness with a rising tide of populism is one of the main sources of the energy and instability associated with the national question in contemporary politics. This form of national consciousness has supplied a rich seedbed for the declinist, anti-political outlook which has emerged within English culture in the last few years. Others, however, maintain that this interest in English-focused ideas and sentiments carries relatively little political significance, as the English remain committed to celebrating their sense of nationality within the arenas of sport and popular culture rather than constitution and state.

Having considered the various leading characterizations of English national identity (in Chapter 2), the considerable body of evidence pertaining to popular attitudes towards English national identification (in Chapter 3), and the variety of cultural sites where this form of nationality has been promoted and contested in recent years (in Chapter 4), as well as the different challenges which the English question has generated for policy-makers and politicians (in Chapters 5 and 6), I conclude that neither of these established views supplies an adequate or accurate understanding of recent developments. While there is considerable evidence to support the contention that the English nation has come to acquire a more powerful and resonant set of connotations, in both cultural and political terms, properly nationalist sentiments are held only by a minority of English citizens.

There are several different reasons why English nationalism has not developed as a mass phenomenon in this period. The first is that, where such a perspective has gained ground, it has done so because it supplies a vehicle and language for the expression of discontent on a disparate range of issues, such as welfare, Europe, and immigration. In this vein, English nationalism plays an important, instrumental role as a carrier for populist currents of opinion, and may well be a further stimulus to such feelings. But it has not, as yet, emerged as an independent source of political mobilization or concerted pressure. This is confirmed by the reluctance of any of the mainstream political parties, including the current populist challenger UKIP, to identify wholeheartedly with English nationalism—though it remains entirely possible that UKIP may shift in this direction in the medium or longer term. This disinclination reflects a probably accurate judgement on the part of these political actors about the extent and depth of such sentiments.

The second reason why English nationalism has not, as yet, become a truly popular cause is that it has, to some degree, been contained by the re-emergence of other, distinct forms and expressions of English nationhood. These, I have suggested, have emerged out of a subtle alignment between several long-standing traditions of political thought and a growing contemporary

focus upon a more avowedly English sensibility. I have drawn particular attention to the renewal of an established seam of conservative Englishness, the
appeal of which has deepened in response to the uncertainties and anxieties
associated with the major economic and social changes of the last twenty years.
And I have also observed how Englishness has been framed and narrated in
liberal terms, harking back to an earlier tradition that posits the civic nation
as transcending the entrenched divisions associated with class, geography, and
cultural difference.

Both of these broad and multi-faceted perspectives have grown out of,
rather than in opposition to, the national tradition vaunted by Oakeshott
and other advocates of 'the British way' in the twentieth century. Within this
paradigm, Englishness has been seen as the whimsical and cultural side of a
national coinage that has imprinted on its other side the more formal, legal,
and civic associations of Britain. The greater emphasis given in cultural terms
during the last two decades to England as an organic kind of national community where the values of belonging, community, and security can be located
remains—for the most part—compatible with this hybrid form of national
self-understanding. Indeed the notion of an unbroken and undimmed English
spirit, which harks back to the pre-industrial past, and has allegedly remained
intact beneath the carapace of Britishness, has been a powerful and recurrent
motif in cultural and political terms since the nineteenth century. It figured
prominently, for instance, in the writings and thought of leading mid-century
intellectuals, including conservative historian Arthur Bryant, on the one hand,
and progressive writers, such as Priestley and Orwell, on the other.[1]

Light has suggested that the insular, parochial, and domestic conception of
England which formed part of this outlook was especially prominent within
the middle decades of the last century.[2] And Jed Esty has maintained that
the shift towards the Anglo side of this form of nationality gained significant
momentum in intellectual terms during the post-war decades, in the context of a rejection of Empire and a rediscovery of a smaller and more rooted
sense of English particularity.[3] But the question of what England, rather than
Britain, actually meant, or should mean—in institutional and political, rather
than simply cultural, terms—was largely ignored until the gathering crises of
the late 1960s and 1970s. In those years, different figures began to reflect more
openly, and often critically, on the nature of the relationship between these
different kinds of affiliation, and to consider whether a loyalty to the British
state represented the best, or only, form of national identification available to
the English.

One telling, though latterly forgotten, example of such a reflection was
offered by novelist John Fowles in an intriguing essay he wrote in 1964.[4] In
this he proclaimed himself to be proudly English, while going to great trouble

to explain why being British was also a vital element within his and his fellow countrymen's sense of nationality. Britishness, he declared, was 'a recent facade clapped on a much older building'. Stiff and formal 'Red-White-and-Blue Britain' was in some respects the mirror-image of the organic 'Green England' that was most fully expressed within the genres of romantic, pastoral, and landscape.[5] Britain represented commerce, Empire, and state, and was all about 'clubs, codes, and conformity', possessing deep roots in the patriarchal ethos of state and family. Green England, by contrast, signalled a feeling of being at home, typified by a sense of place, and a feel for the whimsy and Arcadianism of the retreat to the unspoiled countryside. But, crucially, he insisted that these two patriotic seams were deeply intertwined within the English mind. Fowles was especially keen to establish that England was possessed of its own democratic myths. His belief that a lineage of libertarian Englishness could be melded with the social democratic collectivism of the post-war decades is, from a contemporary perspective, striking and surprising in equal measure. His confidence in their compatibility was about to be shaken by profound political developments. Exactly the kind of collectivist consensus that Fowles celebrated became the target for a new populist expression of English nationalism at the behest of maverick Tory politician Enoch Powell in the late 1960s.[6] The subsequent political ascendancy of Thatcherite conservatism ensured that progressives became increasingly wary of Anglicized expressions of nationhood, and opted to identify instead with the nationalisms emerging in Scotland and Wales, and, in the 1990s, with the civic liberalism associated with Britishness.

Yet the deep connections between the complementary connotations of England and Britain that Fowles evoked reflect a pattern of national sentiment that has continued to flow into the recent period, and has proved sufficiently adaptable and sinuous to be reworked in the more fraught context of recent years. In the wake of the extended bout of soul-searching about Britain's prospects that characterized the 1990s (which were considered in Chapter 1), a more separated conception of the organic community supplied by England, on the one hand, and the civic culture and institutional life of Britain, on the other, has become familiar. Yet, it still remains the case now, as it did when Fowles was writing, that the default understanding of most of the English is that: 'We have to be British and we want to be English.'[7]

One further, significant implication of Fowles's argument was that the English have, in their own quiet and stubborn way, been more effective at resisting attempts to foist onto them a British sense of nationhood than has often been assumed. The form of nationhood which Colley suggested was disseminated from above during the eighteenth and nineteenth centuries reflected the idea of Britain as a '*state*-nation'. But this perspective did not

percolate as far, or as evenly, into the populace, as this historical thesis suggested, and many of the English retained a sense of themselves as a people
whose culture predated, and existed separately from, the state.[8] Englishness
therefore represented a variegated consciousness which developed, in complex
and disparate ways, 'from the bottom up'. Nairn and other leftist critics have,
therefore, fallen into the trap of seeing England as a deviant instance of the
first of these models. But the view of Fowles and various other intellectuals
writing in the last century testifies to the confident, culturally rooted ideas
about England which had never been surrendered in the face of the official
forms of patriotism required by Britain. The strength and adaptability of this
'strange half diffusion of Englishness with Britishness' have been quite considerably under-estimated in recent political and cultural discourse.[9]

The various cultural-cum-political visions of Englishness to which I have
drawn attention in this book, are currently engaged in a largely unnoticed,
but potentially significant, competition over the character and implications
of this re-emerging sense of nationality. While each draws upon earlier forms
of thought, and carries significant political resonances, they have rarely been
directly addressed or recuperated by mainstream politicians. And yet, the
reluctance to engage with these trends means that important questions about
the national and democratic character of the British political system remain
unaddressed, not least whether the English can or will develop a sense of
nationhood that can still be nested within the overarching structures of the
union. Those who hold to the view that any kind of engagement with, and
expression of, Englishness is bound to lead to the politicization of this form of
nationhood need to give greater consideration to the dangers, for the Unionist
cause, associated with non-engagement, as the growing sense of national
awareness among the English is left to the mercies of populist politicians
and street-level demagogues. Equally, greater awareness of a rising sense of
inequity about aspects of the extant systems of politics and governance under
which the English live suggests the need to reflect on whether restoring a sense
of recognition and agency to them as a people might serve to undercut the
reified and absolutist vision of national sovereignty which is associated with
growing hostility to the European Union.

In mainstream politics, it is the Conservatives who are the most likely party
to move confidently onto this terrain. Yet they now face a powerful challenge
from the populist image of the English as the perpetual victims of politicians, the EU, and liberal public authorities. Rather than being drawn into
ideological territory defined by their opponents, Conservatives would do better to re-engage the popular lineage of ordinary English conservatism. At the
same time, Labour leader Ed Miliband's partial embrace of the argot of progressive patriotism does not, as yet, look like the first indication of a more

wholehearted engagement with English identity. However, Labour needs both to rebuild its relationship with vast swathes of England where it performed so poorly at the General Election of 2010, and show that it is more engaged with the values, experiences, and preoccupations of voters. The idioms and values of English nationhood offer an important aspect of any viable response to both challenges. But a still palpable fear prevails in Labour circles that such a move would compromise its appeal as a UK-wide 'one-nation' party, and might alienate Scottish voters and MPs. These anxieties have considerably inhibited the party's engagement in this area. And both parties have failed to get to grips, more generally, with the growing importance of England as a community of attachment, on the one hand, and the deepening disenchantment with the established system of lop-sided and top-down governance that prevails in England. Thus, while the case for 'localism' has, for the most part, been made in technocratic terms, the question of whether significant powers—for instance over the organization and funding of key public services—ought to be delegated to tiers of government beneath the level of the state, would be better framed within the language of national representation and empowerment. Were any of the mainstream political parties to engage more openly and positively with this form of identity, and the various issues—of recognition and representation—associated with it, the balance between the different streams of English sentiment that I have emphasized here might well be significantly altered. For there is an embryonic and fluid quality to these sentiments, which means that Englishness remains open to political appropriation and influence. It is particularly imperative that progressives engage more boldly and confidently with ongoing struggles to define and determine the imagined community of England, and lend support to those seeking to challenge rival versions of Englishness.

The enthusiastic embrace of Englishness by the main parties remains at present an unlikely scenario. However, the prospects for a more incremental engagement in policy terms are better. A majority of politicians at Westminster now accept the danger arising from the pervasive sense that this remains a forbidden national identity, an entrenched perception that represents a rich opportunity for populists. Such a focus would involve addressing some of the particular complaints about the non-recognition of the English which have been considered here. This might involve moves to commemorate St George's Day as a public holiday, playing an English anthem at sporting occasions when England is represented, and including an English option on forms employed by public bodies and authorities. Such an agenda might also involve communicating more clearly and transparently the territorial remit of different departments of state, and of public bodies and authorities more generally. The naming of those institutions that are responsible for key services in England only has, thus far, happened in an uneven and inconsistent way. While the BBC has autonomous operations in Scotland, Wales, and Northern Ireland, as well as distinct English regional divisions, for instance, it has remained wary of developing an overarching English voice, continuing to subsume this within its overall UK programming. The British Council, by contrast, has recently established a 'British Council England', as a counterpart to its affiliates in Northern Ireland, Wales, and Scotland. And, more generally, there are clear signs of a shift towards the recognition of the importance of greater territorial transparency in different parts of the establishment—hence the call in 2013 by the Local Government Association for the introduction of a Secretary of State for England.[10]

A commitment to address the issues associated with the lack of recognition for England in cultural and institutional terms is a natural accompaniment to a greater willingness to accept that the English are, in important respects, denied equality of representation within the current political system. The proposals advanced by the McKay Commission in March 2013 for reforms to the procedures governing legislation that apply only to England, or to England and Wales, speak to this latter issue, and deserve careful consideration by all the main parties. More important than the various concrete amendments that are floated in its report is its willingness (discussed in Chapter 6) to accept that new normative-democratic principles are now required in the context of the establishment of devolution for all of the non-English territories of the UK. I have argued, more generally, that it is important as well to consider those questions of democratic and national principle which are implicated within the shifts in national awareness that have been considered here. Two particular questions are bound to impress themselves upon the UK's political community in the coming years. Is it feasible that the English will remain satisfied with a political conversation among their representatives that is still conducted within a British, not English, framework? And what are the prospects for the development and popularization of a civic, rather than ethnic, idea of the English nation?

The first of these questions arises directly from the development of an increasingly meaningful sense of English community for a growing number of the English in the last twenty years. As these sentiments have become stronger and more salient, there has bubbled to the surface of political life an unfamiliar, but increasingly resonant, set of normative ideas—about the democratic rights of the majority nation within a multi-national state—which have been hard to assimilate within the leading forms of thinking and governance associated with the British state. The strong possibility that this broad trend in national identification will, over time, grow stronger, has led, as we saw in Chapter 5, to the dawning realization that this sense of English identity needs to be more positively and creatively engaged in policy terms. Such recognition is very gradually opening the door, I have suggested, to the reappraisal of the UK as a multi-national state, rather than a polity that can ensure its legitimacy through an image of itself as a *state*-nation.

The need to accept and speak to the implications of this shift is more urgent than most politicians appear to appreciate. The growing and deepening sense of affinity with the imagined community of England has become tangled up with a growing sense of disenchantment about membership of the European Union. And recent polling suggests that this attitude may now be spilling over into many people's perceptions of the United Kingdom itself. The growth of national self-awareness among the English appears to be crystallizing a hardening scepticism about the multi-national associations and wider alliances of which England is a member, and this trend represents a formidable obstacle to arguments in favour of these different involvements that are pitched in the language of national interest. Those who believe that it is preferable for the English to remain involved in the European Union might wish to consider that identifying other areas for the expression of the growing demands for cultural recognition and national sovereignty on behalf of this people might provide important, alternative outlets for English frustration.

More generally, while the English question has, for the most part, been viewed by politicians and commentators alike in exceptionalist terms, it is also useful, as I suggested in Chapter 4, to view this as a local instance of a much more generic fault-line—between the appeal of smaller-scale and more intimate communities of attachment, on the one hand, and the vast, trans-national kinds of action and cooperation that are increasingly imperative in an era of multi-level governance. Devising political narratives that make sense of these seemingly divergent dynamics is a challenge that has not, as yet, been adequately grasped in British politics. In some of its most powerful forms, Englishness carries at its heart the pessimistic proposition that, with the abandonment of Empire, the English should retreat from broader entanglements and avoid grandiose, modern enterprises. Such sentiments are by no means novel. In *The Road to Wigan Pier* Orwell wryly observed that, much as he disliked imperial England, the only alternative to it was 'to reduce England to a cold and unimportant little island where we should all have to work very hard and live mainly on herrings and potatoes'.[11] The sense that the English can only really be true to themselves and their culture by resisting the forces, causes, and entanglements associated with the wider world remains a powerful cultural impulse.

Many members and shapers of political society have interpreted recent geo-political and economic shifts to suggest that the English interest lies in its membership of trans-national association and alliance. The growing sense of

strain generated between the divergent imperatives represented by the calculation of national advantage within the world of high politics, on the one hand,
and the increasingly magnetic pull of identities and loyalties that lie beneath
the state, on the other, renders this one of the most powerful and destabilizing
dynamics within contemporary British politics.

For liberal-minded politicians and commentators this disjuncture throws
up a difficult challenge: how to convince a large number of increasingly
disenchanted citizens of the legitimacy of institutions and associations that
are widely depicted as antithetical to those imagined communities where
a sense of belonging and community tend to be identified. One possible
answer to this question is for politicians to re-embed themselves within
their own national cultures and civil societies, and to engage more fully
with expressions of, and arguments over, the terms and meaning of nationhood, in order to bolster those more outward-facing and culturally confident forms of national consciousness. They might also adopt a more
proactive stance in seeking to delegitimate those forms of nationalism that
are sour, xenophobic, and fuelled by fear and anxiety. For this reason above
all, skirting around Englishness may not now be as wise an option as liberal
orthodoxy suggests.

A second major question, which flows from the recognition of the deep and
challenging nature of this tension, is whether a form of nationhood that speaks
to both of these dynamics—which is, in other words, sufficiently meaningful
to be resonant at a popular level and sufficiently outward-facing to promote
the idea of trans-national cooperation—might be created. Can a brand of
English nationhood be forged that is both civic and popular?

While many critics and commentators remain inherently sceptical about
such an idea, there are good reasons to think that a civic reimagining of the
English nation is more attainable than is widely supposed. Its construction
would, at the very least, require a more concerted and enthusiastic engagement by a range of political voices and civic leaders, conveying a clear sense
that Englishness is both legitimate and valuable as a source of national identification. But codifying Englishness and seeking to promote an orthodox liberal
version of it are unlikely to work. A viable, civic form of Anglo-nationhood
would most likely be achieved through reference to the rich heritage of
national thinking which has interwoven liberal and conservative themes and
ideas, and the redeployment of these in current circumstances. The process
I have described at various points in this book, whereby older conservative
and liberal idioms have been set to work as the bases for politically resonant
narratives about Englishness, illustrates the potential for such a development.
The establishment of a viable form of English nationhood would need to
reflect the strong sense of cultural particularity, place, and tradition that have

been endemic to English culture. In this context, the habit of some progressive patriots of pointing to Scotland, and other 'model' nationalisms in Europe, as a template and guide for the English, constitutes a reflex that itself merits critical examination. Some of the principal coordinates of a prospective civic nationality among the English are likely to emanate from conservative, as well as liberal, sources. From the conservative side, there is a strong sense of Englishness as rooted in places, communities, and institutions. An ethos of respect for the variety of locally rooted customs and traditions, and the extraordinarily varied kinds of associational life that have prospered in the cities, towns, and villages of England, would need to be central to a prospective civic nationality. From the liberal side of this inheritance, the values of civil and political liberty, tolerance, and fairness would most likely be salient. An encompassing form of English nationhood would need to stitch together these different emphases, and harness the various sentiments and values that they evoke. A civically inclined Englishness which has the capacity to appeal across some of the most entrenched cultural, ethnic, and social divides of modern England also needs to find space for the different forms of Englishness which have lately come to the fore. The real promise of a genuinely inclusive national culture is that it would ensure a more equal relationship and interplay between these various characterizations, while also promoting forms of cultural and normative commonality that would ensure that Englishness was both meaningful and 'deep' in character. In this respect the artistic and cultural developments to which I drew attention in Chapter 4 carry significance as they illustrate the potential for a more vigorous set of debates and interplay between these different expressions of nationhood in ways that have not, as yet, been explored in the worlds of politics and political thought.

The potential development of such a national culture depends, above all, upon the willingness of liberals and progressives to engage England as the site for a positive and progressive nationality, rather than continuing to assume that the civic ideal applies only at the level of the UK. It requires also that conservatives turn away from the siren call of a populism that frames England as the authentic, subaltern nation that the political and economic elites are determined to destroy. In fact, as I suggested in Chapter 3, the kind of rooted, conservative Englishness that has quietly returned to the fore in recent years represents an important seam within any putative English national culture. It is reasonably accommodating of cultural difference, pragmatic in its character, and dispositionally restrained in its support for, and opposition to, various forms of political and economic modernization. Such sentiments are all potentially beneficial to the health and perpetuation of a democratic culture in England, providing an important bulwark against the illusions and fantasies that populism promotes.

In the final years of the last century, a number of progressive thinkers and commentators came to believe that the kind of civic culture that democracies require implies a culturally coherent and capacious body of national senti- ment. A meaningful and shared sense of nationhood, it has been argued, offers the most stable and conducive foundation for some of the democratic 'virtues' which are in decreasing supply in representative democracies, including the kind of solidarity required for redistributive systems of taxation and welfare, and the inclination to cooperate and compromise with those from very dif- ferent backgrounds. It is, more generally, through the establishment of what philosopher Charles Taylor has termed a 'shared identity space' that the sense of common endeavour which a successful democratic state requires can best be promoted.[12] Given that it is increasingly open to doubt whether Britishness can any longer play these roles, the case for looking with fresh eyes at a resur- gent Englishness is increasingly strong. Far from being the antithesis of such a space, English nationhood may well represent the best available means of renewing it.

These normative issues aside, I have raised critical questions at various points in this book about the empirical and sociological adequacy of some of the main characterizations of the nature and strength of English nation- hood. The familiar suggestion that a significant rupture with older patterns of national sentiment has taken place in this period represents a misreading of the nature and evolution of English consciousness. It also reflects a ten- dency to exaggerate the extent and appeal of English nationalism. Equally, the notion that Englishness is, by definition, a 'merely cultural', rather than political, phenomenon has led to an under-estimation of the different ways in which a renewed sense of Englishness is filtering into politics. Indeed, the increasing presence of claims about the health and prospects of 'the nation' in public discourse and everyday life may well be linked to the waning appeal of the narratives and ideas emanating from the world of party politics in this period.

In combination, the different narrative versions of Englishness charted here have staked out an imaginative terrain upon which competing visions of the nation are increasingly locked in competition. One of the key features of their interplay has been an intensifying competition over mythical, folkloric, and historic themes. The renewed interest in the national past, the powerful appeal of heritage, and the recurrent focus upon place and landscape within current expressions of Englishness are integral to the contested and fluid process of national reimagining. What England's modernist critics have tended to forget, but increasingly need to appreciate, is that a nation which possesses a past that has been so lengthy and prolific is very likely to have a future which is also replete with different cultural and political possibility. Revived and reimagined notions of English nationhood are being forged from such materials, and informed by the contemporary social and cultural make-up of the country. And a vital struggle over the political soul of Englishness is steadily emerging as the most important of the various English questions that now need to be faced in British politics.

Notes

INTRODUCTION

1. The main volumes devoted to the English question in British politics include: Robert Hazell (ed.), *The English Question* (Manchester: Manchester University Press, 2006); Selina Chen and Tony Wright (eds), *The English Question* (London: Fabian Society, 2000); and Arthur Aughey, *The Politics of Englishness* (Manchester: Manchester University Press, 2007). A number of studies of the British constitution and the nature of territorial politics after devolution also include significant reflections upon this question, including: Vernon Bogdanor, *Devolution in the United Kingdom* (Oxford: Oxford University Press, 2001); James Mitchell, *Devolution in the UK* (Manchester: Manchester University Press, 2012); Christopher Bryant, *The Nations of Britain* (Oxford: Oxford University Press, 2006); and Anthony King, *The British Constitution* (Oxford: Oxford University Press, 2009).
2. The merits and importance of different approaches to nationalism, spanning various disciplinary traditions, are explored in Umut Ozkirimli, *Theories of Nationalism* (Basingstoke: Macmillan, 2010) and Steven Grosby, *Nationalism: A Very Short Introduction* (Oxford: Oxford University Press, 2013).
3. Peter Mandler, *The English National Character: The History of an Idea from Edmund Burke to Tony Blair* (New Haven, Conn.: Yale University Press, 2006).
4. Mandler, *English National Character*. See also Paul Langford, *Englishness Identified: Manners and Character 1650–1850* (Oxford: Oxford University Press, 2000).
5. For a theoretical discussion of the importance of the 'decontestation' of concepts within competing and overlapping webs of ideological thinking, see Michael Freeden, *Ideologies and Political Theory: A Conceptual Approach* (Oxford: Oxford University Press, 1998).
6. For a progressive argument for the importance of these last two myths to early twentieth-century socialism, see Christopher Hill, *The Norman Yoke* (London: Lawrence & Wishart, 1955).
7. Ronald Harwood's *An English Tragedy*, was first staged at the Watford Palace Theatre in Feb. 2008.
8. David Gervais, *Literary Englands: Versions of 'Englishness' in Modern Writing* (Cambridge: Cambridge University Press), 152.
9. Mandler, *English National Character*, 56.

10. Krishan Kumar, *The Making of English National Identity* (Cambridge: Cambridge University Press, 2003), 3.
11. See Hill, 'Norman Yoke'.
12. See Susan Condor, 'Unimagined Community? Some Social Psychological Issues Concerning English National Identity', in Glynis Breakwell and Evanthia Lyons (eds), *Changing European Identities: Social Psychological Analyses of Social Change* (London: Routledge, 1996), 41–68; 'Pride and Prejudice: Identity Management in People's Talk about "this Country"', *Discourse and Society*, 11 (2000), 175–205; 'Sense and Sensibility: The Conversational Etiquette of English National Self-Identification', in Arthur Aughey and Christine Berberich (eds), *These Englands: A Conversation on National Identity* (Manchester: Manchester University Press, 2012), 29–55; and Jackie Abell and Susan Condor, 'Vernacular Accounts of "National Identity" in Post-Devolution Scotland and England', in Karyn Stapleton and John Wilson (eds), *Devolution and Identity* (London: Ashgate, 2006), 51–75.
13. See Steve Garner, 'The Entitled Nation: How People Make Themselves White in Contemporary England', *Sens Publique* (2010); available at: <http://www.sens-public.org/spip.php?article729>.
14. Michael Billig, *Banal Nationalism* (London: Sage, 1995).
15. On the prevalence and implications of such lists in relation to Englishness, see Ellis Cashmore, 'The Impure Strikes Back', *British Journal of Sociology*, 54/3 (2004), 407–14; Christine Berberich, ' "A Peculiarly English Idiosyncrasy?": Julian Barnes's Use of Lists in England, England', *American, British and Canadian Studies*, 13 (2009), 75–87; and Aughey and Berberich, 'Introduction: These Englands—a Conversation on National Identity', in *These Englands*, 1–28, 5–6.
16. John Major, 'Speech to the Conservative Group for Europe', 22 Apr. 1993; available at: <http://www.johnmajor.co.uk/page1086.html>.
17. Julian Barnes, *England, England* (London: Picador, 2005).
18. For some insightful commentary on Willetts's argument, see Aughey and Berberich, 'Introduction', in *These Englands*, 5.
19. George Orwell, 'England, Your England', in *England, Your England and Other Essays* (London: Secker & Warburg, 1953), 192–224.
20. T. S. Eliot, *Notes towards the Definition of Culture* (London: Faber & Faber, 1948), 31.
21. John Betjeman, 'Oh, to be in England', *The Listener*, 11 Mar. 1943, 296.
22. This term figures in Tom Nairn, *The Break-up of Britain: Crisis and Neo-nationalism, 1965–75* (London: New Left Books, 1977).
23. Anthony Barnett, 'Afterword', in Michael Gardiner and Claire Westall (eds), *Literature of an Independent England: Revisions of England, Englishness and English Literature* (London: Palgrave Macmillan, 2013), 340–7, 340.
24. For an extensive assessment of these features of national discourse in British politics, see Aughey, *Politics of Englishness*.
25. Krishan Kumar, *The Making of English National Identity* (Cambridge: Cambridge University Press, 2003).
26. J. G. Ballard, *Kingdom Come* (London: Harper Perennial, 2007).

27. Ballard, *Kingdom Come,* 121.
28. See Andrew O'Hagan, 'The Age of Indifference', *Guardian,* 10 Jan. 2009; available at: <http://www.guardian.co.uk/books/2009/jan/10/andrew-ohagan-george-orwellmemoriallecture>. This is an edited version of the George Orwell Memorial Lecture that he delivered in 2008.
29. O'Hagan, 'Age of Indifference'.
30. Jason Tuck, 'The Men in White: Reflections on Rugby Union, the Media and Englishness', *International Review for the Sociology of Sport,* 38/2 (2003), 177–99.
31. David Marquand, 'Give us a Moral Vision for England', *Open Democracy,* 7 Jan. 2008; available at: <http://www.opendemocracy.net/ourkingdom/2008/01/07/give-us-a-moral-vision-for-england>.
32. Rachel Joyce, *The Unlikely Pilgrimage of Harold Fry* (London: Black Swan, 2013).
33. John McLeod, 'Introduction: Measuring Englishness', in David Rogers and John McLeod (eds), *The Revision of Englishness* (Manchester: Manchester University Press, 2004), 1–15.
34. Peter Ackroyd, *Albion: The Origins of the English Imagination* (London: Chatto & Windus, 2002), 237, 448.
35. Daniel Defoe, *The True Born Englishman: A Satire* (London: Ulan Books, 2012).
36. Ackroyd, *Albion*, 449.
37. Ian Baucom, *Out of Place: Englishness, Empire and the Locations of Identity* (Princeton: Princeton University Press, 1999).
38. Baucom, *Out of Place*, 4.
39. Krishan Kumar, 'Nation and Empire: English and British National Identity in Comparative Perspective', *Theory and Society,* 29 (2000), 575–608.
40. For a historiographical discussion of the various ideas associated with 'Little England', see John S. Galbraith, 'Myths of the "Little England" Era', *American Historical Review*, 67/1 (1961), 34–48.
41. Simon Heffer, *Like the Roman: The Life of Enoch Powell* (London: Faber & Faber, 2008).
42. On the ideological roots of liberal interventionism, see Oliver Daddow and Pauline Schnapper, 'Liberal Intervention in the Foreign Policy Thinking of Tony Blair and David Cameron', *Cambridge Review of International Affairs,* 26/2 (2013), 330–49. On the re-emergence of a conservative politics of place in contemporary England, see John Harris, 'No Mainstream Party in England Truly Understands Conservatism', *Guardian,* 4 Mar. 2013; available at: <http://www.guardian.co.uk/commentisfree/2013/mar/04/conservatism-identity-representation-eastleigh>.
43. Kumar, *Making of English National Identity.*
44. See Julia Stapleton, *Political Intellectuals and Public Identities in Britain since 1850* (Manchester: Manchester University Press, 2001), and *Sir Arthur Bryant and National History in Twentieth-Century Britain* (Idaho Falls, Ida.: Lexington Books, 2006).
45. James Campbell, 'The United Kingdom of England: The Anglo-Saxon Achievement', in Alexander Grant and Keith Stringer (eds), *Uniting the Kingdom? The Making of British History* (London: Routledge, 1995), 31–47, 31.

46. See Liah Greenfeld, *Nationalism: Five Roads to Modernity* (Cambridge, Mass.: Harvard University Press, 1993), and Hans Kohn, 'The Genesis and Character of English Nationalism', *Journal of the History of Ideas*, 1/1 (1940), 69–94.

47. See, for instance, Colin Copus, 'English National Parties in Post-devolution UK', *British Politics*, 4/4 (2009), 363–85, and the discussion of the growing sense of collective interest discernible among the English, in Christopher Bryant, 'English Identities and Interests and the Governance of Britain', *Parliamentary Affairs*, 62/2 (2010), 250–65.

48. Aleks Sierz, *Rewriting the Nation: British Theatre Today* (London: Methuen Drama, 2011), 9.

49. For a trenchant critique of the application of 'nationalism' to the English case, see Richard English, *Is there an English Nationalism?* (London: IPPR, 2011); available at: <http://www.ippr.org/publications/55/1838/is-there-an-english-nationalism>. And for an account of the singularity of cultural forms of nationalism, see John Hutchinson, *Modern Nationalism* (London: Fontana Press, 1994).

50. See, for instance, Benedict Anderson, *Imagined Communities: Reflections on the Origins and Spread of Nationalism* (London: Verso, 2006). On the role of national mythologies, see also Tim Edensor, *National Identity, Popular Culture and Everyday Life* (London: Berg, 2002), and Geoffrey Hosking and George Schöpflin (eds), *Myths and Nationhood* (London: Hurst & Co., 1997).

51. Floriane Reviron-Piégay, 'Introduction: The Dilemma of Englishness', in Floriane Reviron-Piégay (ed.), *Englishness Revisited* (Cambridge: Cambridge University Press, 2009), 1–27, 5–6.

52. David Cannadine, *Ornamentalism: How the British Saw their Empire* (Oxford: Oxford University Press, 2001).

53. These are the words of a 45-year-old 'white', male participant in a deliberative workshop on identity-related issues held with community stakeholders from the South London area, which I organized in collaboration with the Institute for Public Policy Research, Mar. 2008.

54. This distinction is thoughtfully discussed in Peter Mandler, 'What is "National Identity"? Definitions and Applications in Modern British Historiography', *Modern Intellectual History*, 3/2 (2005), 271–97.

55. Mandler, 'What is "National Identity"', 282.

56. These broad trends, and the challenges they pose for political theorists and analysts, are discussed in Michael Kenny, *The Politics of Identity: Liberal Political Theory and the Dilemmas of 'Difference'* (Cambridge: Polity, 2004).

57. See Michael Skey, *National Belonging and Everyday Life* (Basingstoke: Palgrave, 2011).

58. I take my lead in this respect from several recent historical and theoretically informed studies of nationalism, including Anthony Smith, *Ethno-symbolism and Nationalism: A Cultural Approach* (London: Routledge, 2009), and Richard English, *Irish Freedom: The History of Nationalism in Ireland* (Basingstoke: Macmillan, 2006).

59. See esp. Smith, *Ethno-symbolism and Nationalism,* and Ozkirimli, *Theories of Nationalism.*

60. Edensor, *National Identity*.
61. Edensor, *National Identity*, 13.
62. Edensor, *National Identity*, 4.
63. Hutchinson, *Modern Nationalism,* 10.

CHAPTER 1

1. Ben Wellings, *English Nationalism and Euroscepticism* (Oxford: Peter Lang, 2012). This connection was also central to the characterization of Englishness advanced by historian Anthony Smith; see, for instance, Smith, ' "Set in the Silver Sea": English National Identity and European Integration', *Nations and Nationalism*, 12/3 (2006), 433–52.
2. See Colin Kidd, *Unions and Unionism: Political Thought in Scotland 1500–2000* (Cambridge: Cambridge University Press, 2008).
3. For an assessment of the role of exceptionalism in relation to academic characterizations of Britain's polity and culture, see Michael Kenny, 'Politics as an Academic Vocation', in Matthew Flinders, Andrew Gamble, Colin Hay, and Michael Kenny (eds), *The Oxford Handbook of British Politics* (Oxford: Oxford University Press, 2009), 3–24.
4. See esp. Linda Colley, *Britons: Forging the Nation, 1707–1837* (London: Vintage, 1996), and Norman Davies, *The Isles: A History* (London: Papermac, 2000).
5. Ben Wellings, 'Rump Britain: Englishness and Britishness, 1992–2001', *National Identities,* 9/4 (2007), 395–412.
6. Ben Wellings, 'Losing the Peace: Euroscepticism and the Foundations of Contemporary English Nationalism', *Nations and Nationalism*, 16/3 (2010), 488–505.
7. See the discussion of the coalesecence of these ideas in Philip Dodd's *The Battle over Britain* (London: Demos, 1995).
8. Gareth Young suggests that Wellings's argument may underplay the importance of Euroscepticsm in other parts of the UK: 'Euroscepticism: A Very English Disease?', *Open Democracy,* 9 Dec. 2011; available at: <http://www.opendemocracy.net/ourkingdom/gareth-young/euroscepticism-very-english-disease>.
9. Wellings, 'Rump Britain', 407.
10. See, for instance, Andrew Pearmain, 'England and the "National-Popular" ', *Soundings,* 38 (2008), 89–103.
11. See, for instance, Will Hutton, *The State We're In: Why Britain is in Crisis and How to Overcome it* (London: Vintage, 1996).
12. Some of these changes are registered in Hutton, *The State We're In,* and also Anthony Giddens, *The Third Way: The Renewal of Democracy* (Cambridge: Polity, 1998).
13. For a discussion of the appeal and implications of post-national theorizing among intellectuals in this period, see Craig Berry and Michael Kenny, 'Ideology and the Intellectuals', in Michael Freeden, Lyman Tower Sargent, and Marc Stears (eds), *The Oxford Handbook of Political Ideologies* (Oxford: Oxford University Press, forthcoming, 2013), 251–70.

14. Michael Ignatieff, *Blood and Belonging: Journeys into the New Nationalism* (London: Vintage, 1994), 168.
15. Berry and Kenny, 'Ideology and the Intellectuals'.
16. For a much debated counter-blast to this trend, see David Goodhart, 'Too Diverse?', *Prospect*, 20 Feb. 2004.
17. See esp. Will Hutton and Anthony Giddens (eds), *On the Edge: Living with Global Capitalism* (London: Vintage, 2001), and David Held, Anthony McGrew, David Goldblatt, and Jonathan Perraton, *Global Transformations: Politics, Economics and Culture* (Cambridge: Polity, 1999).
18. Paul Ward, *Britishness since 1870* (London: Routledge, 2004).
19. Cited in Michael Collins, *The Likes of Us: A Biography of the White Working Class* (London: Granta, 2004), 229.
20. This contrast between the ethical properties of Britishness and the 'merely cultural' nature of Englishness was central to one of the most important theoretical attempts in recent years to rescue the normative value of nationality for liberals—David Miller's *On Nationality* (Oxford: Oxford University Press, 1997).
21. Ignatieff, *Blood and Belonging*.
22. Lizanne Dowds and Ken Young, 'National Identity', in Roger Jowell, John Curtice, Alison Park, Lindsay Brook, and Katarina Thomson (eds), *British Social Attitudes: The Thirteenth Report* (Aldershot: Ashgate, 1996–7), 141–60.
23. Dowds and Young, 'National Identity', 143–4.
24. Igantieff, *Blood and Belonging*.
25. See the discussion of shifting attitudes towards the Church of England in this period in Cole Moreton, *Is God Still an Englishman? How we Lost our Faith But Found New Soul* (London: Little Brown, 2010).
26. On shifting perceptions of the monarchy in this period, see Andrzej Olechnowicz, *The Monarchy and the British Nation: 1780 to the Present* (Cambridge: Cambridge University Press, 2007).
27. On Britishness see Andrew Gamble and Tony Wright, 'Introduction: The Britishness Question', *Political Quarterly*, 78/supp. 1 (2007), 1–9; and Tony Wright, 'England, Whose England?', in Chen and Wright, *The English Question*, 1–12.
28. Wright, 'England, Whose England?', 8.
29. Wright, 'England, Whose England?', 9.
30. Wright, 'England, Whose England?', 9.
31. For an illuminating discussion of a variety of political ideas about the exemplary and exceptional nature of Britain, see Aughey, *Politics of Englishness*.
32. For a partial exception, however, see Nevill Johnson, *In Search of the Constitution: Reflections on State and Society in Britain* (London: Pergamon Press, 1977).
33. This argument is advanced in Vernon Bogdanor, 'Lions, Unicorns and Ostriches', *Times Higher Education*, 8 Nov. 2002; available at: <http://www.timeshighereducation.co.uk/books/lions-unicorns-and-ostriches/172864.article>, and Jonathan Clark, 'Not Fading Away Yet', *Times Literary Supplement*, 7 June 2002, 3–4.

34. Dodd, *Battle over Britain*.
35. For a discussion of the role of émigré intellectuals in relation to this form of exceptionalism, see Ian Buruma, *Voltaire's Coconuts or Anglomania in Europe* (London: Phoenix, 2000).
36. Ignatieff, *Blood and Belonging*, 166.
37. Barnett, 'Afterword'.
38. Richard Rose, *Politics in England* (London: Faber & Faber, 1982), 29.
39. Cited in Bogdanor, 'Lions, Unicorns and Ostriches'.
40. J. G. A. Pocock, 'British History: A Plea for a New Subject', *Journal of Modern History*, 4/4 (1975), 601–21.
41. For an insightful discussion of this current and its key intellectual assumptions, see Richard Bourke, 'Pocock and the Presuppositions of the New British History', *Historical Journal*, 53/3 (2010), 747–70.
42. Hugh Kearney, *The British Isles: A History of Four Nations* (Cambridge: Cambridge University Press, 2006).
43. Kearney, *British Isles*, 40.
44. Hugh Kearney, *Ireland: Contested Ideas of Nationalism and History* (New York: New York University Press, 2007), 179.
45. Raphael Samuel (ed.), *Patriotism: The Making and Unmaking of British National Identity*, i–iii (London: History Workshop Journal, 1989).
46. See esp. the influential essay by Hugh Cunningham, 'The Language of Patriotism', in Samuel, *Patriotism*, i: *History and Politics*, 57–89.
47. Michael Bentley, *Modernizing England's Past: English Historiography in the Age of Modernism, 1870–1970* (Cambridge: Cambridge University Press, 2006).
48. David Cannadine, 'British History: Past, Present—and Future?', *Past and Present*, 119 (1988), 171–203.
49. Hugh Kearney, 'Myths of Englishness', *History Workshop Journal*, 56 (2003), 251–7.
50. Davies, *The Isles*; Keith Robbins, *Great Britain: Identities, Institutions and the Idea of Britishness since 1500* (London: Longman, 1997); and Laurence Brockliss and David Eastwood (eds), *A Union of Multiple Identities: The British Isles, c1750–1850* (Manchester: Manchester University Press, 1997).
51. For an assessment of the resistance to comparative approaches within political studies in the UK, see Edward Page, 'British Political Science and Comparative Politics', *Political Studies*, 38/3 (1990), 438–52, and Michael Kenny, 'The Case for Disciplinary History: British Political Studies in the 1950s and 1960s', *British Journal of Politics and International Relations*, 6/4 (2004), 565–83.
52. See Peter Flora (ed.) (with Stein Kuhnle and Derek Unwin), *State Formation Nation-Building and Mass Politics in Europe: The Theory of Stein Rokkan* (Oxford: Oxford University Press, 1999).
53. James Mitchell, 'From Unitary State to Union State: Labour's Changing View of the United Kingdom and its Implications', *Regional Studies*, 30/6 (1996), 607–11, and 'The Westminster Model and the State of the Unions', *Parliamentary Affairs*, 63/1 (2010), 85–8.

54. Charlie Jeffery and Daniel Wincott, 'Devolution in the United Kingdom: Statehood and Citizenship in Transition', *Publius*, 36/1 (2006), 3–18.
55. Dodd, *Battle over Britain*, 13–14.
56. Hadlow faced considerable scepticism within the BBC about the prospects for this landmark series; Tristram Hunt, interview with Michael Kenny, 22 Feb. 2008.
57. David Cannadine, interview with Richard English, 20 June 2007.
58. Chris Hastings, 'England is the Country that "Dare Not Speak its Name"', *Daily Telegraph,* 17 Oct. 2004.
59. Cannadine, interview.
60. Michael Wood, *In Search of England: Journeys into the English Past* (Berkeley, Calif.: University of California Press, 2001).
61. Wood, *In Search of England*, 66.
62. *New Statesman,* Special Supplement, 'England, Whose England?', 24 Feb. 1995.
63. Tristram Hunt, 'England and the Octopus', *History Today,* 56/6 (2006); available at: <http://www.historytoday.com/tristram-hunt/england-and-octopus>.
64. Jeremy Paxman, *The English: A Portrait of a People* (London: Penguin, 2007), and Andrew Marr, *A History of Modern Britain* (London: Pan, 2009).
65. Paxman, *The English*, 10–11.
66. Paxman, *The English*, 14.
67. Paxman, *The English*, 17.
68. Paxman, *The English*, 15.
69. For a broad overview of this trend, see Steve Redhead, *Post-fandom and the Millennial Blues* (London: Routledge, 1997).
70. Anthony King, 'Nationalism and Sport', in Gerard Delanty and Krishan Kumar (eds), *The Sage Handbook of Nations and Nationalism* (London: Sage, 2006), 249–59.
71. Simon Heffer, interview with Richard English and Michael Kenny, 21 Feb. 2008.
72. Amelia Hill, 'The English Identity Crisis: Who Do You Think You Are?', *Guardian,* 13 June 2004; available at: <http://www.guardian.co.uk/uk/2004/jun/13/british identity.ameliahill>.
73. Hill, 'English Identity Crisis'.
74. Skey, *National Belonging and Everyday Life,* 95–120.
75. Paxman, *The English*, 21.
76. Skey, *National Belonging and Everyday Life*, 108–11.
77. This fear is a central motif in Ignatieff's *Blood and Belonging.*
78. Jeremy Paxman, 'A Short History of England by Simon Jenkins—Review', *Guardian,* 8 Sept. 2011; available at: <http://www.guardian.co.uk/books/2011/sep/08/short-history-england-simon-jenkins-review>.
79. Andrew Gamble, *Between Britain and America* (London: Palgrave, 2003), 9.
80. Frank Bechhofer and David McCrone, 'Being British: A Crisis of Identity?', *Political Quarterly*, 78/2 (2007), 251–60.
81. Bechhofer and McCrone, 'Being British', 258.
82. Anthony Heath and Jane Roberts, *British Identity: Its Sources and Possible Implications for Civic Attitudes and Behaviour. Research Report for Lord Goldsmith's*

Citizenship Review, 2008; available at: <www.justice.gov.uk/docs/british-identity. pdf>.

83. Heath and Roberts, *British Identity*.
84. For a discussion of the main, pertinent political factors, see Mitchell, *Devolution in the UK*.
85. Kidd, *Unions and Unionism*.
86. Wright, 'England, Whose England?', 9.
87. See Mark Leonard, *Britain TM: Renewing our Identity* (London: Demos, 1997).
88. See esp. Dodd, *Battle over Britain*. He has reflected subsequently on his discomfort at the manner in which his ideas were appropriated by figures in the first Blair government; Dodd, interview with Richard English and Michael Kenny, 8 Apr. 2008.
89. Simon Heffer, *Nor Shall my Sword: The Reinvention of England* (London: W&N, 1999).
90. For a discussion of these themes, see Joel Krieger, 'The Political Economy of New Labour: The Failure of a Success Story?', *New Political Economy*, 12/3 (2007), 421–32.
91. See Alan Finlayson, *Making Sense of New Labour* (London: Lawrence & Wishart, 2003).
92. Kumar, 'Nation and Empire', 593.
93. David McCrone, 'A Nation that Dares Not Speak its Name? The English Question', *Ethnicities*, 6/2 (2006), 267–78, 269.
94. Robin Cohen 'Fuzzy Frontiers of Identity: The British Case', *Social Identities*, 1/1 (1995), 35–62.
95. Cohen, 'Fuzzy Frontiers', 59.

CHAPTER 2

1. Bagehot, 'Alex Salmond, Little Englander', *The Economist*, 21 Jan. 2012; available at: <http://www.economist.com/node/21543150>.
2. Nairn, *Break-up of Britain*.
3. Nairn, *Break-up of Britain*, 12–13.
4. This position is often termed the Anderson–Nairn thesis. For discussions of its subsequent intellectual influence, and impact upon progressive thought, see Michael Kenny, 'Faith, Flag and the First New Left: E. P. Thompson and the Politics of One Nation', *Renewal*, 21/1 (2013), 15–23, and Dennis Dworkin, *Cultural Marxism in Post-war Britain: History, the New Left and the Origins of Cultural Studies* (Duke, NC: Duke University Press, 1997).
5. Nairn, *Break-up of Britain*, 43, and Colley, *Britons*.
6. Nairn, *Break-up of Britain*, 45.
7. Nairn, *Break-up of Britain*, 63.
8. Nairn, *Break-up of Britain*, 78.

9. Nairn, *Break-up of Britain*, 80.

10. Nairn, *Break-up of Britain*, 261.

11. Nairn, *Break-up of Britain*, 262.

12. Nairn, *Break-up of Britain*, 259.

13. Nairn, *Break-up of Britain*, 268.

14. Tom Nairn, *After Britain: New Labour and the Return of Scotland* (London: Granta, 2000).

15. Nairn, *After Britain*, 4.

16. Nairn, *After Britain*, 4.

17. Nairn, *After Britain*, 5.

18. Nairn, *After Britain*, 9.

19. Nairn, *After Britain*, 15.

20. Nairn, *After Britain*, 16.

21. Nairn, *After Britain*, 89.

22. Tom Nairn, 'A Republican Monarch? England and Revolution', *Open Democracy*, 12 Oct. 2011; available at: <http://www.opendemocracy.net/ourkingdom/tom-nairn/republican-monarchy-england-and-revolution>.

23. See esp. Ellen Wood, *The Pristine Culture of Capitalism: A Historical Essay on Old Regimes and New States* (London: Verso, 1992), and the overview in Keith Nield, 'A Symptomatic Dispute? Notes on the Relationship between Marxian Theory and Historical Practice in Britain', *Social Research*, 47/3 (1980), 479–506.

24. See Nairn's *Enchanted Glass: Britain and its Monarchy* (London: Verso, 2011).

25. Marquand, 'Give us a Moral Vision for England'.

26. See esp. E. P. Thompson, 'The Peculiarities of the English', *Socialist Register* (1965), 311–62.

27. J. G. A. Pocock, 'Gaberlunzie's Return', *New Left Review*, 2nd ser. 5 (2000), 41–52.

28. Pocock, 'Gaberlunzie's Return', 48.

29. See also the criticisms registered in Stephen Howe, 'Internal Colonization? British Politics since Thatcher as Post-colonial Trauma', *Twentieth-Century British History* 14/3 (2003), 286–304.

30. Patrick Wright, 'Last Orders for the English Aborigine', 2004; available at: <http://patrickwright.polimekanos.com/wp-content/uploads/pwright-last-orders-for-the-english-aborigine-final.pdf>. This is an expanded version of a speech he made at the National Heritage Lottery's Conference, 'Who Do We Think We Are? Heritage and Identity in the UK Today', which was held at the British Museum on 13 July 2004.

31. Wright, 'Last Orders'.

32. Robert Colls, *Identity of England* (Oxford: Oxford University Press, 2004).

33. Mark Perryman, 'Becoming England', in Mark Perryman (ed.), *Imagined Nation: England After Britain* (London: Lawrence & Wishart, 2008), 13–34.

34. Mark Perryman, 'St George's Day for an Imagined Nation?', *Compass*, 23 Apr. 2008; available at: <http://www.compassonline.org.uk/news/item.asp?n=1642&offset=50>.

35. Kumar, *Making of English National Identity.* He has also acknowledged the considerable influence upon him of Colley's work; email interview with Michael Kenny, 18 Apr. 2007.

36. Kumar, *Making of English National Identity,* 3.

37. See Krishan Kumar, 'Negotiating English Identity: Englishness, Britishness and the Future of the United Kingdom', *Nations and Nationalism,* 16/3 (2010), 469–87.

38. Kumar, 'Nation and Empire'.

39. Kumar, *Making of English National Identity,* 6.

40. See, for instance, Philip Gorski, 'Review of Krishan Kumar, *The Making of English National Identity', American Journal of Sociology,* 110/6 (2005), 1826–8.

41. See the reflections on Kumar's argument offered by John Hutchinson, Susan Reynolds, Anthony Smith, Robert Colls, and his response, in 'Debate on Krishan Kumar's *The Making of English National Identity', Nations and Nationalism,* 13/2 (2007), 179–203.

42. Colls, 'Debate on Kumar's *The Making', Nations and Nationalism,* 13/2 (2007), 193–4.

43. Kumar, *Making of English National Identity,* 410.

44. Alun Howkins, 'The Discovery of Rural England', in Robert Colls and Philip Dodd (eds), *Englishness: Politics and Culture 1880–1920* (London: Croom Helm, 1986), 62–88. See also Jackie Abell, Susan Condor, and Clifford Stevenson, '"We are an Island": Geographical Imagery in Accounts of Citizenship, Civil Society and National Identity in Scotland and in England', *Political Psychology,* 27 (2006), 207–26.

45. Robert Young, *The Idea of English Ethnicity* (London: Wiley Blackwell, 2007), 208.

46. Kumar, *Making of English National Identity,* 272.

47. Kumar, *Making of English National Identity,* 238.

48. Andrew Anthony, 'I'm English But What Does That Mean?', *Guardian,* 30 June 2004; available at:
<http://www.guardian.co.uk/uk/2004/jun/30/britishidentity.andrewanthony>.

49. O'Hagan, 'Age of Indifference'.

50. O'Hagan, 'Age of Indifference'.

51. O'Hagan, 'Age of Indifference'.

52. Matthew Parris, 'With a Shrug of the Shoulders, England is Becoming a Nation Once Again', *The Spectator,* 18 Dec. 2010; available at: <http://www.spectator.co.uk/columnists/matthew-parris/6543693/with-a-shrug-of-the-shoulders-england-is-becoming-a-nation-once-again>.

53. Parris, 'With a Shrug of the Shoulders'.

54. Greenfeld, *Nationalism.* For a discussion that locates her arguments in relation to other recent texts, see Joseph Hardwick, 'Historians and Britishness', *Institute for the Public Understanding of the Past,* n.d.; available at: <http://www.york.ac.uk/ipup/projects/britishness/discussion/hardwick.html>.

55. Adrian Hastings, *The Construction of Nationhood: Ethnicity, Religion and Nationalism* (Cambridge: Cambridge University Press, 1997).

56. Kohn, 'Genesis and Character'.

57. Kohn, 'Genesis and Character', 90.

58. Simon Jenkins, *A Short History of England* (London: Profile, 2011).
59. Jenkins, *Short History*, 8.
60. Jenkins, *Short History*, 10.
61. The concept of 'occlusion' was borrowed from G. K. Chesterton, whose views are summarized thus by John Grainger—'England was the occluded country, occluded by its governing classes, its press magnates, its businesses, its art, culture and science and, above all, by its Empire'—in *Patriotisms: Britain 1900–1939* (London: Routledge & Kegan Paul, 1986), 108.
62. Roger Scruton, *England: An Elegy* (London: Chatto, 2000), 30.
63. Scruton was commissioned in the early 1990s to write a book about Britain. But by the time he came to write it, roughly a decade later, it felt unimaginable that he could or should now refer to Britain, as opposed to England; interview with Richard English and Richard Hayton, 25 June 2008.
64. Scruton, *England*, 36.
65. Scruton, *England*, 257.
66. Scruton's position is here encapsulated by Kearney, in his 'Myths of Englishness', 253.
67. Scruton, *On Hunting* (London: St Augustine's Press, 2002), 87.
68. Scruton, *On Hunting*, 155.
69. Scruton, *On Hunting*, 155.
70. Arthur Aughey, *Nationalism, Devolution and the Challenge to the United Kingdom State* (London: Pluto, 2001), 27.
71. Scruton, *England*, 5.
72. Roger Scruton, 'England: An Identity in Question', *Open Democracy*, 30 Apr. 2007; available at: <http://www.opendemocracy.net/globalization-kingdom/england_identity_4578.jsp>.
73. See, for instance, the arguments of Labour MP and chair of the party's Policy Review process, Jon Cruddas, 'Time for a Truly English Labour Party', *New Statesman*, 29 July 2010; available at: <http://www.newstatesman.com/uk-politics/2010/08/labour-party-english-england>. See also the discussion of different Labour figures' shift towards Englishness in Andrew Mycock, 'The Politics of Englishness', *Policy Network*, 4 July 2012; available at: <http://www.policy-network.net/pno_detail.aspx?ID=4203&title=The-politics-of-Englishness>, and David Skelton, 'Englishness Matters and Politicians Should Embrace it', *Huffington Post*, 22 June 2012; available at: <http://www.huffingtonpost.co.uk/david-skelton/englishness-matters-and-p_b_1618975.html>.
74. Billy Bragg, *The Progressive Patriot: A Search for Belonging* (London: Black Swan, 2007). For a thoughtful discussion of the book's merits and weaknesses, see Bikhu Parekh, 'New Englands', *Times Literary Supplement*, 2 Feb. 2007
75. See, for instance, Paul Ward, *Red Flag and Union Jack: Englishness, Patriotism, and the British Left, 1881–1924* (Woodbridge, Suffolk: Boydell Press, 2011), and Mark Bevir, *The Making of British Socialism* (Princeton: Princeton University Press, 2011).
76. Aughey, *Politics of Englishness*, 57.
77. See Cunningham, 'Language of Patriotism'.

78. Bragg, *Progressive Patriot*, 60.

79. See for instance Jon Cruddas, 'Attlee, the ILP and the Romantic Tradition: The Clement Attlee Memorial Lecture 2011', University of Oxford, 28 Oct. 2011; available at: <http://www.compassonline.org.uk/news/item.asp?n=14018>.

80. Richard Weight, *Patriots: National Identity in Britain 1940-2000* (London: Pan, 2000).

81. For an important counter-argument from the left, however, see Ward, *Britishness since 1870*.

82. See esp. Aughey, *Politics of Englishness*; Stapleton, *Political Intellectuals and Public Identities*; and Mandler, *English National Character*.

83. See also Julia Stapleton, 'England and Englishness', in Flinders *et al.*, *The Oxford Handbook of British Politics*, 501–16.

84. Mandler, *English National Character*.

85. Margaret Canovan, '"Breathes There the Man with Soul So Dead…": Reflections on Patriotic Poetry and Liberal Principles', in John Horton and Andrea Baumeister (eds), *Literature and the Political Imagination* (London: Routledge, 1996), 170–97.

86. Orwell, *England, Your England*, 224.

87. Michael Oakeshott, 'Political Education', in *Rationalism in Politics and Other Essays* (London: Methuen, 1962), 111–37.

88. Aughey and Berberich, 'Introduction'.

89. Aughey and Berberich, 'Introduction', 2.

90. Aughey and Berberich, 'Introduction', 2.

91. Aughey and Berberich, 'Introduction', 12.

92. Iain McLean and Alistair McMillan, *The State of the Union* (Oxford: Oxford University Press, 2005).

93. McLean and McMillan, *State of the Union*, 24–5.

94. Arthur Aughey, 'Anxiety and Injustice: The Anatomy of Contemporary English Nationalism', *Nations and Nationalism*, 16/3 (2010), 506–24.

95. Arthur Aughey, 'The Return of England', *Prospect* (May 2007), 40.

96. The case against seeing Englishness as a species of political nationalism is set out in English, *Is there an English Nationalism?*.

97. Robert Eccleshall, 'Michael Oakeshott and Sceptical Conservatism', in Leonard Tivey and Tony Wright (eds), *Political Thought since 1945: Philosophy, Science, Ideology* (London: Edward Elgar, 1992), 173–95.

CHAPTER 3

1. John Curtice has provided some telling criticism of the wording and ordering of questions used by different polling organizations. See, for instance, 'Is there an English Backlash? Reactions to Devolution', in Alison Park, John Curtice, Katarina Thomson, Miranda Phillips, and Elizabeth Clery (eds), *British Social Attitudes: The Twenty-Fifth Report* (London: NatCen, 2009), 1–24, and *Is an English Backlash*

Emerging? Reactions to Devolution Ten Years on (London: IPPR, 2010). And, in the field of qualitative methods, social psychologist Susan Condor has offered some equally significant observations about the strengths and limitations of different research methodologies. See her 'Unimagined Community?, 41–68; and 'Pride and Prejudice'.

2. For a discussion of these results, see Sunny Hundal, '2/3rds of English Voters Want an English Parliament', *Liberal Conspiracy,* 23 Apr. 2010; available at: <http://liberalconspiracy.org/2010/04/23/23rds-of-voters-want-an-english-parliament>.

3. See esp. Christopher Bryant, 'Devolution, Equity and the English Question', *Nations and Nationalism,* 14/4 (2008), 664–83, 667.

4. See, for instance, Michael Thrasher, 'EU: Immigration Tops List of UK Concerns', *Sky News,* 18 June 2013; available at: <http://news.sky.com/story/1099378/eu-immigration-tops-list-of-uk-concerns>.

5. Ross Bond and Michael Rosie, 'National Identities and Attitudes to Constitutional Change in Post-devolution UK: A Four Territories Comparison', *Regional and Federal Studies,* 20/1 (2010), 83–105.

6. James Tilly and Anthony Heath, 'The Decline of British National Pride', *British Journal of Sociology,* 58/4 (2007), 661–78, 674.

7. For an account of the origins and operation of this methodology, see Luis Moreno, 'Scotland, Catalonia, Europeanization and the Moreno Question', *Scottish Affairs,* 54 (2006), 1–21.

8. John Curtice and Anthony Heath, 'England Awakes? Trends in National Identity in England', in Frank Bechhofer and David McCrone (eds), *National Identity, Nationalism and Constitutional Change* (Basingstoke: Palgrave, 2009), 41–63, 46.

9. John Curtice and Anthony Heath, 'Is the English Lion about to Roar? National Identity after Devolution', in Roger Jowell, John Curtice, Alison Park, Katarina Thomson, Lindsey Jervis, Catherine Bromley, and Nina Stratford (eds), *British Social Attitudes: The Seventeenth Report, 2000/2001* (London: Sage, 2000), 155–75.

10. See Curtice, *Is an English Backlash Emerging?.*

11. The results of this survey, which was conducted by YouGov in 2011, are set out in Richard Wyn Jones, Alicia Henderson, Guy Lodge, and Daniel Wincott, *The Dog that Finally Barked: England as an Emerging Political Community* (London: IPPR, 2012).

12. See esp. English, *Is there an English Nationalism?.*

13. See Wyn Jones *et al.*, *The Dog that Finally Barked.*

14. Ross Bond, Charlie Jeffery, and Michael Rosie, 'The Importance of Being English: National Identity and Nationalism in Post Devolution England', *Nations and Nationalism,* 16/3 (2010), 462–8, 467.

15. For a detailed breakdown of these data see Mark Gettelson, 'Latest Opinion Research and Analysis', *PoliticsHome,* 23 May 2011; available at: <http://www.politicshome.com/uk/article/28510/salmonds_english_allies.html>.

16. Institute of Governance, University of Edinburgh, *Findings from the Leverhulme Trust's Research Programme on Nations and Regions, Briefing 7: Jan 2006: National Identity and Community in England* (Edinburgh: Edinburgh University, 2006); available

at: <http://www.institute-of-governance.org/__data/assets/pdf_file/0007/47374/
IoG_Briefing_16.pdf>.

17. Wyn Jones *et al.*, *The Dog that Finally Barked*.
18. See the report produced by the Office for National Statistics, *Report: 2011 Census Unrounded Population and Household Estimates for England and Wales* (London: ONS, 2012); available at: <http://www.ons.gov.uk/ons/rel/census/2011-census/population-and-household-estimates-for-england-and-wales---unrounded-figures-for-the-data-published-16-july-2012/RPT-2011-census-unrounded-EW.html>.
19. For a commentary upon the significance of these results, see Michael Kenny, 'Our Parties Must Respond to the Rise of Englishness', *New Statesman and Society*, 15 Dec. 2012; available at: <http://www.newstatesman.com/politics/2012/12/our-parties-must-respond-rise-englishness>. It has been suggested by some experts that the ordering of the national identity options on this survey may have contributed to this result; see esp. 2011 Census Programme, *Final Recommended Questions for the 2011 Census in England and Wales: National Identity* (London: 2011 Census Programme, 2009).
20. Richard Wyn Jones, Guy Lodge, Charlie Jeffery, Glenn Gottfried, Roger Scully, Ailsa Henderson, and Daniel Wincott, *England and its Two Unions: The Anatomy of a Nation and its Discontents: The 2012 Future of England Survey* (London: IPPR, 2013).
21. Wyn Jones *et al.*, *England and its Two Unions*.
22. Wyn Jones *et al.*, *The Dog that Finally Barked*.
23. For a methodological objection to the findings generated by this polling (including its reliance upon internet-based responses) see Rachel Ormston, *The English Question: How is England Responding to Devolution?* (London: NatCen, 2012); available at: <http://www.opendemocracy.net/ourkingdom/michael-skey/belonging-and-entitlement-britains-ethnic-majority-and-rise-of-ukip>.
24. See, for instance, Skey, *National Belonging and Everyday Life*; Edensor, *National Identity*; Robin Mann, ' "It Just Feels English Rather than Multicultural": Local Interpretations of Englishness and Non-Englishness', *Sociological Review*, 59/1 (2011), 128–47; Steve Fenton and Susan Condor, 'Thinking across Domains: Class, Nation and Racism in England and Britain', *Ethnicities*, 12/4 (2012), 385–93; Robin Mann and Steve Fenton, 'The Personal Contexts of National Sentiments', *Journal of Ethnic and Migration Studies*, 35/4 (2009), 517–34; Steve Garner, 'A Moral Economy of Whiteness: Behaviours, Belonging and Britishness', *Ethnicities*, 12 (2012), 445–64; and Steve Garner, *White Working-Class Neighbourhoods: Common Themes and Policy Suggestions; Round up, Reviewing the Evidence* (York: Joseph Rowntree Foundation, 2011).
25. Curtice, 'Is there an English Backlash?', 13–14.
26. The concept of 'delineation' is suggestively deployed in Richard Rawlings, *Delineating Wales: Constitutional, Legal and Administrative Aspects of National Devolution* (Cardiff: University of Wales Press, 2003).
27. See Skey, *National Belonging and Everyday Life*.

28. Lord Michael Ashcroft, 'The UKIP Threat is Not about Europe', *Lord Ashcroft Polls*, 18 Dec. 2012; available at: <http://lordashcroftpolls.com/2012/12/the-ukip-threat-is-not-about-europe>.

29. For an analysis of such attitudes, and other ideational features of populism, see Cas Mudde, *Populist Radical Right Parties in Europe* (Cambridge: Cambridge University Press, 2007).

30. Aschcroft, 'UKIP Threat'.

31. Skey, *National Belonging and Everyday Life*, 109–11.

32. This argument was prominent within the McKay Commission, *Report of the Commission on the Consequences of Devolution for the House of Commons*, 2013; available at: <http://tmc.independent.gov.uk/wp-content/uploads/2013/03/The-McKay-Commission_Main-Report_25-March-20131.pdf>.

33. See, for instance, John Sides and Jack Citrin, 'European Opinion about Immigration: The Role of Identities, Interests and Information', *British Journal of Political Science*, 37/3 (2007), 477–504; and Laura McLaren, 'The Cultural Divide in Europe: Migration, Multiculturalism, and Political Trust', *World Politics*, 64/2 (2012), 199–241.

34. Ted Brader, Nicholas A. Valentino, and Elizabeth Suhay, 'What Triggers Public Opposition to Immigration? Anxiety, Group Cues, and Immigration Threat', *American Journal of Political Science*, 52/4 (2008), 959–78.

35. See Ashcroft, 'UKIP Threat'.

36. See Tim Bale, Christoffer Green-Pedersen, Andre Krouwel, and Nick Sitter, 'If You Can't Beat Them, Join Them? Explaining Social Democratic Responses to the Challenge from the Populist Radical Right in Western Europe', *Political Studies*, 58/3 (2010), 410–26.

37. See Mudde, *Populist Radical Right Parties*.

38. Nick Lowles and Anthony Painter, *Fear and Hope: A Searchlight Educational Trust Project* (London: Searchlight Educational Trust, 2010); available at: <http://www.fearandhope.org.uk>.

39. Laura McLaren, *Cause for Concern? The Impact of Immigration on Political Trust* (London: Policy Network, 2010).

40. Lowles and Painter, *Fear and Hope*.

41. Lowles and Painter, *Fear and Hope*.

42. Lowles and Painter, *Fear and Hope*.

43. Wyn Jones *et al.*, *England and its Two Unions*.

44. Lowles and Painter, *Fear and Hope*.

45. Lowles and Painter, *Fear and Hope*.

46. See the contributions to Kjarten Pal Sveinsson (ed.), *Who Cares about the White Working Class?* (London: Runneymede Trust, 2009).

47. Curtice and Heath, 'England Awakes?'

48. Curtice and Heath, 'England Awakes?', 57.

49. This polling was commissioned by the Campaign for an English Parliament (CEP) in 2007. Its results are set out in CEP, 'ICM Poll: 67% Want an English Parliament'; available at: <http://toque.co.uk/sites/default/files/CEP_Press_Release_2007.pdf>.

50. This survey was commissioned for the *Sunday Telegraph* newspaper. Its results are set out in 'English Parliament Opinion Polls'; available at: <http://toque.co.uk/english-parliament-opinion-polls>.

51. Wyn Jones *et al.*, *The Dog that Finally Barked*, 25, and Wyn Jones *et al.*, *England and its Two Unions*.

52. See Michael Kenny, 'Identity, Community and the Politics of Recognition', in Olaf Cramme and Patrick Diamond (eds), *After the Third Way: The Future of Social Democracy in Europe* (London: I. B. Tauris, 2012), 143–56.

53. See, for instance, James Rhodes, ' "It's Not Just Them, It's Whites as Well": Whiteness, Class and BNP Support', *Sociology*, 45/1 (2011), 102–17.

54. Roger Hewitt, *White Backlash and the Politics of Multiculturalism* (Cambridge: Cambridge University Press, 2005).

55. Jon Cruddas, Peter John, Nick Lowles, Helen Margetts, David Rowland, and Stuart Weir, *The Far Right in London: A Challenge for Democracy* (York: Joseph Rowntree Reform Trust, 2005).

56. Cruddas *et al.*, *The Far Right in London*, 188–9.

57. Peter John, Helen Margetts, David Rowland, and Stuart Weir, *The BNP: The Roots of its Appeal* (Colchester: Democratic Audit, 2006).

58. Garner, 'The Entitled Nation'.

59. See Michael Kenny, 'The Political Theory of Recognition: The Case of the White Working Class', *British Journal of Politics and International Relations*, 14/1 (2012), 19–38.

60. CEP, 'ICM Poll'.

61. Data kindly supplied by John Curtice, 2009.

62. Steven Jivraj, *Dynamics of Diversity: Evidence from the 2011 Census* (University of Manchester: Centre on Dynamics of Ethnicity, 2013), 1; available at: <http://www.ethnicity.ac.uk/census/CoDE-National-Identity-Census-Briefing.pdf>.

63. See, for instance, Achim Goerres, 'Why are Older People More Likely to Vote? The Impact of Ageing on Electoral Turnout in Europe', *British Journal of Politics and International Relations*, 9 (2007), 90–121.

64. See for instance Daniel Burdsey, ' "If I Ever Play Football, Dad, Can I Play for England or India?" British Asians, Sport and Diasporic National Identities', *Sociology*, 40/1 (2006), 11–28.

65. Curtice and Heath, 'England Awakes?', 56.

66. Curtice and Heath, 'England Awakes?', 56.

67. Camelot Foundation, *Young People and British Identity: Research Study Conducted for The Camelot Foundation by Ipsos MORI* (London: Camelot Foundation, 2009), 15.

68. Camelot Foundation, *Young People and British Identity*, 17.

69. Susan Condor, Stephen Gibson, and Jackie Abell, 'English Identity and Ethnic Diversity in the Context of UK Constitutional Change', *Ethnicities*, 6/2 (2006), 123–58.

70. Condor *et al.*, 'English Identity and Ethnic Diversity', 135.

71. Condor *et al.*, 'English Identity and Ethnic Diversity', 135.

72. Jivraj, *Dynamics of Diversity*, 1.

73. Wyn Jones *et al., England and its Two Unions,* 24–31.

74. Wyn Jones *et al., England and its Two Unions,* 26.

75. Condor *et al.,* 'English Identity and Ethnic Diversity'.

76. See, for instance, the suggestive findings on this theme reported in Charles Leddy-Owen, '"It's True, I'm English...I'm Not Lying": Essentialized and Precarious English Identities', *Ethnic and Racial Studies,* available online at: <http://www.tandfonline.com/doi/pdf/10.1080/01419870.2012.705010#.Udyj5HaDTcs>.

77. I convened a workshop on questions of identity and nationhood, attended by a range of community leaders and youth workers from different ethnic and cultural backgrounds in Leicester, in June 2009.

78. Mann, 'It Just Feels English', 135.

79. Leddy-Owen, '"It's True, I'm English...I'm Not Lying"'.

80. See Gary Younge, 'Why I'll be Cheering on England this Year', *New Statesman and Society,* 8 June 2010; available at: <http://www.newstatesman.com/society/2010/06/british-football-england>.

81. Younge, 'Why I'll be Cheering on England this Year'.

82. Younge, 'Why I'll be Cheering on England this Year'.

83. George Alagaiah, *A Home from Home* (London: Little Brown, 2006), 261.

84. Kumar, 'Negotiating English Identity', 479.

85. Hanif Kureishi, *The Buddha of Suburbia* (London: Penguin, 1991), 1.

86. On the affective and symbolic dimensions of social and political identities, see Manuel Castells, *The Power of Identity: The Information Age. Economy, Society and Culture,* ii (London: Wiley-Blackwell, 2009).

87. See esp. Cohen, 'Fuzzy Frontiers'.

88. See, in particular, Skey, *National Belonging and Everyday Life*; Edensor, *National Identity*; Robin Mann and Steve Fenton, 'Resentment, Class and Social Sentiments about the Nation: The Ethnic Majority in England', *Ethnicities,* 12/4 (2012), 465–83; Mann, 'It Just Feels English'; Fenton and Condor, 'Thinking across Domains'; Mann and Fenton, 'Personal Contexts of National Sentiments'; and Garner, 'Moral Economy of Whiteness'.

89. See Billig, *Banal Nationalism,* and Michael Skey, 'Carnivals of Surplus Emotion? Towards an Understanding of the Significance of Ecstatic Nationalism in a Globalising World', *Studies in Ethnicity and Nationalism,* 6/2 (2006), 143–61.

90. See, for instance, the various contributions to Sveinsson, *Who Cares about the White Working Class?* For polemical rejoinders on behalf of this constituency, see Collins, *The Likes of Us,* and Owen Jones, *Chavs: The Demonization of the Working Class* (London: Verso, 2012).

91. See Michael Skey, 'A Sense of Where You Belong in the World: National Belonging, Ontological Security and the Status of the Ethnic Majority in England', *Nations and Nationalism,* 16/4 (2010), 715–33.

92. Skey, 'Sense of Where You Belong', 716.

93. Skey, 'Sense of Where You Belong', 730.

94. Skey, *National Belonging and Everyday Life.*

95. Michael Skey, '"I Like Living Here Because it is my Country": Exploring Narratives of Belonging and Entitlement in Contemporary England', paper delivered at the University of East London, 15 Mar. 2011; available at: <https://www.jiscmail.ac.uk/cgi-bin/webadmin?A2=CENTREFORNARRATIVERESEARCH; edbdab7.1103>.

96. Michael Skey, '"Sod them I'm English": The Changing Status of the "Majority" English in Post-Devolution Britain', *Ethnicities*, 12/1 (2012), 106–25, 107.

97. Michael Skey, 'Belonging and Entitlement: Britain's "Ethnic Majority" and the Rise of UKIP', *Our Kingdom*, 3 June 2013, available at: <http://www.opendemocracy.net/ourkingdom/michael-skey/belonging-and-entitlement-britains-ethnic-majority-and-rise-of-ukip>.

98. Skey, *National Belonging and Everyday Life,* 10.

99. Skey, *National Belonging and Everyday Life,* 14.

100. Skey, '"Sod them I'm English"', 119.

101. See esp. Jones, *Chavs.*

102. Andrew Gamble, 'Chavs', *Times Literary Supplement,* 22 Aug. 2011.

103. See e.g. Stephanie Lawler, 'Disgusted Subjects: The Making of Middle Class Identities', *Sociological Review,* 53/3 (2005), 429–46, 443.

104. See Vron Ware, 'Towards a Sociology of Resentment: A Debate on Class and Whiteness', *Sociological Research Online,* 13/5 (Sept. 2008); available at: <http://www.socresonline.org.uk/13/5/9.html>.

105. Ivan Lewis, 'One Nation Labour: Tackling the Politics of Culture and Identity', in Robert Philpot (ed.), *The Purple Book: A Progressive Future for Labour* (London: Biteback, 2011), 231–44.

106. Chris Haylett, 'Illegitimate Subjects? Abject Whites, Neoliberal Modernisation, and Middle-Class Multiculturalism', *Environment and Planning D: Society and Space,* 19 (2001), 351–70, 353.

107. Skey, *National Belonging and Everyday Life*, 20.

108. Haylett, 'Illegitimate Subjects?'.

109. Garner, 'Entitled Nation'.

110. For a discussion of the geographical imagination at the heart of current forms of provincial Englishness, see Pearmain, 'England and the "National-Popular"'.

111. For a historical discussion of the cultural politics of 'Northern' representations of Englishness, see Simon Featherstone, *Englishness: Twentieth-Century Popular Culture and the Forming of English Identity* (Edinburgh: Edinburgh University Press), 2009.

112. Featherstone, *Englishness,* 85.

113. See esp. George Orwell, *The Road to Wigan Pier* (London: Mariner Books, 1972) and Joseph Priestley, *English Journey* (London: William Heinemann Medical Books, 1936; repr. Ilkley: Great Northern Books, 2009).

114. Geoffrey Gorer, 'Some Notes on the British Character', *Horizon,* 120/121 (Dec. 1948–Jan. 1950), 369–79.

115. Gorer, 'Some Notes on the British Character', 370.

116. Charles Townshend, cited in David Hayes, 'Ozymandias on the Solway: England at the Edge', *Open Democracy*, 7 July 2007; available at: <http://www.opendemocracy.net/democracy_power/ourkingdom/edward_first>.
117. Hayes, 'Ozymandias on the Solway'.
118. George Schöpflin, *Nations, Identity, Power* (London: NYU Press, 2000). And for an insightful discussion of his ideas, see Arthur Aughey, 'Englishness as Class: A Re-examination', *Ethnicities*, 12 (2012), 394–408.
119. Joanna Bourke, *Working Class Cultures in Britain, 1890–1960: Gender, Class and Ethnicity* (London: Routledge, 1993).
120. Bourke, *Working Class Cultures in Britain*, 1.
121. For a discussion of the national dimensions of the renewal of cultural interest in the English country house in the second half of the last century, see Peter Mandler, *The Fall and Rise of the Stately Home* (New Haven, Conn.: Yale University Press, 1997).
122. See esp. Mandler, *English National Character*, and David Cannadine, *The Rise and Fall of Class in Britain* (Columbia, NY: Columbia University Press, 2000).
123. Mann and Fenton, 'Personal Contexts of National Sentiments'.
124. Mandler, *English National Character*.
125. Skey, *National Belonging and Everyday Life*, 103.
126. See, for instance, David Matless, *Landscape and Englishness* (London: Reaktion Books, 2001).
127. Condor and Abell, 'Romantic Scotland, Tragic England, Ambiguous Britain: Constructions of "the Empire" in Post-Devolution National Accounting', *Nations and Nationalism*, 12/3 (2006), 452–72, 455. See also Condor, 'Sense and Sensibility'; 'Unimagined Community?', and ' "Having History": A Social Psychological Exploration of Anglo-British Autostereotypes', in C. C. Barfoot (ed.), *Beyond Pug's Tour: National and Ethnic Stereotyping in Theory and Literary Practice* (Amsterdam: Rodopi BV Editions, 1997), 213–53; 'Pride and Prejudice', and Condor *et al.*, 'English Diversity and Ethnic Identity'.
128. Condor *et al.*, 'English Diversity and Ethnic Identity'.
129. Condor, 'Devolution and National Identity: The Rules of English (Dis)engagement', *Nations and Nationalism*, 16/3 (2010), 525–43.
130. Condor, 'Sense and Sensibility', 32.
131. Condor, 'Sense and Sensibility', 35.
132. Condor and Abell, 'Romantic Scotland, Tragic England'.
133. Condor, 'Sense and Sensibility'.
134. John Curtice, 'What the People Say—If Anything', in Hazell, *The English Question*, 119–41, 129.
135. This term has become ubiquitous within mainstream political discourse in the last decade. See, for instance, Peter Oborne, *The Triumph of the Political Class* (London: Pocket Books, 2008).
136. See Stapleton, *Political Intellectuals and Public Identities*.
137. Gilbert Keith Chesterton, 'The Secret People', first published in *The Neolith*, 1907; available at: <http://www.poemhunter.com/poem/the-secret-people-2>.

138. For an assessment of the various uses to which it has been put in recent years, see Wright, 'Last Orders'.

139. See, for instance, the argument advanced in A. A. Gill, *Angry Island: Hunting the English* (London: Simon & Schuster, 2008).

140. See Wellings, *English Nationalism and Euroscepticism*.

141. See Ashcroft, 'UKIP Threat'.

142. Aughey, 'Return of England'.

143. Sveinsson, *Who Cares about the White Working Class?*, and Kenny, 'Political Theory of Recognition'.

144. Garner, 'Moral Economy of Whiteness'.

145. Curtice and Heath, 'England Awakes?', 61.

146. Garner, 'Moral Economy of Whiteness', 459.

147. Mann and Fenton, 'Resentment, Class and Social Sentiments about the Nation'.

148. Mann and Fenton, 'Resentment, Class and Social Sentiments about the Nation', 468.

149. Garner, 'Moral Economy of Whiteness'.

150. Garner, 'Moral Economy of Whiteness'.

151. See Jivraj, *Dynamics of Diversity*.

152. See, for instance, Oakeshott, 'Political Education', and George Santayana, *Soliloquies in England and Later Soliloquies* (Ithaca, NY: Cornell University Press, 2011).

153. See esp. Scruton, *England*.

154. Kumar, *Making of English National Identity*.

155. Matless, *Landscape and Englishness*.

156. James Fenton, 'A Heavy Vase of Irony Broken Over Our Heads', *NYR Blog: New York Review of Books,* 13 May 2011; available at: <http://www.nybooks.com/blogs/nyrblog/2011/may/13/james-fenton-jez-butterworth-jerusalem/>.

157. Raymond Williams, *The Country and the City* (Oxford: Oxford University Press, 1973).

158. Stapleton, *Political Intellectuals and Public Identities*.

159. See the discussion of the inter-war years in Mandler, *Making of the English National Character,* 143–58.

160. Stanley Baldwin, 'On England', speech delivered to the Royal Society of St George at the Hotel Cecil, 6 May 1924, in *On England and Other Addresses* (London: Philip Allan, 1933), 1–7.

161. Baldwin, 'On England', 6–7.

162. The major critique emanating from the New Left of the 1960s and 1970s was influenced by Perry Anderson's essays, 'Origins of the Present Crisis', *New Left Review,* 23 (1963), 26–53, and 'Components of the National Culture', *New Left Review,* 50 (1968), 3–57. On the right, the work of Martin Weiner was especially influential, notably his *English Culture and the Decline of the Industrial Spirit, 1850–1950* (Cambridge: Cambridge University Press, 1981).

163. See Raphael Samuel, *Theatres of Memory: Past and Present in Contemporary Culture* (London: Verso, 2012).

164. Edensor, *National Identity and Popular Culture,* 43.

165. Patrick Wright, *On Living in an Old Country: The National Past in Contemporary Britain* (London: Verso, 1985).
166. Julian Baggini, *Welcome to Everytown: A Journey into the English Mind* (London: Granta, 2008).
167. Baggini, *Welcome to Everytown*, 47.
168. Baggini, *Welcome to Everytown*, 45.
169. Mandler, *Making of the English National Character*, 189.
170. Wright, 'England, Whose England?', 3.
171. Paul Kingsnorth, *Real England: The Battle against the Bland* (London: Portobello Books, 2009), 284.
172. Schöpflin, *Nation, Identity, Power*.
173. Berry and Kenny, 'Ideology and the Intellectuals'.
174. Neal Ascherson, 'When was Britain?', *Prospect*, 20 May 1996; available at: <http://www.prospectmagazine.co.uk/magazine/whenwasbritain>.
175. Christopher Bryant, 'These Englands, or Where does Devolution Leave the English?', *Nations and Nationalism*, 9/3 (2003), 393–412.
176. Anthony Everitt, 'Exasperated Affection', *The Spectator*, 1996, 34–7.
177. Everitt, 'Exasperated Affection', 34.
178. Ackroyd, *Albion*, 448.
179. See for instance Gavan Curley, 'The Revival of Englishness', *Catalyst*, 27 July 2007; available at: <http://www.juliushonnor.com/catalyst/Default.aspx.LocID-0hgnew0wb.RefLocID-0hg01b001006009.Lang-EN.htm>.
180. Archbishop John Sentamu, 'The Triumphs of Englishness', lecture delivered at the *Sunday Times* Literary Festival in Oxford 2009; available at: <http://www.archbishopofyork.org/pages/the-triumphs-of-englishness-.html>.
181. Suzanne Moore, 'I'm Not Alone in Feeling English, Not British: But that has Nothing to Do with Racism or UKIP', *Guardian*, 4 Jan. 2012; available at: <http://www.guardian.co.uk/commentisfree/2012/jan/04/feeling-english-is-not-racism>.
182. Madeleine Bunting, 'If Scotland Goes, All We'll have Left is the Englishness We so Despise', *Guardian*, 15 May 2011; available at: <http://www.guardian.co.uk/commentisfree/2011/may/15/nationalism-scotland-redefine-englishness-britain-england>.
183. Jonathan Freedland, *Bring Home the Revolution: The Case for a British Republic* (London: Fourth Estate, 1999).
184. Ernest Barker, *The Character of England* (London: Greenwood Press, 1947).
185. For an insightful analysis of the national dimensions of his thinking, see Julia Stapleton, *Englishness and the Study of Politics: The Social and Political Thought of Ernest Barker* (Cambridge: Cambridge University Press, 1994).
186. See esp. Cunningham, 'The Language of Patriotism', and Bevir, *Making of British Socialism*.
187. Ed Miliband, 'Englishness', speech delivered at the Royal Festival Hall, London, 7 June 2012; available at: <http://www.politics.co.uk/comment-analysis/2012/06/07/ed-miliband-s-englishness-speech-in-full>.

188. Kumar, *Making of English National Identity*, 272.
189. Curtice and Heath, 'England Awakes?', 62.

CHAPTER 4

1. The number of internet sites dedicated to proclaiming and charting the political dimensions of English identity has mushroomed in recent years. Among the best of these are the linked sites 'Open Democracy' and 'Our Kingdom', which have given considerable prominence to the English question, 'English Icons', 'Devolution Matters', 'What England Means to Me'—on which a large number of personal and political reflections are lodged—and the 'Tocque' site, which carries in-depth coverage of English-related political and policy debates.
2. See Marquand, 'Give us a Moral Vision for England'.
3. Kazuo Ishiguro, 'In Conversation with Alan Vorda', in Brian Shaffer and Cynthia Vong (eds), *Conversations with Kazuo Ishiguro* (Jackson, Miss.: University of Mississippi Press, 1988), 74.
4. See the various contributions to Hosking and Schöpflin, *Myths and Nationhood*.
5. For a stimulating and provocative discussion of the integral character of myths to modern social and political thought, see John Gray, *The Silence of Animals: On Progress and Other Modern Myths* (London: Penguin, 2013).
6. See the discussion of these themes in David Miller's argument for the virtues of nationality, in his *On Nationality*.
7. See George Schöpflin, 'The Functions of Myth and a Taxonomy of Myths', in Hosking and Schöpflin, *Myths and Nationhood*, 19–35, 19.
8. Schöpflin, 'Functions of Myth'.
9. See esp. Edensor, *National Identity*, for a discussion of these elements, and the treatment of myths in various theoretical accounts of nationalism.
10. For an elucidation of the concept of the 'national-popular' in Gramsci's thought, see esp. David Forgacs, 'National-Popular: Genealogy of a Concept', in Simon During (ed.), *The Cultural Studies Reader* (London: Routledge, 1993), 209–19.
11. Edensor, *National Identity*, 40.
12. See the iconic works in this genre by Morton, *In Search of England*, and Priestley, *English Journey*. And for an illuminating analysis of this genre of writing, see Featherstone, *Englishness*, 66–83.
13. See Chris Mawson, *A History of the Shell County Guides* (2012); available at: <http://www.shellguides.freeserve.co.uk/history.htm>.
14. Featherstone, *Englishness*, 82.
15. See Robert Macfarlane, *The Old Ways: A Journey on Foot* (London: Hamish Hamilton, 2012). Numerous books have excavated English culinary traditions and recipes, including Nigel Slater, *Eating for England: The Delights and Eccentricities of the British at Table* (London: Fourth Estate, 2012).
16. See Baucom, *Out of Place*.

17. Sue Clifford and Angela King (eds), *England in Particular: The Commonplace, the Local, the Vernacular and the Distinctive* (London: Hodder & Stoughton, 2006).

18. Richard Mabey, *The Common Ground: A Place for Nature in Britain's Future?* (London: Hutchinson, 1980).

19. See esp. the thinking associated with the so-called 'Red Tory' and 'Blue Labour' currents: Philip Blond, *Red Tory: How Left and Right have Broken Britain and How We Can Fix it* (London: Faber & Faber, 2010), and Maurice Glasman, Jonathan Rutherford, Marc Stears, and Stuart White (eds), *The Labour Tradition and the Politics of Paradox* (London: Lawrence & Wishart, 2011).

20. Kingsnorth, *Real England.*

21. Kumar, *Making of English National Identity.*

22. See the discussion in Julian Mischi, 'Englishness and the Countryside: How British Rural Studies Address the Issue of National Identity', in Reviron-Piégay, *Englishness Revisited*, 109–25.

23. See, for instance, the trenchant arguments of art historian and curator Roy Strong in his *Visions of England: Or Why We Still Dream of a Place in the Country* (London: Vintage, 2012), and a review by a critic who notes the various political uses of 'pastoral': Terry Eagleton, 'Visions of England by Roy Strong—Review', *Guardian*, 1 July 2011; available at: <http://www.guardian.co.uk/books/2011/jul/01/visions-of-england-roy-strong-review>.

24. See Mabey, *Common Ground,* and Iain Nairn, *Your England Revisited* (London: Hutchinson, 1964).

25. Nairn, *Your England Revisited.*

26. These alliances first became apparent during the wave of anti-roads protests that came to public attention during the early 1990s, most notably at Twyford Down in 1991 and 1992.

27. Kingsnorth, *Real England*, 17.

28. See Williams, *The Country and the City.*

29. See, for instance, historian Christopher Hill's discussion of the potency of the mythology of the Norman yoke in his 'Norman Yoke'.

30. See Mischi, 'Englishness and the Countryside', and Neal, 'Rural Landscapes'.

31. See, for instance, Slater, *Eating for England,* Alan Titchmarsh, *England, Our England* (London: Hodder, 2009), Kate Fox, *Watching the English: The Hidden Rules of English Behaviour* (London: Hodder, 2005), and David Crystal, *The Story of English in 100 Words* (London: Profile Books, 2011).

32. David Crystal, *By Hook or by Crook: A Journey in Search of English* (London: Harper Press, 2008).

33. For an illuminating discussion of the importance of nostalgia to the socialist imagination in Britain, see Alastair Bonnett, *Left in the Past: Radicalism and the Politics of Nostalgia* (London: Continuum, 2010).

34. See Patrick Wright, 'An Encroachment Too Far', in Roger Scruton and Anthony Barnett (eds), *Town and Country* (London: Vintage, 1999), 18–33.

35. Wright, 'An Encroachment Too Far'.

36. See Rachel Lichtenstein, *On Brick Lane* (London: Penguin, 2007), and Ian Sinclair, *Lights Out for the Territory* (London: Granta, 1997).

37. Peter Woodcock, *This Enchanted Isle: The Neo-Romantic Vision from William Blake to the New Visionaries* (Glastonbury: Gothics Image Publications, 2000), 4.
38. Madeleine Bunting, *The Plot: Biography of an English Acre* (London: Granta, 2009).
39. Bunting, *The Plot,* 263.
40. Bunting, *The Plot*, 273.
41. See, for instance, Colls, *Identity of England,* 194.
42. Colls, *Identity of England,* 193–4.
43. Condor, 'Devolution and National Identity', 540.
44. Edensor, *National Identity,* 4.
45. Edensor, *National Identity,* 4.
46. Gordon Marsden, 'When was England, England?', in Chen and Wright, *The English Question*, 18–28.
47. Marsden, 'When was England, England?', 27.
48. See Rob Young, *Electric Eden: Unearthing Britain's Visionary Music* (London: Faber & Faber, 2011).
49. For an account of the nature and implications of the emergence of the movement of folk music into the musical mainstream, see Simon Keegan-Phipps, 'Folk for Art's Sake: English Folk Music in the Mainstream Milieu', *Radical Musicology* (2009); available at: <http://www.radical-musicology.org.uk>.
50. Tim van Eyken is a well-known folk musician, and a member of the successful Waterson:Carthy ensemble, who founded his own band, Van Eyken. The latter's version of the traditional English song 'John Barleycorn' won the award for Best Traditional Track at the 2007 BBC Radio 2 Folk Awards. In 2008, he was cast as the Song Man in the acclaimed production of Michael Morpurgo's *War Horse* at the National Theatre.
51. For a fuller account of the rising profile of folk, see Trish Winter, 'English Folk Music as World Music', paper delivered at the International Association for the Study of Popular Music, University of Liverpool, 2009.
52. See Trish Winter and Simon Keegan-Phipps, *Performing Englishness in New English Folk Music and Dance* (London: AHRC, 2010); available at: <http://www.crmcs.sunderland.ac.uk/images/Project%20Closing%20Report.pdf>.
53. Winter and Keegan-Phipps, *Performing Englishness,* 16–18.
54. Critical accounts of the political implications of the collecting practices of Sharp and other folklorists were supplied by Dave Harker, *Fakesong: The Manufacturing of British Folksong 1700 to the Present Day* (Milton Keynes: Open University Press, 1985), and Georgina Boyes, *The Imagined Village: Culture, Ideology and the English Folk Revival* (Manchester: Manchester University Press, 1994). Some of their critical arguments were foreshadowed in earlier studies, including: James Reeves, *The Idiom of the People: English Traditional Verse. Edited and with an Introduction and Notes from the Manuscripts of Cecil J. Sharp* (London: Heinemann, 1958), 8–16.
55. For an account of these aspects of English folk music, see Young, *Electric Eden.*
56. Young, *Electric Eden.*
57. Young, *Electric Eden,* 5.
58. Boyes, *Imagined Village.*
59. Peter Martin, 'Preface', in Boyes, *Imagined Village*, vi–x, viii.

60. For a discussion of the importance of Mary Neal and her troubled relationship with Sharp, see Featherstone, *Englishness*, 28–45.

61. Featherstone, *Englishness*, 145.

62. Harker, *Fakesong*.

63. Harker, *Fakesong*, 190–1.

64. See David Gregory, 'Fakesong in an Imagined Village? A Critique of the Harker-Boyes Thesis', *Canadian Folk Music,* 43/3 (2009), 18–26.

65. See the announcement by the English Folk Dance and Song Society, 'Arts Council Funding Heralds New Era for the English Folk Dance and Song Society', 2010; available at: <http://www.efdss.org/news/newsId/5>.

66. See Eliza Carthy, 'Traditional English Song Has No Links to the Far Right or Nick Griffin', *Guardian,* 26 Jan. 2010; available at: <http://www.guardian.co.uk/commentisfree/2010/jan/26/nick-griffin-bnp-folk-music>.

67. Emma Hartley, 'The BNP and Folk Music, Part Two: A Question of Roots', *Daily Telegraph,* 11 Jan. 2009; available at: <http://blogs.telegraph.co.uk/news/emmahartley/8064367/The_BNP_and_folk_music_part_two_a_question_of_Roots>.

68. For an account of the rationale behind the formation of this campaign, see 'Folk against Fascism'; available at: <http://www.last.fm/tag/folk%20against%20fascism>.

69. Cited in Winter and Keegan-Phipps, *Performing Englishness*, 15.

70. This is a quotation from the cover notes of a compilation album sponsored by *fRoots* magazine and Arts Council England, *Looking for a New England. New Folk: Old Roots*; details available at: <http://www.frootsmag.com/content/freecd/anewengland/#musicians>.

71. *Looking for a New England.*

72. Over 200 festivals are listed on one of the leading sites promoting English folk festivals in 2013; available at: <http://www.bellesoflondoncity.co.uk/>.

73. This is a female quartet of Morris dancers who have become one of the best-known contemporary folk dancing ensembles. Further details are available at: <http://www.bellesoflondoncity.co.uk/introducing.html>.

74. Steve Cox is a member of the folk-cum-pop ensemble, Mr Love & Justice. This quotation is from an interview conducted by James Turner in *Albion*, 2/1 (2005); available at: <http://www.zyworld.com/albionmagazineonline/music3.htm>.

75. For a bold analysis of *Sweet England*, and its potential cultural significance, see Neil McCormick, 'The Reinvention of Folk Music', *Daily Telegraph*, 25 Sept. 2003; available at: <http://www.telegraph.co.uk/culture/music/rockandjazzmusic/3603270/The-reinvention-of-folk-music.html>.

76. This quotation is from McCormick, 'Reinvention of Folk Music'.

77. McCormick, 'Reinvention of Folk Music'.

78. For a perceptive analysis of these trends, see John Mullen, ' "We Need Roots": Englishness and the New Folk Revival', *Open Democracy,* 13 July 2010; available at: <http://www.opendemocracy.net/ourkingdom/john-mullen/%C2%91we-need-roots%C2%92-englishness-and-new-folk-revival>.

79. Steve Anderson, 'Frank Turner: "This Might be the Zenith of my Career" ', *Independent,* 5 Apr. 2012; available at: <http://www.independent.co.uk/arts-

entertainment/music/features/frank-turner-this-might-be-the-zenith-of-my-career-7619015.html>.

80. See, for instance, Nabeel Zuberi, *Sounds English: Trasnational Popular Music* (Champagne, Ill.: University of Illinois Press, 2001).
81. Zuberi, *Sounds English,* 4.
82. Martin Cloonan, 'State of the Nation: "Englishness", Pop, and Politics in the Mid-1990s', *Popular Music and Society*, 21/2 (1997), 47–70.
83. See Cloonan, 'State of the Nation', 58.
84. Her album was chosen as 'Album of the Year' in 2011 by sixteen separate musical publications, and won the Mercury Prize in the same year.
85. Robert Stradling and Meirion Hughes, *The English Musical Renaissance 1860–1940: Construction and Deconstruction* (London: Routledge, 1993).
86. Jean-Philippe Heberlé, '*Hugh the Drover* by Ralph Vaughan Williams, or How to Restore the Englishness of English Opera?', in Reviron-Piégay, *Englishness Revisited*, 68–78.
87. Simon Heffer, *Vaughan Williams* (London: Faber & Faber, 2008).
88. Heffer, *Vaughan Williams,* 23–4.
89. See James Day, *Englishness in Music: From Elizabeth Times to Elgar, Tippett and Britten* (London: Wise Publications, 2007). On the early music revival, see Daniel Leech, *The Modern Invention of Medieval Music* (Cambridge: Cambridge University Press, 2002), and Harry Haskell, *The Early Music Revival: A History* (London: Thames & Hudson, 1988).
90. See Peter Parker, 'Benjamin Britten: The Englishman Who Saved Music', *Daily Telegraph*, 8 Feb. 2013; available at: <http://www.telegraph.co.uk/culture/books/bookreviews/9854826/Benjamin-Britten-the-Englishman-who-saved-music.html>.
91. Roger Scruton, 'We Need the English Music that the Arts Council Hates', *The Spectator,* 16 April 2008; available at: <http://www.spectator.co.uk/features/615311/we-need-the-english-music-that-the-arts-council-hates>.Seealso David Hamilton, 'The Revival of English Classical Music', *Traditional Britain*, 2011; available at: <http://www.traditionalbritain.org/content/revival-english-classical-music>.
92. Scruton, 'We Need the English Music that the Arts Council Hates'.
93. Scruton, 'We Need the English Music that the Arts Council Hates'.
94. Scruton, 'We Need the English Music that the Arts Council Hates'.
95. Patrick Parrinder, *Nation and Novel: The English Novel from its Origins to the Present Day* (Oxford: Oxford University Press, 2006), 14.
96. Simon Gikandi, *Maps of Englishness: Writing Identity in the Culture of Colonialism* (New York: Columbia University Press, 2006).
97. David Gervais, 'The English and the European: The Poetry of Geoffrey Hill', in Rogers and McLeod, *Revisions of Englishness*, 65–80.
98. Parrinder, *Nation and Novel.*
99. For an insightful discussion of Smith's writings, see Nick Bentley, 'Re-writing Englishness: Imagining the Nation in Julian Barnes's *England, England* and Zadie Smith's *White Teeth*', *Textual Practice,* 21/3 (2007), 483–504.

100. John McLeod, 'Black English Writing and Post-British England', in Gardiner and Westall, *Literature of an Independent England*, 254–72.

101. Mike Phillips, 'Migration, Modernity and English Writing: Reflections on Migrant Identity and Canon Formation', *Tate Encounters*, 1 (2007), 1–14, 12; available at: <http://www2.tate.org.uk/tate-encounters/edition-1/Eng-Lit-and-Canon-Formation.pdf>.

102. Andrea Levy, 'This is my England', *Guardian*, 19 Feb. 2000; available at: <http://www.guardian.co.uk/books/2000/feb/19/society1>.

103. Ingrid Gunby, ' "Dying of England": Melancholic Englishness in Adam Thorpe's *Still*', in Rogers and McLeod, *Revisions of Englishness*, 107–20.

104. Adam Thorpe, *Still* (London: Vintage, 1996).

105. Ingrid Gunby, ' "Dying of England" '.

106. See the discussion of this phrase in Raphael Ingelbien, *Misreading England: Poetry and Nationhood since the Second World War* (New York: Rodopi, 2002), 109.

107. See Ian McEwan, *Atonement: A Novel* (London: Anchor, 2003), and Julian Barnes, *Arthur and George* (London: Vintage, 2007).

108. Parrinder, *Nation and Novel*, 406.

109. See Ballard, *Kingdom Come*.

110. Rupert Thomson, *Divided Kingdom* (London: Vintage, 2007), and James Hawes, *Speak for England* (Leeds: Lawson Library 2007).

111. Barnes, *England, England*.

112. See Berberich, 'Whose Englishness is it Anyway?'

113. Vera Nunning, 'The Invention of Cultural Traditions: The Construction and Deconstruction of Englishness and Authenticity in Julian Barnes' *England England*', *Anglia: Zeitschrift für englische Philologie*, 119/1 (2007), 58–76.

114. For a number of broadly similar arguments, see Gardiner and Westall, *Literature of an Independent England*, and Michael Gardiner, *The Return of England in English Literature* (London: Palgrave Macmillan, 2012).

115. Hywel Dix, 'Devolution and Cultural Catch-up: Decoupling England and its Literature from English Literature', in Gardiner and Westall, *Literature of an Independent England*, 273–90.

116. Dix, 'Devolution and Cultural Catch-up'.

117. Christine Berberich, 'England, Devolution and Fictional Kingdoms', in Gardiner and Westall, *Literature of an Independent England*, 236–53.

118. Tony Harrison, *Prometheus* (London: Arts Council of England, 1998).

119. Dalya Aberge, 'Poets Enlist for Quest to Pull St George from Jaws of Far Right', *Guardian*, 24 Jan. 2011; available at: <http://www.guardian.co.uk/books/2011/jan/24/poets-enlist-st-george-liturgy>.

120. Euan Fernie (ed.), *Redcrosse: Remaking Religious Poetry for Today's World* (London: Bloomsbury Academic, 2012).

121. See George Szrites, 'The Englishness of English Poetry 1', 2008; available at: <http://georgeszirtes.blogspot.co.uk/2008/08/englishness-of-english-poetry-1.html>.

122. See Simon Trussler, 'English Acting, Interactive Technology, and the Elusive Quality of Englishness', *New Theatre Quarterly*, 12/46 (1996), 3–5.

123. Ackroyd, 'The Englishness of English Literature', in Thomas Wright (ed.), *The Collection* (London: Vintage, 2001), 328–40.

124. Ackroyd, 'Englishness of English Literature', 334.

125. Ackroyd, 'Englishness of English Literature', 329.

126. Ackroyd, *Albion*.

127. Peter Ackroyd, *Hawksmoor* (New York: Harper & Row, 1986), and *The House of Doctor Dee* (London: Hamish Hamilton, 1993).

128. Woodcock, *This Enchanted Isle*.

129. Alexandra Harris, *Romantic Moderns* (London: Thames & Hudson, 2010).

130. These are collected in Nikolaus Pevsner, *The Englishness of English Art: An Expanded and Annotated Version of the Reith Lectures Broadcast in October and November 1955* (London: Penguin, 1955). See also Harris, *Romantic Moderns*.

131. Sophie Aymes, 'The Line: An English Trait', in Reviron-Piégay, *Englishness Revisited*, 55–67.

132. Harris, *Romantic Moderns*, 293.

133. Niru Ratnam, 'Whose Art is it Anyway?', *The Spectator*, 2 July 2011; available at: <http://www.spectator.co.uk/arts-and-culture/featured/7059853/whose-art-is-it-anyway.thtml>.

134. See, for instance, Simon Jenkins, 'For a Real Exhibition of Modernism, Skip the V&A and Go to Manchester', *Guardian,* 7 Apr. 2006; available at: <http://www.guardian.co.uk/commentisfree/2006/apr/07/comment.society>.

135. Isabel Taylor, 'Interview with Cathy Lomax', *Albion Magazine online*, 5/1 (2008); available at: <http://www.zyworld.com/albionmagazineonline/art5.htm>.

136. For further details of her exhibition, see 'Tabloid Tales at London's Gallery 102', *Collective*; available at: <http://www.bbc.co.uk/dna/collective/A4926675>.

137. See Taylor, 'Interview with Cathy Lomax'.

138. Owen Hatherley, 'How Patrick Keiller is Mapping the 21st-Century Landscape', *Guardian,* 30 Mar. 2012; available at: <http://www.guardian.co.uk/artanddesign/2012/mar/30/patrick-keiller-robinson-tate-exhibition>.

139. Details of this project can be found at: <http://thefutureoflandscape.wordpress.com>.

140. For further details, see 'Simon English: England Revisited'; available at: <http://www.englandrevisited.net>.

141. See Steve Blandford, *Film, Drama and the Break up of Britain* (London: Intellect, 2007), and Andrew Higson, *English Heritage, English Cinema* (Oxford: Oxford University Press, 2003).

142. See, for instance, Mike Leigh's *Life is Sweet* (London: British Screen Productions, 1990), and Ken Loach's *Riff-Raff* (London: Parallax Pictures, 1991).

143. Shane Meadows, *This is England* (London: Warp Films, 2006).

144. The film *Last Orders* (London: Future Films, 2001) based upon Swift's novel, was directed by Fred Schepisi.

145. Blandford, *Drama and the Break up of Britain,* 46.

146. Higson, *English Heritage,* 35.

147. See David Lowenthal, 'British National Identity and the English Landscape', *Rural History,* 2 (1991), 205–30.

148. See, for instance, Richard Dyer, *Only Entertainment* (London: Routledge, 2002).

149. See Higson, *English Heritage.*

150. See, for instance, Alison Goordrum, *The National Fabric: Fashion, Britishness, Globalization (Dress, Body, Culture)* (London: Berg, 2005).

151. See esp. Christopher Breward, Becky Conekin, and Caroline Cox (eds), *The Englishness of English Dress* (London: Berg, 1992).

152. See Goodrum, *National Fabric.*

153. Sierz, *Rewriting the Nation,* 1.

154. Sierz, *Rewriting the Nation,* 105.

155. *The Christ of Coldharbour Lane* was performed at the Soho Theatre, London, in 2007, and *Elmina's Kitchen* at the Royal National Theatre in 2003. The latter was subsequently dramatized by the BBC in 2005.

156. *Playing with Fire* premiered at the Royal National Theatre in 2005.

157. Sarah Kane's controversial play *Blasted* was first performed at the Royal Court Theatre Upstairs in 1995.

158. See Sierz, *Rewriting the Nation,* 225.

159. Sierz, *Rewriting the Nation,* 227.

160. See, for instance, Andrew Marr, 'Evictions, Protests, Unrest—How Jerusalem Saw Them Coming', *BBC News Magazine,* 24 Oct. 2011; available at: <http://www.bbc.co.uk/news/magazine-15427879>, and Libby Purves, 'Jerusalem at The Apollo W1', *The Times,* 18 Oct. 2011.

161. Dominic Cavendish, 'Jerusalem: Why No Fuss about this Radical Play?', *Daily Telegraph,* 23 Apr. 2010; available at: <http://www.telegraph.co.uk/culture/theatre/7265867/Jerusalem-why-no-fuss-about-this-radical-play.html>.

162. See esp. Julia Boll, 'The Sacred Dragon in the Woods: On Jez Butterworth's *Jerusalem*', *Forum,* 14 (n.d.); available at: <http://www.forumjournal.org/site/issue/14/julia-boll>; and Lyn Gardner, 'Why I Love Jez Butterworth's Jerusalem', *Guardian Online,* n.d.; available at: <http://www.guardian.co.uk/stage/theatreblog/2011/oct/25/why-i-love-butterworths-jerusalem>.

163. On the religious connotations of this character, see Boll, 'Sacred Dragon in the Woods'.

164. The play's programme notes included excerpts from his *The Real England.*

165. He is quoted in 'The English Identity Crisis and Jerusalem', *The Invisible Province,* 19 Feb. 2010; available at: <http://theinvisibleprovince.blogspot.co.uk/2010/02/english-identity-crisis-and-jerusalem.html>.

166. See Moreton, *Is God Still an Englishman?.*

167. Gardner, 'Why I Love Jez Butterworth's Jerusalem'.

168. Gardner, 'Why I Love Jez Butterworth's Jerusalem'.

169. Marr, 'Evictions, Protests, Unrest'.

170. See 'Jerusalem: The Play by Jez Butterworth', *Beyond the Zeitgeist*, n.d.; available at: <http://beyondthezeitgeist.wordpress.com/2011/08/05/jerusalem-the-play-by-jez-butterworth>.

171. Michael Goldfarb, 'Who are the English?', *Global Post*, 31 July 2011; available at: <http://www.globalpost.com/dispatch/news/regions/europe/united-kingdom/110729/dr-dee-damon-albarn-englishness>.

172. Dr Dee was an operatic piece created by theatre director Rufus Norris and musician and composer Damon Albarn. Its debut performance was at the Palace Theatre, Manchester, in July 2011. It was subsequently performed at the Cultural Olympiad in London in 2012.

173. Norris and Albarn were heavily influenced by Benjamin Woolley's *The Queen's Conjuror: The Life and Magic of Dr. Dee: The Science and Magic of Dr. Dee* (London: Flamingo, 2002).

174. Prospero, 'Staging a Renaissance Man', *The Economist*, 4 July 2012; available at: <http://www.economist.com/blogs/prospero/2012/07/qa-rufus-norris-director>.

175. Prospero, 'Staging a Renaissance Man'.

176. Prospero, 'Staging a Renaissance Man'.

177. See 'Andrew Marr Interview Transcript', at *Damon Albarn Unofficial*, n.d.; available at: <http://damonalbarn.tumblr.com/post/6736716784/andrew-marr-interview-transcript>.

178. Skey, *National Belonging and Everyday Life*, 114.

179. See Wyn Jones *et al.*, *The Dog that Finally Barked*.

180. Simon Walter and Brendan Carlin, 'Cripes! Boris's Plan to Celebrate St George (and to Blazes with What the PC Brigade Think)', *Daily Mail*, 22 Mar. 2009.

181. See, for instance, the declaration of support for this cause by former Labour MP for Middlesborough, Ashok Kumar, at: <http://www.youtube.com/watch?v=ZngvN19fssk>.

182. See Peter Tatchell, 'St George—Middle East Rebel and Human Rights Defender', *Peter Tatchell*; available at: <http://www.petertatchell.net/multiculturalism/stgeorge.htm>.

183. See, for instance, 'Saint George's Day Marked by Google Doodle', *Guardian*, 23 Apr. 2013; available at: <http://www.guardian.co.uk/lifeandstyle/2013/apr/23/saint-georges-day-google-doodle>.

184. Sentamu, 'Triumphs of Englishness'.

185. See, for instance, '"Cry God for Harry, England, and Saint George!": Celebrating England and Englishness', speech delivered at the Smith Institute, 23 Feb. 2010; available at: <http://www.smith-institute.org.uk/19-John-Denham>.

186. 'George and Drag-on for Leicester', *The Sun*, 3 Apr. 2009; available at: <http://www.thesun.co.uk/sol/homepage/news/article2357727.ece>.

187. On the diverse range of meanings associated with the display of the English flag, see Susanne Reichl, 'Flying the Flag: The Intricate Semiotics of National Identity', *European Journal of English Studies*, 8/2 (2004), 205–17.

188. Andrew Mycock and James McAuley, *Sympathy for the Dragon? Englishness and St George's Day. A Study* (Huddersfield: University of Huddersfield, 2009).
189. Billig, *Banal Nationalism*.
190. Jackie Abell, Susan Condor, Robert Lowe, Stephen Gibson, and Clifford Stephenson, 'Who Ate All the Pride? Patriotic Sentiment and English Patriotic Football Support', *Nations and Nationalism,* 13/1 (2007), 97–116.
191. Isabel Taylor, 'Interview with Kate Fox', *Albion Magazine online,* 2005; available at: <http://www.zyworld.com/albionmagazineonline/books4.htm>.
192. Taylor, 'Interview with Kate Fox'.
193. This is a quotation from a white, male participant, aged 42, at a workshop involving community stakeholders that I organized in the London borough of Barking and Dagenham in 2008.
194. See esp. Skey, *National Belonging and Everyday Life*.
195. Garner, 'Entitled Nation'.
196. Office for National Statistics, *Who we are. How we Live. What we Do* (London: Office for National Statistics, 2011); available at: <http://www.ons.gov.uk/census/2011-census/2011-census-questionnaire-content/question-and-content-recommendations-for-2011/ethnic-group-prioritisation-tool.pdf>.
197. See, for instance, 'Britology Watch: "Deconstructing British Values"'; available at: <http://britologywatch.wordpress.com/2011/03/07/white-and-english-but-not-white-english-how-to-deal-with-the-discriminatory-census-for-england-and-wales>.
198. Curley, 'Revival of Englishness'.
199. Liam Byrne, 'Rise up Englishmen', *The Spectator,* 28 Apr. 2007.
200. McLeod, 'Introduction', in Rogers and McLeod, *Revisions of Englishness*, 3.
201. Anon, 'Shaken, Stirred and Confused', *The Economist,* 3 Nov. 2012; available at: <http://www.economist.com/news/britain/21565681-latest-film-bond-franchise-raises-puzzling-questions-about-hero%E2%80%99s-mixed>.

CHAPTER 5

1. Tony Wright, *British Politics: A Very Short Introduction* (Oxford: Oxford University Press, 2013), 10.
2. Wright, *British Politics*, 25.
3. See esp. Aughey, *Politics of Englishness*.
4. Barnett, 'Afterword', 340.
5. Mandler, *English National Character*.
6. Cited in Vernon Bogdanor, 'The English Constitution and Devolution', *Political Quarterly,* 50/1 (1979), 36–49, 36.
7. See McLean and McMillan, *State of the Union,* for a historical overeiw of the emergence and development of these arguments.

8. House of Commons Justice Committee, *Fifth Report of Session 2008–09*, i, ch. 5, *The English Question* (London: House of Commons, 2009), 50.

9. Wright, *British Politics*, 11.

10. Charlie Jeffery, 'Dis-United Kingdom?', *Juncture*, 19/1 (2012), 14–16, 14.

11. Jeffery, 'Dis-United Kingdom', 14.

12. Jeffery, 'Dis-United Kingdom', 14.

13. Wyn Jones *et al., The Dog that Finally Barked*, 4.

14. Guy Lodge and James Mitchell, 'Whitehall and the Government of England', in Hazell, *The English Question*, 96–118.

15. McKay Commission, *Report of the Commission on the Consequences of Devolution*.

16. On English attitudes towards devolution, see Condor, 'Devolution and National Identity'.

17. Daniel Wincott and Emyr Lewis, 'Written Submission No. 40 to the McKay Commission', 2012; available at: <http://webarchive.nationalarchives.gov.uk/20130403030652/http://tmc.independent.gov.uk/submission-40-daniel-wincott-and-emyr-lewis/>.

18. Colls, *Identity of England*, 312, and Weight, *Patriots*, 726.

19. George Monbiot, 'Someone Else's England', *Guardian*, 17 Feb. 2009; available at: <http://www.monbiot.com/2009/02/17/someone-elses-england>.

20. See Michael Kenny, 'The Many Faces of Englishness', *Juncture*, 15 Dec. 2012; available at: <http://www.ippr.org/juncture/171/10061/the-many-faces-of-englishness-identity-diversity-and-nationhood-in-england>.

21. Richard Rose, *Understanding the United Kingdom: The Territorial Dimension in British Government* (London: Prentice Hall, 1982).

22. Rose, *Understanding the United Kingdom*, 67.

23. See Giles Radice, *Southern Discomfort* (London: Fabian Society, 1992).

24. Charles Pattie, 'Written Submission No. 64 to the McKay Commission', 2012; available at: <http://webarchive.nationalarchives.gov.uk/20130403030652/http://tmc.independent.gov.uk/submission-64-professor-charles-pattie/>.

25. For an in-depth analysis of this bias, see Galina Borisyuk, Colin Rallings, Michael Thrasher, and Ron Johnston, 'Parliamentary Constituency Boundary Reviews and Electoral Bias: How Important are Variations in Constituency Size?', *Parliamentary Affairs*, 63/1 (2010), 4–21.

26. On Scotland, see Douglas Fraser, *Nation Speaking unto Nation: Does the Media Create Cultural Distance between England and Scotland?* (London: IPPR, 2008). And on the nature of Anglicization at Westminster, see Richard Hayton and Andrew Mycock, 'The Party Politics of Englishness', *British Journal of Politics and International Relations*, forthcoming; available at: <http://onlinelibrary.wiley.com/doi/10.1111/j.1467-856X.2012.00543.x/abstract>.

27. For an in-depth discussion of the territorial dimension of party structures, see Hayton and Mycock, 'Party Politics of Englishness'.

28. Kenny, 'Many Faces of Englishness'.

29. Hayton and Mycock, 'Party Politics of Englishness'.

30. Jeffery, 'Dis-United Kingdom'.

31. On how the Conservative party responded to Labour's devolution legislation, see Richard Hayton, *Reconstructing Conservatism: The Conservative Party in Opposition, 1997–2010* (Manchester: Manchester University Press, 2012).

32. David Heathcote-Amory, 'Advertising the End of Britain', *The Spectator,* 1 Nov. 1997.

33. See Bogdanor, *Devolution in the United Kingdom*, 287.

34. See, for instance, Wellings, *English Nationalism and Euroscepticism*, 401–2.

35. William Hague, 'Leader's Speech', Conservative Party Conference—Bournemouth, 1998; available at: <http://www.britishpoliticalspeech.org/speech-archive.htm? speech=144speech>.

36. See, in particular: Hague, 'Change and Tradition: Thinking Creatively about the Constitution', speech delivered at the Centre of Policy Studies, 24 Feb. 1998; 'Strengthening the Union After Devolution', speech at the Centre for Policy Studies, 15 July 1999; and 'Identity and the British Way', speech at the Centre for Policy Studies, 24 Jan. 1999.

37. Hague, 'Change and Tradition'.

38. Hague, 'Strengthening the Union'.

39. Hague, 'Identity and the British Way'.

40. Hague, 'Identity and the British Way'.

41. Roger Scruton, 'Where does England's Loyalty Lie?', *The Spectator*, 15 Mar. 2003; available at: <http://www.spectator.co.uk/spectator/thisweek/10935/part_5/where-does-englands-loyalty-lie.thtml>.

42. For a long-range analysis of the shifting character of Unionist thinking in British politics, see McLean and McMillan, *State of the Union*.

43. David Davis, 'Equality for the English', *Conservative Way Forward*, May 2001; available at: <http://toque.co.uk/david-davis-equality-english>.

44. Davis, 'Equality for the English'.

45. Davis, 'Equality for the English'.

46. Tim Montgomerie, 'Pro-Nuclear, Gay Friendly, Barely Unionist, Very Eurosceptic… Meet the Next Generation of Tory MPs', *Conservative Home,* 3 July 2009; available at: <http://conservativehome.blogs.com/goldlist/2009/07/pronuclear-gay-friendly-barely-unionist-very-eurosceptic-meet-the-next-generation-of-tory-mps.html>.

47. Colin Kidd, 'The End of Labour?', *London Review of Books,* 8 Mar. 2012; available at: <http://www.lrb.co.uk/v34/n05/colin-kidd/the-end-of-labour>.

48. For an analysis of the development of Labour's thinking on devolution, see Bogdanor, *Devolution in the United Kingdom*.

49. Jack Straw, 'Living with West Lothian', *Prospect*, 139 (2007), 19–20.

50. These comments were made on the BBC Radio 4 programme *Brits*; see BBC News, 'English Nationalism Threat to UK', 9 Jan. 2000; available at: <http://news.bbc.co.uk/1/hi/uk/596703.stm>.

51. See Andrew Sparrow, 'Soccer Yobs are Distorted Patriots, says Straw', *Daily Telegraph,* 17 July 2000; available at: <http://www.telegraph.co.uk/news/uknews/1349000/Soccer-yobs-are-distorted-patriots-says-Straw.html>.
52. This quotation was from an article he wrote in *The Times* in 1999, which is discussed in some detail in 'Ministry of Justice Commission Britishness Poll', *Tocque,* 13 Mar. 2008; available at: <http://toque.co.uk/ministry-justice-commission-britishness-poll>.
53. William Saunders, *Municipalisation by Provinces* (London: Fabian Society Tract No. 125, 1905).
54. For a helpful discussion of these documents, see Hugh Atkinson, 'Democracy, Accountability and Identity in the English Regions', *Teaching Public Administration,* 20/1 (2000), 26–38.
55. See Regional Policy Commission, *Renewing the Regions: Strategies for Regional Economic Development* (Sheffield: Sheffield Hallam Press, 1996).
56. John Tomaney, 'The Evolution of Regionalism in England', *Regional Studies,* 36/7 (2002), 721–31.
57. See the discussion of these factors in Gerry Stoker, 'Is Regional Government the Answer to the English Question?', in Chen and Wright, *The English Question,* 63–79, and Mark Sandford, 'What Place for England in an Asymmetrically Devolved UK?', *Regional Studies,* 36/7 (2002), 789–96.
58. National Centre for Social Research, *British Social Attitudes Survey 2001* (London: UK Data Service, 2001); available at: <http://discover.ukdataservice.ac.uk/catalogue/?sn=4615&type=Data%20catalogue>.
59. Local Government and the Regions Department for Transport, *Your Region, Your Choice: Revitalising the English Regions* (London: Stationery Office Books, 2002).
60. Local Government and the Regions Department for Transport, *Your Region, Your Choice.*
61. BBC News, 'North East Votes "No" to Assembly', 5 Nov. 2004; available at: <http://news.bbc.co.uk/1/hi/uk_politics/3984387.stm>.
62. Dept for Communities and Local Government, *Strong and Prosperous Communities: The Local Government White Paper,* 2006; available at: <http://www.official-documents.gov.uk/document/cm69/6939/6939.pdf>.
63. See John Tomaney and John Mawson, *England: The State of the Regions* (Bristol: Policy Press, 2002).
64. Bogdanor, *Devolution in the United Kingdom,* 269.
65. See the contributions to Matthew Flinders and Martin Smith (eds), *Quangos, Accountability and Reform: The Politics of Quasi-Government* (Sheffield: St Martin's Press, 1999).
66. Sarah Ayres and Graham Pearce, 'Building Regional Governance in England: The View from Whitehall', *Policy and Politics,* 33/4 (2005), 581–600.
67. Gerry Stoker, 'New Localism, Progressive Politics and Democracy', *Political Quarterly,* 75/supp. 1 (2004), 117–29.

68. David Miliband, 'More Power to the People', speech delivered to the Annual Conference of the National Council for Voluntary Organizations, Feb. 2006; available at: <http://www.guardian.co.uk/society/2006/feb/21/localgovernment.politics1>.
69. See Guy Lodge and Rick Muir, 'Localism under New Labour', *Political Quarterly*, 81/supp. 1 (2010), 96–107.
70. See, for instance, Michael Kenny and Guy Lodge, *An Elected Mayor for Every English Town and City* (London: IPPR, 2008); available at: <http://www.ippr. org/press-releases/111/2242/an-elected-mayor-for-every-major-english-town-and-cityon mayors under labour>.
71. See New Local Government Network, *Beyond SW1: Elected Mayors and the Renewal of Civic Leadership* (London: NGLN, 2002), and Michael Kenny and Guy Lodge, 'More Mayors for England', *Prospect*, 24 May 2008; available at: <http://www. prospectmagazine.co.uk/magazine/moremayorsforengland/#.Ub47cXaDT5o>.
72. See, for instance, Adam Marshall and Dermot Finch, *Civic Leadership: Giving City-Regions the Power to Grow* (London: Centre for Cities, 2006).
73. David Blunkett, *A New England: An English Identity within Britain* (London: IPPR, 2005); available at: <http://www.ippr.org/publication/55/1336/a-new-england-an-english-identity-within-britain>.
74. Further details are available at: <http://www.hannahmitchell.org.uk>.
75. See, for instance, Brown's 'Liberty' speech delivered at the University of Westminster, 25 Oct. 2007; available at: <http://news.bbc.co.uk/1/hi/uk_politics/7062237.stm>.
76. Michael Wills, 'The Politics of Identity', speech delivered at the Institute for Public Policy Research, Mar. 2008. The partial reading of the survey data which Wills commissioned, and upon which his argument rested, was revealed, following an FOI request, by Gareth Young; see Young, 'BME: Black and Minority English', *Tocque*, 30 Oct. 2008; available at: <http://toque.co.uk/bme-black-and-minority-english>.
77. See Simon Lee, *The Best for Britain? The Politics and Legacy of Gordon Brown* (London: OneWorld, 2007).
78. *The Governance of Britain* (London: HMSO, 2007); available at: <http://www. official-documents.gov.uk/document/cm71/7170/7170.pdf>.
79. Douglas Alexander and Gordon Brown, *Stronger Together, Weaker Apart* (London: Fabian Society, 2007).
80. Cruddas, 'Time for a Truly English Labour Party', and 'Attlee, the ILP and the Romantic Tradition'.
81. Miliband, 'Englishness'.
82. Kenny, 'Our Parties Must Respond to the Rise of Englishness'.
83. See, for instance, Anthony Painter, *Democratic Stress, the Populist Threat and Extremist Threat* (London: Policy Network, 2013).
84. Matthew Goodwin, *Right Response: Understanding and Countering Populist Extremism in Europe* (London: Chatham House, 2011); available at: <http://www. chathamhouse.org/sites/default/files/r0911_goodwin.pdf>.
85. Heffer, *Nor Shall my Sword*.
86. See the discussion of the CEP in Aughey, 'Anxiety and Injustice'.
87. Gareth Young, interview with Guy Lodge, May 2008.

88. Eddie Bone, 'Why Labour should Support an English Parliament', *New Statesman,* 9 July 2012; available at: <http://www.newstatesman.com/blogs/politics/2012/07/why-labour-should-support-english-parliament>.

89. See Ben Quinn, 'English Democrats Could Become "Electorally Credible" as BNP Decline', *Guardian,* 25 Sept. 2011; available at: <http://www.guardian.co.uk/politics/2011/sep/25/english-democrats-electorally-credible-bnp>.

90. Peter Davies was the elected Mayor for Doncaster from 2009 to 2013, and resigned from ED in 2013, citing as his main reason for leaving the influence of its growing number of recruits from the British National Party.

91. BBC, 'Profile: English Democrats' Leader Robin Tilbrook', *BBC News,* 8 Apr. 2010; available at: <http://news.bbc.co.uk/1/hi/uk_politics/election_2010/8610149.stm>.

92. See Quinn, 'English Democrats'.

93. Jamie Bartlett and Mark Littler, *Inside the EDL: Populist Politics in a Digital Age* (London: Demos, 2011).

94. See Bartlett and Littler, *Inside the EDL.*

95. See, for instance, Matthew Taylor, 'English Defence League: Inside the Violent World of Britain's New Far Right', *Guardian,* 28 May 2010; available at: <http://www.guardian.co.uk/uk/2010/may/28/english-defence-league-guardian-investigation>.

96. Jon Garland and James Treadwell, 'Masculinity, Marginalisation and Violence: A Case Study of the English Defence League', *British Journal of Criminology*, 51/4 (2011), 621–34.

97. Paul Jackson, *The EDL: Britain's 'New Far Right' Social Movement* (Northampton: University of Northampton, RNM Publications, 2011).

98. Garland and Treadwell, 'Masculinity, Marginalisation and Violence'.

99. Bartlett and Littler, *Inside the EDL.*

100. Bartlett and Littler, *Inside the EDL.*

101. Bartlett and Littler, *Inside the EDL.*

102. Bartlett and Littler, *Inside the EDL,* 6.

103. For a balanced discussion of the dangers and merits of such comparisons, see Goodwin, *Right Response.*

104. Matthew Goodwin, *New British Fascism: Rise of the BNP* (London: Routledge, 2011).

105. Rhodes, ' "It's Not Just Them, it's Whites as Well" '.

106. David Hannan, 'The Rise of English Nationalism', *Identity* (Oct. 2007), 14–17.

107. Hannan, 'Rise of English Nationalism', 15.

108. Hannan, 'Rise of English Nationalism', 16.

109. Hannan, 'Rise of English Nationalism', 15.

110. Hannan, 'Rise of English Nationalism', 16.

111. Wellings, *English Nationalism and Euroscepticism.*

112. Peter Kellner, 'Small Island', *Prospect,* 16 Nov. 2011; available at: <http://www.prospectmagazine.co.uk/magazine/small-island/#.Ub5SsXaDT5o>.

113. Kellner, 'Small Island'.

114. See Mark Daniel, *Cranks and Gadflies: The Story of UKIP* (London: Timewell Press, 2005).

115. On UKIP's growing appeal to working-class citizens and the implications of this trend for the Labour party, see Max Wind-Cowie, 'Labour's UKIP Problem', *Prospect*, 1 May 2013; available at: <http://www.prospectmagazine.co.uk/blog/ukip-nigel-farage-labour-liberalism/#.Ub71BHaDT5o>.

116. Guy Lodge, 'English Patriotism is One of the Overlooked Reasons for UKIP's Rise', *The Spectator*, 3 May 2013; available at: <http://www.ippr.org/articles/56/10736/english-patriotism-is-one-of-the-overlooked-reasons-for-ukips-rise>.

117. Ashcroft, 'UKIP Threat'. See also Rob Ford, '5 Things People Get Wrong about UKIP', *Guardian*, 6 May 2013; available at: <http://www.guardian.co.uk/commentisfree/2013/may/06/ukip-5-things-people-get-wrong>.

118. Ashcroft, 'UKIP Threat'.

119. Ashcroft, 'UKIP Threat'.

120. Ashcroft, 'UKIP Threat'.

121. Wyn Jones, *et al.*, *England and its Two Unions*.

122. See IPPR, 'UKIP is Becoming the Patriotic Party of England', 3 May 2013; available at: <http://www.ippr.org/press-releases/111/10732/ukip-is-becoming-the-patriotic-party-of-england>.

123. See 'New UKIP Policy on the Union: An Unintended Confederation', *Bloggers4UKIP*, 10 Feb. 2013; available at: <http://www.bloggers4ukip.org.uk/2013/02/new-ukip-policy-on-devolution.html>.

124. See 'A Union for the Future', *UKIP*, 12 Sept. 2011; available at: <http://www.paulnuttallmep.com/wp-content/uploads/2011/09/Union-for-the-Future-FINAL.pdf>.

125. For a discussion of Nigel Farage's evolving approach to this issue, see 'Nigel Farrage on an English Parliament', *Tocque*, 14 Sept. 2010; available at: <http://toque.co.uk/nigel-farrage-english-parliament>.

126. See Wyn Jones *et al.*, *England and its Two Unions*.

127. See Bryant, *Nations of Britain*.

128. See, for instance, Katie Schmuecker, Guy Lodge, and Lewis Goodall, *Borderland: Assessing the Implications of a More Autonomous Scotland for the North of England* (London: IPPR, 2012); available at: <http://www.ippr.org/publication/55/9885/borderland-assessing-the-implications-of-a-more-autonomous-scotland-for-the-north-of- england>.

129. Michael Kenny and Guy Lodge, *The English Question: The View from Westminster* (London: IPPR, 2010).

130. Kenny and Lodge, *The English Question*, 4–5.

131. Arthur Aughey, 'Whatever Happened to the English Question?', *Policy and Politics*, 40/2 (2012), 297–302, 297.

132. Aughey, 'Whatever Happened to the English Question?', 301.

133. See Wayne David, 'The One Nation Labour Debates', 4 Apr. 2013; available at: <http://www.progressonline.org.uk/2013/04/04/the-one-nation-labour-debates-labour-and-the-new-era-in-politics>.

134. Neal Ascherson, 'Will Scotland Go its Own Way?', *New York Times*, 26 Feb. 2012; available at: <http://www.nytimes.com/2012/02/27/opinion/independence-for-scotland.html?pagewanted=all%20>.

135. See for instance, Andrew Gamble, 'A Union of Historic Compromise', in Perryman, *Imagined Nation*, 173–95.
136. For an in-depth discussion of the idea and content of the social union, see Iain McLean, Jim Gallagher, and Guy Lodge, *Scotland's Choices* (Edinburgh: Edinburgh University Press, 2013).
137. Patrick Hennessy, 'David Cameron Backs Jerusalem as English Anthem', *Daily Telegraph*, 14 July 2012; available at: <http://www.telegraph.co.uk/news/politics/david-cameron/9400486/David-Cameron-backs-Jerusalem-as-English-national-anthem.html>.

CHAPTER 6

1. Marquand, 'Give us a Moral Vision for England'.
2. See, for instance, Michael Keating and Nicola McEwen, 'Introduction: Devolution and Public Policy in Comparative Perspective', *Regional and Federal Studies*, 15/4 (2005), 413–21.
3. See James Mitchell, 'Two Models of Devolution: A Framework for Analysis', in Klaus Stolz (ed.), *Ten Years of Devolution: The New Territorial Politics in the United Kingdom* (Augsburg: Wissner-Verlag, 2010), 56–71, 59.
4. Jeffery and Wincott, 'Devolution in the United Kingdom', 9.
5. Arthur Aughey, 'Fifth Nation: The United Kingdom between Definite and Indefinite Articles', *British Politics*, 5 (2010), 565–85.
6. See Guy Lodge and James Mitchell, 'Whitehall and the Government of England', in Hazell, *The English Question*, 96–118.
7. Justice Committee, Fifth Report, *Devolution: A Decade On* (London: House of Commons, 2009), section 2, 'Devolution and the Centre'.
8. See Jeffery and Wincott, 'Devolution in the United Kingdom', and Charlie Jeffery, 'Devolution, Britishness and the Future of the Union', *Political Quarterly*, 78/suppl. 1 (2007), 112–21.
9. See Mitchell, 'The Westminster Model'.
10. Philip Norton, 'The Englishness of Westminster', in Aughey and Berberich, *These Englands*, 174–92.
11. Norton, 'The Englishness of Westminster'.
12. Jeffery and Wincott, 'Devolution in the United Kingdom'.
13. Charlie Jeffery, Guy Lodge, and Katie Schmuecker, 'The Devolution Paradox', in Guy Lodge and Katie Schmuecker (eds), *Devolution in Practice* (London: IPPR, 2010), 9–31.
14. Aughey, 'English Questions', *Prospect*, 27 Aug. 2006; available at: <http://www.prospectmagazine.co.uk/magazine/englishquestions/#.UcMjXnaDT5o>.
15. Lodge and Mitchell, 'Whitehall and the Government of England'.
16. Simon Lee, 'Gordon Brown and the Negation of England', in Aughey and Berberich, *These Englands*, 155–73, 156.

17. Henry McLeish, 'Evidence to the Commission on Scottish Devolution', 12 Sept. 2008, 20–46; available at: <http://www.commissiononscottishdevolution.org.uk/uploads/transcript-12-September.pdf>.
18. Jim Gallagher, 'So, What About England?', *The Scotsman,* 21 Nov. 2012; available at: <http://www.scotsman.com/news/jim-gallagher-so-what-about-england-1-2647129>.
19. See, for instance, BBC News, 'Scots MPs Attacked over Tuition Fees', *BBC Home,* 27 Jan. 2004; available at: <http://news.bbc.co.uk/1/hi/scotland/3432767.stm>.
20. Philip Cowley, *The Rebels: How Blair Mislaid his Majority* (London: Politico, 2005).
21. Cited in Meg Russell and Guy Lodge, 'The Government of England by Westminster', in Hazell, *The English Question,* 64–95, 72.
22. Rachel Ormston and John Curtice, 'Resentment or Contentment? Attitudes towards the Union 10 Years On', in Alison Park, John Curtice, Elizabeth Clery, and Catherine Bryson (eds), *British Social Attitudes: The Twenty-Seventh Survey. Exploring Labour's Legacy* (London: Sage, 2010), 155–78, 156.
23. See, for instance, 'The West Lothian Question Personified', *Ian Dale's Diary,* 8 May 2006; available at: <http://iaindale.blogspot.co.uk/2006/05/west-lothian-question-personified.html>.
24. See 'Alan Duncan: Almost Impossible to Have Scottish PM', *Conservative Home,* 3 July 2006; available at: <http://conservativehome.blogs.com/torydiary/2006/07/alan_duncan_alm.html>.
25. For a discussion of some of the historical aspects of this issue, see Vernon Bogdanor, 'The West Lothian Question', *Parliamentary Affairs,* 63/1 (2010), 156–72.
26. See Robert Hazell, 'An Unstable Union: Devolution and the English Question', State of the Union lecture, University College, London, 11 Dec. 2000; available at: <http://www.ucl.ac.uk/spp/publications/unit-publications/66.pdf>.
27. Field's thinking on this issue was set out in 'The Strange Death of Labour England? Revisiting Bagehot's English Constitution', lecture at the University of Hertfordshire, 3 June 2008; available at: <http://toque.co.uk/frank-field-strange-death-labour-england>.
28. Field, 'Strange Death of Labour England'.
29. See *Strengthening Parliament: The Report of the Commission to Strengthen Parliament* (London: Conservative Party, 2000); available at: <http://www.conservatives.com/pdf/norton.pdf>.
30. See BBC News, 'Tories Ponder English Only Voting', *BBC News Channel,* 28 Oct. 2007; available at: <http://news.bbc.co.uk/1/hi/uk_politics/7065941.stm>.
31. Nicholas Watt and Paul Kelbie, 'Tories will Hand Crucial Powers to English MPs', *Observer,* 28 Oct. 2007; available at: <http://www.guardian.co.uk/politics/2007/oct/28/uk.conservatives>.
32. Sir Malcolm Rifkind, interview with Richard Hayton and Michael Kenny, 5 Apr. 2008.
33. Fraser Nelson, 'Clarke Waters Down the West Lothian Answer', *The Spectator,* 1 July 2008.

34. Conservative Democracy Taskforce, *Answering the Question: Devolution, the West Lothian Question and the Future of the Union* (London: Conservative Party, 2009).
35. Kenneth Clarke, interview with Michael Kenny and Guy Lodge, 8 Sept. 2008.
36. Rifkind, Evidence to Justice Committee, Fifth Report, *Devolution: A Decade On*, i. 56–7.
37. Conservative Democracy Taskforce, *Answering the Question*, 1.
38. Clarke, interview.
39. Clarke, interview.
40. Conservative Democracy Taskforce, *Answering the Question*, 2.
41. Lord Charles Falconer, 'Speech to ESRC Devolution and Constitutional Change Programme', Queen Elizabeth II Conference Centre, London, 10 Mar. 2006; available at: <http://www.dca.gov.uk/speeches/2006/sp060310.htm>.
42. See, for instance, David Cameron, 'Leader's Speech to Conservative Party Conference, Birmingham, 2008; available at: <http://www.britishpoliticalspeech. org/speech-archive.htm?speech=153>.
43. See the analysis of one of these keynote speeches in Alan Trench, 'David Cameron Speech to the Scottish Conservative Party Conference', 12 Feb. 2010; available at: <http://devolutionmatters.wordpress.com/2010/02/12/david-camerons-speech-to-the-scottish-conservative-conference>.
44. HM Government, *The Coalition: Our Programme for Government*, 2010; available at:<https://www.gov.uk/government/publications/the-coalition-documentation>.
45. For a detailed account of the thinking behind this Bill, see Harriett Baldwin, 'To the Bitter End: Lessons Learned from a Private Member's Bill', *Total Politics,* 28 Sept. 2011; available at: <http://www.politics.co.uk/comment-analysis/2011/09/28/to-the-bitter-end-lessons-learned-from-a-priv>.
46. See esp. Vernon Bogdanor, *The Coalition and the Constitution* (London: Hart, 2011).
47. This issue is not mentioned in the accounts of the negotiations between the Lib Dems and Labour supplied by two of the main protagonists within them: David Laws, *22 Days in May: The Birth of the Lib Dem-Conservative Coalition* (London: Biteback, 2010), and Andrew Adonis, *5 Days in May: The Coalition and Beyond* (London: Biteback, 2013).
48. Bogdanor, *The Coalition and the Constitution*, 40.
49. Jim Gallagher, *England and the Union: How and Why to Answer the West Lothian Question* (London: IPPR, 2012).
50. Gallagher, *England and the Union*, 26.
51. Sir Roger Sands, 'Evidence to McKay Commission', Submission No. 4; available at: <http://webarchive.nationalarchives.gov.uk/20130403030652/http://tmc. independent.gov.uk/submission-4-sir-roger-sands/>.
52. See the discussion of this and other occasions when the Labour government relied on Scottish MPs in Russell and Lodge, 'The Government of England', 72–3.
53. See Gallagher, *England and the Union*, annex 2, 'Public General Acts of 2006 and their General Suitability for an England-Only Legislative Process', 37–9.
54. Bogdanor, *The New British Constitution* (London: Hart, 2009).

55. See, for instance, Bogdanor, *The Coalition and the Constitution*.

56. See, for instance, Russell and Lodge, 'The Government of England'.

57. George Foulkes MP, *Hansard*, 21 Jan. 2004, col. 1394.

58. Cited in Gallagher, *England and the Union*, 3.

59. Bogdanor, 'The West Lothian Question'.

60. Bogdanor, 'The West Lothian Question'.

61. Bogdanor, 'The West Lothian Question'.

62. Robert Hazell, 'Conclusion: What are the Answers to the English Question?', in *The English Question*, 220–41, 239.

63. Iain McLean, 'Two Possible Solutions to the West Lothian Question', paper presented at a meeting organized by Open Democracy and the IPPR, 30 May 2007.

64. Justice Committee, *Devolution: A Decade on*, ch. 5, 'The English Question', para. 186.

65. Keating, 'Evidence to McKay Commission', Submission No. 25; available at: <http://webarchive.nationalarchives.gov.uk/20130403030652/http://tmc.independent.gov.uk/submission-25-michael-keating/>.

66. See Keating, 'Evidence to McKay Commission'.

67. Gerald Holtham, 'Evidence to McKay Commission', Submission No. 48; available at: <http://webarchive.nationalarchives.gov.uk/20130403030652/http://tmc.independent.gov.uk/submission-48-gerald-holtham>.

68. See Holtham 'Evidence to McKay Commission'.

69. Peter Behrens, 'Evidence to McKay Commission', Submission No. 50; available at: <http://webarchive.nationalarchives.gov.uk/20130403030652/http://tmc.independent.gov.uk/submission-50-paul-behrens>.

70. Behrens, 'Evidence to McKay Commission'.

71. McKay Commission, *Report of the Commission on the Consequences of Devolution for the United Kingdom*.

72. Adam Tomkins, 'A West Lothian Answer?', *Scottish Constitutional Futures Forum*, 28 Mar. 2013; available at: <http://its-ewds1.ds.strath.ac.uk/scf/Opinionand Analysis/ViewBlogPost/tabid/1767/articleType/ArticleView/articleId/1395/Adam-Tomkins-A-West-Lothian-Answer.aspx>.

73. Clarke, interview.

74. Peter Riddell, 'Evidence to McKay Commission', Submission No. 18; available at: <http://webarchive.nationalarchives.gov.uk/20130403030652/http://tmc.independent.gov.uk/wp-content/uploads/2012/06/120419_Submission_18_Rt-Hon-Peter-Riddell.pdf>.

75. This claim is central to Wyn Jones *et al.*, *The Dog that Finally Barked*.

76. See McLean and McMillan, *State of the Union*.

77. See Iain McLean, 'Financing the Union: Goschen, Barnett and Beyond', in William Miller (ed.), *Anglo-Scottish Relations: From 1900 to Devolution* (Oxford: Oxford University Press, 2005), 81–94.

78. Iain Mclean and Alistair McMillan, 'The Distribution of Public Expenditure across the UK Regions', *Fiscal Studies*, 24/1 (2003), 45–71, and *State of the Union*.

79. For a detailed account of these years, see Russell Deacon, *Devolution in Britain Today* (Manchester: Manchester University Press, 2006), 62–89.
80. McLean, 'Financing the Union'.
81. See esp. Ormston, 'The English Question', which argues against strong claims that there has been a further increase in English resentment on this, and other, issues.
82. John Curtice and Rachel Ormston, 'Evidence to the McKay Commission', Submission No. 28; available at: <http://webarchive.nationalarchives.gov.uk/20130403030652/http://tmc.independent.gov.uk/wp-content/uploads/2012/05/120509_Submission_28_John-Curtice-and-Rachel-Ormston.pdf>.
83. Justice Committee, *Devolution: A Decade On*, 4.
84. Iain Dale, interview with Michael Kenny and Guy Lodge, 5 May 2008.
85. Sir Brian Barder, 'Evidence to McKay Commission', Submission No. 46; available at: <http://webarchive.nationalarchives.gov.uk/20130403030652/http://tmc.independent.gov.uk/submission-46-sir-brian-barder/>.
86. See Bryant, 'Devolution, Equity and the English Question', 668.
87. Curtice and Ormston, 'Evidence'.
88. Curtice and Ormston, 'Evidence'.
89. See Wyn Jones *et al.*, *England and its Two Unions*, and the discussion of these figures in McKay Commission, *Report of the Commission on the Consequences of Devolution for the United Kingdom*, 15.
90. McKay Commission, *Report of the Commission on the Consequences of Devolution for the United Kingdom*, 7.
91. McKay Commission, *Report of the Commission on the Consequences of Devolution for the United Kingdom*, 9.
92. McKay Commission, *Report of the Commission on the Consequences of Devolution for the United Kingdom*, 46.

CONCLUSION

1. See, for instance, Stapleton, *Political Intellectuals and Public Identities,* and *Sir Arthur Bryant and National History*.
2. Light, *Forever England*.
3. Jed Esty, *A Shrinking Island: Modernism and National Culture in England* (Princeton: Princeton University Press, 2003).
4. John Fowles, 'On Being English But Not British', in *Wormholes* (London: Random House, 1998), 79–88. This essay was first published in 1964.
5. Fowles, 'On Being English But Not British', 87.
6. See, for instance, Baucom, *Out of Place*.
7. Fowles, 'On Being English But Not British', 84.
8. See, for instance, Bernard Crick, 'Do We Really Need Britannia?', in Andrew Gamble and Tony Wright (eds), *Britishness: Perspectives on the British Question* (London: Political Quarterly, 2009), 149–58, 150–1, and Robert Colls, 'British

National Identity', *History Today*, 62/8 (2012); available at: <http://www.historyto-day.com/robert-colls/british-national-identity>.

9. Barnett, 'Afterword', 340.
10. See Christopher Hope, 'Give the English a Voice in Whitehall says LGA's Merrick Cockell', *Daily Telegraph*, 16 June 2013; available at: <http://www.telegraph.co.uk/news/politics/10123462/Give-the-English-a-voice-in-Whitehall-says-LGAs-Sir-Merrick-Cockell.html>.
11. Orwell, *Road to Wigan Pi*, 148.
12. See Charles Taylor, 'Democratic Exclusion (and its Remedies?)', in Alan Cairns, John Courtney, Peter MacKinnon, Hans Michaelmann, and David Smith (eds), *Citizenship, Diversity and Pluralism: Canadian and Comparative Perspectives* (Montreal: McGill-Queen's University Press, 1999), 265–92.

Index

Abell, Jackie 102–103, 166, 246n, 265n, 276n
Ackroyd, Peter 9, 16–17, 126, 156,
    247n, 273n
Agboluaje, Oladipo 160
Alagiah, George 104
Albarn, Damon 150, 163, 164, 275n
Alexander, Douglas 190, 281n
Anderson, Benedict 22, 248n
Anderson, Lindsay 158
Anderson, Perry 53, 266n
anglicization 5, 180, 200–204, 278n
Anthony, Andrew 63, 255n
Ascherson, Neal 125, 203, 266n, 283n
Ashcroft, Michael 93, 199, 260n, 283n
Aughey, Arthur 52, 69–70, 72–73, 201, 208,
    245n, 246n, 250n, 256n, 265n, 281n
    The Politics of Englishness 73–75
Aymes, Sophie 157, 274n

Baggini, Julian 123, 266n
Baker, Kenneth 211
Baldwin, Harriet 215
Baldwin, Stanley 9, 121–122, 266n
Ballard, J.G. 13, 246n
    Kingdom Come 154
Barder, Brian 228
Barker, Ernest 73, 127, 267n
Barnes, Julian 155, 246n, 273n
    England, England 9
    Arthur and George 154
Barnett Formula 5, 201, 205, 218, 224–227
Barnett, Anthony 11, 246n
Barnett, Joel 224
Baucom, Ian 17–18, 135–136, 154, 247n
Bawden, Edward 157
Bechhofer, Frank 44, 252n
Behrens, Peter 221
Berlin, Isaiah 36
Betjeman, John 9–10, 19, 135, 246n
Billig, Michael 9, 106, 166, 246n
Blair, Tony 2, 45, 55, 92. 171, 176, 181,
    187, 189, 190, 209, 219, 245n, 247n,
    253n, 285n
Blunkett, David 71, 128, 190, 281n
Bogdanor, Vernon 188, 215, 218, 219,
    245n, 250n
Bond, Ross 81, 87, 258n

Bourke, Joanna 112, 264n
Boyes, Georgina 145–147, 270n
Bragg, Billy 41, 71, 257n
    The Progressive Patriot 70
British National Party 98, 147, 194, 196–198
British Union 36–37, 45–47, 75, 128, 169,
    173–174, 190–191, 202, 214
    Conservative Party 180–184
    Labour Party 184–185
Britishness 1, 11, 20–21, 32, 34, 39, 41, 44,
    46, 48–49, 59, 71, 75, 78, 81, 84, 88, 100,
    102, 104, 119, 125, 129–130, 149, 169–
    170, 190, 197, 200, 206, 208, 234–235,
    236, 242, 250n
Britten, Benjamin 151–152
Brockliss, Laurence 39, 251n
Brown, Gordon 92, 165, 182, 187, 190, 208,
    210, 281n
Bryant, Arthur 19, 118, 234
Bryant, Christopher 125, 245n, 248n,
    258n, 266n
Bryce, James 37
Bunting, Madeleine 127, 268n
    The Plot 140
Burke, Edmund 67, 69, 123
Buruma, Ian 36, 251n
Butterworth, Jez 161–163
Byrne, Liam 169, 277n

Calman Commission 209, 227
Cameron, David 204, 213, 215, 247n
Campbell, Menzies 212
Cannadine, David 22, 41, 248n, 251n, 252n
Carthy, Eliza 147, 149, 270n
Centre for Policy Studies 182, 279n
Chesterton, G.K. 118
Clarke, Kenneth 213, 223
Clifford, Sue 136, 268n
Cloonan, Martin 150, 271n
Coalition government 118, 176–177, 215
Cobbett, William 137
Cohen, Robin 48, 253n, 263n
Colley, Linda 39, 53, 235, 249n, 255n
Colls, Robert 59, 61, 140, 254n, 255n, 289n
Condor, Susan 8, 101, 103, 114–115, 140,
    166, 246n, 255n, 258n, 260n, 262n, 265n,
    276n, 278n

Cox, Steve 149, 271n
Cruddas, John 71, 98, 128, 190, 256n, 257n, 261n, 281n
Crystal, David 137, 169n
Cunningham, Hugh 70, 251n
Curtice, John 81, 83–84, 86, 92, 97, 99, 101, 116, 119, 130, 210, 229, 250n, 258n, 259n, 265n, 285n, 288n

Dalyell, Tam 211
Davies, Norman 39, 249n, 251n
Davis, David 165, 182–183, 211, 279n
Defoe, Daniel 16, 247n
Democracy Taskforce 213, 223
Denham, John 71, 109, 128, 165
devolution 2, 4, 20, 27, 29, 30, 40, 45–47, 48, 49, 54–56, 66, 76, 78, 80, 81, 82, 84, 86, 87, 91, 100, 108, 116, 129, 130, 132, 143, 149, 154, 155, 164
    English question 171–177
    Conservative Party 180–183
    Labour Party 183–187
    UK Style 206–210
Dickens, Charles 133
Disraeli, Benjamin 172
Dodd, Philip 35, 249n, 253n, 255n
Dowds, Lizanne 33, 250n

Eastwood, David 39, 251n
Edesnour, Tim 26
Edgar, David 161
Eliot, T. S. 9–10, 246n
Emmerson, Simon 147
empire 10, 15, 17–18, 34, 36, 44, 60–61, 126, 128, 135, 152–153, 163–164, 185, 203, 234–235, 239
English backlash 84, 87, 173, 225, 258n
English Defence League 194–196, 282n
English Democrats 193–194
English Grand Committee 212, 216, 230
English Nationalism 14, 21–22, 27, 47, 51, 56, 58–60, 79, 86, 99, 108–110, 118–120, 129, 132, 138, 171, 181–182, 185, 194–195, 197–200, 208, 233, 235, 242, 248n, 249n
    European Union 29–30
English parliament 80, 87, 91, 97, 99, 207, 218, 221, 258n, 261n, 281n, 283n
    Conservative Party 181–183
    campaign for 192–193
    English Democrats 193–194
    BNP 197

UKIP 199
English votes for English laws (EVEL) 91, 182–183, 210–211, 213–214, 216
    against EVEL 217–219
    in favour of EVEL 219–224
English, Simon 158
Englishness
    interpretations 11–13
    diversity 15–17
    terminology 21–23
    causality 31–33
    popular culture 42–43
    absence of 62–64
    class 97–100
    ethnicity 100–104
    fairness 114–117
    expressions of 117–128
    landscape 134–140
    arcadianism 5, 11, 25–26, 57, 64, 111, 121–122, 137, 148, 235
European Union 22, 28, 29–30, 44, 47, 69, 80, 118, 177, 193–194, 202, 229, 236, 239
Everitt, Anthony 126, 266n

Falconer, Charles 214
Farage, Nigel 199, 283n
Ferguson, Niall 41
Field, Frank 211
Folk 7, 12, 18
    narratives 25–26
    aesthetic 133–134
    folk music 142–144
    politics 147–148
    popular music 150–152
    the novel 52–157
    fine Arts 157–158
    cinema 159–160
    theatre 160–164
Forsythe, Michael 211
Fox, Kate 166, 269n
Freedland, Jonathan 127, 267n
Future of England Survey 87–88, 95, 97, 102, 165, 199, 229, 259n
    tables 89–92

Gallagher, Jim 209, 216, 284n, 286n
Gamble, Andrew 44, 249n, 250n, 252n, 263n, 283n
Garner, Steve 98, 119–120, 167, 246n, 260n, 263n
Gaskell, Elizabeth 113
Gervais, David 7, 245n, 272n
Gikandi, Simon 152–153, 272n

globalization 28, 31–32, 68, 96
  anti- 137
Gorer, Geoffrey 112, 264n
Gorman, Theresa 181
Gramsci, Antonio 134, 268n
Greenfield, Liah 65
Gregory, David 146
Griffin, Nick 147, 197

Hadlow, Janice 40
Hague, William 181–182, 192, 211, 279n
Hannan, David 197, 282n
Hare, David 32
Harker, Dave 146
Harrison, Tony 155, 273n
Harvey, P.J. 150
Harwood, Ronald 7
Hastings, Adrian 65, 256n
Hawes, James 154, 273n
Haylett, Chris 110, 264n
Hazell, Robert 219, 245n
Heath, Anthony 44, 81, 83–84, 97, 101, 119,
  130, 253n, 258n, 259n
Heffer, Simon 42, 46, 151, 192, 247n,
  252n, 253n
Hewitt, Roger 98, 261n
Hill, Amelia 42
Hill, Geoffrey 153–155
Hitchens, Christopher 9
Holst, Gustav 151
Holtham, Gerald 221
Home Rule 37, 173, 211
Howkin, Alun 62, 255n
Hughes, Simon 165, 212
Hughes, Ted 155
Huhne, Chris 165
Hunt, Tristram 41, 252n
Hutchinson, John 26, 248n, 255n

Ignatieff, Michael 31, 36, 250n, 252n
Industrial Revolution 10, 12, 61, 111, 134,
  142, 143
Institute for Public Policy Research
  (IPPR) 87, 216
Ishiguro, Kazuo 133
Islam 94, 102, 120, 194–195, 196

Jenkins, Simon 66, 256n 274n
Johnson, Boris 165
Joyce, Rachel 14–15

Kane, Sarah 161, 275n
Kearney, Hugh 38, 251n, 256n

Keating, Michael 221, 284n
Keegan-Phipps, Simon 143, 269–270n
King, Angela 136, 268n
Kingsnorth, Paul 72, 124, 136–139, 162, 266n
Kinnock, Neil 46
Kohn, Hans 65, 248n, 256n
Kumar, Krishan 8, 47, 49, 63, 104, 130, 246n,
  247n, 252n, 255n, 262n
  Edwardian moment 16–18, 67, 137
  Anglo-British nationhood 51
  English moment 60–62, 74, 145
Kureishi, Hanif 104
Kwei-Amiah, Kwame 160

Landscape 15, 17–18, 62, 111, 124, 134–140,
  152, 153, 157–158, 162, 235, 242
Larkin, Philip 155
Leddy-Owen, Charles 103, 262n
Leigh, Mike 159, 274n
Levy, Andrea 153, 272n
Lewis, Ivan 109, 264n
Liberal-Constitutionalism 35, 74
Lichtenstein, Rachel 139
Liddington, David 209
Light, Alison 10
Loach, Ken 159, 274n
Lomax, Cathy 158

Mabey, Richard 136–137, 268n
MacCulloch, Diarmaid 41
McCrone, David 44, 47, 252n, 253n, 258n
McEwan, Ian 154, 273n
Macfarlane, Robert 135, 268n
McKay Commission 176–177, 202, 215–216,
  222, 229, 238, 260n
McLean, Ian 75, 220, 225–226, 257n, 277n,
  279n, 287n
McLeish, Henry 209
Mcleod, John 15, 247n, 272n
McMillan, Alistair 75, 225, 257n, 287n
Major, John 9, 29, 246n
Mandler, Peter 3, 6, 8, 24, 73, 124, 126, 172,
  245n, 248n, 264n
Mann, Robin 103, 119, 260n
Marquand, David 14, 57, 247n
Marr, Andrew 41, 163, 252n, 275n, 276n
Marsden, Gordon 142, 269n
Meadows, Shane 159
Miliband, David 189, 280n
Miliband, Ed 71, 190, 236, 267n
Millan, Bruce 186
Mitchell, James 40, 245n, 251n, 253n,
  277n, 284n

Monbiot, George 177, 278n
Moore, Suzanne 127, 267n
Moray, Jim 149
Moreno, Luis 82, 88, 102, 258n
Morpurgo, Michael 143
Morton, A.V. 135
Motion, Andrew 156
Mullen, John 149, 271n
multiculturalism 2, 12, 15, 17, 95, 98, 103,
    119, 124–128, 147, 153, 196, 260n, 261n,
    264n, 276n
  Scruton 67
  Multicultural Englishness 165
  BNP 197

Nairn, Tom 11, 34, 51–59, 71, 73, 76, 124,
    137, 178, 236, 246n, 253n, 254n
  The Making of English National Identity 60
Namier, Lewis 36
Nash, Paul 135, 157
Norris, Rufus 163–164, 275n
Norton, Lord 212
Nuttall, Paul 199

Oakeshott, Michael 52, 73–75, 120, 234,
    257n, 258n, 266n
O'Hagan, Andrew 14, 63–64, 247n
Ormston, Rachel 210, 229, 260n, 288n
Orwell, George 9–10, 73, 112, 115, 123–124,
    137, 234, 246n, 264n
  The Road to Wigan Pier 239

Parrinder, Patrick 152, 154, 272n
Parris, Matthew 65, 255n
pastoral themes 10,12, 19, 57, 140, 235
Paxman, Jeremy 9, 41–42, 44, 252n
Perryman, Mark 59, 255n
Pevsner, Nicholas 156–157, 273n
Piper, John 135, 157–158, 135, 157–158
Pocock, J. G. A. 38, 57–58, 251n, 254n
Powell, Enoch 18, 54–56, 58, 235
Prescott, John 186
Purcell, Henry 151

Ravilious, Eric 157
regional government 185–191
Reid, John 210
Reviron-Piégay, Florence 22
Riddell, Peter 223
Rifkind, Malcolm 212–213
Robbins, Keith 39, 251n
Roberts, Jane 44, 253n
Rokkan, Stein 40

Romanticism 54, 151, 156–157
Rose, Richard 37, 178, 251n, 278n
Rosie, Michael 81, 87, 258n, 259n
Rushdie, Salman 153

Salmond, Alex 52, 253n
Samuel, Raphael 39, 122, 251n, 266n
Sands, Roger 216
Schama, Simon 41
Schöpflin, George 112–113, 124, 134, 248n,
    264n, 268n
Scottish referendum 177, 210, 227
Scruton, Roger 51, 66–72, 151–152, 182,
    256n, 269n, 272n, 279n
Searchlight Educational Trust 95–96
Sentamu, John 126, 165, 267n
Sharp, Cecil 144–147, 151, 270n
Sierz, Aleks 20, 160, 248n
Silk Commission 177, 210
Sinclair, Iain 139, 269n
Smith, Anthony 61, 255n
Smith, Zadie 153
St George 14, 42–43, 108–109, 121, 156,
    164–167, 169, 237
Stapleton, Julia 19, 72–73, 247n, 257n
Starkey, David 20, 41
Straw, Jack 185–186, 279n
Swift, Graham 155, 159
Szirtes, George 156, 273n

Thatcher, Margaret 39, 114
  Thatcherism 31, 35, 235
Thompson, Edward 56–57
Thomson, Rupert 154
Thorpe, Adam 153–154
Tillbrook, Robin 194
Tilley, James 81
Tomkins, Adam 222
Turner, Frank 149, 271n

United Kingdom Independence Party 30,
    93–94, 96, 118, 194, 198–200, 202, 233

Van Eyken, Tim 143, 270n

Ward, Paul 32, 250n, 257n
Ware, Vron 109, 264n
Weight, Richard 71–72
Wellings, Ben 28–30, 33, 118, 198, 200, 249n
West Lothian Question 84, 91, 99, 173–174,
    176, 205, 210, 219, 221–224 227–228
  tables 86 92
  proposals for reform 211–217

Whiggism 13, 28, 35, 37–40, 62, 66, 190
Wilde, Oscar 69
Williams, Vaughan 54, 143, 151
Wills, Michael 185, 190, 281n
Winter, Trish 143, 270n
Wood Michael 41, 252n
Wright, Patrick 58, 123, 139, 158, 254n, 265n, 266n, 269n
Wright, Tony 34, 124, 171, 173, 245n, 250n, 277n, 289n

Wright, Tony 124, 171, 173, 245n, 250n, 258n, 277n, 289n

Yeo, Tim 210
Young, Ken 33, 250n
Young, Robert 62, 144–146, 255n, 269n
Younge, Gary 103, 262n

Zephaniah, Benjamin 147
Zuberi, Nabeel 150, 271n

Importance of community, but needs to develop organically, Integration means diversity & open-ness of an identity comm, hence it isn't closed & is open to the world - it is based on values — not on ethnicity.

How would it be important for the politics of today? - It will offer another focus for politics - + one which can have wide appeal - + it can have both open & inward aspects which would also be important for blunting the edge of reaction - people can express themselves - in terms of imagination, etc, can help to provide unity - + if it is a modern identity then it is useful for helping to resolve issues of inequality as well - as now there are competing narratives -

— Community / organic dev. / intellectuals who all part of the org dev. who describe it / integration / open-ness as a US policy

— community - sense of needs to be allowed its organic dev. with intellectuals who study it + describe it - integration is necessary with open-ness to new groups who become English - e, a. it isn't just an ethnic thing.

Integrations - world com + at home. Values